THE MANAGEMENT QUADRILLE

Douglas Foster

PITMAN

PITMAN PUBLISHING LIMITED
39 Parker Street, London WC2B 5PB

Associated Companies
Pitman Publishing Pty Ltd, Melbourne
Pitman Publishing New Zealand Ltd, Wellington
Copp Clark Pitman, Toronto

658.4
F62a

Printed and bound in Great Britain
at The Pitman Press, Bath

ISBN 0 273 01344 0

Contents

Preface

In the last three decades in particular, management has been inundated with a torrent of so-called new techniques. Each has been eulogised by some of its originators, often far beyond its true capabilities. Practitioners lacking perception, have rushed to apply these new concepts, often regardless of their suitability for the tasks in hand. The haste with which some persons applied these new ideas, without much thought, suggested perhaps incorrectly, that they were keen to cover up their own inadequacies, lack of intelligence, managerial ability or whatever. This usage regardless of their suitability was unfair to many of the new ideas. Properly applied they can be helpful or beneficial to executives struggling against an ever-increasing load of problems and complexities and of the basic knowledge needed for effective management in a growingly hostile business environment. It is not surprising, therefore, that management performance in most countries has declined since the end of the Second World War. This decline has been more pronounced in the last decade when economic, international and political matters have also become complex, defying understanding, never mind effective control.

So the need for this book arose. It developed from a series of informal discussions with executives of Pitman Publishing and academics and business people generally, over a period of nearly five years. The author has also been researching and studying the idea more formally for some years as part of his general interest in management problems and their solution. The common thread that ran throughout was the vital need for executives to return to the first principles of successful management and cut free from the bewildering plethora of management techniques on offer. They had also to refresh their memories on what good, effective management is all about and learn of the common failings or pitfalls met in business management. The book had to avoid detailed explanations of the techniques and concentrate instead on the correct approaches, mental processes and applications that were needed. Nor should it offer yet further complex theories which in time may prove to be just additions to the many gimmicks that already masquerade as important management concepts. The last do not offer harassed executives any workable solutions to their many, real problems and often just confuse the issues involved. In addition, academics saw the need for a book that would be a cautionary tale to students and graduates, one that stressed that the possession of theoretical or arcane knowledge was not enough if they wished to become effective and successful managers.

This book grew around the simple concept of the need for integrated management involving total and continuous cooperation between all facets of a business. It also recognises that this cooperation comes most of the time, through packages of four activities — hence 'the quadrille concept'. Understanding what the more usual foursomes are and how and why they work is essential for success. It was also necessary to show why management fails from time to time even with so-called cooperation, and to illustrate the main points by recalling some well-known case histories.

Considerations of length necessitated that readers already understood the basic concepts and principles of management. There was no room for a straightforward detailed text on these as well as an exhaustive discussion of the main purpose of the book. Readers would have to have recourse to formal textbooks on the various disciplines of management. Nonetheless the book is intended for students, graduates and executives and is relevant to most countries. With executives it will be appropriate for refreshing their memories and bringing their abilities up to scratch. For students it would be essential reading to keep the realities of management in their minds, saving them from being submerged in the ill-conceived belief that mastery of theory is all that is needed for effective management. For graduates moving on to their second degrees, it is an essential reminder about the keys to effective management.

Above all else, this is not a standard textbook giving glib, precise answers to stereotyped problems. It is meant to be a thought-provoking book, intended to show readers how to identify problems and the thought processes necessary if unique solutions that fit the individualised situations of a corporation are to be found. This is essential, since each corporate situation varies considerably from those operative in other companies. Standard textbook solutions can be irrelevant to the actual conditions facing executives. It is thus a work that aims to help people to *think about and through* the difficulties they will face in their work. If it does nothing more than start arguments or discussion between established and would-be executives and academics then it will have more than served its purpose.

Douglas Foster
London, 1979.

Acknowledgments

Copyright holders for Figures 1.3, 1.4, 4.3 and 5.5 have been acknowledged at the foot of the relevant illustration. Unfortunately the copyright holders of Figures 7.5, 7.6 and 7.7 have not been traced, but if they should contact the author he will gladly make full acknowledgment in any future printing. The remaining illustrations have been provided by the author.

To my dear wife Elizabeth, a constant and loving source of encouragement and support.

'It is one thing to show a man that he is in error, and another to put him in possession of the truth.'

John Locke (1632–1704)
Essay on the Human Understanding,
Book iv, chapter 7, section 11.

1 Management today

Once upon a time management of an enterprise was a relatively straightforward operation. Companies were of limited size, easily controlled by one, or a
few, people. Competition was limited and occasionally non-existent. Labour
and material costs were reasonably stable. Simple skills were required. Supply
and demand were more or less in balance. Capital was, by current standards,
cheap and generally available. Prices and profit margins did not fluctuate too
much. Markets were easily identifiable and were supplied by a limited number
of companies of which one or two were dominant. Most companies enjoyed
viable market shares. Market and competitive conditions were usually known
to all of reasonable intelligence and especially those with a flair for their
business, i.e. the true entrepreneurs. Changes occurred at a decent pace,
measured in years rather than months. It was a relatively simple task for the
chief executive or proprietor of an enterprise to consider these facts and arrive
at simplistic decisions about the management and conduct of the business.

By comparison with conditions by the mid-1970s, this early stage of modern
business management reads like a fairy tale. Of course some companies were
very successful. Others were successful to a degree sufficient for their own
needs. Yet others got things wrong and paid the appropriate penalties. *Uncertainty* existed but not to the level of the *insecurity* that predominates today.
Mistakes in management were not *necessarily* fatal and minor corrections to
corporate action could contain most of them. Major upheavals were the
exception rather than the rule. Management education and scientific methods
of management engaged the attention of a few executives considered avant
garde by the majority, and a few deep-thinking academics seen as being
somewhat 'long-haired' (whatever that may mean!).

For the British, who gave the Industrial Revolution to the world, dominance
in most industries and markets appeared to offer a secure present and future.
Beneficial, general wealth was produced even if during the first three centuries
of expanding trade and industry, this wealth was rather unevenly distributed.
While large numbers of people were lifted from the primary poverty of the
barest means of subsistence there were many more who did not at first benefit
from this improvement. The numbers that remained depressed varied from
country to country. In the leading industrial nations they tended to be a small

percentage of the total working population. This small percentage nevertheless represented a substantial number of people. In undeveloped nations and the colonised regions the depressed represented a much greater proportion of the total population (e.g. 70–90 per cent). Yet this was considered a temporary impediment in a society moving steadily, if slowly, towards greater prosperity.

The expectation of life and its quality improved every decade. There were signs that material endowments seemed capable of infinite growth. The increase in wealth was manifested in the acquisition of material property. The income of the middle classes grew so that each household acquired the power equivalent of medieval kings and barons. The social consequences developing from these advances called for more growth and innovation and the continuing, if slow, abolition of squalor and poverty.

Until the First World War, Britain was the predominant industrial nation. After the Great Depression and the resurgence of economic activity Britain, the U.S.A., Western Europe (especially Germany) and Japan (in some activities) were the major industrial powers. However, in the main, competition was limited. It could perhaps be described as 'more gentlemanly' than the present cut-and-thrust approach.

1.1 The dream fades

It was *too* much like a fairy story or a dream. Like all dreams, it began to fade quite early, in fact some fifty years ago in the mid-1920s. The Great Depression did much to prove the concepts of that era were at best, naïve and at worst, dangerously misleading. Industry and services could not provide an endlessly increasing stream of goods and services. Education does not necessarily provide or create new wealth, nor solve social and economic problems. The benefits of growth do not necessarily benefit the majority of people, leaving only a minority still submerged in poverty. (In fact, the way things have developed by the mid-1970s it seems that increased wealth accrues mainly to those who already have a sufficiency of it!)

Finally, education does not lead naturally to a better understanding of the environment and the increasing complexity and problems of modern society by humanity at large. Ultimately in all human endeavour there is a finite limit to economic and technological growth. Wealth accrues to those who have it and is only lost by them through some unforeseen disaster, like the Great Depression. Education is effective only in so far as the innate capabilities of the individual can benefit from it.

By the late 1920s executives began to wish to learn from the mistakes that caused the Great Depression. It was clear that more scientific approaches to management were needed, though many were slow to accept this. Even more did not know which path to take. However, a business policy course was in existence at Harvard University in the U.S.A. as early as 1911. Others were not long in following. For the most part these early courses were down to earth attempts to instil the basics of good management practice into the students.

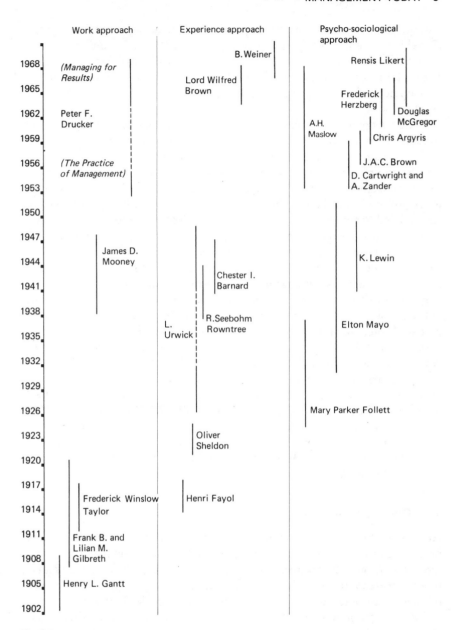

Fig 1.1

The early techniques were also very sensible basic aids to good management.
So-called 'modern management' can perhaps be traced back to about 1902
with the first efforts to improve the management and output of workshops or
the factory floor. Henry L. Gantt, perhaps best known for his straight-line
(Gantt) charts, worked on a bonus system for rewarding labour for improved

output. However, he is considered less of a giant in management development thought than others who were operating in his time or after him. The latter included Frederick Winslow Taylor, Frank and Lilian Gilbreth and others. Figure 1.1 gives the names of some of the people who contributed most to the development of new concepts. The illustration itself is in the form of a Gantt chart.

The development of management ideas can be segregated into three distinct streams or approaches. First there was the 'work approach' of Taylor and others. These were attempts to improve the efficiency and performance of specific groups in their work situations. The earliest attempts were directed to shopfloor factory workers. Later ones were aimed at executives and management groups in marketing, financial and personnel activities. The second stream tried to apply the 'experience and knowledge' gained to devise a set of rules or guidelines for those coming along in later years. It tried to discover why some groups were successful and others were not. Finally, a more recent stream is the 'psycho-sociological', which attempts to apply developing psychological and sociological theories to work situations.

Readers who wish to refresh their memories on the work and achievements of the people shown in Figure 1.1 have two possible courses. They can either plough through the books by these people — a formidable task — or read the book by Harold R. Pollard, *Developments in Management Thought* even if the latter is one man's limited, subjective view of the subject. They will see that slowly at first and then more rapidly, after the Second World War, the techniques became more complicated as the size of a business enterprise itself increased and became more complex. The small proprietor-company was for the most part replaced by bigger, ever increasing in size, public corporations active in many countries and markets and often in several technologies. Nevertheless these corporations were based on fairly simple principles and were developed along reasonably logical lines.

1.2. The seeds of confusion

However, while the 'great names' were developing useful, constructive and practical concepts, others were sowing the seeds of confusion that would beset the 1970s. At first they were sown thinly but by the mid-1970s they had taken root and were multiplying fast. Management thought and actions were soon to become a veritable jungle of misconceptions and feeble thinking.

By the beginning of the First World War there had been a fairly drastic change in industrial organisation. The single entrepreneur and partnership enterprises, responsible to their creditors for literally every penny invested in them, had generally been replaced by the joint-stock company. Shares were being issued in ever smaller denominations. With companies requiring larger capital sums, this led often to the dissolution of the traditional controlling interest. As trading conditions worsened or became more competitive, further amalgamations and associations resulted. This aggravated the trend. Logical and necessary rationalisation, although needed, did not occur and the pursuit of self-interest led to increasing internal conflicts. Control of a business became less effective. The accusations of Adam Smith, John Stuart Mill and others, that directors of joint-stock companies were likely to pursue their own interests rather than those of the shareholders as a whole, gained credence. Enterprises that remained owner-controlled, especially by a dominant personality, were relatively more successful. Some cases of the latter existed even into the 1960s.

(It is perhaps worth noting here, however, that by the late 1970s the rapidly growing size and interest of the institutional investors (i.e. the pension funds, insurance companies etc.) has seen these occupy positions where they could exercise some control over the activities of businesses. They have been reluctant to exercise such control and thereby appear to have condoned the continuation of relatively inefficient management. Further, thought is being given to the benefits that could flow from the encouragement of smaller companies. 'Big' is no longer seen as being necessarily 'beautiful' especially as rising costs, inflation and the shortages of capital and other resources begin to bite. If present thoughts and studies continue, they may reverse the trend to large-scale operations.)

1.2.1 The early economists

In the 19th century a group of academics began to call themselves 'economists' and became involved in formulating theories about the behaviour of firms and the allocation of resources. Their chief concern seemed to be the refinement of the theory of competitive markets. With interest and support from outside their own circle, their doctrine of competition gained support. They believed that if all enterprises pursued their own self-interest, seen mainly as the maximisation of their profits, they would produce maximum satisfaction for the community. Competition between them would ensure that only those commodities that people wanted would be produced. Also, those that produced the right products but inefficiently, would not survive.

Such is the persuasive power of economists that this belief represents the view of many top managers, even today, of the role of business in society. However, for the greater part of the 19th century the economists concentrated their thoughts on the theory of *perfect competition*. Surprisingly, they ignored for the most part the possibility of *imperfect competition* arising. Commentators suggest this was simply because they saw no need to consider it. Nor did they see cause to differentiate between the different sorts of competition that could arise. Indeed, it was only towards the end of that century that definitions of competition were attempted. Yet it was the means whereby free enterprise was supposed to regulate itself in society's interest.

While a few economists in the early part of this century were aware that the basic concept mentioned above posed problems, it was not until 1926 that Piero Sraffa spelt it out (see 'The Laws of Returns under Competitive Conditions': *Economic Journal*, XXXVI). It seems obvious today, and it is one of the main reasons for mergers and acquisitions, that even with substantial internal economies of scale, each enterprise cannot continue to expand indefinitely. Ultimately it will encounter the limits of market demand. As that limit is approached so marketing expenses increase as the firm strives to attain further increases in sales. It will ultimately have to reduce unit sale prices to achieve further growth in unit sales. That is, it will be on the classic downward-sloping demand curve.

It came to be appreciated that if the main limit to growth, even with reducing unit costs, was the difficulty of selling the increased output, resolved only by increasing marketing effort and expenses and reducing unit sale prices, then the condition of *perfect competition* did not exist in the market place. An enterprise's products became differentiated from those of other firms. The market supply curve for a commodity had little relevance since each company would produce different commodities. The study of *monopolistic* and *oligopolistic* conditions gained slowly in popularity. Economists began to consider how far the theory of competition could be developed towards covering a monopolistic situation! Attempts were made to salvage some elements of competitive theory, mainly by Professor Joan Robinson (*Economics of Imperfect Competition*) and Edward Chamberlin (*Theory of Monopolistic Competition*). These works were both published in 1933, the worst year of the Great Depression!

Despite these books, economists failed to save their initial basic concept of the theory of the industry. Their studies were forced towards another concept, that of the firm. The emphasis swung away from the study of market behaviour. This appreciated the fact that the firm may operate in many kinds of markets and (especially in the 1960s and 1970s) find itself active simultaneously in more than one kind of market. The enterprise has to make individual decisions on the nature and the character of the products it will produce, the methods and means of producing them, the quantities to be produced and the prices that should be charged. The decisions are as complicated as the variety of markets selected for the company's operations. The managerial thought processes and the management methods required become increasingly complex also.

By the late 1930s industry in most developed countries was comprised substantially of the larger joint-stock companies. Their former association with inefficiency and mismanagement in the minds of economists had been overcome. They were seen now to be the more efficient brethren in industry. The larger companies were thought to be able to take advantage of economies of scale, leading to reduced unit costs as output increased. Thus most of the concept that the efficient working of the forces of supply and demand rested on the existence of perfect competition lay in ruins. In the larger companies the concept arose that managers handled the day-to-day problems and policy decisions. The shareholders (stockholders) who had put up the capital took little or no interest in management aspects of the business. Indeed they seldom bestirred themselves, even when crucial or major policy decisions affecting the whole future of the company arose.

Add to this the proliferation of new economic and other concepts, theories and sub-theories after the Second World War and one can perceive the beginning of the present-day troubles. Management, management decisions and the economic and other theories on which they depended, became immensely complex, especially as gimmickry was substituted more and more for relevance or appropriateness.

Concepts on how management efficiency could be improved also became very complicated. The real problems that had to be solved were obscured more and more by the gimmicks that were introduced. Starting with the sensible, simple idea of studying the work that had to be done and how best to do it within the time and cost constraints that applied (*The Work Approach:* Figure 1.1) the subject edged into sensible application of experience gained by the enterprise and its individual sub-units (*The Experience Approach:* Figure 1.1). In more recent times, the *Psycho-sociological Approach* (Figure 1.1), involving the study of individual and group behaviour and attitudes in the company and its markets and the interactions between them, has enjoyed growing credence. Now in the late 1970s a few voices can be heard querying the basic tenets of growth, size and the interaction of the forces of demand and supply. There is a growing feeling in some quarters that in industrial terms at any rate, being 'big' is not necessary good for the firm. In fact there is no clear-cut, generally accepted theory that can be applied in each and every management case. About the only certainty is that economists and other management theorists will continue to differ widely on what is right and what should be done to increase efficiency and productivity.

As one group propounds one concept, others can be counted on to challenge that and to offer their own concepts and views. Is it surprising therefore that mere executives and planners at enterprise level — forgetting the more complicated conditions existing at national, international and government levels — can become more and more confused on every aspect of what they should be doing, how they should do it and the decisions they should make? Given the greater internationalisation of business and of life in general, the confusion underlying the operation of free- and state-enterprises, and the resultant deterioration in the quality of their decisions and activities, can be appreciated.

The world in general and industry in particular is entering, if it is not already well into, a confused age of mediocrity. This may be due to deterioration in the standards of education and management training. It may be due to individuals' preference for 'La Dolce Vita', or simply, laziness and the desire to earn more and more for less and less effort. It is certainly in part traceable to the plethora of theories and concepts on offer, all of which could be right, wrong, or partly right and partly wrong. It may be due to the fact that many of these theories are being applied to conditions or situations for which they were never intended. It is also due in part to attempts to relate theories and techniques where no inter-relationships exist.

No managerial discipline is immune to this last error. Mass production is fine if mass demand exists. Strict financial controls are excellent if it were not necessary from time to time, to take risks, especially when some new or untried venture is necessary for long-term survival. A knowledge of human behaviour is helpful, provided it is remembered that individuals in any specified group do sometimes behave in ways far removed from the norms enunciated for the group. Each managerial discipline could pursue its own interests, isolated from related disciplines in the enterprise, if overall managerial success did not depend on close, continuous cooperation between disciplines; or if the optimisation of success by each discipline led automatically to the optimisation of success of the whole, which it does not, not even in state-run industry. Good industrial relations are always an important aspect of any business endeavour but they cannot be bought at costs which push market prices beyond what customers will pay. And so on.

1.2.2 Need for reappraisals

Worldwide situations in the late 1970s indicate clearly that management has reached the point where a thorough reappraisal of all concepts is vital for the survival of free enterprise. A return to the first principles of good management is unavoidable. One of these is the acknowledgment of the need for total cooperation between all facets of a business. This must be linked with a simplification of the application of proved techniques of each management discipline. Techniques should be carefully selected for their relevance to the problem or activity in hand. Gimmicks should be avoided at all costs. Whatever the apparent reasons for management failures of the present day, all can to some degree be traced to failure to appreciate these simple rules. Another contributory factor is poor, or ineffective communications within the organisation.

In the economic storms of the late 1960s and the hurricanes of the 1970s, too many enterprises were found to be no more solidly based than the proverbial house built on sand. After a severe 'storm' the survival or viability of the organisation is threatened. Indeed many edifices have crumbled with alarming rapidity and completeness. Discarding the operations that were never really viable in the long term and only appeared so because of some misleading or momentary financial or freak economic condition, many failures were due to ignorance of some basic facts of business life. This includes refusal to bring operations and techniques up to the standards necessary to meet current conditions. In addition some concepts or techniques have been misused while others were applied in some over-complicated manner. Yet other techniques were developed beyond the mental and physical capabilities of mere men and women to use them. The growing amount of supporting hardware made available to executives added to the problem of presenting a bewildering array of choices to executives. Much of this was aggravated further by the reluctance of managers both to talk and to listen to each other, especially when managerial decisions have to be made.

In many instances executives were latter-day Leonardo da Vincis. They may have had brilliant glimpses of original approaches to modern business problems but they lacked all the means to turn these ideas into practical, workable solutions. The more gimmicky a so-called new management technique, the larger was the gap between its theory and likely practice. Far too many of the post-Second World War techniques have been gimmicky. It is significant that the most successful 'modern' methods employed today are old, well-tried techniques. Admittedly many have been altered, almost beyond recognition, to keep pace with the advanced hardware (e.g. computers) or greater experience and improved knowledge (e.g. in statistics) existing today. A wide-ranging series of studies in depth, yet to be done, may well show that the more brilliant the academic thought behind the development of a 'new technique', the less likely is it to be capable of useful, practical application. The need today is, and always will be, for more efficient practical minds; people who will not be swept away by the current fad of super-enthusiasm for any new idea just because it is new. These people too must be willing to cooperate at all times with colleagues from other departments of a firm.

Other complications arise because some traditional views are maintained without due regard to their relevance or suitability to current conditions and needs. While it is good to continue with proved methods that have worked in similar situations, tradition for tradition's sake is as damaging to managerial proficiency as the rush to use every new technique, regardless of its relevance. The dominant traditionalism encountered in every country and all industries from time to time, is that of the strict compartmentalisation of areas of work. Each department is regarded as a self-contained and separate entity. Members of other departments or disciplines are warned off at all costs. (For example, woe betide the marketing person who takes an interest in manufacturing matters even if that enlightened executive is doing so because it is realised that closer understanding and cooperation between these two departments are vital for sustained business success.) Much of the in-fighting that goes on, openly or secretly, is based on this misguided concept.

In business education also, staff are too often held rigidly to the exercising of their knowledge of the specialism to which they have been assigned. Little regard is paid to the fact that their practical and theoretical knowledge of other specialisms, especially those peripheral to their main subject, could be better utilised. Sometimes a person may be incorrectly assigned to a specialism due to some misinterpretation of their achievements. Alternatively, the rigidity of staff establishments in colleges may require them to be placed in a particular department regardless of their true capabilities. Other locations which could better utilise the total skills of the person concerned have then to be ignored. By these and other means, confusion is compounded.

Many readers will be able to recall instances of these problems within their own experience. They will recall also the stubborn way some executives cling to methods and techniques regardless of their relevance to the task in hand. Instances include the random use of all marketing techniques even if, for example, the bulk of the business is in national and local tenders. In this case a little market and product research to identify the tenders the enterprise should strive for, and a little corporate advertising to keep the name of the firm in the minds of those who issue the tenders may be all that is required. Or further, as in the 1960s and mid-1970s, there may be insistence that the company has an expensive computer system when all that it may have needed was some time-sharing arrangement with another appropriate system. For example the travel industry has various arrangements to tie in with the major airlines' computer systems. The trouble is that once a computer is installed, work for it will be created to keep it loaded at least to its theoretical economic level. The fact that much of this work may not be necessary is ignored and the resultant waste of resources is not appreciated.

Other examples of wasteful use of resources exist. A common one is insistence on there being a detailed marketing research programme. This may provide vast amounts of information and data which the company may not be able to use. Either the rest of the management system is not sophisticated enough to use the data or it lacks the number of executives, because it cannot afford them, to process the data in time. Then much of the information obtained will not be used. This wealth of information may just confuse the issue. The real problems or answers may be hidden under the weight of data provided and the more information there is the more likely it is to be misinterpreted. Then there are the misapplications or misuse of operational research and behavioural science techniques. All management techniques have their uses but in the haphazard and unthinking ways in which they are applied their usefulness is often negated.

1.2.3 Myths and taboos

The human being is a mixture of rational and irrational thoughts, words and deeds. The exact rational/irrational mix depends on the stresses and strains appertaining to a given time and subject. Sociological considerations such as status, occupation, income level, social class, educational and religious backgrounds also influence this mix. When a person becomes a manager he or she does not automatically become a more rational being. In fact, depending on the prestige of the job and its inherent stress, the person may well become a less rational being, at least in thought and action. This is so even when the executive, with innate cunning, covers up this irrationality with a façade of resolute assurance presented to the world at large. Graham Cleverley, a former director of manpower development for the International Publishing Company in Britain, in his book *Managers and Magic* (Longman, 1971) suggested there were parallels of behaviour between today's managers and members of the 'superstitious societies' of earlier times. Since 1971 some other writers and academics in business studies have ventured similar views. Several senior practitioners in management will agree with these views, if reluctantly.

Managers' behaviour seems to be conditioned and guided by actual taboos concerning things that must or must not be done in given conditions regardless of their true relevance. This is more pronounced the more senior an executive becomes. For example, there are many taboos surrounding the 'cabinet decision and responsibility' approach of board decisions. Once a decision is agreed, it is considered treachery if a board member speaks out publicly against the decision. Only in dire circumstances is the view of the board challenged. Institutional non-executive directors, though they are on the board to protect the considerable investment of their own share- or stock-holders in the company, seldom if ever speak out on any point. This is so even when they know that incorrect and costly decisions have been taken by the board. In several instances they have not stirred even when it was fairly clear the company was heading into serious trouble or bankruptcy. The breaking of these directorate taboos cause at best a feeling of unease in the minds of the violator and the violated and at worst creates such antagonism on the board that ultimately the violator has to resign, or is ignobly sacked. These and other taboos have become so firmly entrenched and are held so strongly even when greatly irrational in concept, that they are applied even in situations where trouble or retribution for breaking the taboo is never likely to occur.

The wide range of these taboos may be judged from the following list. Company chairmen (or presidents in the U.S.A.) visit their factories at set times in a year. (If British companies have an operation in the Caribbean or in Southeast Asia, a safari is usually arranged for December, January or February. For American presidents or vice-presidents, visits to European subsidiaries usually take place in the Spring or Summer). Although the purpose is said to be to see the operation on the ground and check on efficiency and productivity, the preparations for the visit and the time consumed by the visit and its attendant genuflections mean in reality that productivity and efficiency decline during the visit. If it proved to be a traumatic visit, in some sense, for the visited, then productivity and efficiency may remain depressed for some considerable time. In some cases they never recover!

Another associated taboo is that local people, if suitably qualified, are picked to run their own national operations. This is on the sound basis that local people know their own conditions and markets best. So why visit them except very occasionally to let them see they have not been forgotten? It is far better to get them to visit the parent company. For most other reasons the implications are that the right people are not in post perhaps because they do not exist. Or in the early days of the emergence of their countries local appointments may at times have been dictated by political considerations. However, business education and the internationalisation of business has become so widespread in the last two decades that the selection of the wrong person for a job should rarely occur or be due to some defect in the selection process. In these cases visits by suitable personnel executives, with far less formality, would be more effective and less disruptive to overall operations.

Then for some there is the marketing taboo of the advertising/sales ratio. Many organisations maintain a near strict adherence to such ratios which, in any case, only suggest the norms for a particular industry, market or product. The actual apportionment of an advertising budget for any given sales target is, however, dependent on many other factors. These include competition, product quality, image of company and products in selected markets, price and profit margins, market shares and the amount of money that can in fact be afforded (to mention a few). Trauma and stress should not be allowed to arise if a company is found to be well outside the indicated ratio, provided the objectives or purposes of the advertising are sound and correctly based on marketing and corporate objectives. Yet executives will squander money, or underspend in relation to needs and so cause havoc to the actual profits earned through sticking, unthinkingly to some advertising/sales ratio. At best, these ratios indicate only how different one's business is from the declared norms. At worst, they offer the inexperienced executive an approximate guide to expenditure.

In manufacturing an oft-met myth is that summed up by the dreaded phrase 'economy of scale'. It is a widely held belief that the greater the output, the lower will be the unit cost of production. So, it goes on, there is a certain scale of production that will give optimum economy measured in terms of unit costs. While this is theoretically correct, blind adherence to this rule ignores factors such as market demand. It does not matter how cheaply a product may be produced in quantity, benefits will not occur if the quantity made cannot be absorbed by its market. The actual production costs will represent partial or total loss depending on how much of the output remains unsold. If the product is out of date in design, quality, performance etc., it does not matter how cheaply it is produced; it will not sell. It may have to be cleared from inventories at prices well below cost or even written off entirely if customers cannot be persuaded to buy it.

In the financial department the taboos met with frequently concern the rate of return, or the period over which a project must recoup all costs and show a profit and the return on investment which an operation must be targeted to achieve. If these are not within some norm set by the financial department or the board, the ideas are not approved by the accountants. Frequently, little thought is given to the long-term development plans and objectives of the company. Nor is much appreciation shown, at times, for the fact that survival and growth of an enterprise may make it unavoidable for it to run a project or two that will never do much more than break even. Happily, in the more enlightened companies, these taboos are dying and accountants and executives are becoming more interested in risk reduction, if the long-term objectives are right, rather than in the impossible task of trying to eliminate all risk.

On the personnel side of business, a common taboo is the strict adherence to the need for references in the appointment of a new employee. Yet the laws of most lands regarding libel and slander are such that no-one, except the bold or foolhardy, would issue a bad reference, even if it were true. In practice, a truly bad reference may help a candidate if the personnel executives believe that no-one could be so bad! Further, few executives seem to realise that a person may be useless in one job but good in another. It all depends on the chemistry of the situation, the personality and desires or preferences of the candidate, the type of colleagues involved and the general atmosphere pervading the department or company for which the candidate is aiming. All these factors may have been wrong in the previous employer but may be right for the candidate in the new situation. Thus previous poor performance and even bad behaviour may count for little in the new job. Most references are not worth the paper they are written on, yet referees still have to experience anguish and spend much time and thought on this chore.

Finally, on a minor note, many companies produce house journals whose worth and usefulness are in doubt. With widespread or large businesses the journal may help to keep each unit informed of what the others are doing and how individuals are contributing to the overall enterprise. The cost and trouble involved in producing the journals, however, far outweigh any benefits. Often the journals are given only a cursory glance; many are consigned straight to the wastepaper basket; or they are seen simply as vehicles to boost the ego of extrovert members of staff or to promote the image of a few favoured for promotion by senior executives. If not carefully written, some article or report may merely create extra friction or new conflicts. Recent examples in Britain were articles concerning possible wage and salary increases under conditions of government-imposed constraints. Even though these were trying to sell sensible ideas on new wage bargaining and other procedures, they provided useful vehicles by which the trade unions or individuals could mount powerful counter-offensives before the ideas had had a chance to be debated or investigated rationally.

Every reader could add examples drawn from personal experience. These perhaps just illustrate the widespread nature of taboos and myths and the potential harm that adherence to them can do to a corporation. Frequently they emphasise that the situation is '*my mind is made up—do not confuse me with facts*'. They show that executives are often not prepared to acknowledge that circumstances and conditions have changed and that new approaches are necessary to face up to these changes successfully.

Many of the current taboos seem to be based either on blind faith or a sceptical attitude to management. Because something seems to have worked in the past, it is tried again and again regardless of different circumstances. If it appears not to have worked, it is rejected out of hand without investigation to discover why it has not worked. On the other hand, even sceptics rush to implement 'new' techniques regardless of their worth or relevance. It may be in their scepticism they have accepted that new things are the current fad, so all new things must be right for today! Much of this attitude may be due to the fact that managers work in an atmosphere of insecurity and, in some organisations, fear. They do not understand the system in which they must operate nor the forces having play in, or effect on, the system. So if myths do not exist, executives tend to create them; and if the people survive for a sufficient period of time, the myths are translated in their minds as new taboos to be followed relentlessly.

1.2.4 More modern complications

Several more recent developments have further complicated the world of management. When mankind 'invented' money, inflation was also 'invented'. The latter has worried executives for a long time. However it is only since social, economic and political forces began to play an increasingly major role in affecting inflation that it became a nightmare. Greater involvement in business and economic matters by home governments (i.e. the government of one's home country) and with the internationalisation of business, by host governments (i.e. the government of a foreign country in which a company is operating), have added greater complexities. It was only a few years ago that governments worried about apparently high inflation rates of 3 per cent per annum or so. Now after rates in the 20 to 30 per cent per annum range (with some countries achieving 200 to 300 per cent!) most governments and executives would consider 3 per cent as stability!

With increasing world trade there are increasing balance of payments problems. If one or two world markets decline several nations may experience an economic slump, for which the modern euphemism is 'recession'. All the forces at play are little understood. Witness the many conflicting, often diametrically opposed 'solutions' suggested for identical conditions. Many people just hope that someone, somewhere will have the answers that work and until that Messiah appears, they will cling to established taboos and myths.

It is clear from study of the records of most governments and quasi-governmental bodies, that no-one really understands how an economy works. There is a considerable body of opinion that says that any national economic problem would correct itself even if the government did nothing. Others believe that an economy corrects itself *despite* official action. Where government measures appear to have worked, partial hindsight showed that undesirable side-effects had occurred and that the economy had already begun to recover before the remedies were introduced. Further, many of the remedies in fact retarded or minimised recovery or ensured that another recession would occur shortly. (Note the long and tedious arguments in Britain during the 1950s to 1970s about the 'Stop-Go' policies followed by every government of that period. The regular slide into credit squeezes and recessions due to many people's reluctance to work harder and accept methods that would increase productivity, was dubbed the 'English disease'. However as other countries succumbed to the same problem in the 1970s, it was obviously not a purely 'English' problem. By 1977 some six million or more people were out of work throughout Western Europe. In the U.S.A. the unemployment rate exceeded 8 per cent for a substantial period.) Even in the more successful countries there is scant evidence that official action produced any remedial results. Indeed, the more successful nations had governments that took minimal action.

Time and again, business spokesmen claim that people are in business to make profits. Some go on to state that unless profits are earned a business cannot survive. (However, some unprofitable businesses take an extremely long time to die!) While profit is not the sole criterion of success, it is a basic rationale of business. Unfortunately, many executives do not work to earn profits for the company. They are obsessed with power, self-esteem, social status and, sometimes, comradeship. If they kept the profit motive in mind — even made of it a new taboo — then many of today's business problems would no longer exist. Without profits, a free-enterprise company will eventually founder although some can take a very long time to struggle to oblivion. With state-owned industry, however, survival is paid for through increased injections of capital, adding to the burden of the taxpayer, and ever-rising prices until the consumer revolts and refuses to pay exorbitant prices. The record of state-owned enterprises in Britain in several instances bears this out.

Next, just as religions of all kinds postulate the existence of supernatural forces, so managers assign such powers to the share- or stock-holder. In practice, the power of the shareholder is limited and seldom exercised. This belief, another taboo, is used as an excuse for the behaviour patterns of many executives. It is used to cover their sins of omission and commission. The chief rite of absolution is the annual general meeting. It is usually required by law that an annual general meeting is held, but it is also often seen as an annual incantation to the gods (i.e. the shareholders) to keep them happy (i.e. a propitiation of the gods) and so persuade them to keep their powers dormant. Happily, there are signs that the gods are becoming restive. However, until the major gods (i.e. the institutional investors) stir themselves, the annual general meeting ritual will survive in its present form for some time to come.

Another part of the creed concerns the apparent supernatural powers of the company. In fact, a company is just (we hope) a heterogeneous group of people who are supposed to be working to common goals. 'The company' can do nothing, decree nothing, except what the people who comprise it agree it should achieve. Yet, often, a powerful personality is allowed to impose his or her will on the organisation, in the name of 'the company', regardless of the correctness of that person's decisions and actions. (The dangers of one-person rule are discussed later.) Sometimes 'the company' is deemed to be the persons of the shareholders but so long as they are inactive, such a 'company' does not exist in practice.

Companies also have their 'high priests'. They include not only senior executives with powerful personalities but also specialists deemed to have arcane knowledge and skills. If they have achieved some modicum of success in the past, their skills and knowledge are believed to extend beyond the bounds of their expertise. Ordinary managers will then believe that they can never aspire to such heights and allow themselves to be convinced by the 'high priests' that certain actions and decisions are essential. Managers then do not query the opinions of these people often enough and accept without criticism, or constructive investigation, the advice given by these so-called experts. They forget one definition of an expert: a person who knows more and more about less and less! If managers were more critical, in a constructive manner, of expert opinion proffered to them they would not face so many problems in the future.

Also, executives do not check the trustworthiness of the expert. Human nature being what it is, all experts tend to proffer information and views which help to support their reputation as experts in their own subjects. Checking the reliability of the sources of information is essential. Experts are useful, however, in suggesting other persons who could also give advice. When these are not seen as experts, or do not see themselves as such, their information and suggestions may be more reliable. Finally, many executives do not take the common-sense precaution of seeking information from more than one source and then comparing or checking the advice and 'facts' so obtained.

It is unnecessary to go on. Enough has been stated to indicate why business activity has become so complicated and why it can go off course so easily. If taboos and myths can be seen for what they are, out-of-date concepts and half-truths, perhaps more executives will have the courage to explore other approaches. Some may be new but many will be simply a return to the first principles of management on which most successful enterprises base their activities.

Greater use of common sense will also help. So will a willingness to throw textbook solutions out of the window when this is necessary and a determination to evolve unique solutions for a company's own circumstances and conditions. In this way workable solutions to company problems, present and future ones, will be found more easily.

1.2.5 Size and growth

A widely held belief, especially by top managers, is that the task of management is to balance the divergent interests of shareholders, customers, employees and creditors, according to the resources and capabilities of the company. Since resources, whether of money, people or plant, are always limited, the only way to ensure increasing satisfaction for all parties is to increase the resources of the company. This then becomes another major aim of management. However, this latter point assumes the existence of a unity of purpose; that the company should grow and prosper as rapidly as possible in the interest of all who are dependent on the enterprise.

By the mid-1970s that view was under scrutiny. First, cases are developing which show that mere size is not always beneficial. The bigger an organisation, the more difficult it becomes to maintain efficient control of all facets of the business at all times. There are many reasons for this. First, the problems thrown up by size may simply be beyond the capabilities of the executive team. Or the resultant conglomeration of activities may be too diverse, or unrelated, or too scattered or too small individually to offer long-term survival prospects. Many of the taboos and myths may have too much sway on decisions and operations. Ignorance of the new businesses, markets or countries of operation could also be contributory factors to poor performance.

Other causes of problems and failures inherent in the size of the organisation include the fact that the larger the company, the greater are the number and levels of decisions which have to be taken. The communication and decision channels may be too long and complex. This is particularly inhibiting when decisions have to be made speedily. There may be too much information requiring constructive analysis and this too will increase the time required to arrive at correct decisions, increasing the time delay and reducing further the chances of good decisions being taken at the right times. The real danger is that all these points increase the chances of incorrect decisions being made for expediency.

The technical aspects, whether of technology, markets or finance, of each problem also become more complex. So do the decision-making processes, further complicating the communication network. Also, the human element of business (i.e. the thoughts, views, expectations, prejudices and desires of employees and customers) cannot be considered carefully, if at all, in the time available. So further chances of friction or dissatisfaction are created.

Thus, large size can be a serious handicap rather than an advantage. One solution may be to break up the enterprise into autonomous, sensible and workable smaller profit centres; but this too has its problems. How should one divisionalise, and what subsidiaries should be formed? What activities should be allocated to each? What are the implications for, and interactions between, each unit? Neat, tidy, self-contained blocks of operations are almost impossible to achieve and may in the long term not be workable, given the wide spread of activities of a large enterprise. Some consider the most workable idea is to keep each unit to a particular number of employees, 250, 500, 1000, 2000 etc. However, this ignores the product-market operational considerations which will not break down into such convenient sub-units of equivalent manufacturing and marketing activities. It also begs the questions posed above.

Breaking up the operation by product lines also poses similar problems. Then the existence of such sub-units could lead to lack of uniformity or consistency in policy and in coordination between the sub-units. The dynamics of the enterprise must also be considered and will influence decisions on the correct way to achieve the divisionalisation of the company. If the enterprise's basic industries or technologies are expanding rapidly, too great a burden may also be placed on the group's top management as well as on its subsidiaries.

Not one of the possibilities mentioned represents a general or common solution to the question of divisionalisation. Each company will have to work out a solution which is appropriate or unique to itself. There are no textbook solutions and, in the end, compromises will be necessary, with the final result deviating by various degrees from what may be considered the ideal solution. The success or failure of other enterprises gives little guidance. The operating and other circumstances of the other companies will usually be different, often very different, from those of the company seeking a solution. There is no alternative to analysing the basic principles of operation applying to the enterprise and seeking custom-built solutions. Some companies have managed it, and the first names that spring to mind are General Motors of the U.S.A. and Thomas Tilling and the Norcros Group in Britain, but their methods of operation are quite different. The objectives of their solutions could also be quite different.

Growth, and whether or how an enterprise should achieve it, is another hurdle. Until recently, growth in absolute terms was a major target of most businesses. Growth had to be achieved, often at any cost and was thought to be a never-ending possibility. Provided the resources could be marshalled and periods of consolidation allowed for, growth into the unknown long term was considered possible. This too is now in question.

Economic developments in the 1970s have thrown further doubts on these views of size and growth. The desire of all emerging nations to have their own industries to support or supplement their basically agricultural economies, has increased competition and reduced the possibility of unlimited growth for industry in developed countries. Developed nations with their higher labour and other costs find themselves at a disadvantage. Nor are the world's resources infinite. Even if new reserves of oil and other important raw materials continue to be discovered at present, ultimately there is a limit. Even if these resources are unlimited, one other resource, skilled workers, is not. While population growth has been explosive in nature, there has been a slowing down of this in the 1970s. Further, the supply of suitably skilled labour of all kinds has not kept pace with demand made by industrial growth. Also, some nations are now worrying about the ageing characteristics of their populations. They are wondering how an ever-declining workforce of younger people will be able to produce enough to support everyone. Hopes pinned on technological development have also dimmed as the limits to technological development and the increasing problems associated with it (e.g. escalating development costs; lack of hardware of the right standards and quality) become clearer. Even if sufficient skilled people existed to man the factories and farms, the earth has a finite limit to the number of people it could house, feed, educate etc.

As nations become overpopulated the chances of major epidemics increase. Nature has a way of balancing things and major world epidemics wiping out large numbers of people is a natural expectancy, a way in which nature corrects imbalances. Other natural hazards (e.g. plagues of locusts, droughts, floods etc.) will also inhibit efforts for economic and industrial growth. The problems associated with the handling, education, feeding and employment of large numbers of people over a long-term period will also be beyond the capabilities of mankind if present results are any indication of the future. Even with today's population, mankind has enough troubles. Extreme poverty and hardship exist in many countries regardless of efforts to remedy the situation. Only another major leap forward in intellect and skill would allow solutions to today's economic and business problems. There is also need for an increase in humanitarian thought for the less fortunate and a willingness by nations and people at large to sink their own selfish interests to help the disadvantaged improve their lot.

1.2.6 Managers — a key resource

Peter Drucker (*People and Performance*) affirms that managers are the basic, vital resource of a business enterprise. Other textbooks on management make similar statements, or the view is implied by the text. Noteworthy amongst fairly recent publications are *Fundamentals of Management* by Donnelly, Gibson and Ivancevich and *Management and Organisation* by Sisk (Southwestern 1973). Only a few highly automated operations (e.g. oil refineries) can function efficiently on a handful of skilled technical people, but even they must have a core of highly trained and experienced managers. Indeed, the more automated a process, the more highly trained and skilled must be its managers.

Where the abilities of managers fall below the standards needed, the operation will encounter many problems. The number of difficulties that arise seems to be in some geometric relationship with the shortfall in managerial skills and experience. Yet there are cases of companies which manage to survive to some degree despite the inefficiencies of their managerial teams. In general though, problem-fraught enterprises favour the remedy of a massive reorganisation of their workforce. This may merely shift people from one task to another, or recruit some new employees, or (most often) declare some of the workforce to be redundant. (The days of simple sackings for incompetence are gone, and now one is made 'redundant'.) Yet in many cases the workforce so affected may be innocent victims. The correct solution may have been to sack incompetent managers or move them to jobs that they can do well, and recruit people who are trained, experienced and qualified for the jobs that have to be done.

Until recently there has been scant recognition that managers represent the most expensive resource of a company. Their gross cost to an enterprise is much greater than that of a skilled blue-collar worker or technician. They cost more to train also. In addition, they represent a resource that depreciates quickly. With the increased rate of change experienced in most sectors of the business environment (technology, finance, marketing etc.) executives should be retrained at planned, regular intervals, if not continuously. This resource also requires regular supplementation and at times, replenishment, depending on the increasing demands that a business places on its executives' abilities. How well managers control the work of their departments and how effectively they themselves are managed, governs the degree of success in achieving the corporate objectives of an enterprise.

Yet it is only in the last two decades in Europe, admittedly longer in the U.S.A., that management training and development has featured in any degree in corporate thinking. In some countries (e.g. Britain) the first attempts to improve executive development have been only qualified successes. Too many universities and colleges are still preoccupied with the achievement of their own academic ideals and ideas of excellence, regardless of relevance to business needs. The author recalls, not so long ago, querying the practical relevance of proposed changes in a major business studies course only to be rebuked by the head of the faculty concerned with: 'I am not interested in what industry wants, only in the attainment of the academic objectives of the course.' That is fine, if these objectives match the real and urgent needs of industry. If they do not, only long-term disaster awaits the business community and perhaps, the unfortunates on the course. As Peter Drucker has recorded so often and eloquently, there have been many exhortations underlining that a manager's task is to manage the people in their charge so as to get them to realise, constantly, the objectives to which they should strive in their work. He calls this 'downward communications'. Yet when engaged in discussions many managers seem preoccupied with 'upward communications', that is trying to impress their superiors and striving only to respond to their imagined views and reactions. This happens in the academic world also. They seek to maintain the goodwill of their superiors, without regard to the fact that in doing so, they may be working against the real objectives of the enterprise and their own true, long-term welfare. Yet doing the right things and achieving objectives is the only real way to ensure the approval of one's superiors.

Drucker quotes the case of Henry Ford's rise and decline; and the revival of the company under Henry Ford II, his grandson. He states that Ford eventually failed because he was firmly convinced that a business did not need managers or management. All that was required was the owner and a trusted group of helpers. If a person dared to act as a manager should, it is alleged, he was fired or sidetracked regardless of his abilities. Failure was due not to personality conflicts, nor temperament, but to the failure to realise the need for a competent management team and sound management. The grandson ousted many of his grandfather's executives and brought in a new management team whose competence saved the company and set it on the road to being a powerful, international enterprise. Of course, from time to time fresh problems and difficulties were met and overcome. Henry Ford II applied the opposite thesis to that of his grandfather, one that some twenty years earlier, had been tried and found to be successful by Alfred P. Sloan Jr. when he became president of General Motors. Sloan's work raised General Motors from being a poor second to Ford, a collection of operations stitched together financially, to the world leader it remains today. (In Britain today a similar example has been the Norcros Group.) Both men created efficient management structures and teams. They showed that in any enterprise, other than those of limited size, efficient management is a prerequisite for sustained success in business. Even if management is just the delegation of the top person's, or owner's, job, the complexities involved in running an enterprise of any size makes it impossible for one person to control all its activities with consistent success.

The U.S.A. has had several men like the first Henry Ford but it has also had many people like Alfred P. Sloan Jr. and other self-made persons who saw the importance of having efficient and successful management teams to run their businesses. Indeed, the U.S.A., West Germany and to a lesser extent, Japan, seem to have more than their fair share of successful self-made people who understood what management was all about. Is it a coincidence that these same countries have the most consistently successful business records since the Second World War? While all that emanates from a foreign country may not be beneficial or appropriate for other nationals, concepts that have proved themselves to be sound are always worthy of study to see if in some modified form they could be helpful in other countries.

With hindsight, one can see the considerable element of truth in such contentions. On a national basis, post-war West Germany, Japan and the U.S.A. (and in the 1980s, perhaps S. Korea) are the best proofs of that view. On industrial levels, companies succeed when they have dynamic management and fail when that successful management is replaced by more lethargic executives, due to the retirement or transfer of the original teams. When the next generation of youngsters shows marked disinterest in personal achievement, or when ill-conceived educational aims and techniques are allowed to dampen the interests of up-and-coming generations, then the national drive for achievement wanes. Former leading nations can very soon degenerate into 'also-rans' or 'has-beens'. In the 1970s many cases appeared to bear out these contentions. It would be worth the trouble of full-scale surveys by social scientists, with an understanding of business concepts, to see how far these ideas are correct in practice. For when such trends are coupled with an indiscriminate rush to grasp at all the latest techniques regardless of their relevance, or to ape others (the easy way out as it is easy to copy, so difficult to work things out for oneself), difficult economic and business times must be the outcome for the unfortunate individuals and nations so afflicted.

1.2.7 Effects of taxation on initiative and motivation

High levels of taxation, especially when the bands between rates of taxation are narrow and taxation thresholds are low, are great disincentives to executive initiative. When these are coupled with substantial periods of severe pay restraints, not only is disincentive at its highest but motivation of executives and shopfloor people is almost impossible. The end-on effects are considerable enough to have serious adverse consequences on a national economy.

For example, in Britain in the 1970s, high taxation and relatively narrow bands between successive rates, coupled with unemployment relief payments considered by many to be too generous, often made it more advantageous for skilled blue collar workers with families not to seek employment. Either the net pay was so little more, or even less, than the total unemployment benefit that could be drawn that it was just not worth the effort involved in working. Thus high levels of unemployment were maintained and national output potential was not realised. The economical and profitable operations of all businesses were subsequently threatened and Britain's performance in the world's industrial league deteriorated, aggravating a wide range of economic problems. The total human resource capabilities of the nation were not being fully utilised. In other countries (e.g. India) where rates of taxation were high in relation to pay levels and increases in taxation for increases in pay were so big that promoted executives took home less pay than before promotion, the disincentive was at its greatest. Not unnaturally, many executives refused to accept promotion. The greater responsibilities and risks involved in more senior posts were not acceptable given the lower net financial rewards.

In addition, senior executives, in particular in Britain, took a depressing view of pay and promotion generally. They saw themselves as being discriminated against by government pay policies which affected them more adversely than other groups of workers. Pay differentials were being eroded. The morale and motivation of executives, especially in big companies, were damaged. The incentive to work harder for the good of all was considerably reduced. More than nine out of ten executives interviewed in a survey in Britain (*Survey of the Motivation of Top Management*, Opinion Research Centre, London, 1978) considered the government's approach to the taxation of managers as unfair. Some 85 per cent held the same view of the government's attitudes to pay differentials while more than 75 per cent considered that the government did not appear to regard the work of managers to be important or worthwhile! Over 90 per cent of senior managers considered themselves badly paid, in net terms, in comparison with junior groups of management and skilled labour. Expanding on the theme that high levels of taxation act as disincentives on managers, the survey showed that a startlingly high level of executives (84 per cent of senior managers and 50 per cent of all executives) agreed that government attitudes to pay and taxation encouraged people to break the law. Significant numbers of executives were refusing to accept promotion because of the effects of taxation on subsequent pay increases.

Nor were these attitudes confined only to Britain. Surveys by *Eurosurveys*, at about the same time in other European countries, identified similar dissatisfaction amongst executives, though not to such a pronounced degree. This was despite the fact that these countries were considered to treat executives and taxation of executive pay better than in Britain. (The U.S.A. was considered to offer a more favourable attitude to managers than European countries.) These surveys indicate how essential it is for governments to see taxation, especially at the higher levels of income, as having considerable effect on the attitudes of executives to their work, net remuneration and resultant incentives and motivation to improve their performance. Pursuing taxation policies for political motives without due regard to economic and social considerations can hinder and retard the economic development of a nation. (*See also* Section 7.4.3.)

1.3 Communication barriers

The seeds of confusion are nurtured by the existence of communication barriers in an organisation. These barriers are encountered in life generally, so it is not surprising that they occur in the business community also. They are the direct results of the nature of the human animal, an egotistical often selfish and self-centred individual, more often than not interested only in its own well-being and progress and with an inflated opinion of its own abilities and powers. No-one is free from these failings to some degree or other (alas, not even the author!). Thus from time to time we will be secretive or uncommunicative, especially if we have taken umbrage at something done or said when no offence was intended by the third party. Far worse, perhaps, in the business community are those persons who are unable or unwilling to listen to what others are saying to them or to understand the written word put before them. These failings may be due to lack of intelligence, simple ignorance of the subject being discussed, overwork (which in the resultant rush can distract the executive's mind or attention), or some other character defect. Whatever the cause, the result is chaos in the organisation and a lowering of operational efficiency and profitability.

People's individual natures, characters and behaviour patterns lead to wide variance in the ready acceptance of a communication's intended meaning, whether in spoken or written form. A few receive and accept a message as it was intended. Many others seem always able to misinterpret it. Some, probably a larger number than realised, will resist or resent the import of the communication as a result of a total misunderstanding of it or due to some remote, deep-seated prejudice. Even with the simplest form of communication, one person speaking to another, there is the situation of two individuals trying to understand each other when, perhaps, their backgrounds, outlooks, concepts, expectations, fears etc. are quite different. Thus there is always the possibility that each will place a different meaning on the words used, when the message that is sent is not what is received in terms of meaning. If their educational, family and religious backgrounds are very different, then the degree of misunderstanding or misinterpretation is likely to be greater. Even if no prejudice or antagonism exists between them, their different backgrounds and experiences will lead to the placing of different meanings on the communications quite naturally. All these factors help to distort the true meaning of the communication.

In business, the size of the organisation can also help to increase the distortion factor. The greater the number of layers of supervision or management, or its physical or geographical spread, the longer are the lines of communication. The inter-staff relationships are also more complex so the communication network itself is also a complex one. In these conditions it becomes more difficult to maintain a good and effective communication system which is free of distortion at all times. The basic problem here is often that many will be 'talkers' or initiators of communications but few will listen carefully to what is being said to them. Or they may accept the words at face value without trying to get to the meaning behind the words.

As stated earlier, the difference in corporate and social status will also determine the variance between points of view on the subject being communicated. When a subordinate listens to a superior, the receiver will evaluate the message received in terms of their background, position, status, experience and so on. The receiver will also unconsciously evaluate the sender and will find it difficult, even when aware of the points made earlier, to set aside any prejudice held about the sender. Motives are applied to the message which the sender never dreamed of, nor intended. A regular example of this is the adverse interpretations which trade union representatives place on management statements, especially those dealing with pay and conditions of service. They have a fixation (another taboo or myth which cannot be abandoned?) that management's prime aim is to undermine the power and authority of the unions. Similarly, the reverse is true. Many executives view with suspicion anything said by a trade unionist, especially the leaders of a union (a managerial taboo or myth also?).

Even the house journal or company newspaper tends to be seen as a propaganda organ or mouthpiece of management to be read by workers with suspicion. The truth of the communications is not appreciated. Indeed, one suspects that companies do not really have manufacturing, marketing or any other problems. They are just outwards manifestations of some communications problem or breakdown. Either the system has broken down or ineptitude or slackness in the formation of the communication has led to misunderstanding. If this is not cleared quickly, the passage of time will lead to further distortions of the truth and greater misunderstanding until the real cause of the failure of the communication will be lost or forgotten.

Thus, much more consideration should be given to a company's communications network and system than has been given in the past. Also, regular reviews of the system and its effectiveness and efficiency are advisable since the company and its business environment are subject to many changes and developments. The system will therefore require modifications from time to time even if it were originally effective and efficient. The problem of executives who do not listen to their subordinates should receive constant attention. The reason may stem from a belief that the juniors are not worth listening to or it may be due to some other pressing problem occupying the executive's mind. The former means that the executive is applying the status barrier in reverse, i.e. they consider it is beneath them to give much time or consideration to utterances by juniors. Time often shows the error of such attitudes, but by then the damage has been done and the juniors begin to build on their misconceptions of the ability and intelligence of their superiors. Given that in most organisations communications are not a person-to-person matter but involve many executives at different levels, the escalation of the problems that poor communications will bring can be appreciated. Also, senior executives would be well advised to devote more time to ensuring that their executives are really both talking and listening to each other!

1.3.1 Resistance to change

Another result of poor communications is the degree to which workers resist any change, regardless of the essentiality of the need to make some changes. This resistance to change is a natural phenomenon of the human animal. We are all guilty of it in our daily lives. We cling desperately to the familiar or known, and are scared of anything new or untried. It is not surprising that this, really unhealthy, attitude should be carried over into the business community.

Now every listener seems to have some form of inbuilt filter that receives, accepts or rejects messages. (As you study this book, you are doing just all that! You will be accepting some of the points made but will also be rejecting, probably vehemently, other contentions, depending on your loyalties.) If the communication or proposed change is an unpleasant one, or the message conflicts with firmly held beliefs, the filter rejects it to an extent that the receiver genuinely does not remember having received it. If oral communications are involved the receiver may not hear the message at all, so efficient is the filter in keeping out unpleasant news. It is totally effective of course if the receiver on hearing the news goes into a state of shock.

Alternatively, the receiver will hear only what he or she expects or wishes to hear. The power of this barrier to communications depends on the sense of insecurity, degree of fearfulness, worry or antagonism a person has towards the organisation or a superior. A senior executive knowing this about a subordinate is sometimes tempted to play upon these fears or aversions for the executive's own selfish ends. This is a short-sighted approach, since it will only create more friction, resentment and hostility towards the executive, with colleagues of the unfortunate person probably lining up with him or her against the senior executive. The result is a long-term problem for the company and perhaps eventual disaster for the senior executive.

The attitudes mentioned above also condition the amount of resistance to change which will be encountered. There are several causes, but the seven most frequently encountered as responsible for a person's attitude to change are listed below. However, it should be remembered that there are complex interactions between them and the persons involved. So each and every organisation needs to study this problem from its own individual viewpoint. The seven factors are:

1.   the extent of the feeling of insecurity felt by people;
2.   the amount of trust existing between management, the trade unions and the work groups;
3.   the manner in which changes are introduced and implemented;
4.   the predisposed feeling about change of any kind;
5.   the views held of immediate historical events relevant to the change, and sometimes even irrelevant or irrational ones;
6.   specific apprehensions or expectations about each particular change; and
7.   the prevailing cultural beliefs and norms which might be in conflict with the change and may in part be the result of background, education, upbringing and experience.

Research that has been done into this subject suggests that:

a.   change is more acceptable to people who have participated in planning for it than to those on whom change is imposed;
b.   change is more acceptable when it is not seen as a threat to any individual or group but rather as an opportunity for greater achievement and endeavour;
c.   change is more acceptable to those who are not affected by it than those

who are; the latter will tend to defend the structure or event which they see as being under attack;

  d. change is acceptable to persons new on a job;

  e. change is more acceptable in organisations trained to accept that change from time to time is a normal development and a continuing necessity in present day circumstances; and

  f. substantial changes are more readily accepted after partial changes have been implemented successfully; i.e. a step-by-step approach is more acceptable than a major leap forward.

Although these points were well aired in the 1960s and featured in some management books of the early 1970s, including an earlier one by the author (*Planning for Products and Markets*), there is little evidence that much practical note has been taken of them. If these simple truths are ignored barriers to change and all communications will result. Enterprises will then be forced to spend a considerable amount of time and effort in making their ideas acceptable. This is effectively a waste of time and money which could otherwise be put to more productive purposes, those that improve the overall performance and profitability of the enterprise.

1.3.2 Overcoming resistance to change and improving communications

Many writers acknowledge that perfect understanding may not be possible in every case, but certain simple rules will help to achieve a high degree of understanding. The most important, in the author's view, is to develop the art of effective listening which, in turn, requires greater sensitivity to the world of the receivers. This means understanding the background, motivations and aspirations of the receivers. This will help the sender to gauge the impact and interpretation that would be attached to the communication. Then realising the way in which receivers use words and the meanings they place on them, a message reasonably free of potential ambiguity and misunderstanding can be devised.

It means also really listening to the receivers and what they say and analysing the actions that result. Just giving the impression of listening is not sufficient. Further, an executive who hears for the sole purpose of finding fault is not really listening or appreciating the receivers' points of view. Better communications and overcoming resistance to change require the setting aside of prejudices or bias. While there is no need to agree completely with the speakers, it is essential to try to understand them and why they adopt certain attitudes and use certain phrases or presentations.

It may also be advisable to use more words that would be necessary if sender and receiver were of identical status, outlook, motivations and aspirations. The more remote the receiver's world from that of the sender, the greater could be the use of words that would, in the former case, be considered redundant or superfluous. However, too long-winded a statement could create confusion and more misunderstanding. So the art of communication lies in devising messages which clearly explain the matter under discussion, especially if it is a complicated subject.

A method of analysing written communications was developed in the U.S.A. and called the 'fog index'. It aims to quantify the clarity of a message by methods which have nothing to do with the style of writing. The index is classified by age groupings and types of persons (i.e. their status) most likely to be encountered. This idea has been taken up in Britain by the Staff Training Centre near Windsor and has been, more kindly, called the 'clarity index'. The approach is simple and involves counting the number of words in a sentence and the proportion or percentage of words with more than two syllables. For example a sentence with twenty words of which 10 per cent have more than two syllables would have an index number of thirty. This is said to be the reading standard of sixteen year olds.

The lower status of the recipient, or the younger the person, the smaller the index number should be. Indeed, messages with the lowest possible index number are most easily understood. However, if the number is too high, e.g. over fifty, the chances of the message being clearly understood, even by senior people, are reduced. Though it is not a perfect system and its usefulness has still to be established for general use, a study in the *Sunday Times* (in the United Kingdom) of March 20th, 1977, suggested that in one major company's case, the more important the message the more obscure was the text. Also it found that too often, converted verbs (e.g. 'commitment') were used instead of simpler nouns (e.g. 'promise'). Further, the passive mood was preferred to the active and the mixed use of tenses was nothing short of chaotic. Widespread misunderstanding resulted, apparently.

1.4 Small may be beautiful

It has been stated that in several countries doubt is being thrown on the formerly held belief that large size may be of advantage in an industrial enterprise. The difficulties of running a large corporation have been mentioned. However, in some countries, like Britain, these problems may be accentuated because industrial activity started with small enterprises and has remained so for most of the time since. At least executive thinking has remained, for the most part, on the level of small-scale enterprises. Even when big corporations have evolved, they have done so through the amalgamation or take-over of smaller units which are then not fully integrated into a single operation but left to continue in a fairly autonomous way. This perpetuates the concept of smallness.

Executives then develop an automatic inclination to think small, i.e. running their own small business even if it is a tiny part of a much larger operation. Experience, expectations, desires and even training all tend to perpetuate this small or limited approach to management activity. Not unnaturally there is also some fear of large operations and, correctly or incorrectly, a deep-seated, often unrealised opinion exists that they cannot handle big operations as well as small. Certainly many executives display reluctance to take on the challenge of a large corporation. They do not seem to possess the mental attitude needed to deal effectively with the complicated techniques encountered in large companies.

With certain honourable exceptions, executives in such countries also lack the knack of being able to merge and manage large operations successfully. While the relationship with trade unions remains on the same aggressive and oppressive levels as exist today in these countries, inhibiting innovation, executives can be excused for feeling that the effort of trying to master the necessary techniques is not worthwhile. With smaller businesses personal involvement is easier, communications are on an easily established face-to-face basis and the achievement quotient is greater. Hard work and good results are more easily identified and can be rewarded effectively. There is greater vitality and thus the possibility of innovation is improved. While these ideal situations do not apply in every small organisation, they are easier to achieve in them than in large corporations. In present-day conditions it would be sensible for governments to encourage more small businesses.

For large corporations the lesson is that the large intimidating operation is seldom as advantageous as it is believed to be. It is often too impersonal in the view of the employees who feel themselves to be merely small cogs, or numbers, in a very big operation. They feel isolated or forgotten and believe that human dignity has been sacrificed on the altar of efficiency of the big companies. Major corporations should therefore study the possibility of breaking down their activities into smaller, self-contained units, on a human scale comparable with smaller enterprises, despite the problems encountered and as mentioned in Section 1.2.5. Improved results should then follow.

In countries like Britain another prerequisite is for the massive quantity of rules and regulations constraining businesses, which seems so often to hinder the smaller company most, to be modified or discarded. In the Britain of the 1970s, such legislation inhibited those who might otherwise have been prepared to plan and operate on a smaller scale.

For those wishing to create new small businesses another essential need is the availability of capital at reasonable terms. Large operations are usually capital intensive and the more of the former that exist the greater will be the amount of capital swallowed up by them. A readjustment of the money supply/demand position is needed to make a better share of capital available for the smaller operations. Given that a majority of executives have the background, training and inclination to operate more efficiently in smaller operations, not to encourage this is a serious defect by governments. Given that small enterprises tend to employ more people in total, readjusting a nation's industrial activity in this direction can help with the unemployment problem. If small operations are what the nation does best, then encouraging them will also help solve many of its economic problems. The entire attitude to this subject must be thought through by all those involved, whether officials or private individuals in business. The studies should be on national, regional and enterprise bases.

1.5 Causes of corporate collapse

Joel E. Ross and Michael J. Kami (*Corporate Management in Crisis: Why the Mighty Fall*, Prentice-Hall, 1973) give perhaps the best analysis of the most common reasons why companies fail. They open with a broadside. They state that (in the early 1970s) the top 500 U.S. corporations accounted for 65 per cent of corporate sales and 75 per cent of profits earned, *yet many of them were woefully behind in terms of managerial ability and sustained success*. If that statement is true the mind boggles at what the achievements would have been had the European-held myth of American management efficiency been true for most American companies.

Of course European businesses cannot be smug about this for the current decade, especially in Britain, has shown how woefully inadequate many management teams have been. Comparable figures are not available for Britain or Europe but private studies have indicated that in the United Kingdom only about 20 per cent of all enterprises are achieving consistently near-optimal performance. This 20 per cent seldom included any of the 'big names'. However, there is no gainsaying that considerable improvement in performance is possible for all enterprises if they can follow the precepts of sound management and take note of the more common causes of corporate collapse, aiming to avoid these traps in the future. Ross and Kami summarise what many others have found, that failure stems from overlooking or ignoring what they call the 'Ten Commandments of Management'. These are as follows, modified a little by the author.

1. *Develop and communicate a strategy* (i.e. unified sense of purpose and direction) to which *all* members of the organisation can relate.

2. *Develop effective overall controls* (especially *cost control*) to achieve the plans, programmes and policies stemming from the agreed strategy.

3. *Exercise care in the selection of executives*, especially senior ones and the board of directors (or executive vice-presidents) and require that the latter *actively* participate in management.

4. *Avoid one-person rule.*

5. *Provide depth of management*, or managerial talent.

6. *Keep the corporation fully informed of changes taking place in its business environment* (and those of customers) and be ready to *react positively to change* (when necessary).

7. *Do not overlook the customers and their newfound power* (i.e. the growth of their purchasing power and the evolution of consumer protection etc.).

8. *Use but do not misuse computers* (and other so-called modern management aids).

9. *Do not engage in accounting manipulations.* (Recent legal developments in many countries are aimed to prevent these.)

10. *Provide for an organisational structure* that meets the needs of customers and employees.

They might also have added an eleventh commandment, the theme and purpose of this book:

11. *Achieve a constant and truly integrated approach to management* involving continual interdepartmental cooperation which acknowledges the interdependence of *all* management decisions and actions.

They support their contentions by depth analyses of then current American case histories, e.g. A.& P., (the Atlantic & Pacific Tea Company), A.T.& T., Chrysler, Lockheed and 20th Century Fox and, for good measure, Britain's Rolls-Royce. Although subsequent events may be overtaking some of their views, most remain valid as causes of corporate collapse. Their book is worth study by executives interested in avoiding these common failings.

1.5.1 Strategy

Misunderstanding about the meaning and role of strategy is widespread both in relation to business enterprises and national economies. Yet this is probably one of the more important concepts for top management in today's conditions. Some readers may disagree and suggest that sound financial and cost control, or marketing, or production management are at least as important. In operational terms, this is true, but until a corporate strategy has been agreed no executive can be sure what comprises sound control, marketing or production management. Until everyone in an organisation has a clear, precise understanding of the basic philosophy of a company's continuing existence and development (i.e. what they are in business to achieve), clear and successful objectives and plans cannot be agreed and implemented. There is no direction or purpose to which day-to-day and long-term decisions can be related.

Without a strategy that is practical an organisation is like a rudderless ship, blown hither and thither by the winds of chance and change. When there is no strategy, any road will do; and all usually lead to disaster. Platitudes like 'to make a profit', 'to develop and grow', 'to give satisfaction to our workforce', and so on, are not sufficient. They do not give a unified direction to management decisions and actions; they are too vague for these purposes.

An example of a successful strategy was that of I.B.M. in the U.S.A. They expressed the intention of developing each specific end-use market by the development of new generations of computers and office equipment, with appropriate software, to meet the problems of each customer group. In addition they linked this with the aim of prompt attention to calls for help from their customers. In contrast, it is often quoted that the two-part strategy of Lockheed (let defence contracts pay for research and development and let these also carry the lion's share of the business) was ill-chosen. More than 90 per cent of the company's business was in defence projects with the growing commercial market left almost entirely to Lockheed's major competitors.

Many good books exist on the subject of corporate strategy. Executives are well advised to study some of them carefully, especially those appropriate to their own operations. They should also read some of the many good case studies that exist.

1.5.2 Effective controls

Many books have been written and courses held on controls for financial experts, non-financial executives and newcomers to the executive ranks. Yet many enterprises in several countries still survive with inadequate or ineffective control systems. On the other hand, some have such elaborate systems that it is not surprising that rigor mortis seems to have set in and operational problems abound. Others seem to control their activities by rough figures pencilled on the back of an envelope in the pocket of the chief executive. Still others survive on information and data retained in the head of a key executive. Yet others seem to ignore completely the systems they are supposed to be using and which, probably, were devised with considerable expenditure of effort, time and money. (In the late 1960s there was a British group which had an elaborate control system that required senior executives at head office to check through some one hundred and sixty odd forms every month. It was impossible to check them all with equal thoroughness and this led to an unbalanced control of the group's operations. Integrated management and control was impossible and the executives found themselves rushing to deal with one crisis after another with little thought given to the total corporate system.)

Effective control systems, especially for costs, require the setting of standards, the measurement of performance against these standards, analyses of the causes of any operational variances encountered (both positive and negative) and the planning and implementation of corrective action to balance deviations from the standards. Further, the system used should be as simple as possible, covering what is essential and involving executives responsible for given segments of the work. The executives should, however, have reasonable cognisance of the rest of the control and financial systems and the overall corporate objectives that must be achieved. Otherwise they cannot be effective in their own spheres of responsibility. Massive, complex systems involving too much paperwork and too many executives merely hinder the operations. (In another British group, head office confined its day-to-day and planning involvements to reaching agreement with subsidiaries on what the corporate objectives should be and the contribution each subsidiary would make towards them. The main effort at head office centred on the formulation of strategy and policies, the attainment and utilisation of the capital needed and checking corporate progress. The management of the subsidiaries was held responsible for the control of their own activities within this corporate framework.)

Executives who do not feel competent to deal with control systems should seek professional help in setting them up and professional advice on how to operate them. Attendance at carefully selected conferences or courses and study of appropriate books are also necessary to learn about effective control systems. Good management and control is not letting a company be run, for example, by engineers for engineers. Appropriate financial experts and other financially aware executives must also be involved in control activities. More detailed comments on the key areas of control will be found in later chapters.

1.5.3 Active participation by the board

In many countries boards of directors have specific legal responsibilities they must meet. They cannot avoid them, but the degree to which they honour the law can vary considerably. However, just meeting these requirements is not enough. Directors (or executive vice-presidents) must take an active interest in the work of the company and participate in the work of management especially in the departments for which they hold (nominal) board responsibility.

Too often a board may merely endorse the actions of a powerful chief executive or other director with a strong or dominating personality. In such cases the role of the board degenerates into whatever the powerful personality wants it to be. The last thing that such persons want is 'interference' by a strong board. However uncomfortable it may be, a strong board is a prerequisite for sustained managerial success. Thus a board must not be content only to receive the regular reports of the company on the results being obtained. It must be prepared to probe deeply into the figures and reports to find out what is really happening, what results are actually being obtained, why the results are as they are, why variances are occurring, what else may or may not be going according to plan and, in conjunction with line managers and other executives, initiate studies to indicate the best remedial action that should be taken and to ensure that such action is actually taken. In doing this boards should not abrogate the responsibilities and authority of line executives. Members of a board should be seen as valuable, constructive members of the management team and should act as a guide, prompter and sometimes even a ringmaster to their executive groups.

Many boards do not seem prepared to give the time and interest necessary for these purposes. Often they do not even keep themselves fully informed on what is happening in 'their' departments, never mind the company as a whole. Thus they are not in a position to be certain that they are taking the right decisions on any matter. They are acting as their inclinations, hunches or prejudices guide them. Other boards are manifestations in business of the Three Monkeys — 'See no evil; hear no evil; speak no evil; — and there may even be a fourth monkey present, 'Think no evil'. In countries where corporation law is not comprehensive, or correctly applied, the board may just be an adornment. Then it is intended to keep the timid share- or stockholder happy and quiet, giving the misconception that responsible senior executives are in control of the business and that line managers are themselves being kept under some sort of surveillance. Other boards may be preoccupied with policy matters. While these are important, all the other responsibilities should not be sacrificed to them. Such boards as mentioned above, are not really looking after the interests of the company's financiers, nor of the company itself, nor of its employees. The laxity of view of the big institutional investors towards the boards and activities of the companies in which they are investing does nothing to improve matters.

Unfortunately, there is no generally agreed view on the role and duties of a board. Luckily in some countries, including Britain, thought is being given to this matter by interested bodies (e.g. the Institute of Directors, London). Perhaps in due course a detailed code of conduct will evolve for most industrialised nations. In trading communities, like the European Communities (the 'European Common Market') community rules will eventually emerge on this subject. (*See* Section 1.7.5 for further comments on board involvement.)

1.5.4 One-person rule

When a weak board exists, one-person rule generally dominates a company. Either it will be the chief executive (or proprietor, who perhaps is the only one who has the right to impose his or her own views on the organisation) or some other strong personality. A variation of this is rule by a small caucus, usually the chief executive and financial director or vice-president, though other powerful personalities could be included. The last need not necessarily be members of the board. The weakness of this approach is that characteristically, the strong person normally does not seek advice or help from anyone. If the person's decisions are right, all is well! However, the complexities of modern business are such that it is difficult for any one person to be right all the time and be able to control an enterprise of any size. He or she needs the help, advice and cooperation of specialists in other disciplines. In the case of a caucus, opportunities may be opened to sycophants. The results could be disastrous.

Nevertheless there is always room for the true entrepreneur in a business. Nor must successful chief executives such as Harold Greneen of I.T.T., Tom Watson of I.B.M. and others be belittled or constrained, but the chances of men and women of this calibre coming forward in sufficient numbers under present conditions are slight. Only a very few of such calibre will emerge at any time. Those companies who have such chief executives are most fortunate. For the majority, cursed with having to survive with ordinary mortals, the rules and principles of sound management cannot be ignored. Also for them, a return to basic principles and careful study, and the possible rejection, of available management techniques is the only approach that offers the prospect of sustained success. Companies should beware also of persons with reputations for being successful. Few are consistently so. Most have scored one, perhaps two, successes at some period of time. They need not be successful again! Perhaps their skills and abilities were right for bringing success at those times, but they may not be relevant to current situations or may be out of date.

1.5.5 Depth of managerial talent

Good managerial talent is in short supply. However this is no excuse for trying to run an organisation with the necessary skills spread very thinly on the ground. Capable managers are a company's greatest asset and it pays to have the best available. There should also be some back-up facilities in case of death, illness, a move to other subsidiaries, departures or some other personal disaster. Where the skilled people do not exist the training of staff with development potential should be undertaken even though lazier companies who will not try to train their own staff attempt to steal fully trained personnel. The obverse is also true. Companies should avoid keeping too many good managers in comparative idleness, since this leads to dissatisfaction, friction or lethargy in management. It should be noted that lack of managerial depth is experienced most often in companies struggling under one-person rule.

Examples quoted in books and articles suggested that one of the main contributory factors to major problems faced in earlier times by such diverse operations as Lockheed, Penn Central, A.& P., British Leyland (now B.L.) and the former Rolls-Royce company stemmed from lack of managerial talent in sufficient quantity to be able to tackle all the work that had to be done. Such contentions may or may not be true. However all readers will know from their own experience of smaller but just as disastrous examples. (*See also* Section 3.1.)

1.5.6 Reaction to change

The problems of resistance to change by employees have been discussed earlier. Whether for this reason, or simple lethargy too many executives do not react or respond to important changes in their business environment until forced to do so by competitors' actions. They then find themselves rushing to catch up with events and, meanwhile, the success and profitability of their companies are threatened. While most executives react to important product changes or developments (e.g. xerography) there are other more subtle changes which must be considered. For example, there was the development of the mini-car which was ignored for a while by other manufacturers. When they finally realised they must compete in this market they were involved in costly rush or panic tactics. In some cases, it was reported, the move came too late and proved too expensive.

Then there are all the obvious changes (but often with subtle implications and interactions) in consumer spending patterns and habits. The biggest of these in recent times was the growth of the importance of supermarkets which made them the centre of suburban shopping. Then there were the changes in tourism habits and demands, tourist expenditure, home labour-saving devices, bulk and direct mail order buying, and so on. Each changed established activities quite fundamentally. Executives must consider how such changes are likely to affect their future business directly or indirectly and plan to alter their operations, policies and strategy accordingly.

1.5.7 Customer attitudes

Changes in customer or consumer attitudes occur from time to time. They can affect much wider subjects than just commercial aspects. For example in recent years attitudes have changed not only towards the degree and nature of protection that should be accorded to consumers, protecting them from the excesses of unscrupulous operators, but also to concern about pollution, conservation and social responsibilities as a whole. All of these have some effect on the business environment and business prospects. Changed consumer attitudes are thus not always due only to changing economic conditions, or income structures or other, more obvious, commercial relationships. People's attitudes and expectations alter as social attitudes change or as they see the quality of their lives changing; or because of their increasing desire that their life patterns should change for the better. For example while at some time the apparent price benefits of house brands seemed attractive, if people become convinced that the price savings do not justify the lower quality, or they wish to enjoy better quality products as their incomes rise, then they will turn away from house brands to proprietary ones. Also gimmicks, like trading stamps, which once were attractive and helped to sell goods, may no longer be seen to be so, or the consumers may in difficult times, as in Britain in the 1970s, prefer straight price reductions to trading stamps or other 'free gifts'. Changed attitudes will then lead to a move away to alternative retail outlets, products and methods of purchasing which in turn could change the future business prospects of the affected organisations.

If the public lose confidence in an activity, or the corporation promoting it, they will turn away and seek other suppliers. Better education and greater awareness of basic economics help to make the consumer a better informed person and more likely to change attitudes and actions. Further, despite the economic problems of the second half of the 1970s, people's spending power in Western Europe and North America appears to be continuing to rise. With this has come also, through being better informed, greater ability to judge the real value of a product or service and thus whether it should be purchased or used. The critical abilities of consumers is increasing as education becomes more widespread and comprehensive. Interest in social aspects in areas unrelated to commercial activity is also making ordinary consumers much more conscious of important facts relating to their lives and how they should live them. The power of the consumer, in every meaning of that phrase, is increasing and cannot be ignored much longer by 'big business'. ('Little business' has long since learnt the truth of this.)

There is also the increasing interest in spiritual values with a resultant turning away from pure, selfish materialism. People are becoming less concerned with themselves and more anxious about the millions of greatly disadvantaged and impoverished people. While this is not yet a major, or pronounced trend, it could become so and thus alter beyond recognition, consumer behaviour patterns and attitudes. All these developments are turning the average consumer from a fairly set — some said, bovine — creature, with well-engrained habits to a person willing to change attitudes and behaviour to be in accord with new-found views, values and standards. Consumers are ready to accept wider responsibility towards society at large. Corporations ignoring these trends do so at their peril and the cost to them in future will be considerable.

1.5.8 Misuse of techniques and hardware

The misuse of management techniques and hardware by executives has become widespread. This is especially true in relation to more advanced technological developments. There is also a failure to relate the capabilities of each technique to the others they propose to use. For example, why use very sophisticated marketing research methods if the company is not mentally or physically equipped to use the results efficiently and effectively? Why use operations research methods when simpler ones are available? Why rush to every new fad or fashion as it is announced? Nor is much thought given in many cases, about how different management activities relate to or depend on other operations. If the answers to these questions are not known, the techniques are being misused. This is a costly affair and merely squanders scarce resources.

Allied to this is the common belief that new techniques are infallible. Computer systems are the most quoted example of this. Computer systems can and do break down; and they do give incorrect outputs (i.e. information) if the wrong data has been fed into them. (This is the famous 'garbage in, garbage out' condition). As recent articles (1978) in the British press and elsewhere have shown, they are also open to criminal misuse which cannot be detected early enough or easily. When they are, companies are reluctant to prosecute the criminals to avoid adverse publicity. Apart from this, computer systems can produce incorrect production and other schedules adding further to costly errors and wastage of resources. Eternal vigilance and a sound knowledge of the techniques used are vital if these pitfalls are to be avoided.

1.5.9 Accounting manipulations

Most countries have laws designed to prevent the more blatant accounting manipulations, though a few misguided persons still try some 'juggling' even if they usually pay the appropriate penalty. However, other manipulations that still get through the law include payment of large dividends when a company's performance and results do not justify this. The company may in fact be making heavy operational losses. (See the case illustrations at the end of this chapter for further variations and examples of this.) Then there were those executives who, during the acquisition period in the 1960s, were only concerned with the stock- or share-market prices of their equities. Little thought was given to the real value of the acquisition; provided they kept the acquirer's share prices high and rising that was all that mattered.

Another manipulation tried some years ago involved taking the notional profit margins of finished goods, stocks or inventories and adding this to the trading profit of the enterprise to show more favourable total profit figures. While this was done in most cases from an honest point of view (i.e. that this reflected the 'true' performance of the operations in the year concerned), and there was no dishonest motive, the financial world viewed such moves with distaste. Shareholders responded by selling the stock and the share-market prices plummeted to new lows. Some companies have never recovered from this in the sense that their share prices never again reached the level enjoyed before this 'manipulation'. Such a move does not of course take account of the possibility of sales of this inventory not being achieved, nor the reduction in actual profits that would occur as a result of any write-down of prices or write-off of stocks, due to the items remaining unsold.

1.5.10 Organisation

Organisation structures tend to be like Topsy, one finds they have just 'growed'. In some cases they do not grow enough, or relevantly, to handle a corporation's expanding activities. Or work was not apportioned in packets that the people who had to carry it out could manage. Nor were their capabilities and experience taken into account. Further, the needs of the business (i.e. the type of business, the speed at which decisions had to be taken, spheres of responsibility, delegation of work etc.) were not considered sufficiently thoroughly. Sufficient time and thought were not allocated to the question of organisational structure or to the reorganisation that was needed.

Whether to reorganise or not is another area of this work which executives find difficult. In many instances it may be advisable to leave well alone, even if in the future succession problems will arise. When everything is working well organisational change may be inadvisable. It may work well because of the personalities and qualities of executives running the business. They may fit into a good and effective working relationship rather than because the logic of the organisation or the suitability of the administrative system are theoretically correct. If the workforce has confidence in the executive team any disruption of the team may destroy their confidence. Where an organisation is not working well, the logical application of the basic principles of management can put to right seemingly insoluble problems. These problems may seem mundane to a consultant experienced in organisational matters but to the executives concerned they may cause considerable problems. Getting the organisational concepts wrong can loosen essential rivets in the fabric of the organisation and its operations. Is it any wonder that some companies do come apart at the seams? (*See also* Section 8.1.2.)

1.5.11 Capital investment

Corporations may also fail to survive because of faulty or inadequate capital investment. Finance may be poured in without regard to the corporation's short- and long-term objectives and targets at the whim of the board or one dominant personality on it. Or more usually, not enough capital is invested in the business. In this case development towards long-term goals is not possible. Plant and machinery become out-of-date or reach the end of their useful, profitable life. Manufacturing resources decline and cannot meet new demands or changes in competitive activity. Short-sighted investment policies are a considerable waste of scarce resources. They confine the manoeuverability of the company into very limited areas of activity. This in turn makes future, long-term and more important investment and development difficult, if not impossible, to achieve.

Many instances of these shortcomings have been recorded from time to time and in the 1970s much was debated on this subject in Britain. British industry it was claimed was not investing enough for future needs. This was due to political and economic uncertainties, the rising cost of capital and galloping inflation. On the other hand, the almost total re-equipment of West Germany and Japan (the former's industry especially having been devastated by the end of the Second World War) involving massive reinvestment programmes, are seen as the main reasons for those countries' outstanding performance. This gave them economic and industrial dominance in the world. (The subject of investment is discussed further in Chapter 7, Section 7.3.)

1.5.12 Integrated management

Enough has been written to show that an integrated approach to management, with a thorough investigation of all aspects of major problems and decisions, is an essential element for sustained business success. Some companies have some form of integrated management but these do not generally go far enough. They do not embrace *all* the activities, decisions and planning needed. The rest of this book sketches out the thought processes necessary to work out how and where integrated management is needed and assumes that basic knowledge of the work and techniques involved are known. If they are not, then they can be learnt by studying the many good books on the various disciplines and specialisms of management. Attending appropriate courses over a period of time is also necessary. Of course the courses chosen should be those that have shown themselves to be effective for the purposes required, i.e. ones that have attained the objectives or aims outlined for them.

1.6 Problem-solving decisions

Many executive teams waste a lot of time in arriving at decisions that will solve or circumnavigate specified problems. They utilise their time poorly due to failure to identify the five phases involved in problem-solving work. These are:

1. define the problem;
2. analyse it;
3. develop alternative solutions;
4. decide which is the best solution consistent with the company's short- and long-term objectives; and
5. convert the decision into effective action.

Nor do they allocate the appropriate amounts of time to each stage. Defining or identifying the real problem, analysing the reasons for it and deciding the alternative solutions possibly need the most time and attention. However, if the corporate objectives have been set correctly, the best solution will usually be apparent and little time is needed for this stage of the work. No time should be needed for 'selling' this right solution to the executives responsible for carrying it out. If the management approach is right, these executives too should appreciate what is the correct solution. Finally, sufficient time must be allowed for the necessary actions to be carried through to a successful conclusion.

It is worth remembering also that the real problem is often not the one that appears at first study. The most visible symptoms are the least revealing ones. Whatever the problem, the real causes of it may lie in other areas, for example a poor management structure, or a clash of personalities in some critical area of work, or bad communications. High unit costs may not be due to manufacturing methods but could be caused by poor design, the use of the wrong materials, or the over-marketing of the product resulting in excessive marketing costs. There may be an apparent organisational problem, but the real cause may be lack of clear-cut objectives for the operation.

A company may try to cut production costs over many years (as one British furniture manufacturer and several American and European companies did) without improving profitability only to find the real problem was that the product mix offered did not match the demand of market segments offering the greatest potential and profitability. Sales were below economical levels of production and thus profit targets were not attained. If the profitability problem is one of too high unit prices inhibiting sales, a reduction of selling prices or the dependence on price for sales appeal often mean that even less profits will be earned. Finding the critical factor of any problem is not easy but Peter Drucker (*The Practice of Management*) and others have suggested simple ways in which this can be done successfully. Readers are advised to study these books.

1.7 Other causes of management failure

This section deals with the more common causes of management failure. Space limitations prevent a more exhaustive study being made of the less frequent reasons that arise from time to time.

1.7.1 Management conflict

Perhaps the most common cause in this group is the incidence of management conflict. While some friction will always exist between departments and if properly used or interpreted it can be creative, too much friction is utterly disruptive. There are many executives who do not hesitate to harm their organisations in the relentless pursuit of their own, personal, limited interests. They seem determined to create as many in-house feuds as possible. If the reason for this is some personality defect then transfer to less sensitive posts, or dismissal, may be the only solutions.

Again, some executives are excessively friendly and helpful to colleagues from other, competitive groups but are correspondingly obstructive and antagonistic to their own departmental colleagues. Some hard decisions may be needed to deal with this problem though good industrial relations and the retraining of the executives can save them from self-destruction.

Then there are the conflicts created by fear, even fear by a senior for a subordinate. Time and again people have been transferred to other jobs, or sacked, because the senior feared for his or her own position because of the existence of a junior with better training or apparent ability. The junior was thought to threaten the senior's position and future prospects. It is not unknown for executive directors or vice-presidents to be pushed off a company board because the chief executive feared them or their ability.

Some countries now have job protection laws which limit the possibility of unfair dismissal and require the affected person to be suitably compensated. However, many executives are still prepared to have their companies pay considerable amounts in redundancy compensation in order to safeguard their own positions and future. In any case the conflict and friction will continue until human nature changes for the better. Even if not under direct threat, some executives may smother their initiative and drive in order not to run the risk of finding themselves in similar positions of direct conflict. Some observers believe this is one reason why so many board members remain passive. They do not wish to run the risk of losing their jobs and status! They believe the loss of the latter can ruin their standing in their home environment.

There are other common situations which cause this malevolence, or guerrilla activity, to arise. First is when a company or department has been taken over. The incoming management alarms the existing executives and the easiest solution to the difficulty is for the winners to get rid of the losers. A more beneficial answer involves a study of the purpose of the take-over and the synergy that should flow from it. Then all the executives can be better matched to the new roles that have to be carried out. Retraining of some may be necessary and should not be avoided if fairness in these decisions is to be achieved. The cost of retraining will be more than offset by the greater goodwill and improved performance that would result.

Another reason for conflict, met with internationally, is the over-promotion of executives. (This is the 'Peter Principle', which professes that eventually people will be promoted beyond their capabilities. It is sometimes cynically described as: 'the scum always rises to the top'!) In these cases the poor people thrash around in desperation, trying to do the job but perhaps only too well aware of their inadequacies. The resultant stress and anxiety leads to the picking of unnecessary quarrels as they try to protect their position or status. As these quarrels increase so the position is further undermined.

One such case concerned a manufacturer of air-conditioning equipment whose chief executive was a brilliant engineer. However, he appeared to lack the abilities needed of a chief executive. He was fearful of his position within the holding group and imagined himself to be inadequate when it came to handling group procedures. He insisted also on making all decisions himself and challenged every suggestion made to him by senior and junior executives. He even challenged executives more senior to himself from head office. He saw his position under threat and responded with aggression and extreme sensitivity. In the end he was replaced. A different approach, seeking to learn, acknowledging his shortcomings and asking for either help or training in his weak areas, would have made this unfortunate action unnecessary. In the end, he, the company and the group suffered for a time.

The reality of the generation gap in business is another cause. Younger executives with better training and mastery of the newer techniques often have little respect for older, senior management. This enhances the natural drive in juniors to unseat their superiors and take over. They feel, often mistakenly, that they can do better. Whether they can is doubtful, since business success requires both theoretical knowledge and suitable experience. Perhaps the educators can help here by stressing this fact to their students and that considerable experience is necessary before a high degree of proficiency can be achieved.

Acknowledgment by juniors of the important role played by older, experienced executives is also essential. Similarly, the seniors should not allow themselves to fear brilliant young people joining their organisation. They should develop a partnership mentality that will be to their mutual good and that of the company.

One variation on this theme is the over-emphasis by seniors that newcomers must gain experience before they can be effective. This may be true to varying degrees but continually harping back to this point, with ruthlessly maintained obstructionism at all times, only leads to conflict that can harm everyone including the enterprise. Strangely, the existing executives' fear of newcomers is greatest before the latter arrive and do anything. Waiting is apparently always the worst part of life. A better understanding of human relations and behaviour would perhaps help to reduce the incidence of this cause of managerial conflict.

Another cause of friction arises when the enterprise slides into one of the serious crises that can menace its continued existence, e.g. severe decline of cash flow, profitability, sales, labour relations or a threatened take-over and failure in product design and customer acceptance. The tension and worry produced by these, especially concerning threats to future employment, create more friction and conflict. It is a sad sight to see executives of a threatened company indulging in savage in-fighting when their energies should be directed to a unified, determined effort to save the company. Apart from keeping the company out of trouble, the only way of minimising this type of conflict is to have strong leadership from the top, directing all effort towards recovery.

Finally, the failings and foibles of human nature can create conflict especially when the failings are manifested as strong dislike of certain colleagues, whether for logical or illogical reasons. Most dislikes are based on fantasies and the persons disliked may be totally innocent and unaware of the charges against them. They may not even know that they are disliked. Even when a person has done something to warrant the dislike (e.g. some quirk of personal behaviour, sneaking to senior executives, pinching kudos or being hyper-critical of people, etc.) this attitude is a sterile one at best, or a festering sore on the corporate body at worst. Self-discipline is the only apparent solution.

Of course, where a person spreads lies about another senior or junior colleague, hard measures may be necessary to stop the contamination spreading. A sharp warning to mend his or her ways by a specified date is needed. It should also be made clear that if the deadline is not met then dismissal may be the only remedy. (Current labour laws in some countries may require a much more long-drawn-out procedure, e.g. several oral warnings followed by one or more written ones; at all times the person concerned is allowed to query the charges being made; at the end a formal written notice of dismissal stating the reasons may have to be given. Even then the person may have recourse to an appropriate union and/or some industrial tribunal.)

1.7.2 Non-consultation

Without falling into the bad ways mentioned earlier (Section 1.5) many executives succeed too often in giving the impression that they are consulting with colleagues and subordinates when in reality they are doing nothing of the sort. It is a wonderful, if damaging charade to observe. Some ploys are however less subtle than others.

First, there is direct or indirect intimidation. The former is a crude statement meaning: 'do it my way or else!' backed by blatant stressing of who grants salary increases, or recommends them and promotion. The latter consist of many more subtle approaches but their meaning is quite clear. Usually this type of pressure is not aimed at someone who is popular and who would attract the sympathy or support of the other members of the team. It is usually slashed at some weak or unpopular member of the group. The older executive and the lower achievers are especially vulnerable to such tactics. Or there may be an appeal for support, in private before a meeting; but the receiver is left in no doubt of the disasters awaiting him or her if that support is not forthcoming without question.

The simplest method of all is of course for the executive to surround him- or herself with 'yes-people'. The danger of this approach is that the team, so busy agreeing with the boss, will not see the approaching dangers of wrong decisions. It will not be able to warn the executive that things are really turning sour and the operation or company are heading for some disaster or other. Readers can put their own case examples to these points from their own experience.

Other ploys that can have disastrous results include falsifying the documentation or arranging for data to be so set out that it 'proves' the leader's points. Readers will know that the same set of statistics can be assembled to stress different points of view. However, given a dominant leader of the 'I'm always right' type, it is difficult and dangerous to try to prove that a different interpretation of the facts is possible. This problem arises more frequently in discussions on marketing and manufacturing matters.

For example, a managing director of the biggest company of a British manufacturing group that started with a dominating market position (80 per cent market share in highly technical products) insisted that all was well as sales continued to rise substantially. He ignored the fact that total demand was growing at a much faster rate and the company's market share was declining at an alarming rate. He did not recognise his error, or could not be persuaded to that view, until the market share had dropped below 60 per cent. The problem had been made worse as he seemed able to read a sales graph but not a market share one. Having been an engineer in his early life, in his own words, he did not understand 'all that marketing mumbo-jumbo'! By the time remedial action was agreed and started to take effect, the market share had fallen below 40 per cent in a total market that had meanwhile increased to double that when the problem was first pointed out to him. The consequences for the company were severe. The remedial action that had to be taken was far more painful than it would have been had it been taken when its need was first pointed out to that executive. Inability to read figures and graphs correctly, in this instance, was linked with fear that his position was threatened by younger men with 'smart' ideas. He resisted any action which might be interpreted as agreement that he was ageing, losing his grip and not keeping up with new marketing ideas.

In this case the manufacturing/technical director also weighed in with the view that as sales were increasing there could not possibly be anything wrong with the products. He was deaf to arguments that technological changes had made alterations to the formulation of the products essential. He took the view that the long-established reputation of the company would continue to protect the company from competition. He also stated that if customers were foolish enough to use the products of competitors, inferring that they were inferior, more fool them. Using highly technical jargon and arguments he was able to hoodwink board colleagues as he was the only technical man on the board. It was thus doubly difficult to expose the true position of the company.

The manufacturing director's ploy in this case is also used in other situations and is simply based on blinding others with science or one's own expertise. It is achieved by providing such a wealth of impressive data that lesser mortals find it difficult to argue against the expert. If they try, recourse to intimidation or bullying is the response. This ploy is a favourite of some senior financial executives.

Then there are others who pontificate at length on any subject, even ones in which they are not qualified. This is met on occasions in the academic world but businesses are not immune from it. Usually these people are very good in their use of words and can so use them that opponents' arguments are turned against them and the latter are left floundering. Often the spoken word is very impressive so that in the end the collective decision becomes the one expounded by the pontificator. Yet if the statements could be written down and studied carefully, they would be found to be meaningless or highly polished nonsense.

A variation of the above is the person who is good at summing up, especially after long and complicated discussions. However, this is done so skilfully that the summing-up agrees with that person's view. Or the argument can be so skilfully put that it obscures the real issues and thus the correct decision that should be taken. This seems to be most effectively done if the correct decision is likely to threaten the status and future of the executive doing the summing-up!

1.7.3 No room for self-development

All management practitioners, educators and observers stress, from time to time, the need for the self-development of middle and junior executives. That is, through their own study, reading of books and attendance at courses, with increasing understanding of the general and special natures of their companies, these executives develop and increase their competence and knowledge. In reality this does not happen too frequently as the executives are seldom given the time and opportunity. The amount of work that they have to do may not allow them any spare time or energy for self-development. Or, for the reasons mentioned earlier, their superiors may place various obstacles in their path to ensure that they do not become too proficient or knowledgeable (the fear syndrome again).

Learning calls for intensive mental application. After a full day's work, probably also loaded with family problems and difficulties of all kinds at home (e.g. balancing the family budget, worrying about the children and their education, neighbour problems, difficulty with an in-law or parent, and even worrying about what the spouse is up to when the other partner is away!) many executives cannot find the interest or energy to generate this level of mental activity in the evenings. Staring vacant-eyed at the television set seems all that they can do before it is time to retire to bed.

With the accent in recent years given to management and technical training and in countries like Britain where a training levy is put on all companies, more senior executives are giving serious consideration to self-development by their subordinates. More time is being made available for this. However, many more companies have still to adopt positive policies on self-development. Educators can also play a bigger role in helping companies in this by finding the best ways that senior executives can help subordinates to improve their knowledge and performance. They should not only confine themselves to offering and running set and established full- or part-time courses (day release and evening classes) but should suggest to companies associated self-development programmes that students should follow, according to their interests and prospects, when they have completed a course. This will involve providing students with programmes for further study, including recommended books, articles and magazines to be read. Perhaps they could also indicate that, at the end of a stated period of such study, the former students are ready to consider other more advanced or specialist courses to continue to improve or add to their capabilities and knowledge.

Even when managers accept the need for development, difficulties can arise. The more common difficulties centre on finding effective appraisal systems, encouraging sufficient organisational support and finding suitable learning experience. If the aspirations of junior management have been aroused, they will become resentful and alienated if these ambitions are frustrated. This frustration arises if either the learning opportunities available are inadequate or they find that their new-found skills do not fit their company's needs or are not properly used by their organisations.

1.7.4 Departments are reflections of their managers

A truism of management is that every department is the reflection of its manager. The style of management, aspirations, attitudes, priorities and prejudices of middle management are usually reflections of those held by their bosses. The latter prescribe the authority style and method of operation of their subordinates. This fact progresses right down the executive ladder. Each subordinate, often unconsciously, apes his or her superior but this is done consciously when subordinates desire to please their managers, or to appear successful and so win favour and appreciation. Thus if the manager is inefficient, lax or prejudiced then the department will generally exude similar attitudes and be equally inefficient or lax. The more authoritarian the manager, the more difficult will subordinates find it to develop into fully-rounded executives of high capability, ripe for promotion.

The repercussions for an enterprise can be serious. When competent managers leave there may be no-one of comparable calibre to take over, only under-trained and under-prepared executives. The operation may take on a mediocre air and soon become mediocre. Management education experts have tried to devise various systems to overcome this problem. They have identified the five stages of management development. These are listed below.

1. Assess the firm's short- and long-term needs for managerial resources.
2. Assess current competence and potential by relevant, systematic appraisal systems.
3. Devise in-house and external learning situations (projects, training programmes, secondments, courses etc.) (*See* Figure 8.4.)
4. Evaluate their effectiveness.
5. Maintain a continual process of assessments.

Results obtained have not been very exciting. As stated earlier, the main difficulties lie in devising appraisal and assessment systems that really mean something to the work of the corporation and its executives. However, the real reason why the results have not been good may lie with the attitude of the executives themselves. They tend to view training as a waste of time, a bit of window dressing. Their hearts often are not in it because too frequently the training has a very high academic flavour and approach. Executives doubt if they could apply what they are being taught to their own practical work situations. If earlier experiences have been negative, this reinforces their antagonism to training. There is a two-fold remedy. First, educators must make sure that the courses and programmes not only contain a large practical slant but they must also be seen to do so. Second, executives should be motivated to take greater personal interest in their training as an essential part of their own self-development. They must be given time for this in working hours and be encouraged to do more in their own time.

At times of economic depression and high unemployment amongst executives, there emerges a very strong self-preservation motive to take self-development seriously. In boom times people tend to sit back and enjoy a rest! Senior executives can maintain motivation in good times as well as bad by getting subordinates to consider, regularly, the answers to critical performance questions. These are given below.

1.   How can I improve the results I am getting in my present post?

2.   How can I improve the job satisfaction I derive from my work?

3.   How can I improve the methods I use so that either my performance is improved and/or operational costs are reduced?

4.   What do I wish to achieve in my work and private life, and how will success in my job help me in this? (Sometimes the executive will realise here that he or she should get another job whether within or outside the present corporation!)

5.   What are my strengths and weaknesses? What do I do well, and badly? How can I build on my strengths and avoid, or overcome, my weaknesses?

6.   How can I improve the cooperation between myself and colleagues?

7.   How can I keep myself better informed of the corporation, its goals, work and achievements?

If this sort of mentality can be developed, executives will be able to help to overcome the problems associated with in-job self-development. A powerful motivational development would perhaps be to link pay increases and promotions to the success executives are achieving in their self-development programmes.

Executives must also know the sources of information and advice which would help them to answer these questions. The usual sources are given below.

1.   One's immediate boss.

2.   Other senior staff as appropriate and colleagues. The former should not exclude the more remote, godlike, hierarchical people.

3.   Customers, including not only people external to the organisation but also colleagues who depend on the executive's work and results to be able to function properly themselves.

4.   Family and friends, including those with knowledge of the executive's type of work, business and corporation.

5.   The executive's own subordinates.

6. Fellow professionals and others in professions affected by the executive's work or who can influence it (e.g. all executives can benefit from detailed discussions with accountants, financial executives, legal advisers etc.).

7. By personal input/output analyses (the input of effort to achieve different outputs of work; how results are achieved?).

With all this it helps if the educators, whether employed by the company or retained from universities and colleges, act more in the role of friend and personal adviser rather than an all-knowing, high-powered specialist or professional in the subject of management development. (*See also* Sections 8.1.5 and 8.2.2.)

1.7.5 Top management involvement

Top management must become more closely involved with the work of line managers. They should not be content to be either the benevolent fathers, or the stern whippers-in and fault-finders seeking the culprits for any failure. Managers must also realise that their work follows certain similarities of routine. This requires recognition that the work of executives —

a. involves all jobs being built on routines and constantly recurring tasks (meaningful job descriptions cannot otherwise be written and operated);

b. requires specialisation in management functions;

c. that management technology has advanced beyond the usual training of managers but nonetheless, executives have somehow to operate within this advanced technology (which is like giving an untrained blind person a micrometer and expecting that person to be able to check the measurements of a product with precision); and

d. new management techniques, even if they are viable and relevant, make impossible demands on executives and may also be beyond their comprehension.

Top management's role should also be, therefore, to help and encourage line executives in a positive way. Their greater involvement will require them to take on new tasks and responsibilities including the following.

1. Evolve a 'science' for every major element of a line manager's job, replacing former rule-of-thumb approaches. [The sophisticated nature of these 'sciences' should be modified, and methods adapted to suit, the capabilities of the management team; conformity for its own sake (the hobgoblin of the mediocre) must be avoided].

2. Executives must receive the training and help necessary to improve their performance; new executives should be chosen for their knowledge, experience and appropriateness for the tasks they must do and the 'science' they should follow. They will need regular training too as will all executives earmarked for possible promotion.

3. Top managers should have a close working and cooperative relationship with line executives, providing help and encouragement at all times.

4. They must see that the work is correctly apportioned between line and top executives and that this top management support at departmental level does not abrogate the authority and responsibility of line or departmental executives.

This changed approach should not be allowed to compress executives into a mindless work role, stifling initiative. Nor should it result in the use of meaningless or irrelevant techniques.

1.7.6 Research into management methods

Study of management procedures and techniques, the results they can achieve under different conditions and the performance of various management organisational structures has become an established part of the management scene. Substantial sums of money are spent annually in most developed countries on these studies. It has become 'big business' in its own right. Annual expenditure in Britain in 1972 (the last available figure) exceeded £1½ million and kept several hundred researchers busy. The growth in expenditure, until the recession in 1976, was running at about 40 per cent per annum. Expenditure in the U.S.A. and in Europe was considerably greater, especially if the work of the major business schools and universities are included.

With all this expenditure why does management performance continue to be at such low levels of efficiency, especially in Britain, as numerous articles and reports continue to point out? The main reasons seem to be: first, that while the studies satisfy some academic whim or a perfectly valid theoretical point, they bear little relevance to the hard practical problems facing management in action. Or there is little follow-up effort to adapt theoretical findings to practical situations. Second, even when the studies are relevant to business needs, the findings may be written up in terms that satisfy fellow academics rather than for easy comprehension by practising managers. While some papers are readable, easily understood and provide valuable guidance, too many are just torrents of academic outpourings and jargon. They may even bewilder fellow academics! Many of the perennial arguments on various aspects of management stemmed from such obscure papers with overcomplex statistical analysis and presentation that they defied correct interpretation. Thus the arguments continue indefinitely as each group supports one particular interpretation or another. Meanwhile the country and its industries ride on to ruin.

Once again the solution lies in getting the objectives of any research right. It may sound naïve to some, but all research studies, before they are approved and undertaken, should be made to state clearly what they are supposed to achieve, not only in advancing knowledge but also in providing workable solutions to real, practical problems. Investment in research should also be tested to see what return should be obtained. This return should be measured in terms of immediate solutions to problems and the resultant financial benefits that would accrue. The financial benefits could be in terms of cost savings or

reductions, reducing wastage of all kinds, improving performance and profitability and so on. These gains should be measured for both the immediate, or
short term, and the longer term.

Such an approach would build rapidly on managerial knowledge of processes and methods used, the relevance of techniques and the solution of problems, especially those unique to each company. It may be necessary therefore
to divide research into management into: first, that adding to a company's
overall knowledge of management subjects and procedures; and second,
specific problem-solving research dealing with urgent, current difficulties.
The former could be based in part on possible future needs, though short-term
requirements should not be completely ignored. The latter would be orientated mainly to the present but should also not forget possible long-term
problems which may be forecasted by, or be inherent in, the companies'
long-term corporate plans. For example if long-term development requires
evolution into new technologies and markets, thought should be given to the
operational problems these may bring in their wake.

In addition, the ideas or prognoses for all research studies should be tried out
on independent people, within and outside the corporation, to seek their views
on the proposed studies and whether the concept, terms of reference or
proposed brief are clear, concise and free from ambiguities. These discussions
should also test the definitions and assumptions used. Obviously the research
team must be carefully chosen for the work in hand and their work and
evolving results should be monitored carefully as the work progresses. Then,
alterations can be made to the research brief if preliminary findings show this
to be necessary. Finally, the results of the research should be discussed with
the researchers to check that the results will be appropriate to the problem they
are intended to solve. Check should be made of what other benefit or spin-off
might result. Learning from each study made will assist in the more effective
planning necessary for subsequent management research. Decisions should
also become more effective. Indeed, research into management methods and
concepts should be planned, activated, monitored and assessed with the same
exactitude required for normal marketing research, if success and usefulness of
them is to be assured.

1.8 The Civil Service

Since government and thus the Civil Service involvement in business activity is
growing in all countries, it is worth noting that the Civil Service is not immune
from the main problems discussed earlier. There have been and will continue
to be many instances of 'management' failure in the Civil Service. The most
common causes of these have been the lack of objectives for their work and
maintenance of the attitude that time is of no real consequence. Also, there
may be great and strong insistence on excellence and thoroughness of the study
and its findings. Yet in striving for excellence, the task may have taken so long
that the problem it was meant to deal with has changed, or has grown to such

proportions that things are, by then, totally out of control.

There are no precise business criteria that would prove common to every aspect of the work of the Civil Service. The time scales involved will also vary with the task, especially its size or complexity. Yet ignoring the degree of urgency that applies will ensure that the problem the work is meant to solve will certainly occur and will become more and more disruptive while the study progresses on its unhurried way. Thus millions of pounds and dollars will be wasted in doing unnecessary things in the meantime to try to stem the problem. Even when the results and the decisions that should be taken are known, developments in the meantime would have made these results irrelevant.

Admittedly, running a country is very different from running a business but the major criteria still have relevance. Thus the Civil Service should set clear objectives for each major task and indicate the time in which the work must be completed. Each major case may also have to be treated individually and the criteria that have to be used will vary. It is pointless to apply similar criteria to different tasks unless their conditions, prognoses and situations are similar. The nature of problems, it must be remembered, has the awkward habit of differing from one situation to another. Further, the present, apparent, secure system of employment results in a kind of managerial castration, protected by the appearance of ministerial responsibility via an obscure and irrelevant parliamentary system of so-called accountability. These defects must be overcome if the management of a nation is to be more efficient.

Another contributory factor to ineffectiveness is the often established practice of recruiting new staff straight from the universities. They may be bright young people with exciting ideas but they will not have had the hard experience of practical realities of the situations they are supposed to control or influence if they have not had previous experience in the world of business administration. As an article in the October 1976 issue of the magazine *The Director* ('Why the Civil Service cannot manage': Neville Abraham) states, these people are 'bright as diamonds and green as chlorophyl'. While the British Civil Service is good at picking young people with all-round intelligence, balanced judgment and common-sense appreciation of matters, good for a consultative approach to management, they lack the experience to select the right solution from alternatives, or to assess the chances of real success of their decisions. Examples that support these contentions include the many senior civil servants who retire early to take up senior business appointments. As the realities bear down on them often they will criticise government policies and actions, many of which they helped to formulate and recommend! In some cases they had forced these through despite the resistance of the business community and politicians with business experience. The incongruity of such volte-face does not appear to strike them.

1.9 The 'people concept' of management

Management systems and organisations can fail when senior executives forget that 'management' is a collection of people, i.e. individuals; not a machine that can be switched on and off at will. Each person is a unique mix of expectations, inhibitions, preferences, dislikes and prejudices. A management department, corporation, government department and academic institution are all social groups whose collective abilities and performance is some amalgam of those properties of the individuals who comprise the groups and the interactions existing in their working conditions. A 'company' is in fact the product of many individuals' ideas, concepts and effort. These individuals interact with each other so the sum of their efforts is not the simple arithmetic addition of their individual effort.

The hierarchy, reporting structure and procedures are the results of human aptitudes and attitudes, not only of those currently in post but also of those who have gone before. The latter were the reason why the company evolved its historical preference for certain techniques and systems, the way it works best or likes to operate. The former will modify and set the pattern for the present and immediate future. The end-products of 'management' have a high personal content to them and are not just mechanistic things. Every executive must have constant awareness of this 'people concept' of management. It is when this is ignored that a company is beset with personnel problems. It is essential that in the creation of management systems, especially if a computer is involved, this concept is not forgotten. Luckily the human element in management is being appreciated more and more and hence, the growing interest in study of human behaviour via the behavioural sciences. It is suggested that executives with more than a passing knowledge of this subject are likely to be more successful in the future than those who see management as a purely mechanistic structure.

An executive may get away with riding rough-shod over others for a while but once the latter are treated, all the time, as mere cogs in some great impersonal machine, labour relations and other problems arise. Often the problems will appear to have nothing to do with labour relations, but deeper analysis will show that the seeds of dissension and conflict were sown there, usually because someone has treated others in a totally impersonal manner. Thus personnel executives have a vital role to play in management. They must strive to maintain good inter-personal relationships throughout a company, advising other executives on human relations aspects relevant to their activities. This simple truth has yet to achieve universal appreciation. The important role of personnel executives is seldom adequately recognised; hence, the frequency with which these executives are relegated to the position of 'third class citizens' in an enterprise. Further, many companies are still locked in that sterile conflict between unions and management. The former feel forced to try to buttress the dignity of human labour through aggressive, but to them positive, action. The latter view labour with suspicion and as a constant threat to the maintenance of easy, convenient methods of controlling the business. All this results from the belief held by executives that everyone else is just a small, if vital, cog in the *machina* of the company's operations. (*See also* Section 8.3.)

1.9.1 Relating to feelings

Notwithstanding the above, many executives find it difficult to relate to human feelings. While this may be due simply to an inability to do so, a desire not to relate is engendered by the general belief that executives are strong and self-sufficient. They fear that any other attitude would lose them the respect and deference of their subordinates. Yet executives should have the skill and courage to be aware of their own and others' feelings and to learn how to deal with them. For many organisational problems arise from persons' inabilities to cope openly and effectively with emotions aroused in the performance of their work. Thus if executives develop their ability to relate to feelings, theirs and others', and to deal with them effectively, they can achieve greater proficiency in the performance of executive functions.

The failure of attempts to improve executive performance at work is partly due to the erroneous assumption that attention should be focused only on the tasks and techniques involved. If there is no relation to human feelings, everything that is provided for the executive to manage people more effectively becomes a mere gimmick. Its efficacy is short lived. While executives are trained to become 'doers' in order to succeed in the world of action, nothing is done to help them explore the world of emotions. Indeed, many courses imply that feelings must be controlled and channelled, being forced into acceptable modes; in other words repressed. Executives are told how feelings should be expressed and what and how they should feel. In business, feelings are seen as nuisances and possible threats to the effective functioning of the organisation. There is implied fear also that any expression of feeling will injure the personal relationships existing in the company. The less feelings are recognised by executives the less able are they to deal with the feelings of themselves and the people they must manage, or work with daily. The less skilful executives are, the more threatening feelings may seem and the more vehemently will their existence be denied.

It should be remembered that executives usually have high achievement needs. They desire to be able to measure unambiguously and accurately the extent of their achievements. This is not difficult to do in the world of work and action. However, achievement in the unstable world of feelings and personal relationships are hard to perceive and measure.

1.9.2 Leadership

Leadership is one quality executives should possess if they are to be successful managers. Alas, little is done to try to develop the leadership potential inherent in many executives. It is true that in any given situation, the leader of a group will emerge and who the leader is will depend on the experience, interests and skills that are required for the task. For example when an aircraft is in flight the captain is obviously the leader. However, if it crashes into a jungle and the captain is not knowledgeable or experienced in jungle survival, the leadership will pass to a passenger who is. However, in the rigid hierarchy of management, the chances of a leader emerging according to circumstances is very slight. Management development work should therefore be geared more to seeking and encouraging the flowering of latent leadership qualities.

This aspect of management is ignored when, on occasions, the properties demanded for real leadership, e.g. the ability to grapple and deal with emotions, may be considered as 'soft' or 'cissy' by colleagues and senior executives. There is also too widespread a belief that being tough, ruthless and uncompromising are the essential characteristics of an effective leader. Nothing could be further from the truth. Many writers, including Peter Drucker, maintain that leadership cannot be taught or learned. They hold that it is something which is or is not born in a person. They state that management cannot create leaders. This is a hard cynical view.

The author does not subscribe to this view. Conditions can be created under which potential leadership qualities are encouraged to develop and can become effective. Executives can be given certain guidelines which, if studied, will help them to lead effectively even if they do not possess the flair or élan of the so-called natural-born leaders. (*See* Section 2.6.)

It must be agreed that the inherent leadership qualities of any national will vary because of variances in educational standards and opportunities and the size and nature of the business activity of a country. If business is limited in size and total then opportunities to gain experience and learn and so develop leadership qualities will be restricted. So the stage that a country has reached in its economic development will determine how many chances exist for leaders to emerge or be trained. The developed nations appear to have more leaders only because their greater development and advancement has provided far greater opportunities for leadership to develop. Nationals of under-developed countries, especially those that are poor in resources, have become accustomed to being told everything they must, or must not, do. It is not surprising therefore that they tend to develop sheep-like personalities rather than become leaders. However, many developing nations have shown that leadership increases amongst its executive ranks as the countries develop. More leadership qualities are displayed by increasing numbers of their executives.

Therefore, it becomes the responsibility of the more fortunate to help the less favoured to develop what is a latent aptitude in all human beings. Situations and systems should be evolved which will help people to develop the attitudes that encourage leadership qualities to flower. Witness the many who, having been considered as useless, when given the right opportunities, develop and display leadership ability. Often this is much greater than 'experts' in management development had thought possible.

On this subject the sweeping generalisations made by some people show the danger of applying general concepts to every situation. If we believed such views, all senior executives would think that people displaying leadership qualities are as rare as Messiahs and would not bother to consider any other employees for promotion. So they would not discover that some executives possess leadership talents when placed in the right jobs. It must be remembered also that leadership takes several forms. These range from the rough, tough, front-end-of-the-arrow type to those that can inspire their teams to greater effort in various, more subtle ways. Sometimes the method used is so subtle it may appear as if nothing is being done, the team just happens to achieve high levels of performance. Also, while some people may have leadership qualities suitable for one job, they may not be sufficiently interested, or motivated, to take the leader's role in another. Fitting the right person to every job is therefore an important task for senior executives to perform, even if in this bald statement, it may appear an impossible one. This does not excuse the executives from not trying.

Companies must also stop placing people in jobs because they are not disqualified from holding them. They must place people in roles because they are qualified for them. Executives must also be able to differentiate between apparently 'born leaders' who fizzle out in a short while, and those who will be stayers. The former occur either for natural reasons (their real abilities are limited) or because they are too opinionated to keep themselves abreast of developments in business and management techniques. Then there are the young executives who are so 'sharp' they may cut themselves one day! If they also cut the company's throat in the process, then the unbridled support of such people will prove to be unwise. (*See also* Section 2.6.)

1.9.3 Executive silence

One general myth existing today is that the society of most countries is egalitarian in nature. Unfortunately in all nations some citizens are 'more equal' than others. This is so even in states with Communist governments and seems to be an immutable fact for even some animals are 'more equal' than others! Because of their experience, training and knowledge of economic, business and industrial matters, including of course the financial aspects of business, executives are numbered amongst the 'more equal' group. The 'most equal', of course, are senior executives by nature of their greater experience and positions in the more important activities of their enterprises. It is a pity then, and a great loss to their nations, that executives as a tribe are reluctant to comment publicly on matters of importance or concern to the nation. This is particularly a sad loss when the topics are economic, financial, international trade, taxation, fiscal matters and other critical areas where government involvement is increasing.

Because executives tend to shun personal involvement in important and controversial issues not directly related to business activities, a nation is deprived of the collective experience, judgement and insight of one of the most responsible and influential leadership groups. There are of course exceptions to this fact in most countries but the numbers prepared to speak up and be seen to be amongst those who are keenly concerned about national development, are still too few. On the other hand, the extreme left and right of the political spectrum in all countries except the Communist ones, are increasing in vociferousness. The academic community, students, educators and administrators are also becoming increasingly vocal. However the great silent majority, which include most executives, continues to be silent. At times, when pushed too far they will cry out, but for the most part they do not take any role in the great debates on issues vital to a country's well-being.

Executives, from board chairmen (and presidents) to directors and managers, shrink from expressing publicly their positions on issues vital not only to the well-being of their companies but also to the economic system which gives them their livelihood and to the survival of their nations. It is as if they do not care about the conditions and system their children will inherit.

The depressing result of this self-imposed intellectual and social reserve is that countries are being starved of high-grade, practical experience and judgement by the best people to give it, in areas where such advice and help is sorely needed. The executive group possesses considerable potential to make a powerful impact and influence national destinies. With society becoming more and more polarised between left and right wings, the moderate centre cannot allow itself to be devoured while it watches with calm detachment. When executives devote considerable time and energy to public service it is usually on the local or community level in non-controversial civic, charitable or cultural activities. These may be described as being in areas that avoid controversy. The rationale seems to be that as it is impossible to please everyone all the time, executives should avoid being involved in controversy. Share- or stockholders, civil servants, politicians and others it seems, must not be goaded into criticism or hostility towards corporations. There seem to be two main reasons for this silence. First, executives are reluctant to do anything that may jeopardise their security and success within their companies. The second is the fear that, by being outspoken on vital matters, their corporations or enterprises may become identified with their personal views. There is thus the feeling that one must tread carefully; conformity or orthodoxy are solid and respectable and should be pursued almost at all costs. There are other reasons too for keeping clear of involvement, but these seem to be the main ones.

Undoubtedly it is difficult to express conscience about any major national subject and maintain the neutrality of the enterprise, as distinct from the people who work for it. The company should not be identified with the views of executives on matters which are not substantially related to business matters unless the executive is identified clearly as speaking for the corporation on such matters. Yet the press, seeking for sensational news, will always tend to link the individual views of executives to their employers even when no such association exists. The trouble is greatest when the executive views expressed are on highly controversial political and social matters. If imputed to the company, then both the organisation and the executive are called to account. Where the subject is one involving considerable public disagreement the result for the corporation could be serious.

Stock- or shareholders will complain, probably as will any craven finance organisations that have provided the company with capital. Even those who do not disagree with the views expressed might feel that it is regrettable that the corporation's executives have become embroiled. At the extreme, there may be loss of business and goodwill. If the subject is politically sensitive then governments, politicians and trade unions may be offended and there will be the risk of retaliation of some sort. However, there is need for a clear view of the perspectives of the matter. While employees of the company operate under the direction of its management in the discharge of the obligations of the enterprise to customers, shareholders and so on, in other areas such as personal views, thoughts, aspirations and fears, their lives are their own.

There is no ready or general solution to this problem but a good start would be made if corporations would enunciate clearly as corporate policy that their executives enjoy freedom of expression in their own right and that personal statements by executives do not represent the view or attitude of the corporation. If it does, then this can be claimed by the corporation when endorsing an executive's statements. There are signs that a start has been made in this direction with a few articles appearing with the by-line that they do not express the view of the employer in the matters discussed. This will not eliminate all the risks for the enterprise mentioned earlier, for whenever a position is taken on an important issue, hostility will be evoked from some section of society.

However, in a democratic society there is no substitute for the airing of all points of view; but if sensible decisions are to be reached on critical matters then the positive contributions of all concerned people are required. If restrictions are placed, even for good reason, on the opinions of intelligent persons then dissatisfaction will result. Indeed, in this more enlightened era, with improved education, there have been instances of senior executives and others leaving what they consider to be intellectually sterile organisations to work elsewhere where freedom of expression is allowed. Silence and conformity are in fact the hallmarks of totalitarian states and support only the façade of tranquillity. In democracies the democratic system can only flourish in a climate of the free expression of divergent views. It is important, therefore, that business executives feel free to express personal views on all important matters and for the public at large not to assail their employers when this happens. When executive silence ends, more successful government will result and the economies of nations, industries and corporations will benefit.

1.9.4 Fables and foibles of planning

Planning is undoubtedly a very important component of management. The degree of success achieved in planning will determine the success achieved by management. However, many fables and foibles have been built around this important activity. Most stem from ignorance, or the ignoring of the 'people concept' in management.

Fable 1 is that once a good plan has been evolved the company will necessarily achieve success. This ignores the fact that changes in the business environment will require changes to the plan. Also, if the people operating the plan are not sufficiently trained, experienced or motivated, then the plan may well fail. *Fable 2* is that good plans do not need regular monitoring. Indeed they may need as much or more checking than bad plans, especially if the company is operating in a climate of change and uncertainty. In time, initial assumptions may be found to have been wrong, or no longer relevant, and adjustments to the plan will be necessary. *Fable 3* is the belief that plans foisted on executives from on high (the board) will be faithfully carried out. Depending on the resentment felt and executives' views of the board and its competence (*see* Sections 1.3 and 1.3.1) such plans may, or may not, be implemented. There may be pretence at following them, but much would be ignored or poorly done.

Foible 1 is that planning is done formally only at one set time of each trading year. In fact some element of planning is needed whenever events demand, e.g. a major change in the business environment or in the company will demand instant reconsideration of existing plans and some replanning. *Foible 2* concerns the involvement only of senior or key executives in the planning work. Everyone at some time or other should be called upon to make his or her contribution to planning considerations, especially where individual experience and knowledge can contribute usefully to the work, e.g. field sales force, on sales aspects, competition and customer reactions. Note also that those who have not participated in the planning will be most resistant to the plans, especially if they involve some major change. *Foible 3* involves the belief that there is no need to report progress to all who have participated in the planning or have been affected by the plans. They must be kept informed and often the result of this will be greater cooperation and contribution to the whole planning process, and the work generally, by those who feel they have been taken into the confidence of top management.

These are the main fables and foibles in planning. There are others which will be discussed in later chapters where they are of greatest relevance. Readers wishing to gain full insight into these problems could start by reading a very erudite book by David Hussey (*Corporate Planning; Theory and Practice*). Then there is the book edited by C. Margerison and D. Ashton (*Planning for Human Resources*) and that by J. Valerie Grant and Geoffrey Smith (*Personnel Administration and Industrial Relations*). There are also many good books by Rosemary Stewart and others.

1.10 The U.S.A.

Non-American executives have long thought that their U.S.A. colleagues were generally free from the failings and problems faced in less favoured lands. This, of course, has never been true and is becoming less so as pressures on American executives for changes in their approach to the management task are increased. The standards of performance, particularly of boards, has been under serious attack and all the signs are that this process will intensify. Society is demanding a much higher standard of performance and ethics from those in positions of trust. The development of movements like *Consumerism*, *Antipollution*, *Human Rights* and *Social Responsibility* have broadened the scope and intensity of such pressures.

1.10.1 New boardroom image

All this is due first, to a change of public attitude, especially towards the way that the affairs of public corporations have been conducted. During the second half of the 1970s, much debate has taken place on the role of company directors who are being called upon to account for their actions and decisions not just to share- or stockholders but also to the community at large. Corporations are now being seen to play 'quasi-public' roles either because of their size and subsequent effects on the economy, or because of their functions or areas of activity. Thus they can no longer conduct themselves on purely economic bases. Social considerations also play an important role.

Second, regulatory bodies have ceased to act as benevolent societies. They are taking more positive action to enforce their views of the public requirements. Leading in this has been the Securities and Exchange Commission. New laws are being enacted and enforced. Old ones have been revitalised after years of lying dormant or being ignored. Readers will find the article by Anthony W. Perry ('The American Director gets caught in the crossfire') in the August 1974 issue of the magazine *The Director*, interesting reading on this subject. More recent events have underlined the points made by Perry.

However, all the signs are that share- or stockholders still tend to be speculative investors. They will sell their holdings when a company performs badly rather than demand changes in the company to protect their investments. If this continues to be true, boardroom and other management reforms will have to come from the boards themselves or the managements of companies. The pressures on executives, especially board members is thus increased. They must be constantly watchful and be prepared to introduce modifications and changes when these seem mandatory for the continued survival and prosperity of their enterprises.

1.10.2 Non-executive or 'independent' directors

If executives are to ensure that balanced decisions are being taken, without help or prompting by shareholders, they must turn to other expert opinion. One of the best ways of doing this is to have a number of non-executive directors on the board. This aspect has also engaged the minds of American executives in the late 1970s. Mr. Harold Williams, chairman of the Securities and Exchange Commission in 1978 became one of the outspoken advocates in favour of reforms in 'corporate governance'. The aim is to make corporations more accountable and responsive to social goals or needs. His suggestions, meant to be more guides than a blueprint for change, include the following. First, the board should be comprised mainly of independent or non-executive directors to whom management is clearly accountable. Thus management would be represented on boards only by the chief executive. Second, the chief executive should not also be chairman of the board.

Third, if there are a number of management representatives on a board, committees composed exclusively of independent directors to audit decisions and operations, nominate other directors, recommend executive remuneration and terms of reference, adjudicate in areas where conflict of interests arise, and ensure that corporate policy is in accord with public policy and intentions, seem essential. Fourth, commercial and investment bankers and those thought to be suppliers hired by management for their expertise, and therefore not truly independent, should not be board members. Potential conflicts of interest exist from their business relationships with the company. Finally, new mechanisms should be created to judge management in terms of its responsibilities to both the owners and to society, and to balance short- and long-term profitability, taking into full account the public's social and political expectations of the company.

While these views cannot be ignored they have not gone unchallenged. Early in 1978, the Business Roundtable, a group of top executives from over 190 of America's largest corporations, issued a study titled *The role and composition of the Board of Directors of the large publicly-owned corporation*. In this they argued that the actual constraints on business belied the myth of unchecked corporate power. They cited factors such as competition, market conditions, legal and other regulatory requirements such as shareholder suits, anti-trust and environmental laws and various 'consumerist and environmentalist causes'. They rejected such formal reforms as the requirement that the roles of chairman and chief executive should be kept separate or that only one management executive should sit on a board. However, they endorsed several other emerging trends in the structure of company decision-making processes.

They backed the idea of an audit committee of non-executive directors and also the trend towards boards having non-executive committees responsible for decisions on remuneration and management succession. This recognises the trends of the last decade when major companies have been responding to criticisms of their decision-making processes by introducing these and other changes in board structure. However, critics contend that these reforms may be little more than tokens and will not fundamentally alter the decision-making processes of corporations. They point out that, while the overall figures indicate significant changes in board structure, many are not altering their traditional policies on board appointments.

The proprietary rights of shareholders would undoubtedly be limited by reforms of company boards in response to long-term social needs. Short-term commercial pressures would be less dominant. Ironically therefore, for those who view the U.S.A. as the last bastion of unfettered private capitalism, parallels between what is happening in Europe can be seen to be emerging in the U.S.A. in the second half of the 1970s. In Europe, the proprietary rights of shareholders on decisions made by the company are being diluted by pressures from within the corporation for trade union or employee representation on boards. In the U.S.A. similar pressures are coming from outside the corporations. These take the form of demands that the corporate decision-making process should be reformed to make companies more responsive to the needs of society. They could have considerable influence on how major American corporations conduct their affairs, as much perhaps as does co-determination in Germany or as demands for worker representation on British boards could have.

It is not just the apparent sins of business which are provoking calls for reform in America and Europe. There is also the growing realisation that shareholders are not using their voting power effectively. They do not play an effective role in making management accountable for their actions even for the narrow economic interests of the business, never mind the wider social interests. There is increasing demand for social interests to be taken into greater consideration when companies make major decisions. The proposed reforms would ensure that large corporations which have become 'quasi-public' institutions would be more clearly accountable if they had boards comprised mainly of outsiders. This in turn, it is believed, would help companies to command greater public confidence and make their power more legitimate. Others question whether these reforms would have such a happy outcome. They feel the reforms would only further subvert the freedom of the private sector and thus society.

1.11 Some case histories

It would perhaps be helpful to record here brief summaries of some well-known company case histories to illustrate some of the points made in this and subsequent chapters. Many of these cases have been written up in detail in newspapers, magazines and even books. They have been discussed, some almost continuously, by management and academic experts and 'popular' business journalists. Many analyses, interpretations and opinions have been expressed by commentators and the author does not necessarily agree with all, or any, of them. However, it does no harm to record them here if they help to emphasize the points made by this book. It may prove useful to those who will come later.

1.11.1 Penn Central

This is perhaps one of the best known 'cases' of recent times emerging from the U.S.A. It is a good illustration of the problems that mergers, especially between large corporations, can pose to executives.

The 1920s were the golden age for railroads (railways) but even before the Second World War they had begun to make substantial losses. Many railroad companies throughout the world were affected. By the end of that war most privately- and even state-owned railways were making substantial losses and there seemed no way out of this trouble. Two exceptions to this generalisation were Union Pacific and Southern in the U.S.A. As freight and passenger traffic moved to other forms of transportation the situation deteriorated beyond recovery. It is not surprising therefore that by 1970, Penn Central (the product of a merger between the Pennsylvania and the New York Central Railroad Companies) was, apparently, bankrupt. However, many observers saw the series of events leading to bankruptcy as 'one of the most incredible stories' in American industrial history. Joel E. Ross and Michael J. Kami (*Corporate Management in Crisis: Why the Mighty Fall* Prentice Hall, 1973) claim that the management of Penn Central not only violated most fundamentals of management but also invented some new ones.

Since the war, railway operations in many countries including the U.S.A., have been hamstrung by regulations, laws, political decisions, court decisions and poor labour relations. Unlike manufacturers, when earnings declined they could not make major alterations immediately to their product-market strategies and policies, prices, operations, management and sales effort. Proposals for any change were subject to time-consuming arbitration, public examination and public and political pressures. If any proposed change survived to implementation it was in some emasculated form that probably added to, rather than cured, the original problem.

In Penn's case, court-appointed trustees put forward the suggestion that the company's problems could be summarised as being due to ignoring the theory of *rational costs*. This is the thesis that railways should only absorb costs that were rational. The basic argument of this is as follows.

1.   If only x per cent of routes are profitable, the remainder (100-x) per cent, should be abandoned. (This proposition is only workable if a substantial percentage of routes is profitable. It means also that if less than 50 per cent of routes were profitable, under present economic and cost conditions, the only real solution would be to close down the entire operation. Otherwise losses and subsequent government subsidy would be unacceptably high.)

2.   Tariffs should be based on a variable costing principle and below-cost rates abolished. (If prices currently being charged represent the best that markets could bear, such a revision would result in higher prices and an increase in the flow of traffic away from the railways, worsening the situation mentioned in point 1.)

3.   Work rules should be altered to give rational manning, or a government subsidy should be provided. (The first ignores the fact that union antagonism and resistance would be increased. The second takes little notice of all the political problems that would be involved and would be an open-ended commitment. Cf. the experience of British Rail where this suggestion, or a variation of it, was made some years before and, happily, ignored.)

However the management protested that it was the absorption of non-rational costs that was the real reason for its problems. Investigations revealed facts that were quite different. The real cause, according to Ross and Kami, lay in mismanagement. First, the merger between the two railroad companies, seen by many to be a panacea for all their problems, was doomed to fail because of organisational difficulties consequent on the merger. There were the problems of amalgamating routes and the need to rationalise some of them. Then there were the personalities involved, especially of the two presidents, both of whom held unshakeable and opposed views on how to organise and run a railroad.

The task of combining these two giants presented an enormous problem which would have existed even if all other difficulties had not. Other old railroad hands saw the merged corporations as suffering from corporate schizophrenia which at operating levels only polarised executives to identify themselves with one or other of the factions, never with the new Penn Central concept. Conflict had broken out in the new corporation; the strong personalities were striving, if not consciously, to impose one-person rule and there was resistance to change. The organisational structure could not be recast to cope with the operational tasks that had to be done. Then there was the too common problem of a squeeze on the cash flow and this diverted the attention of executives from their true purpose of running a railroad operation. (Between 1963 and 1969, when the net income was just $2 million, the company paid dividends totalling $292 millions. American experts found it hard to believe that responsible and informed executives should continue to pay substantial dividends while the company was experiencing negative cash flows.) This accentuated the big gamble taken on diversification.

The top management team seemed intent on forming and running a conglomerate in which a railroad would play a relatively small part. The return on investment, outside railroads, was potentially greater but this was no excuse for such a massive change of strategy, especially if managerial talent is limited. The consequences of such a move were not, apparently, fully considered and checked as being within the capacity, resources and skills of the existing management.

American observers also stated that the board was of the 'See no evil, hear no evil' type and did not discharge its duties in what is regarded in the U.S.A. as an acceptable manner. Shortcomings listed included failure to supervise —

a. the selection of a correct corporate strategy;
b. capital acquisition and distribution; and
c. the railroad operations themselves.

On the operational side, delaying the maintenance of track and equipment in order to conserve cash for other purposes, seems to have been the order of the day. In a post-bankruptcy enquiry a trustee, former Secretary of Labour, Willard Wirtz, is on record as stating:

'... the policy at the time was to put the best conceivable face on the facts, to the point that these facts were dubious allies of the truth'.

One effect of this policy was to diminish the supply of serviceable rolling stock, especially the essential freight cars. Service deteriorated and accelerated the loss of business. This, in turn, worsened the cash flow position and the vicious circle was completed.

The detailed comments, including those not referred to here, by American experts and commentators may or may not be complete and accurate descriptions of what caused the collapse. With hindsight and from this remove, the comments and post-bankruptcy testimonies given at the official enquiry, seem to bear them out. However, the basic lessons that can be learnt from this case are summarised below.

1.   Careful study must be given to any intended merger and the difficulties that might be encountered in the merging of two disparate operations. This point is ignored at one's peril.

2.   Integration of the two organisations must be a complete one. There is no evidence that retaining the two chief executives after a merger, except for a very short time, works well. If they are retained their respective spheres of responsibility and authority must be clearly defined and each must accept and adhere to this. One of them must always be *the* chief executive. If the other does not like this, and continually tries to usurp authority, dismissal or early retirement is unavoidable for the sake of the corporation's future and sanity.

3.   The corporate strategy established for the new corporation should be correct for the merged operations and intentions. Then the executives should follow it and not wander off along inconsistent lines.

4.   The new board must participate fully in all the work, from the amalgamation of the merged companies to the operations of the new corporation. They should not be just a cipher of the strongest personality in senior management.

5.   The temptation to diversify beyond the skills, resources and agreed strategy of the company should be avoided. Not to do so will not solve any problems, only create fresh ones.

6.   The survival of the corporation should not be sacrificed by resorting to short-term or dubious ploys aimed at putting an artificially beneficial face on the operations.

7.   The final organisation should fit the corporate strategy and intended operations of the new corporation.

1.11.2 Rolls-Royce

This is perhaps the best known case coming out of Britain in recent years. There are differences of opinion about the date when British industry went into decline relative to the rest of the world. Some say it started as early as the late 19th century; others that the country exhausted itself in the Second World War and the decline set in in the 1940s. Whatever date is correct, the biggest shock to Britain's industrial pride was when Rolls-Royce went bankrupt, officially on February 4th, 1971. This great name, synonymous around the world for beautiful cars and powerful, smooth-running and efficient aero engines, all made to very high standards of quality, workmanship and technology, was bankrupt. This seemed almost unbelievable. As the newspaper the *Guardian* reported, ' . . . to the British the news . . .was like hearing that Westminster Abbey had become a brothel'!

The company, founded in 1906, was well established by the First World War and with growing demand for aeroplanes, they switched from the 'Silver Ghost' car which was the cornerstone of their business, to making aero engines. The first successful engine was the 'Eagle' which went into many warplanes and was the one used by Alcock and Brown for their celebrated Atlantic flight. Then there was the 'R', a V-12 engine fitted to the Supermarine seaplane that broke the world's air speed record in 1931. The 'Merlin', a development of this, was fitted to Spitfires and Hurricanes. During the Second World War production was expanded and many engines were built.

By 1945 the company was predominantly a builder of aero engines rather than cars. The latter formed a small, but significant, part of its operations. At the end of the war, it was clear that demand for warplanes would decrease. What business strategy, then, should the company follow? The basic decision was not to diversify but to build on their considerable expertise in high technology engineering, developing new engines including jets, for civil aviation. The manufacture of cars, understandably stopped for the duration of the war, was also to be restarted. It was a successful strategy and from it and the 'Welland' engine (the only new one to go into service during the war) came other famous names such as 'Nene', 'Tay', 'Tyne', 'Avon', 'Conway', 'Dart' and 'Spey'. By the second half of the 1960s the company employed 90,000, was the leading aero engine company in Europe, if not in the world, and could match or better anything the Americans produced. Its high technology abilities and standards were acknowledged throughout the world and its reputation stood high.

In 1961 thoughts were being directed towards a new, large engine of advanced design and when work started on this (a 25,000 lb thrust engine, designated the RB178) in 1963, the stage was set for the problems that would arise eight years later. In 1966 work was begun on another engine with three shafts (the RB178 had two). This was called the 'Trent'. It was soon after this that work on the RB178 was stopped because of heavy financial strains resulting from a substantial research and development programme. The company lacked the necessary finance to sustain all its projects.

The decision to stop work on the RB178 was seen by experts to have had far-reaching effects. Many of the technical problems that later were to bedevil the development of the RB211 might well have been solved in the development of the RB178. The latter was being designed for Boeing's jumbo jet (the 747), but Boeing preferred to buy American. Buying a foreign engine might have undermined the reputation of a country that prided itself on its technology, or technological ability. This decision by Boeing put Pratt & Witney and General Electric many years ahead of Rolls-Royce in the development of big engines. The government support given to these two American companies to develop large engines for the big military C5A plane played an important role in this advancement.

A market survey done for Rolls-Royce in the mid-1960s showed that as a result of the development of widebodied aircraft, a large demand was developing for big jet engines that could power these planes efficiently and economically. The demand for engines then being made by the company was expected to fall from £100 million in 1965 to about £3 million per annum by 1975. It was also appreciated that the company was well behind its American rivals on the appropriate technical developments. It was clear that despite past successes, Rolls-Royce could never benefit from the mass market demand for American planes unless it could break into the American aircraft industry on a major scale.

The company took the courageous decision to carry the fight right into the American market by building a big engine (the RB211) that could be sold to the Americans. Executives were counting on the strength of the company's legendary reputation as engineers and the belief that it had a few technical developments to surprise the Americans. These included the use of an annular combustion chamber in the engines, three shafts and a new material (Hyfil) instead of titanium for the turbine blades. The last would reduce engine weight giving improvements to the power/weight ratio. The company was by then the seventeenth largest company in Britain with sales around £300 million ($720 million at the then exchange rate of $2.4 to £1). Eighty per cent of this was in aero engines and these engines were used by 180 airlines and 60 air forces.

The inspectors who conducted the official enquiry into the collapse of the company, Messrs. MacGrindle and Godfrey, in their report stated that in launching into this most challenging project there was 'no special cause for confidence'. True the 'Spey' developments were successful but development cost to 1962 when it went into service was about £30 million. The 'Tyne' development was unsuccessful, despite expenditure of £17 million and the 'Medway' and 'Trent' developments were cancelled, as was the RB178. In 1967 the development costs of the RB211 was estimated at an incredible sum of £60 million (with £40 million from the government) with the sale price of each engine — not mass-produced, but virtually handmade — put at £250,000. In practice, each new production batch incorporated about a dozen improvements or modifications from the previous batch with some resultant increases in costs. At the time these estimates were made, the company hoped to sell more than 3000 engines in the ten years 1970 to 1979 at prices around £$^{1}/_{4}$ million each and to make a profit of £264 million before loan interest was taken into account. When these estimates were made the company's turnover was, as stated £300 million, with profits at about £20 million. The RB211 was planned to become the cornerstone of the business, absorbing a considerable proportion of the total assets of the company.

The development of such a project required substantial effort and assets (in plant, skilled labour and money). It should be recalled that the development of engines for the C5A by General Electric cost $450 million (or about £200 million at the then rate of exchange), all of which was provided by the U.S. government. The estimate of £60 million seemed woefully inadequate for the RB211 given that half this amount had been needed for the 'Spey', a quite different and simpler proposition.

By 1969 development costs had been revised to £100 million and the cost of each engine was expected to be £187,000 instead of the 1968 estimate of £153,000. Other revised forecasts showed there would be a loss of £16 million on the project rather than the original estimated profit of £47 million. These forecasts were made by the subsidiary (Derby Engine Division, 'D.E.D.') responsible for the engine's development. The adverse swing in forecast was not apparently reported to the main board.

At the end of 1969 the chairman of the group reported that the programme was being put on an emergency basis and one month later (in November) D.E.D. executives reported that 'unless some very special steps were taken we would not have an engine that works at all'. In March 1970 a Hyfil fan blade failed and the engine virtually exploded. The trouble with this material was that while it was successful for blades in normal conditions it was insufficiently impact resistant to birds drawn into the engine while an aircraft was in flight. Eventually it had to be abandoned for this use and the company had to develop titanium blades, at considerable extra cost to the company. This increased the weight of an already overweight engine. Launch costs were further revised to £135 million and each engine was then estimated to cost £205,000 to build.

A few days later, launch costs were further revised to £151 million and engine costs upped to £217,000. In May the test engines ran for only 125 hours instead of the planned 300, because of the many technical problems that had developed and were continuing to develop. (Incidentally in April 1969 it had been estimated that the engine would cost about $12\frac{1}{2}$ per cent more than the original estimate of two years earlier. This fact was not reported to the board. What they were told was that the engine had demonstrated full thrust on test and that 'the total task is still a formidable one but it is, we believe, achievable.') However, by the end of 1970 it seemed as if all the problems would be overcome, although with enormous extra costs and well outside the contractual period. In 1971 a new set of estimates showed that launch costs would be £203 million and each engine would cost £281,000. More technical problems emerged, pushing the engine nearer its design limits and several engines failed. Disaster was just around the corner.

The terms of the Lockheed contract for the RB211 also contained seeds for disaster. These included the requirements that the engine should —

    a. be twice as powerful as the next most powerful in airline use;

    b. use new materials untried in commercial jets; and

    c. be delivered in 1971 for a development cost of $156 million (or about £65 million at the current exchange rate).

The contract was also virtually a fixed price one, based more or less on fixed costs with each engine to cost no more than $450,000 (then equivalent to about £193,000). When the contract was signed the thrust equivalent of the engine had been increased 19 per cent to 39,576 lb. The price had been increased to $565,000 each (or about £235,000), adjusted to allow for the devaluation of sterling. That was the price to Lockheed. Other tough clauses existed, usual when competition is fierce, and there were heavy penalties for late delivery and cancellation. Provision for escalation in price due to cost inflation was minimal. The 1971 estimate of unit costs at £281,000 showed a loss per engine of £46,000 even before any profit margin was added.

Other seeds for disaster probably lay in the fact that the group chairman at the time was a very powerful personality who was said to have stood 'head and shoulders' over the main board. He was also the effective head of D.E.D., the division charged with developing the RB211. So the effects of one-person rule could be said to have come into play twice over in this case. Also in 1961 the accounting procedures were changed so that future jet development costs could be paid back when engines were delivered. Thus profits could be declared earlier but disaster was unavoidable if development costs ever got out of hand, as they appeared to do for the RB211. Actual costs were viewed as paper costs with the attitude, let the costs rise, they will be paid back when production starts.

Then there was the unbalanced top management team with a preponderance of engineers over accountants. There was, apparently, no balance to the organisation. In high technology operations like this the creative technical person or engineer tends to rise to the top and then surrounds himself with similar types of executives. Maintaining production costs, finance and marketing within planned control limits is difficult in these circumstances. The emphasis tends to be on producing the high technological results demanded, almost at any cost, until disaster strikes. The inspectors made particular note in their report of this imbalance at the top. They also reported that the board did not participate effectively in this development. They relied on reports by the chairman and were stunned when they were eventually told the company was insolvent. The management apparently did not know the extent of their troubles until disaster struck.

In fact, while the financial function may not have been any worse than that of many other companies, the company's financial voice was not heard at top levels soon enough. While accountants may argue interminably about the wisdom of the accounting changes made in 1961, even by the mid-1970s there were no firm rules or regulations on this point. However, they may have misled executives into believing all was well because the changes showed published profits in a more favourable light than they were in reality. The sheer size of the operation ensured that the outcome in the circumstances could only be bankruptcy. Also, while costing data seems to have been abundant, witness the several revisions of cost estimates, no-one of any importance appeared to take notice or recommend remedial action. There were plenty of messages and warnings but the messages did not, apparently, get through to the main board.

The company also appeared not to respond to change effectively or soon enough. It appears to have missed both the technical and market buses. It had lost touch with market trends and was well behind the Americans in associated technology. The strategy adopted would have worked, perhaps, in 1960/62 but by 1965 the odds were too great. Events showed that the wrong decision had been taken. (However, by the late 1970s after the 'rebirth' of the organisation the picture has changed again. The strategy adopted in the 1960s now seems right for the 1970s and 1980s.)

Although the company was not overtrading, with hindsight, the RB211 and the contract terms it had to meet combined to produce a project that was too large and financially restricting for the company and its available resources. They might have made it had the company stuck strictly to the fundamental laws of good management (good planning, control etc.) and had the contract been less severe. However, the full implications of what the company was attempting and the consequences of the terms under which it had to succeed, apparently escaped notice. No-one apparently realised the facts. Indeed the government of the day encouraged the chairman to drive on hard, to what was in the end, unavoidable disaster. It did not help that the chairman of the board appeared to be master of it rather than its servant.

It was Robert Heller, editor of the magazine *Management Today*, writing at that time in the *Observer*, who stressed the argument that the chief executive should be the servant of the board and not its master. Rolls-Royce at the time did not benefit from having both a chairman and a chief executive. Thus there was not one senior manager (a chief executive) responsible with colleagues for the formulation of major decisions and policies and another (the chairman) acting as a check or judge on the decisions and work of the chief executive. Heller pointed out also that the inspectors failed to understand the role of the financial function in the company. If the serious cash position had been appreciated and something was done about it quickly, the company might have been saved. There was lack of response by top management to financial data, not a lack of data. He pointed out also that the company's legendary skills did not exist in sufficient quantity any more. He stated further, that he thought the inspectors should have laid more blame on management for continuing to pay out substantial dividends when the true profit, rather than the declared profit, did not cover them. He thought too that greater blame should have been placed on executives for not ensuring that the company was in a fit state financially to tackle such a big project. This is essential even for a sound new project. It was vital, he said, for a project like the RB211.

Other commentators considered that a further contributory factor was the excessive generosity shown by the banks to Rolls-Royce when it was ailing. Because so many very senior personalities, including those from the government, were involved in some way with the negotiations for bank loans, it was natural to expect only traditional prudence to be shown to requests for loans. Yet even this minimal requirement appears not to have been met. The banks loaned the company a further £88 million just three months before the insolvency was announced. The company's gearing was also high throughout the decade of this saga and interest charges absorbed a significant percentage of profits. In addition, while inflation had yet to reach the horrific heights of the mid-1970s, it was affecting cost escalation sufficiently to have a significant effect, given the fixed cost clauses of the Lockheed contract.

Another contributory factor was the growing involvement of government in industry and the attendant problems that it brought. The objectives for greater involvement are greatly different from the business objectives the affected company must follow in its normal activities. The former are judged by political, not economic, criteria. Reconciliation of what are often irreconcilable targets and aims is an impossible task and lies at the root of the major industrial problems and failures of recent years. Given the enthusiastic encouragement Rolls-Royce received from the government, a reason for glossing over the insurmountable problems is apparent.

Yet this case has a happy ending, or rebirth. A large proportion of the aero engine activity and the car division was rescued and resuscitated and is currently operating well. The new company, Rolls-Royce (1971) Ltd. by July 1974, less than three and a half years after rising from the ashes of the old organisation, had delivered 300 RB211 engines, representing a turnover of about £200 million. By 1977 it had travelled a long way from the disaster of February 1971 and can hold its head high again in the world's aircraft industry. However the rehabilitation took time. Just grafting on a new head (chairman) and a new board does not automatically cure an ailing company. It takes time to resolve the many problems concerning assets, systems and people. Nor had it reached by the mid-1970s, in management terms, the very high standards of excellence formerly enjoyed by its engineering.

Some slight touches of former arrogance were still surfacing occasionally. As Tom Lester reported ('The Fightback at Rolls-Royce', *Management Today*, September 1977), one senior executive expressed the view that the company was more intelligent and had more qualified people per 1000 employees than any other company in Britain, judging by their suppliers! The company has never lacked brainpower or individually competent managers. What it lacked, Lester continued, was a management system able to form this considerable brainpower and individualism into a strong wealth-creating organisation.

Some parts of the company it is further stated, still are deficient in realistic commercialism. Undoubtedly the company has always done two things well. The marketing and sales efforts were good and they helped to earn the company the reputation for design skills second to none. However, even these are not enough without matching excellence and consistency in other management departments and procedures, overcoming for example, the refusal to face up to financial data and warnings provided. The present management gives much more attention to costs, profit and the return on investment and these have assumed a much greater significance in management philosophy. Greater objectivity is also being displayed in all decision-making processes which, with a better operational structure and delegation of areas of responsibility, gives the company a better chance of dealing successfully with the problems inherent in this type of business.

Profit planning and budgetary control systems operate and there is wider interest being shown in the financial side of all operations and projects. Executives operate in a very cost-conscious environment and there is now personal commitment by managers in all the budgets and plans that are prepared and executed. Greater emphasis is placed on better communications and on man-management, especially in relation to training policies. Progress has also been made on the manufacturing side with design engineers giving considerably more attention than hitherto to costs, the problems encountered in manufacturing and their control. Manufacturing executives are also involved in the study and planning of new designs.

The application of improved management discipline occurs not only in the design of new products but also in the redesign of existing ones. For example, design executives no longer continue to spend money on redesign to improve product performance without regard to marketing factors and demand. They follow careful evaluation procedures up to and including the chairman's committee. The company now tries to deploy its resources in the most effective way. Ideas are dropped if it is necessary to concentrate resources on other more important and potentially profitable products. This need for careful choice has further emphasised the need for careful planning whether in development, management, use of capital or marketing.

All this represents a very considerable managerial achievement. It is based on a return to basic management disciplines and concepts. There are many lessons that can be learnt from this case history. Readers and students of management would do well to consider them carefully and in depth.

In April 1978 it was announced that Rolls-Royce had reached agreement with Pan Am to supply £115 million worth ($200 million) of RB211 engines and spares. If the additional options are taken up the order would be worth £250 million ($400 million). These are to be used in the airline's new Tristar aircraft. The order represents Rolls-Royce's major breakthrough into the American market and indicates that the original strategy decision may yet prove correct for the 1980s. Given that Pan Am is an acknowledged pioneer in civil aviation with a reputation for making thorough investigations of the technical and commercial implications of its decisions, it is likely that other airlines, American and foreign, will follow its lead. Thus this order, which took fourteen months of negotiations is a valuable prize for the company.

With this order Pan Am has bought the technical excellence of the 524B version of the RB211, the product that due to its great appetite for design investment, finally pushed the original Rolls-Royce company into bankruptcy. The marketing team set out to prove that none of the investment had been wasted. It also held the philosophy, justified by this order, that no matter how impossible the chances may appear, if maximum effort is put behind obtaining an order for an excellent product then, sometimes, the impossible is achieved. In the 230-odd meetings that took place the company was able to prove with figures to the airline that the fuel consumption of the engine was competitive (vital when fuel charges account for 33 per cent of total running costs and fuel prices are rising) while performance was improved. The next highest cost item is engine maintenance (31 per cent of total) and again figures proved the engine's robustness reduced maintenance as the engine needed to be removed from aircraft at one-fifth or even one-sixth the rate necessary with competitive products. These figures of better performance and maintenance costs were obtained from airlines who already had operating experience of the RB211, including the American companies, TWA and Eastern Airlines. The technical team also used its flair for convincing airline engineers that behind all the figures was a real engine with outstanding performance capabilities in daily operation. They also had confidence to invite Pan Am engineers to the Derby, England works to witness the stripping down of an engine that had come in from Saudia Air after months of tough service on desert runways. The engineers saw for themselves how the engine resisted wear and that all the close tolerances had been maintained.

Another reason for success is the 'continuous marketing' approach of Rolls-Royce. The company is in competition with General Electric and Pratt & Witney for a limited number of airlines and airframe manufacturers. Marketing is thus not just a series of presentations and negotiations when an order is in the offing. For years, although Rolls-Royce had never sold anything to Pan Am, all the senior personnel of the airline were known to the company. The latter had been showing to the airline personnel films, reports and technical data for a number of years. They believed that one day all this careful preparation would produce its reward. The April 1978 order appears to have justified this view. (In 1979 Boeing adopted the RB211-535 engine for its new 757 aircraft.)

In this industry there is also a close relationship between an airline's operating efficiency and that of its engine builders. Too many strikes at the latter would hold up the supply and major maintenance of engines and ground aircraft and result in heavy revenue losses. So it was no surprise that Pan Am made a thorough investigation of Rolls-Royce's industrial relations record and situation. Their findings increased their confidence in the company.

In December 1978 it was announced that the Company had had a record sales year. Aero engine sales agreements signed during 1978 were worth more than £2,000 million. The Chairman said that provided the company remained competitive in costs and delivery times and continued to sustain further developments of its product range, its long-term commercial viability was assured. The company has certainly recovered from the debacle of the original RB211 contract and seems poised to write the next illustrious chapter in the history of a very illustrious organisation, notwithstanding the economic problems being faced by Western nations in the late 1970s. Nonetheless, the development of big jet engines will pose several financial problems for the company.

1.11.3 The great A. & P. (Atlantic & Pacific Tea Company)

The great A. & P. in the U.S.A., considered a colossal near-monopoly, had by the early 1970s developed a lesser image. Food sales were no greater than they had been a decade earlier and earnings had declined. A. & P. had lost nearly 10 per cent of its share of the total grocery chainstore sales. The reasons were many but have been summarised by observers as 'hardening of the corporate arteries' leading to strategic, merchandising and organisational problems.

The company was under the shadow of its past. This led to the development of a heritage of attitudes which may well be summed up as an attitude of 'no change'. This was applied also to the organisation itself which, in the end, resulted in structural defects and an inability to respond to the changes in its business environment. Its strategies and policies also followed the 'no change' line. This was seen to be the major reason why there was no growth and why profitability declined.

For example, its product strategy failed to keep up with the changes in supermarket and chainstore operations. In the early part of this century, groceries had been its line and in this the company had been an undisputed champion. In the second half of the century, grocery operations mean more than just handling and selling groceries. They involve also dealing with more profitable, non-food lines. The refusal to handle these new items was summed up by an executive who agreed that while non-food lines enjoyed greater margins, they were not A. & P.'s business. By comparison, those corporations which had added such lines to their range (including the British companies Sainsbury, Tesco and Fine Fare) were more successful. This attitude was perhaps a reflection of John Hartford's dictum that the company was interested in volume lines and would rather sell two pounds of butter at a profit of one cent than one pound at two cents profit. Then there was the rigid adherence to the promotion of its own house brands to the detriment of national brands. Relations with suppliers were strained by the maintenance of this policy even though house brands accounted for only 12 per cent of total sales. A. & P.'s brands were given priority in promotional campaigns and shelf space.

Also, the company's growth strategy was based on a passive or conservative approach. Innovations and policies that its competitors were finding successful in ensuring growth, were not followed or were not pressed home vigorously. This included decisions on the broadening of product lines and mix, trading stamps and other promotional devices, Sunday opening and so on. (In the late 1970s in Britain, trading stamps had become less popular to the public who found the appeal of price reductions more attractive in difficult economic times.) Competitors took the lead and when they were successful A. & P. had to follow. In effect, competition dictated the policy that had to be followed. Yet many of the additional products or lines which should have been offered could have been handled by the company's outlets at little extra cost. This historical approach to its business nearly brought disaster to the company in the Great Depression of the 1930s.

A. & P. was forced to move into the supermarket operation. In the 1960s more profitable competitors were setting up outlets in the suburbs, following their customers to the newly preferred surburban shopping centres. A. & P. did not and, apparently, its management was convinced that another depression would follow shortly. While its chief competitor, Safeway, was moving new outlets west of the Mississippi where major income and population growth was taking place, A. & P. continued to concentrate on the older, stagnant, more trouble-prone eastern and southeastern metropolitan areas, especially in and around New York. The more aggressive strategy of Safeway produced substantially greater growth and profitability than that managed by A. & P. Then in an attempt to save the situation, in 1972, A. & P. decided to go into the discount food business. They turned their 4000-odd outlets into WEO ones (their acronym for 'Where Economy Originates'). Another near disaster resulted. Considerable price cutting occurred in the biggest and costliest price war in the history of the food industry. This move by A. & P. is said to have led to, or been partly responsible for, the industry's loss of some $4 billion in profit.

The general theme of austerity was also applied extensively. The group's stores were plain and unadorned while competitors made theirs more decorative and inviting. It was also reported that management lacked depth and the continued habit of growing their own management from within their organisation meant that new, dynamic approaches to problems and activities were few and far between. Their merchandising and promotional concepts were also limited. As one chairman (Mel Allridge) is on record as stating: 'We are in the food business. We do not want to, nor do we need to, promote'. In current society, success in the supermarket business requires considerable skill in merchandising and selecting the right merchandising strategies. Not promoting one's activities, products and services means that the consumer will shop at stores whose names remain in mind as a result of regular advertising and other promotional activities. In A. & P.'s case, few changes of approach were apparently made. Since few of the executives of the company had worked elsewhere, management attitudes were ingrown and set. Replacing personnel and gaining acceptance of new ideas in these circumstances is almost impossible.

The lessons to be learnt from this case include the following.

1. There must be acceptance that change is unavoidable from time to time and strict adherence to the past does not produce good enough results.

2. A company and its management must avoid getting into a rut (of concept or activity) simply because it is more comfortable, for a while, to be so than to initiate change of any sort.

3. It is also necessary not to rush into any change just for change's sake or when it is too late to emulate other industry leaders' successful efforts.

4. Management skills should be imported when existing ones are inadequate for the tasks in hand. While some in-house growth of talent is advisable, complete exclusion of new blood is not.

5. There is no reason to be afraid of younger talent or new ideas provided they are well tested before complete acceptance is granted.

6. Strategies need to be modified or changed as changes in the business environment dictate this to be a vital necessity.

7. Sticking to old-fashioned and outdated concepts and policies only bring disaster eventually.

8. Avoid unnecessary price wars especially if they will harm the company and the industry.

9.   Up-to-date market information is vital if successful innovation and thus growth, are to result.

10.   The company should be kept abreast of relevant developments and one-person rule must be avoided. The autocratic ruler cannot these days be stretched to handle effectively all the complex situations existing in business.

1.11.4 The Fairey Group

Once one of the best known names in the British aircraft industry, Fairey had ceased to be an aircraft company in Britain by the late 1950s. In its aircraft days, the first forty-five years of its life, it designed and built such well-tried planes as the 'Swordfish', 'Firefly' and 'Gannett', to mention a few. In 1956, only a short time before it was forced by a government drive for rationalisation of the aircraft industry to leave aircraft manufacturing, its 'Fairey Delta 2' established the world speed record for the first aircraft to exceed a speed of 1,000 m.p.h. In 1959 when the government of the day (Conservative) finally decided to rationalise the industry, Fairey Aviation and its factory at Hayes, Middlesex, England, were sold to Westland Aircraft, Britain's largest helicopter manufacturer. At the time it was unlikely that Fairey could have completed its development of the 'Rotodyne', a big helicopter, because of the company's limited resources.

Fairey was left with aircraft factories overseas but at home was in various engineering and marine activities and in air surveying. It had been turned from an aircraft manufacturer with support operations, into an untidy, small conglomerate the market viability of whose activities had not been thoroughly checked. The company's management were not to blame here as they had to accept a government *dictat* on aircraft manufacturing. Not surprisingly, as economic conditions worsened, a receiver was called in in October 1977 to liquidate the business. Things had been made worse by difficulties over a nuclear power generating station contract and major problems with their Belgian subsidiary. The insolvency of the latter put additional financial strains on the parent company. This was at a time when it was already struggling under the consequences of enforced emasculation (from official quarters) and several failed attempts to graft other operations on to it.

The company had entered the nuclear engineering field in 1946 and was a founder member of the Atomic Power Constructions consortium. It was awarded the Dungeness 'B' station which was based on the advanced gas-cooled reactor, then regarded as a triumph of British technology. The project ran into many technical and labour problems and, to make matters worse, the main sub-contractor was another subsidiary, Fairey Engineering. A move to merge with the AVIMO instrument manufacturer failed, as did the move to sell the light aircraft business in Belgium because the company could not meet the government's requirements on redundancy payments. Also, the Belgian authorities refused to release the expensive tools and jigs for the aircraft until Belgian credit claims had been met. The insolvency problem here, bearing on the parent company and resulting in the calling in of a receiver, was an unfortunate development for other group subsidiaries which were operating at a profit and had substantial order books.

This case is a cautionary tale with many lessons that should be learnt. First, enforced hiving-off of a major activity will often leave a small, weakened operation. Government officials and civil servants in particular, but also the board of the blighted company, should consider more carefully the short- and long-term effects of the proposed action before it is forced through. Plans which may seem right for political or even general economic reasons could spell disaster for the rest of the company.

Second, when government enforced action is unavoidable, the executives of the company should get down to detailed discussion and planning on how the remainder of the company can be developed into a strong viable operation. This will cover identification of new areas of activities, product-market situations and technology, all of which should be considered in depth and without unseemly rush. (In other words, a thorough corporate plan for the future revitalisation of the company is needed.) Third, when considering new areas and technologies, the skills, remaining capabilities and resources of the company must be taken into careful consideration. The takeover of other companies must be carefully and thoroughly studied before any approach is made to ensure that it is successfully concluded. The occurrence of unsuccessful bids, especially in circumstances like these, does nothing to enhance the confidence of shareholders and financiers in the company trying to rebuild from the ruins of enforced partial nationalisation. The planned takeovers must of course be compatible with the corporate plan for rebirth and existing activities and market knowledge. If they are not, the company must have the ability to recruit and hold the new skills and resources that will be needed and the will to make the new acquisition succeed. These shortcomings apparently did not exist in the Fairey case, but even then success eluded them. This stresses how big the problems in such situations can be and this is why some observers believe that in situations like this one the only real solution may be to go into voluntary liquidation.

When entry into a new, highly technical field is being considered, care must be taken to ensure that all the necessary resources and skills have been made available in sufficient quantity for the intended operation. Even if this condition is met, a company should move cautiously in case the new activity is subject to enthusiasm beyond the existing knowledge of technical capabilities and forecasts of future demand. Market forecasts for new ideas tend to be notoriously over-optimistic especially when the developers of the ideas make the forecasts. Reality is often only 10 per cent of hopes. The demand for nuclear power generation was one such recent example. Of course, no company can ever be sure that unforeseeable labour problems will not arise to upset the finest forecasts and plans.

Careful planning is especially important when the base for development is relatively small scale. There is little room to accommodate mistakes or setbacks either financially or in managerial terms. In fact, current conditions suggest that the smaller a company the more it should adhere to basic managerial concepts, especially projections of its future business prospects. The viability and advisability of new ventures should be based on the technical and marketing inter-relationships of these activities and careful asssessments of the long-term prospects of ideas for future operations. It may also be prudent to call in appropriate experts to assist with the planning and investigations.

A report in the *Daily Telegraph* of May 5th, 1978, noted what it called one of the final chapters of this case. It was the first creditors' meeting of this company. It went into receivership in November 1977 owing some £28 million. The major question that had to be settled concerned the repayment of £11 million of outstanding liabilities, which excluded debenture-holders. Of this, £6 million related to guarantees secured on the Belgian business. According to this report, this case bristled with loose ends, including the part played by directors and professional advisers in the bullish statement which accompanied the previous half-year statement.

The final lesson is perhaps that when a company contemplates operations in a foreign country it should investigate thoroughly the different operational conditions, laws and regulations that would apply. This should also be extended to what would be demanded should the company, for perfectly valid reasons, decide to close down foreign activities. What financial and other liabilities will be enforced? Companies tend to go into overseas operations with (naturally) considerable optimism and little thought is given to difficulties that might be encountered and the cost that would be met in pulling out of them. As this case shows, blocking action by a foreign government can bring total disaster to the entire company.

In 1977, after the rationalisation of its overseas aircraft problems, the engineering companies remaining in the Fairey Group were taken over by the National Enterprise Board (NEB) and became one more State-owned corporation. This was despite a takeover bid from the private sector of industry (Trafalgar House). Critics challenged the logic of the NEB acquisition and saw it as just spending public money on purchase of operations which were wanted by the private sector. Those who believed that the NEB has some strategic role to play in British industry were also hard pressed to explain the move. However, over a year later, *Fairey Holdings* as it was renamed, showed signs that it could well become a thriving concern. If the board's plans for the new group are realised, the logic of the NEB move might well be justified.

Fairey needed a breathing space. The problems on its aircraft side had denied the engineering companies the finance and direction they needed to expand and in one or two cases, to survive. The NEB appointed a new Chairman (Mr. A. Murray, who had helped to turn round the Redman Heenan group) and a new Chief Executive. The Chairman appointed new board members with a bias to non-executive directors with experience of engineering or the Group's customers' industries. Monthly accounts and reports were then requested and these formed the basis of liaison between the Group and the NEB. The latter also requested the formulation of a corporate plan and forward profit plans. The new management was then left to get on with the job it had to do.

The Group's strengths lie in the areas of hydraulics and in filtration equipment. Emphasis was placed not on acquisitions for their own sake but where the Group already had a technological lead. The filtration side is probably the most promising growth area and as with hydraulics, export orders form a high percentage of total sales. The Group continued to look for overseas manufacturing facilities, particularly in the U.S.A. What the Group has gained from over a year under the NEB umbrella is the time and encouragement to develop its strengths while being able to close down, or hive off, those activities not central to the attainment of its goals. The planning procedures introduced also helped to concentrate its thoughts and activities on the Group's goals and objectives. Despite the economic and other problems facing most industrialised nations in the late 1970s, the future for the revitalised Group looked promising.

1.11.5 B.L. (formerly British Leyland)

This is perhaps the best known case history in Britain in recent years. At time of writing it is still a developing case and it may be some time and many developments more before a solution, one way or other, is found. The comments of observers mentioned here seemed correct at the time they were made but may become less relevant as the management struggles to some final solution to the many difficulties that have beset this major group. Much has been written about this case and much more undoubtedly will appear from time to time. Many analyses have been made to try to identify the reasons for its continually recurring problems. Some of the things written about it are open to doubt and criticism. It is arguable if all the reasons given are the real culprits.

Perhaps the main cause of past failures is traceable to a few simple things, such as poor communications, lapses in leadership and poor labour relations. Freelance economist and writer, and former B.B.C. economic correspondent, Graham Turner believed that the many problems of such a large organisation were the result of poor leadership; ('Leyland, a failure of leadership' in the *Sunday Telegraph* of March 6th, 1977). In what he described as 'a long and unhappy story, reminiscent of a Greek tragedy', he saw British Leyland as 'an unwholesome child, overmanned, under-invested, light on cash and heavy on people'. He stated further that its first chairman, Lord Stokes, a brilliant salesman, was 'long on enthusiasm but short on effectiveness'. Further, attempts to thin out the manpower and the plethora of plants proved to be unsuccessful and much union opposition was encountered.

More seriously, the blue collar workers believed that the people running the organisation had not the faintest idea how to direct an enterprise of this size and complexity. (The preference of British executives for small operations was perhaps, again producing difficulties for those caught up in something much bigger?) Turner continued that even the new deal brought in by the National Enterprise Board (the 'N.E.B.') under Lord Ryder, when the company became state-owned, had done little to rectify the problem of poor leadership. The people chosen for the senior posts were there because of their talents in financial control but, at the time he wrote his article, Turner was of the opinion that they seemed light on leadership qualities and industrial relations judgement. The matter had sunk to such a low level that Britain had the unedifying sight of a Parliamentary Committee cross-examining some senior executives on the clarity and verbosity of the written directives they had issued.

The trade unions too, he stated, must carry some of the blame for the problems. While the then management had gone some way to cleaning up the mess, especially on the design and marketing of new models, too much energy was still being wasted in internal fights. The government of the day also had to accept some blame for having accepted a report whose assumptions were fatuous. (Turner described them as 'pure moonshine'.) Nor is it any use for Ministers of the government to threaten the company. Once they had accepted the financial commitment of keeping the company going, they were fully committed. It would be political suicide for them to withdraw aid to the company. Yet the Ryder Report on which the current operations were based, as was the takeover of ownership by the N.E.B., lost the company a chance of achieving a priceless and successful opportunity to carry out drastic reorganisation. If this is carried out at some time in the future, the cost will be extremely high. However, before any successful and major reorganisation is possible, good leadership must somehow be re-established. Even then a more positive commitment is required from the shopfloor. Otherwise British Leyland will die slowly and at great cost to the British taxpayer. The consequences for British industry, where some 40 per cent or more of activity is directly or indirectly connected with the motor industry, would also be very serious.

Yet the company had many things going for it. For example, in 1972 it exported more cars to the E.E.C. countries than all the foreign manufacturers were exporting to Britain. (Lord Stokes: interview with the magazine *Marketing*, August 1972.) By 1978 it looked as if 50 per cent or more of all cars sold in the United Kingdom would be of foreign make. Also Leyland's sales had dropped below the 33 per cent share that had been forecast by the Ryder Report as necessary for a profitable operation. In that same interview (1972) signs of complacency were apparent. When the interviewer asked if some models were somewhat outdated, he was forced to specify which ones. Then the reply was that as the company could sell every one of these models it made there could not be anything wrong with their design concepts. This ignored what competitors were doing, changes in taste and attitudes then becoming evident with consumers, what their market shares were and how they were apparently declining.

Further, because of labour disputes and other difficulties, the company seemed unable to exploit to the full even its very successful models. For example, 'Landrover' production failed to meet world demand for the eight-year period ending 1975. Long delivery dates, seldom honoured, slowly but surely eroded its supremacy in many markets. World penetration which had been 53 per cent in 1969 had fallen to 44 per cent by 1973 and was believed to have fallen further by 1977. By contrast the corresponding figures for Toyota were 25 per cent in 1969, 37 per cent by 1973 and was approaching 50 per cent by 1977. Production of vehicles which languished around 60 per cent of planned output only jumped to 100 per cent by December 1974 when it was clear that the company was in deep financial trouble and many jobs were threatened. This response by the labour force did not last and shortly after state-ownership, production had slumped again because of industrial relations problems and other reasons.

The problems faced by British Leyland had also existed in the original companies that eventually made up this giant. However, as usually happens, as the size of the operation grew so did the problems; some stated, in geometric progression. The first chairman (Lord Stokes) had apparently always managed the original Leyland Company in Lancashire as an omniscient figure in control of every aspect and decision. No decision could be initiated or implemented without the personal authority of Stokes. It is seldom possible for a person used to this form of management to achieve change in his attitudes of mind to give successful management to a vast organisation. Yet, patently, autocratic one-person rule is not possible in a corporation the size of British Leyland (or Rolls-Royce, or Penn Central, or A. & P. for that matter).

An attempted first solution was the evolution of an organisational structure based on line and staff functions. The complications of this approach which embodied many persons answering to several bosses and twenty-one directors and managers reporting to the managing director are indicated by Figure 1.2. This was an impossible situation. Each major constituent company was similarly organised on a line and staff basis with every function duplicated by a central staff department situated either in London or the Midlands. All export sales activities had also been removed from the individual companies to an international division in London. There was strong opposition to this development from the factories and much of this friction continued into the second half of the 1970s.

In the cause of rationalisation, or 'commonisation' as it was called, there was a proliferation of weekly, monthly and, in some cases, daily reports. Profit planning was given paramount importance but, unfortunately, as some executives commented, more time was spent on planning profits than on making them. Meetings multiplied and, as they will, fed on each other. Minutes were mandatory and informal discussions no longer permitted or were no longer acceptable. The leavening of a limited amount of informal agreement was lost on the altar of strict formality in the decision-making process. So many people had to be kept informed that formality was perhaps unavoidable. Circulating paperwork abounded.

Decisions had to follow certain rigid concepts. For example, market penetration was planned to suit the demands of the profit planners and was not apparently related to the possibilities in the market, measured by total demand, competition and the ready acceptance of models by potential custom-

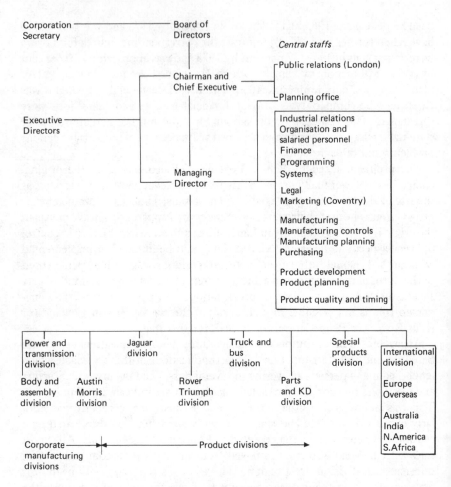

Fig 1.2

ers. It was also based on other imponderables, given the company's labour record, of likely production for some months ahead and the total volume of sales to the home market. The trouble was that remote control, and the formal procedures demanded, made quick decisions almost impossible. This was particularly so with modifications to programmes to match real and changing circumstances in markets and manufacturing. Overbuilding and overstocking (unsold inventories of finished products) of the wrong models occurred. No-one felt solely responsible for anything and no-one could be held accountable for any errors. Advice and instructions flowed in from many directions and were often contradictory. More meetings had to be called to study the problems and by the time their deliberations were known the problems had grown worse. It was a 'Catch 22' situation.

A further complication was the increasing frustration experienced by executives. There were frequent changes in staff and organisation with the resultant decay of morale. The basic truth of organisation work, viz. that no matter how right, neat or logical an organisational structure may look, without the right persons in various posts it will not work, was apparently ignored. Even the post-Ryder, N.E.B. control, organisation failed to operate as efficiently as was necessary (Figure 1.3). There was a preoccupation with neat, paper organisational charts and no-one apparently realised that even an untidy organisation will be more successful than a tidy one, if the right people are in the key jobs and able to motivate others.

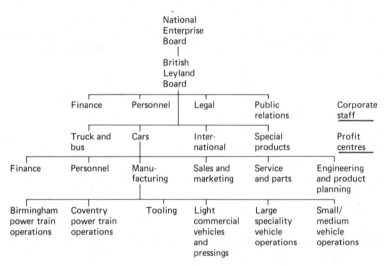

Fig 1.3   Source: *Financial Times* of May 3rd, 1977

As Joan Woodward commented in her book *Industrial Organisation—Theory and Practice (Oxford University Press):*

'... the only conclusion to be drawn was that the systematisation of the information obtained in the way described had produced entirely negative results. No relationship of any kind had been established between organisational and other characteristics ... to a research team based in a college that spent so much time and effort on the teaching of management subjects, the lack of any inter-relationships between business success and what is generally regarded as sound organisation structure, was particularly disconcerting.'

The incentive to the individual to do more than the minimum demanded by the job had gone and with that went job satisfaction and the feeling of relative security. When not only blue collar workers but also clerks and managers feel threatened or are uneasy, the seeds for extensive industrial unrest are sown.

British Leyland's continuing drift to deeper trouble in the mid-1970s is in sharp contrast to the now successful, fully-centralised Ford organisation.

Although in the 1950s, Ford ran into consistent labour problems it managed to resolve these more effectively than British Leyland seemed able to do in the early 1970s. Although Ford, like others, runs into labour problems from time to time it seems able to resolve them before they turn into long-lasting sores.

By 1977, Leyland in its first two years of state-ownership had gone through one major reorganisation and several revamps and reshuffles of its organisation and methods. All this chopping and changing, even the workers admitted, led to the weakening of management. Some observers trace to these reorganisations, the other problems of overmanning, weak control and low productivity. For example, overmanning was compounded as there was rapid proliferation of staff departments to handle more sophisticated systems of industrial engineering and financial control. The slide in confidence to this date was manifested by blue and white collar workers being reluctant to admit at social gatherings that they worked for British Leyland! Senior managers talked quietly about leaving the company if the situation did not improve.

The lessons to be learnt from this case are similar to those drawn from the preceding case histories, but are specifically in the areas of communications, leadership and labour relations. These are the three areas that throw up problems which seem to be common to most industries and countries. But some companies and countries seem to be more troubled by such problems than others. What makes the problems so spectacular in this case history is the fact that British Leyland is a big agglomeration of essentially separate units. In each case the problems tend to be writ large, often it seems, larger than life. The corporate situation is then chaotic.

Here again, one-person rule worsened the inherent problems and the depth of management, although numerically substantial, was not sufficient for the extremely complex tasks thrown up by the size of the enterprise. The organisational structure seemed totally inadequate if the operational and control problems are any measure of the success, or lack of it, being achieved. Methods and procedures were too rigid and there was strong suggestion that there was insufficient flexibility throughout, i.e. in concepts, strategy, policies, methods of operation and control. Executives must be suitably trained and experienced for the tasks they have to handle. For example, executives in charge of manufacturing should have had appropriate experience on the shop floor, either as operatives or as supervisors. Taking apparently brilliant young people straight from business school, but without suitable experience, is seldom successful in terms of practical performance, even if their heads are full of new academic ideas.

Not only should the organisational structure and the management methods be the ones that work best for a given corporation, but its product-market policies should be in accordance with the market and competitive conditions that would be met. If this is not so, there will be erosion of the market share and loss of product and corporate reputations. Sales and turnover and subsequent profits will decline and competitors will attain dominant positions and in effect, dictate policies to the enterprise. The corporation will then find itself trying frantically to catch up with the new market leaders. Cherished hopes, views or myths, especially of product supremacy and security must not be allowed to dominate the thinking in these areas of planning and activity. Communications and cooperation between all departments, especially those where cooperation is vital for sustained success, must exist. Changes in consumer tastes and preferences and in technology, economic, legal, political and other social matters cannot be ignored. Even if they demolish cherished concepts, they must be taken into account. Otherwise potential customers will turn to competitors whose products or services are more in accord with these changes. Correct pricing and trading terms must also be operated. (This is discussed more fully in later chapters.)

In every instance the ideal book solution may be a useful starting point for consideration. However, ultimately, each enterprise must evolve practical solutions correct for its own unique situations. Often this will mean considerable adaptation of theoretical solutions and sometimes require book ideas to be thrown out of the window. The company will then have to pioneer new solutions for itself, often resulting in the modification of existing theory or even developing new theories on the management of the enterprise.

The systems selected should be those that take account of the way executives and executive teams work best for greatest efficiency and productivity. They should also be based on a realistic assessment of the skills, abilities and resources available to the enterprise, or that could reasonably be obtained. In the case of personnel at all levels, correct recruitment, training and retraining programmes are needed. Planning in all areas should be realistic. Large organisations and the proliferation of departments should be avoided. When a corporation grows to an immense size, solutions must be found to the problems of divisionalisation into truly autonomous profit centres with their own chief executives responsible to the main board for the attainment of agreed targets or objectives. Many American corporations have achieved this and in Britain the two examples that spring to mind are the Thomas Tilling Group and Norcros. These cases are worth study by students of management and practising executives wishing to improve their proficiency.

While this book was being written the case of British Leyland continued to develop. In October 1977 a new full-time chairman was appointed. He was Sir Michael Edwardes, formerly chairman and chief executive of the (British) Chloride Group, referred to, with some aspersion by one senior Leyland executive, as scarcely bigger than Leyland's spares and parts division, and not so profitable! It was an interesting appointment not only because of Sir Michael's record, but also because he has no pretensions to being an engineer (formerly almost a prerequisite for any senior appointment in the motor industry). Nor is he a salesman (like the first chairman, Lord Stokes), nor a financial man. That experiment according to some observers, had been tried and failed. He is essentially an organisation man. The author has long propounded the danger of having in the top, key post, a person closely identified with one discipline, especially if his or her mind is constrained to a specialism.

Success depends on having at the top a person with an unbiased, all-round view of the operation, controlling it and giving the right balance to all facets of the business. An organisation person should have these abilities and not be prejudiced towards one management discipline or another. It seems to have worked at Chloride and it now remains to be seen if the much larger entity, Leyland, will respond in similar fashion. Since his appointment there have been further changes in the organisational structure, the main aim appearing to be to remove the highly complex structure that existed and to exclude the centre from over-involvement in day-to-day planning and control. The names of the divisions have also been changed.

The basic concept now being followed can be gleaned from the statement that Sir Michael made to the press shortly after his appointment. Describing the hectic eighteen-month period in the early 1970s when he turned Chloride upside down, he said:

> 'In place of one chief executive (managing director) and one six-man executive team, we established four companies with four managing directors (each) with a five-man executive team; we redeployed two hundred managers while making only one redundant. We brought in a total of eighteen successful managers from group companies at home and overseas. I firmly believe that high calibre, highly paid management is the best investment a company can make.'

At almost the same time as his appointment was announced the news broke of a dramatic slump in Leyland's car sales in the United Kingdom. In October 1977, the company held only about a 20 per cent share of the total market, compared with just over 25 per cent in the summer of 1977. (In July 1978 it was reported that its share of the United Kingdom market had slumped to 17.7 per cent in June, the second worst month ever, the worst being April 1978 with 16.7 per cent. Ford's share by comparison remained at 29.4 per cent.) It should be remembered that Lord Ryder's original plan on which the purchase of Leyland by the N.E.B. was based, envisaged Leyland as holding a 33 per cent share of the British market and that this figure was vital if the company was to achieve acceptable profit levels. The slump in sales called into question not only the ability to expand but whether the company's then size and organisation could be justified.

The major contribution to market share problems has been the continuing labour relations problems in the organisation. Various small but vital strikes occurred resulting in the loss of a considerable volume of production. For example, in July 1978, 640 press workers at one plant went on strike and no body panels for most of the company's models were made. These include the volume sales models, the 'Minis', 'Maxis', 'Allegros' and 'Marinas'. This strike hit Leyland just when the government and the company were alarmed that 1978 might prove the worst year yet for loss of the home market to foreign imports.

Mr. Eric Varley, then Industry Secretary (Minister) is reported as having said: 'The truth is that the British (motor) industry is just not producing the goods. If deterioration and contraction goes on then we shall find ourselves in even worse trouble and unemployment'. It was not unexpected that Leyland would have problems on the volume side of their range since it is accepted, generally, as being an ageing and largely unattractive range of models in comparison with many of its competitors. However, as a report in the *Sunday Telegraph* of May 28th, 1978, put it, what was alarming the company was that stocks of its most attractive models (Rovers and Jaguars) were also piling up.

At the end of 1978 the problems facing Sir Michael and his team were still formidable. However, Sir Michael possesses a rare attribute, that special difficult-to-define, managerial appeal that brings out the best in colleagues. It remains to be seen if this will be the catalyst needed to salvage Leyland from its long-standing difficulties. One former colleague from Chloride described him at the time as 'a genuine charismatic leader . . . head and shoulders above everyone'. He consults with managers and works out acceptable goals in partnership with them but then lets them get on with the job. Central staff members at Chloride were not allowed to 'order' line managers to do anything. They had to assert themselves by the strength of their arguments and persuasions. However, once line managers' tasks had been worked out and targets mutually agreed, they were not expected to run back to head office on any detail. It will be interesting to see how time and developing events will write the final chapters to this case. In the meanwhile there is sufficient food for thought for practising managers and researchers.

In September 1979 yet another plan was proposed for B.L. This envisaged the closing of some plants and the loss of about 25,000 jobs. By this time B.L.'s share of the U.K. market had fallen to 19 per cent.

1.11.6 In summary

This chapter has outlined some of the many roads to corporate decline. However Figure 1.4 illustrates simply the more common cycles of corporate decline. This featured on the front cover of the magazine *The Director* (April 1978 issue) though the illustration featured here is a slight modification of the original. It is worth careful contemplation by all those involved in management, especially those who have to study management problems. (The author is grateful to the editor of *The Director* for permission to reproduce the diagram.)

1.12 Why 'quadrilles' of integrated management?

Readers may be wondering at the inclusion of the word *'Quadrilles'* in the title and the text. The answer is quite simple. When one analyses the working of successful, integrated management it is seen that sustained success results because of the close and continuous cooperation between foursomes of related activities or departments. There are several major, or key, quadrilles in action supported by other quadrilles composed of associated supporting or service activities. The groups themselves also work closely with each other so that two or more quadrilles combine in an eightsome reel, to continue the analogy.

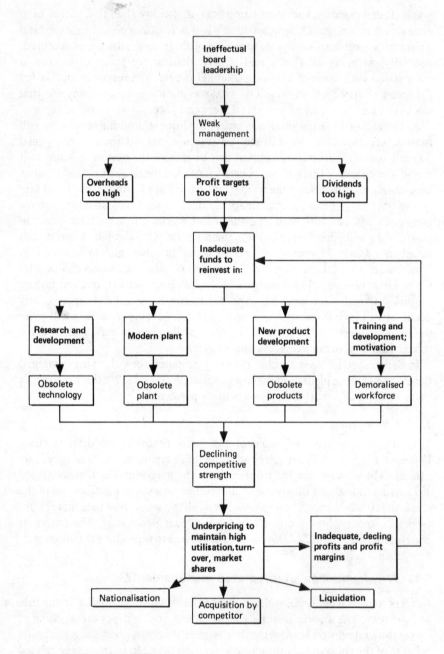

Source: *The Director*, April 1978

Fig 1.4

For example consider the *general management 'quadrilles'* illustrated by Figure 1.5. The main quadrille is comprised of *marketing – manufacturing – finance and accounting – personnel and manpower* activities. If full and continuous cooperation between these major departments is not achieved then consistent success in the company's operations, sustained over the long term, is not usually possible. Short-term success of some sort or other is always a possibility, even for the most disorganised enterprise, but this is due to luck and not planned intentions. The second quadrille, where consistent cooperation is needed concerns *technical services* of all kinds – *research and development – engineering* or equivalent activities – *administration and control.* The vital axle around which both of these revolve is shown as 'G.M.', the general management of the company which would include the corporate planning function. Of course from time to time other temporary quadrilles will have to function in close cooperation, as requirements demand. For example in *new product*

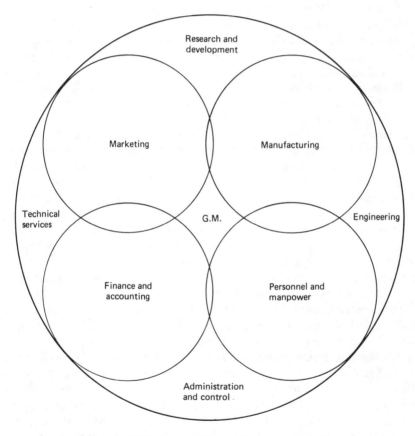

G.M. = General Management (directors, company secretary etc.)

Fig 1.5

development, marketing, research and development, manufacturing and engineering form the critical foursome for this work. For *product modification* or *quality improvements* the foursome could be either marketing, research and development, technical services, finance and accounting, or marketing, research and development, manufacturing and engineering, depending on the circumstances. With *capital utilisation*, *injection of new capital*, or *capital utilisation replanning*, the quadrille would be finance and accounting, marketing, manufacturing and general management (or the board). Other 'temporary quadrilles' will be brought into play for different purposes.

In the case of the *marketing quadrille* illustrated by Figure 5.1, the main quadrille comprises *marketing research and information – personal selling – promotional activities – physical distribution*. The chief support quadrille is made up of *product development and management – marketing development and management – pricing – packaging and merchandising*. Temporary quadrilles will be operative as other needs arise. For example, work to improve marketing performance would involve either product and market management, personal selling and promotional activities or, if promotional work is sound and distribution may be faulty, physical distribution will feature rather than promotional aspects. Marketing management (director/vice-president and marketing manager) form the axle here.

The *manufacturing 'quadrille'* as shown in Figure 6.1 has, as its main foursome, *production planning and control – manufacturing – quality control – costs*. The chief support quadrille is made up of *procurement – labour and plant utilisation – technical services – research and development*. As in the other cases, temporary quadrilles can be formed for specific tasks. For example when major cost reduction programmes are envisaged the critical quadrille could be either manufacturing, labour and plant utilisation, quality control and the costing teams. Or if quality control is no problem and must be kept constant but this requires some new development, quality control executives could be replaced on the team with research and development staff. The quadrille would then consult quality control people from time to time or submit for the latter's comments, the propositions which the team intend to put to top management before they do so. The senior management of the department form the axle around which all else revolves.

The *financial 'quadrille'* is shown in Figure 7.1. The main foursome is *capital and financial planning* (covering investment, utilisation and funding) – *cash flows – budgetary control – management of funds*. The support quadrille is made up of *resource allocation – credit control – project appraisal – acquisition and merger* work. Again temporary quadrilles are formed when specific tasks, other than the usual ones, are involved. Thus for major diversification work, the quadrille could comprise capital and financial planning, acquisition and merger, project appraisal and the department's senior financial management team (e.g. the chief financial executives and his or her staff). The last also form the axle around which the work of the department takes place.

Finally, the *personnel 'quadrille'* is shown in Figure 8.1. As will be seen the

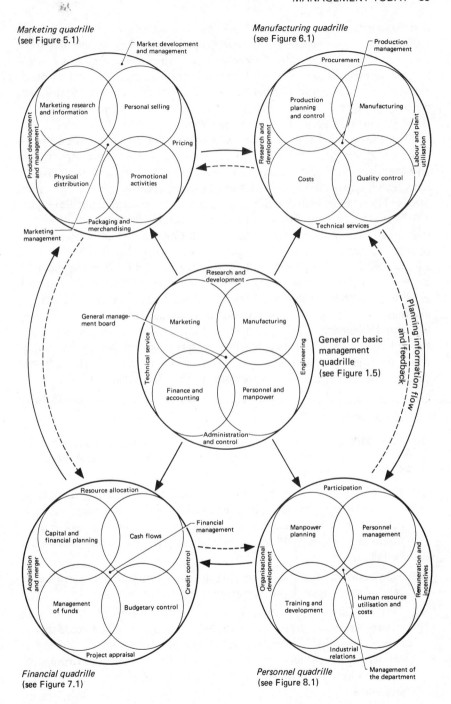

Marketing quadrille
(see Figure 5.1)

Market development
and management

Marketing research
and information

Personal selling

Product development
and management

Pricing

Physical
distribution

Promotional
activities

Marketing
management

Packaging and
merchandising

Manufacturing quadrille
(see Figure 6.1)

Production
management

Procurement

Production
planning
and control

Manufacturing

Research and
development

Labour and plant
utilisation

Costs

Quality control

Technical services

General manage-
ment board

Research and
development

Marketing

Manufacturing

Technical service

Engineering

General or basic
management
quadrille
(see Figure 1.5)

Finance and
accounting

Personnel and
manpower

Administration
and control

Planning information flow
and feedback

Resource allocation

Financial
management

Capital and
financial planning

Cash flows

Acquisition
and merger

Credit control

Management
of funds

Budgetary control

Project appraisal

Financial quadrille
(see Figure 7.1)

Participation

Manpower
planning

Personnel
management

Organisational
development

Remuneration and
incentives

Training and
development

Human resource
utilisation and
costs

Industrial
relations

Personnel quadrille
(see Figure 8.1)

Management of
the department

Fig 1.6

main quadrille is *manpower planning—personnel management—human resource utilisation and costs—training and development*. The chief support foursome comprises *organisational development—participation—remuneration and incentives—industrial relations and welfare*. As with the other cases, temporary quadrilles will form to work together on special requirements or work that falls outside the normal operations of the department. The senior management of the department is again the axle around which all the work revolves.

Thus the *'quadrilles' of integrated management* for an organisation can be represented by Figure 1.6 which also stresses the planning information flow and feedback that should occur. These links do of course exist directly between all departments, e.g. between financial and manufacturing departments. This is represented in the main general management quadrille (Figure 1.5) by the overlapping of the four circles representing the main constituents of that quadrille. The same direct information links should exist between the activities comprising the support quadrilles and also that between any one support service and members of the main quadrilles of other departments or work groups. For example research and development information links will exist directly between that department and marketing and that department and manufacturing, or the financial and/or personnel departments. In this way integrated management is fully achieved and maintained. Divorce any one of the activities shown from its partners in its quadrille and the activity and the whole work of the department or company will run into difficulties. It may collapse entirely when counter-pressures grow substantially.

1.13 Questions

1. How have the characteristics and nature of business changed since the First World War? What further changes have taken place since the Second World War?

2. What myths and taboos exist about management and management techniques? How do they affect businesses adversely? Taking any industry or company of your choice, show what the practical implications of these myths and taboos could be and indicate the remedial action that should be taken?

3. Why is one-person rule so limiting to a company's progress? How does lack of managerial depth aggravate these problems?

4. Discuss fully all the implications of the need to effect change in an enterprise. Why does resistance to change build up and how could this be overcome? Why is it important for executives to respond quickly to major, permanent changes taking place in their business environment? Why do you have to take particular notice of competitors in these situations?

5. Why and how do communications barriers develop? How can these problems be solved or avoided?

6. What implications are there for business executives when the questions of size, growth, inflation and competition have to be faced? Choose an industry or company with which to illustrate your answer.

7. Why are customer attitudes important? How do they play a role in upsetting the plans and operations of a poorly led or managed company?

8. What organisational (structure) problems are encountered in business and industry? Why is it important to 'get the organisation right' for all activities? How does failure to do so lead to corporate collapse?

9. Discuss the other major or main reasons for corporate collapse. How can executives avoid these pitfalls?

10. When does conflict between managers arise? How does an attitude of 'no consultation' aggravate the situation?

11. Why is 'self-development' so important for executives?

12. What common mistakes are made in business planning and what could be their short- and long-term effects?

13. Discuss the importance of leadership in business enterprises.

14. Why is 'executive silence' so damaging to business these days? What is the answer to the resultant problems?

2 The awakening
or Plain Tales from the Managerial Raj

Readers may be forgiven if, after reading the preceeding chapter, they believe that *every* management team in the western world is overwhelmed with problems and operating at a very low level of efficiency, if not a high level of inefficiency! This of course is not true and the author hopes that such a generalisation will not be held by all students of management. However, all companies, no matter how efficiently they are run, could achieve further improvements in their operations if they got their objectives and management techniques right. It is true also that some, a small proportion unfortunately, are very efficient and are the world's managerial pacesetters. Regretfully, many more are operating below their optimal efficiencies and others still struggling along inefficiently.

Happily, there are signs of a growing awakening to the reasons why management inefficiency has increased in recent years. More practitioners and academics are querying the methods and techniques in vogue, misused in too many instances, and calls for a return to the first principles of management are being heard. Also there are the calls for a thorough re-thinking of many of the so-called 'new' management processes. More people are asking if all these new ideas or concepts really have any value in practical business situations under current conditions of economic, political and other turmoil. If at the end of all this some cherished concepts have to be abandoned in order to achieve better standards of management, it would not be a bad thing. At least national industrial salvation will become possible. Britain in particular may see the end of 'Stop-Go' economic policies. At least that could be so if government and civil service policies and methods also followed a practical, down-to-earth approach based on economic and business realities and not political expediency.

Each 'new' technique has its group of supporters (or developers) who tend to shout its virtues and capabilities from the rooftops. Unfortunately their claims for it, especially that the technique is the long-awaited salvation of management, are seldom borne out by events. Given the plethora of techniques available to executives since the Second World War and the strident claims for them, it is not surprising that after some 'new' technique has been introduced, executives tend to sit back and wait for the miracle cures. Critical analysis and appraisal of the efficacy or appropriateness of the new ideas to individual company situations in which they are used, are seldom carried out. Thus there is no check that the ideas have any practical value. Only too slowly and too late does it dawn on the more intelligent executive that the new ideas may not work in practice or may not be suitable for the particular type of operation.

This lethargy also manifests itself in other ways, for example, in the benefits that particular activities are likely to bring to an organisation or the nation. A recent example in Britain was the belief that the discovery and exploitation of North Sea oil and its anticipated riches would go a long way to solving the country's economic and balance of payments troubles. In fact, the boost that this development will give is limited and could be short-lived. What happens when the oil runs out and the oil revenues of earlier years have been squandered on non-essentials instead of being used to revitalise ailing industry by massive reinvestment? Complacent politicians and others will awake one day to find that particular cash flow exhausted and they will still have only outdated, inefficient plant to face a growingly competitive future. Yet a lot of the present plant is producing chronic problems of low productivity and uncompetitiveness in international markets. The equivalent in a business enterprise is complacency or smugness over some cherished, or long-established, or prestige product. Even if it is achieving targets set for it, changes taking place in economic and technical fields, in consumer needs and social attitudes ensure that there is no assured long-term future for even the best products. Indeed, changes are becoming unpredictable in current world conditions so that the 'future' may in fact be tomorrow. Thus a rude awakening will also await executives caught up in this daydream.

Complacency forms a very real threat as far as the engineering industry is concerned. The danger is highlighted if one realises that this industry in many countries, employs about one-third of all those working in manufacturing industry. In Britain this large workforce produces only about one-quarter of the total industrial output. Yet even now this side of manufacturing in the United Kingdom shows up particularly badly when compared with other countries' manufacturing industries. Reports in 1977 showed that the price competitiveness, especially of mechanical engineering, declined badly and was only 'saved' by Sterling's weakness on the foreign exchange markets at that time. The government's efforts to keep Sterling depressed to retain this 'advantage' in international trade only ensured that the high levels of inflation then bedevilling the country, would continue. (It is a sad commentary that the country that gave the Industrial Revolution to the world can now compete in world markets only by depressing its currency. The real solution lies in improving quality standards and the efficiency of production without excessive increases in cost.) In the case of metal products manufacturing, output per person showed up badly, in 1977, when compared with similar figures from other E.E.C. countries.

However, the poor performance of British industry was due not only to the use of outdated plant and poor investment but also to overmanning and the haphazard and careless use of management techniques. In the last instance too many executives still hanker after an easy time and are reluctant to face up to difficulties. Such effort, it is feared, might add further troubles to their lives. Too many seem only to want to lead quiet self-indulgent lives. Happily, some twenty 'big names' (companies) in industry have always done well and, in 1977, were planning to improve overall production and efficiency. Many others were also awakening to these problems and gearing themselves to do something about them, if slowly. If this growing awareness to the realities of the situation continues then vast improvements in business performance are possible.

2.1 Management and managers

Peter Drucker (*The Practice of Management*) describes the manager as the dynamic life-giving element in every business. Without managerial leadership the resources of production remain just resources and never become production. In a competitive economy, the quality and performance of managers determine the degree of success achieved by a business. This success is necessary if the company wishes to survive for a substantial period of time into the future. It expresses the basic belief of western society. This is that economic change and improvement can be obtained by controlling society's livelihood through the systematic organisation of economic resources. However, Chapter 1 has shown some of the reasons why western society seems to have diverged considerably from its high ideal, first expressed over 50 years ago.

If its performance, competence and integrity can regain former high standards, management will be decisive in helping the industry of the free world regain its former prosperity. The competence, skill and responsibility of management, rejuvenated to much higher levels of proficiency, will play an important role in deciding whether free enterprise or the Communist system will dominate world industrial and economic activity in the future. If management fails in its performance the door will be open to Communism. In Britain since the Second World War there has been a decided move to the Left buttressed by the introduction of various Socialist concepts and policies. With these have come also, greater involvement of government and quasi-governmental agencies in business activity. Some were introduced as measures to help the less-advantaged members of society but many others seemed to be foisted on the nation purely to satisfy political dogma. Nationalisation and other controls of business activity seem to fall into this latter (dubious?) category. Whatever the reason (and it is a sound principle that the better-off should help the less fortunate) this trend has posed even greater challenges to management. It remains to be seen whether British management can rise to these challenges.

Since the basic responsibilities of management have been submerged by these political developments and the plethora of techniques available, causing confusion in many minds, it is worthwhile restating these responsibilities here. Management's first function or responsibility is to ensure that every decision and action leads to satisfactory levels of economic performance. Management can only justify its existence and authority by the economic results it produces. This truth is acknowledged, if only subconsciously, by most people in western industry. Witness the loss of authority and ability to manage by management teams that have failed to perform satisfactorily. Management has failed this responsibility when it is unable to produce goods and services which consumers want at prices they are prepared to pay. Management has failed also if it does not maintain, or preferably improve, the wealth-producing capacity of the resources entrusted to it.

Management's next responsibility is to manage the enterprise in its trust so that economic development and the development of the enterprise itself, are ensured. This is measured by its business performance, including allowing executives to perform at the peak of their capabilities. While management may never be able to master its business environment since too much depends on third parties not within its control, and there are so many uncertainties involved, it must strive to turn what is wanted ideally into what is actually possible. Management therefore, should be a creative force and should become so and honour its responsibilities by the attainment of carefully planned and declared corporate objectives.

2.1.1 The gamesman

In the mid-1970s in America, a new type of executive was seen to be emerging. This type was dubbed 'the gamesman' by Michael Maccoby, whose book on the subject was published by Secker & Warburg in the United Kingdom in October 1977. This type of executive seems to fit the leadership needs of modern organisations which are based on the following.

1. *Competition* — the need to match and outstrip activities by competitive enterprises.
2. *Innovation* — continual creation of products and services to gain an advantage over competitors, to meet changing market needs and ensure the continued growth of an enterprise.
3. *Fast-moving flexibility* — changing plans and activities quickly to counter changed business conditions, which requires managers to motivate their craftsmen and other colleagues to make decisions much more quickly than hitherto, consistent with the minimisation of risk where possible.
4. *Interdependence* — the creation of interdependent teams whose coordinated efforts develop, discover and market the products or services required, at acceptable levels of profit.

Some may question whether all these points are beneficial for society in modern conditions. For example, innovation that leads to unnecessary proliferation of new products or services, no matter how successful they may be, may conflict with concepts on conservation of scarce resources and the maximisation of the utilisation of existing raw materials even if this means that corporations will have to sacrifice some element of potential profit.

The gamesman loves change and wants to influence it. He (or she, though the female of the species does not appear to have emerged as yet) takes calculated risks. Perhaps the big drawback is his fascination for new techniques and new methods. The danger is that these may be grasped and used even when their relevance to the situation in hand is minimal. He sees projects, human relations and his own career as options and possibilities, as if they were a game. Carried to extremes, this could mean that he is in fact devoid of human feeling for colleagues and subordinates, reducing them to counters that may be discarded if they hinder possibilities, keeping them only if they advance the game to his benefit. Often in these instances the 'game' is defined in his mind as his own career progression.

He is cooperative but competitive, detached and playful but compulsively driven to succeed. He is a leader but also a rebel against bureaucratic hierarchy. To a certain degree he is fair and unprejudiced so long as this suits his 'game'; but he is also contemptuous of apparent weakness. He is tough and dominating but not destructive. However, if his 'game' is threatened he can take 'tough' action without realising that in time this would be destructive, either to the company, his department or himself. His main goal is to be seen as a winner and his greatest fear is that of being labelled a loser. Sometimes, in his eagerness to be known as a winner, he may gamble everything on a simple opportunity, staking all that he has achieved to date in a sometimes desperate attempt not to become a loser. By comparison, the cautious company executives might produce an inferior product too hurriedly in order to have something to sell. The careful craftsman, driven by hope of designing the ultimate product, might hold off until it was too late and the company has been overtaken by more adventurous competitors. On the other hand, the gamesman's attitude seeks to avoid both of these extremes.

While the situation in the U.S.A., with high technology corporations and a general willingness to drive hard and fast at objectives, are ideal for the development of this character, the British class system tends to work against the innovative, irreverent and risk-taking gamesman. Some European countries (e.g. Germany) and Japan also have conditions conducive to the development of gamesmen. Although it can be questioned whether a nation really needs gamesmen, Britain needs to change its general attitude towards management and adopt the better portions of a gamesman's philosophy if it is to break away from recurring economic problems, low productivity and slow innovative approaches.

However, there is a bad side to the gamesman. He does not initiate social programmes that leave his enterprise in an unfavourable competitive position. He trades anywhere he can, whether or not he approves or disapproves of the régime. He cannot bear to pass up any big win in the market. He will pollute the environment if the actions causing this produce the right level of profit, even though privately he may support the environmentalists. He will respond to anti-pollution drives only if laws exist that compel his company to do so on pain of serious penalties. He will produce and advertise any product that will sell well unless food, drug or other laws forbid this. Even when he believes the government spends too much on armaments, he will produce them if they make sufficient profit for him. While he values privacy (especially his own!) and is outraged by illegal intrusion of the individual's affairs, he will continue to produce high technological products that make this possible (e.g. computer systems with interlocking data banks which can be abused in use without this apparently, being traceable. When some are traced the company is reluctant to prosecute the offenders because of the adverse publicity). He is certainly not 'his brother's keeper' and from a social viewpoint is not a particularly acceptable character.

Perhaps what western society really needs is a gamesman approach with constant awareness of the human and social responsibilities of business; the gamesman without all his bad characteristics. In this situation society's rules will be made and adhered to rigidly by all concerned, even if heavy penalties are needed at first to get organisations to comply with the spirit as well as the letter of the law. Given the greed, love of power and prestige found too often in business society, clearly defined rules applied without fear or favour, are essential if society is to survive. Such fair-minded gamesmen may then be as good as modern society can expect and may produce beneficial results without any destruction of the higher, but non-profit making, values of modern life.

2.1.2 Management skills

The skills required by executives, especially senior ones, have been classified by Henry Mintzberg (*The Nature of Managerial Work*) into eight groups.

First, there are the *leadership skills*, measured by the ability of the executive to deal with and motivate subordinates. These include the ability to train subordinates, providing help and dealing with problems. Next there are the *peer skills*, the executive's ability to enter into and maintain peer or key relationships usually at senior level. The executive must know how to establish contacts with other parties that serve mutual needs, building on the network of contacts to bring the favours and information the executive needs to do his work efficiently. Executives must also be able to communicate with equals on formal and informal bases and be able to negotiate, especially in the trading of resources. For senior executives, *consulting skill* (a peer one) is also necessary in cases where an expert/client relationship exists. Finally, another important peer skill is *political skill*. Having this will allow executives to survive conflict and the infighting that characterise most major corporations these days.

Decision-making skills, the third group, are also essential parts of an executive's armoury. They are especially important in situations where ambiguity or uncertainty, or lack of information are involved in the decisions that have to be made. Here there must be the ability to decide what decision is needed, to diagnose the situation and its unknowns, search for possible solutions, evaluate their possible consequences and then select the optimal one. (*See* Section 1.6.) Managers also have to juggle with a number of decisions at any one time and seldom have the luxury of being allowed to consider only one problem at a time. Possession of decision-making skills, the ability to make the right decisions at the right time despite complications or other pressing matters, is vital if the executive is to survive and prosper. Thus this is perhaps the most critical group of skills needed and its lack is often the reason why executives and whole corporations fail. Happily this subject and the preceeding two groups of skills are being extensively taught in universities, colleges and in in-company schemes to varying degrees of success. Whether deficiences in these areas will ever be totally overcome is open to question, if only because new entrants into the executive ranks will be deficient in these fields and will need training. Some may first need to be convinced they are not 'god's gifts to business' and that they too need training in these important areas. Also, academics must relate the essential theoretical groundwork to the real, live and difficult practical situations existing in business and industry.

Skill in resource allocation probably ranks second to the above since all executives are faced with the task of allocating limited resources to many conflicting needs. As resources move into situations of being in short supply this skill will become increasingly important. In resource allocation, executives have to choose between conflicting demands and decide which combination of alternatives will produce optimal results for the company. Until the mid-1970s many executives viewed this work as being the least important because it can be easily delegated to juniors. The hard economic times of the second half of the 1970s showed them the error of this attitude. The work is far from being simple and more executives, especially senior ones, are giving greater attention to it. Academics are also studying the subject in much greater depth and detail. Perhaps as a result of this awakening, the old 'British sickness' will begin to disappear from British industry?

Also placed in this group by Mintzberg are the skills needed in the allocation of the right amount of time that should be given to each decision and resource allocation problem. Associated with this are decisions on what can be allocated to subordinates, especially in the retrieval or supply of the information needed for correct decisions to be taken. Other aspects of these skills include the ability to decide on the formal and informal structures which will be used by the organisation, and passing judgement on past actions and results. All these decisions, especially resource allocations may have to be decided quickly.

Skills of resolving conflict are also required since inter-departmental and individual conflicts arise far too frequently in modern corporations. The ability to handle disturbances so that the long-term harmful effects on the enterprise can be minimised, is not too commonly possessed by executives.

Information processing skills are also essential elements of an executive's armoury. In all businesses a substantial amount of information has to be collected, collated and analysed before major decisions are taken. Knowing how to do this, how to build an efficient information network (externally and inside the company) and how to identify the right sources of information and their veracity, are abilities vital to executives keen on making successful decisions consistently. They should also know how to disseminate information, who should receive the different pieces of data and how to express their ideas clearly and effectively and thus be able to create a sound communication network within the enterprise. Happily, these aspects of a manager's work are also receiving more attention in companies and by educators so that opportunities to improve these skills exist. (*See also* Sections 1.3 and 8.3.4.)

Entrepreneurial skills are also very helpful but unfortunately true skills of this nature tend to be born in a person. However the less fortunate can evolve some sort of ability in this direction if they are prepared to learn from past experience, especially from mistakes. They involve not only an instinctive feel for any situation but an intuitive ability to select decisions or actions that always prove right. The true entrepreneur can seldom explain how he manages this. More realistically, other executives must develop the ability to identify problems and opportunities before they become apparent to others. While the true entrepreneur is rare, the ability to forecast events and prospects to acceptable degrees of accuracy can be developed by most executives with moderate intelligence and above-average ability. If training programmes teaching the theoretical aspects of management methods can continue to add substantial practical applications to the work then many executives will find that their abilities in these skills will be greatly improved.

Finally, there are the *introspection skills*. Executives should have the ability, by introspection or even meditation, to gain a more thorough understanding of the task in hand and their performance to date while remaining sensitive to their own impact on the organisation. In other words, this means getting a true understanding of oneself and how this true self relates to performance. Then the executive's effectiveness on the job and the impact on the activities of colleagues and subordinates, and thus the company's performance, can be gauged more accurately. This aspect of executive skills has not yet been universally accepted as being important in improving executive performance. A better understanding is needed on how the human mind works and how the many latent powers can be awakened and harnessed to the many problems faced in managerial tasks. Much more research into the subject is needed before useful development programmes can be devised.

However, the development of leadership skills is enhanced by the ability to use introspection constructively. If the development of leadership qualities is important in improving management performance (and most commentators agree that it is) then the development and use of introspection skills is long overdue. If substantial progress in this area can be made all corporations should find that they can achieve more effective development and application of all the other skills expected of an executive. This will be especially important to senior executives: directors, vice-presidents and departmental managers.

Management development has perhaps concentrated too much on techniques and not enough on their practical application to real, live situations. More emphasis is needed on the latter and especially how to forecast and analyse problems and the short- and long-term consequences of possible decisions. Inherent intelligence should also be encouraged so that executives become 'thinkers' as well as 'doers'. There is nothing so pathetic as an executive who knows the theory backwards but is unable to put this into successful practice. This requires also, a more complete conceptualisation of the aims and purposes of an enterprise before the selection of suitable techniques and the construction of appropriate plans of action can be achieved. This conceptualisation should also be checked regularly against the results being obtained and changing conditions in the business environment. Just stumbling along because 'we have always done things this way' is not enough. Again, realisation of the truth of these points is gaining ground. It needs to be given greater impetus.

2.2 Management development

This subject will be covered in more detail in Chapter 8 but it is worth mentioning a few key points here. So much has been written about management techniques that the important function of management, having a clear idea of what is being managed and why, gets overlooked. Executives are involved not just in managing people and projects. They are concerned with a complete enterprise, from ideas for products or services, through the maze of technical, engineering and other production aspects, to the marketing of the finished items and the financial and personnel activities associated with such work. With such a wide range of involvement, there is need for an integrated approach to management.

However, many executives especially senior ones are, by the very nature of their normal activities in management, non-technical or non-scientific people. They are not experts in every aspect of the company's operations. How then can they achieve the ability to see the corporation's activities as a whole? How can they be certain that the enterprise's strategy and policies (or philosophy?) are right for what has to be achieved? How can they organise and control operations efficiently? How can they be certain too that their responses to change are correct?

The case histories in Chapter 1 make it clear, for example, that to run a successful motor manufacturing organisation one needs more than engineering and technical skills. Also needed are marketing, financial, organisational and personnel skills of many kinds. The last is particularly important if the continuance of workable industrial relations is to be secured. The marketing must also be backed up by very sound marketing research and forecasting if the product range is not to become obsolete.

In aerospace, while technical, scientific and engineering skills must lead, marketing, financial and personnel skills and abilities must also be of a high order. The British motorcycle industry was effectively wiped off the world map because it failed to identify what potential customers wanted in the shape and performance of the final product, the motorcycle. Many other corporations ran into difficulties because of the imbalances that were permitted to grow within the management organisation. Further, if marketing and technology are not managed as a combined effort there may be no real future for any product, nor for the company making and trying to sell it.

There is need not only for integrated management in business enterprises but also greater integration between industrialists and academics. There should also be that same high degree of integration between academics and financial and other professional institutions, industrialists and professional institutions and academics, industrialists and politicians. The last is particularly important since politicians are playing an increasing role in business decisions, whether directly or indirectly by the laws and regulations they impose on their countries. For those who dislike the growing incidence of government intervention in industry, the case history of the British motorcycle industry from 1973 onwards provides a cautionary tale for everyone. As a leading Tory politician of the day stated, it is a warning to all those who believe that politicians (and civil servants) should 'play god in the marketplace'. It is not the *métier* of politicians (or civil servants); and it is not their money which is at risk.

What began as a commitment from public funds of £5 million had risen by 1978 to £25 million and this is not expected to be the end of the story. The case, as a rescue operation, was a disaster from start to finish. Every mistake that could be made was made, both in strategy and tactics. Government Ministers it is claimed, abused their legislative powers to support a very shaky enterprise. Trying to second-guess a market is not a strong point of Ministers. Picking winners and saving losers it is argued, is not the business of governments. Commercially viable projects will always obtain the necessary capital from the market and companies heading for bankruptcy should be allowed to do so. The paper dealing with this case is worth study by all executives, politicians, professional people and civil servants. [*Meriden: Odyssey of a Lame Duck*; J.Bruce-Gardyne, Centre for Policy Studies (U.K.), 1978.] Perhaps this tale indicates the need for another quadrille in business, this time at a high level, between Executives – Academics – Politicians – Professional Institutions?

2.2.1 Managing minds

In the first half of the 1970s, various management surveys highlighted another managerial problem. This is the apparent inability of executives at all levels to manage their own minds! Either mankind's mind is incapable of dealing with the complex problems of modern times or executives' minds have not been properly trained to make them able to handle complex business situations. The pessimists believe the former prognosis is correct and the optimists, in the majority, believe the latter. If the optimists are correct there is yet hope, for suitable programmes can provide training on how to handle complex situations. However, academics as a rule have given scant attention to this problem though a few pioneers are beginning to study it. If the pessimists are correct there is little hope. The only answer may lie in the painful scaling down of the entire economic framework in which modern business operates. Already there has been recourse to barter systems in international trade because of the insoluble problems, in some areas, in international finance.

The mental deficiencies can be classified into seven groups which seem to be common throughout management in developed countries. Disturbingly, the most common is the *lack of concentration*. For various reasons executives at all levels fail to maintain their concentration on the tasks in hand, especially the important ones. This results in poor standards of work which increase anxiety and increase the inability to concentrate. It is a vicious circle. If truth be told, this is not a problem peculiar to management but afflicts every walk of life and activity. This is probably the prime reason why so many bad decisions are taken, in business, politics and the Civil Service. Sufficient thought is not given to the eventual consequences of decisions taken because the people responsible just cannot hold their concentration on the subject for long enough. So bad laws are enacted and false hypotheses are drawn to support or justify bad decisions in legal, sociological and management subjects.

Closely associated with the above is the *inability to remember* important facts and data, earlier correspondence, appointments, faces and names. In former, less hectic, times the successful executive included in his armoury of skills, the power of being able to recall where the necessary information had been filed, or could be found, even if the full details could not be recalled at first. Now, students cannot remember lectures given the week previously, politicians forget what they said or claimed a month earlier (or is this a convenient device?), civil servants fail to recollect the correct Act of law applicable to the question under study and executives forget the purpose and objectives of their enterprises and their own departments. All of these failings may be the result of the development of more liberal forms of education in developed nations. It may have been tedious to have to remember multiplication tables (now a pocket calculator does it all for one, without expenditure of effort), but this was in fact the first step in developing and training the memory. The modern trend to employing convenience methods rather than training youngsters to remember and understand the basic principles involved in mathematics and other subjects may make life easier but it means that the human memory is undeveloped. Students and graduates may be able to do complicated calculations in seconds thanks to the calculators and computers available today but when something goes wrong, do they understand how the systems they have been using work? Unless they do, they will have difficulty in finding out the cause of the failure. Academics must awaken to this problem and devise ways in which the memories of their students can be trained or developed to former high standards of ability.

Next are all the activities normally considered to be the products of *creativity*. A growing number of executives claim to have little or no creative ability. This may be why so many poor marketing, promotional and design performances are being encountered. What is worse, is that the lack of creativity or originality of mind leads to poor corporate and departmental planning, especially organisational planning. The business and academic worlds are fully aware of these problems and are striving to correct the situation but the real solution lies in encouraging the young to be creative in their formative years, whether this is done through art, literature, music or any other subject. Once the creative abilities have been awakened in the early years of a person's life he or she should have little difficulty in developing this ability in the business field.

Then there is the question of *negotiations*. Whilst most executives open any negotiation with confidence, sure that they have mastered the key facts, they often leave meetings confused, uncertain, frustrated and disillusioned. They may not know what really went wrong. This is another manifestation of their inability to concentrate on the subject of the negotiation and to remember correctly all the relevant facts associated with it. Existing training programmes are aimed at improving performance in the typical negotiations that executives have to handle. They are particularly good when dealing with personnel and industrial relations subjects. However, unless the programmes also tackle the memory problem, they cannot be as successful as their promoters would wish.

Another variation on this theme concerns *meetings*. In business these have increased in number, duration and degree of boredom. Many executives leave meetings wondering why they were called at all. The causes of this aspect of the problem are: first, that the objectives or need for a meeting have not been clearly thought out before the decision to call it has been made. Second, meetings are being used more frequently to save executives from taking responsibility for making decisions. Ducking responsibility is an often witnessed pastime of too many executives.

The problem is made worse by the fact that few executives, politicians, civil servants and others make good chairmen at meetings. They either lose sight of the objective or reason for the meeting or are too weak in controlling it. They seem unable to identify the critical points and unable or unwilling to steer discussion to them. They are also prone to let a powerful personality or erudite, verbose person take and hold the floor for far too long. Rambling waffle and waste of time result. Again this problem is fully appreciated these days and many training courses exist on how to run and control meetings. More could be done on how to identify whether meetings are necessary and in identifying the objectives or purpose of them.

Reading is another problem area. So much is pouring from the presses, demanding study, that executives find themselves without the time to study in depth all that seems relevant to their work. This matter is made worse where people lack concentration, reasonable memory and creativity. Yet simple instructions on how to select material for study and the use of speed reading in the first instance to help with the selection of items worthy of deeper study, would go a long way to resolving this problem. Courses on reading seem few and far between, despite its vital importance to executives. It may be that executives consider such courses low key, fine for their juniors but too infantile for themselves. It may also be because executives do not see the problem as failings on their part but rather that there is too much to read. Fuller realisation of the true aspects of this problem is needed, as is the training and retraining of all executives from time to time on the whole question of reading. Again, associated training to improve concentration and memory is required.

Finally, there is the subject of *interviewing*. Few executives know how to select the right interviewing techniques and how to conduct interviews, especially lengthy ones. If an interview stretches over a period of time, with several days or weeks intervening between interviews, executives' inability to recall key facts quickly adds to the problem. Faulty memory again disrupts the process. Lack of creativity prevents executives from identifying the candidates that should be interviewed and the important points that should be explored. Also novel ways in which the latter can be done to solicit more information than may be obtained with a straightforward approach are beyond the executive's abilities. Lack of concentration also worsens the problem. Courses exist on this subject but most of the effort is aimed at personnel and manpower executives. In fact they should be provided for all executives including senior managers and board members. It can be argued that all discussions in business are forms of interviewing, whether trying to negotiate a sale, gleaning information from every source, negotiating for or allocating resources and so on; not just when dealing with personnel selection. Greater awareness of the importance of good standards in interviewing is necessary.

Too often executives will use the fact that they are growing older as an excuse for their failings in the seven areas mentioned above. In reality, the human brain improves with age and experience if it is properly stimulated and assisted in the learning process. Only if it is not correctly stimulated will it decline in performance capability. Witness the 'failure' who on being given a job that interests him (or her) will 'suddenly' blossom out to be a high quality performer. There is nothing sudden about this; only that the right stimulation had not been provided before. Also, people with many interests outside their work retire and lead full and often long lives. Those with no interest other than their work tend to die soon after retirement. It is, again, all a question of motivation and stimulation.

There are many ways in which executives can provide help for themselves. First, by reading carefully selected material. Time should be set aside each day, even if it is only half an hour, for reading. The subject matter should not be restricted to things relevant to the executive's work but include peripheral subjects. For example, marketing executives would benefit from studying simple works on production planning and control, quality control and so on. There should also be an element of more general reading on subjects which have nothing to do with business but which expand general knowledge and interest and thus stimulates the brain. Needless to say superficial glances at a page or two is just a waste of time. Training oneself to read quickly; to be able to take in a bracket of words rather than each word individually; to get the context or sense of the matter, is another good piece of self-help and development. Then there is the occasional participation in carefully selected and appropriate seminars and conferences. Again, these can be on subjects dealing with current problems but should also include an element of those that extend existing knowledge. Also study on how one's mental powers can be increased will be useful.

The human brain is capable of great flexibility and possesses considerable untapped potential. It is said that most people only use one-tenth of their potential brain power. An increase in a percentage point or two of one's brain power is all that separates the ordinary person from identified genius. In the developed countries organisations exist who can help business executives to benefit from the growing knowledge on how to develop brainpower. Enormous strides can be made in improving the effectiveness and efficiency of individuals, eradicating some if not all of the problems mentioned earlier.

2.2.2 Rust prevention

Like everything else, executives too can 'rust up' for the reasons mentioned in the preceeding sections. In these cases, productivity and performance decline and the executives appear unable to keep up with growing demands of their work and the development of new ideas. However this 'rusting up' is an attitude of mind rather than a function of age. In many instances it has been found that the older executives are more flexible in their mental attitudes to work situations and more willing to try new things. They are supported by knowledge gained from long experience. The younger executives, having found one panacea that appears to work, cling to it for dear life, regardless of its relevance because they are conscious of their lack of practical experience. Further they may derive little job satisfaction from their work and may feel insecure, so rigid adherence to a well-tried formula is seen as a safe decision. Their operations become routine and their brains are not stimulated. They begin to atrophy and a mental rusting-up takes place often followed by physical rusting, i.e. several physical ailments appear though these are often psychosomatic in nature.

To prevent this happening ways must be found first to stimulate mental development and then increase job security and satisfaction. In addition to worthwhile remuneration and rewards for progress and development, the work must be seen to be important, in fact essential, and the executives made aware of the importance of their contributions to the corporate entity. Good health, financial security, work and mental tranquility (especially in their domestic environment) are also important ingredients. It is significant that in the 1970s in some countries, more executives found time to attend courses on meditation. Some enterprises even organised these on a corporate basis. For executives, carefully planned courses on how to meditate may obtain for them not only spiritual enlightenment but also managerial awareness. This could be of mutual benefit to all, executives, corporations and customers. Some have claimed that even when job and financial security have been low, meditation engendered a calmness of mind that improved concentration, creativity and memory. In giving executives time to think deeply about important aspects of their work, meditation led to better decision-making even under conditions of stress. At least the executives were no longer aware of the factors that created the original stress conditions.

However, back on a materialistic plane, the corporation must avoid diluting work packages so that they become dull, routine and apparently meaningless. If longer-term effectiveness is to be improved, executives must be encouraged and helped to grow and develop in their jobs and be suitably motivated. What motivations are used will depend on the personalities of the executives. Mere achievement may not be the main driving force. This subject is covered more fully in Chapter 8.

However, it is worth recalling here the following points about motivation. First, executive motivation is strongest when the executives are realising their full potential, becoming what they have the desire and capacity to become. Motivation is at its lowest when unnecessary restrictions and frustrations exist. It is also stronger the higher up the executive ladder a person happens to be; top management are usually the most highly and easily motivated. Motivation is strongly related to the supervisory style of the immediate superior. 'Developmental' bosses, i.e. constructive personalities, those seeking to help their subordinates to develop and improve their performance, can motivate their people more easily. Positive approaches to past failures, not to apportion blame but to find the reasons for the failure so that they can be avoided or overcome in future, also stimulate motivation of subordinates. Restrictive or 'reductive' bosses, relatively destructive personalities, are those who almost constantly seek to impart blame, seldom give praise and are chiefly interested in themselves and their own progress. They have little interest in their subordinates and operate through the power of fear rather than cooperation. They inhibit, rather than stimulate, motivation. They are also insensitive to this last fact but still see themselves as good performers as developmental bosses. Executives prefer the latter regardless of their own values or the style of supervision they practise themselves. The basic differences in attitude between the highly motivated and poorly motivated executives are shown in Figure 2.1.

Other key ingredients that increase motivation include the provision of opportunities for executives to mix and interact with their peers, or superiors, on both a formal and informal basis. Supervision of their work should be on a considerate, consultative and participative basis. There should also be opportunities for participation in varied and challenging duties with a high degree of responsibility for control of the work done and the pace at which it is done. Finally of course, good pay, seen as being of the right order for the work and responsibilities involved and good promotion prospects tied to achievement or performance are also good motivating factors.

2.2.3 Participation

Participation in management became yet another management fad in the early 1970s. Like most fads it was over-merchandised and over-sold. As with Management by Objectives ('MBO') that has already passed through the oversell-disillusionment stage, participation has suffered from the fallacies and gimmicks that have been allowed to creep into a very sensible attitude to what management is all about. Participation (like MBO) cannot be imposed on subordinates by an imperial edict from the boardroom. When it is attempted it has always failed. It requires the full and enthusiastic acceptance and support of all executives, especially the senior ones, if it is to stand a chance of succeeding.

Highly motivated	*Poorly motivated*
Easy to approach and talk to even when under pressure; always available to subordinates.	Difficult to approach at any time; must pick time carefully when needing to talk to this executive.
Tries to see the merit in ideas submitted by subordinates without losing sight of the objectives and difficulties. Approach is always a balanced one.	Because he is boss tends to assume his ideas are always the best. Often loses sight of the objectives. Tends to give ill-considered, erratic or unbalanced opinions/decisions.
Tries to help subordinates and others to understand company objectives.	Lets people figure out for themselves how company objectives apply to them.
Tries to give subordinates and colleagues all the information they need or want.	Provides people with as much information as he thinks they need and little that would undermine his position and authority.
Has consistently high hopes and expectations of subordinates.	Expectations of subordinates are changeable and usually minimal. Attitude may change daily.
Tries to encourage people to reach out in new directions, to develop and grow on the job, i.e. to be self-motivating.	Tries to prevent his subordinates from taking risks; sees self-motivation and development as threats to own status and future.
Takes mistakes by subordinates in his stride, so long as they learn from them.	Allows no rope for mistakes, especially those that embarrass or threaten his position.
Tries to correct mistakes, discover causes and seeks ways to avoid the same errors in future.	Primarily concerned with finding out who was to blame and chastises the subordinate. Little attempt to seek ways of avoiding recurrence in future.
Expects subordinates to improve performance and gives credit when this is achieved.	Expects adequate performance and does not praise or reward superior performance.
Encourages subordinates.	By not encouraging subordinates in fact discourages them.
Keeps personal problems out of work situation but helps subordinates when they have personal problems.	Carries personal problems into the work situation and leaves subordinates to sort out their own problems while expecting them not to let their own problems impinge on the work situation.

Fig 2.1 Typical attitudes of highly motivated and poorly motivated executives.

Participation should begin at the top and the bottom of the organisation simultaneously, if the many successful case histories from around the world mean anything. However, few middle-rank executives have displayed the commitment and force to act as catalysts for this development and in many instances have strongly opposed the concept. They see it as a threat to their positions and future. If the senior executives are committed to the concept and the majority of employees (blue collar and junior white collar) are enthusiastic about it and feel convinced it will work, sufficient force can be applied to both ends of the middle executive stratum to overcome its lethargy and resistance to the idea.

Participation is not a particularly comfortable concept for many managers. Its success depends partly on the need to listen to the views of others, including juniors. Strangely, it is the lower end of the management ladder who may find it difficult to do this. They are required to listen to the views of foreman, shopfloor supervisors and blue collar workers generally and they may see this as somehow lowering their own status, calling into question their ability and authority. The concept is an attempt to improve corporate performance by breaking down the traditional barriers (the 'Them and Us' concept) that has existed between executives and shopfloor personnel. Until this happens the enterprise is not a truly cooperative, cohesive team. The concept seeks to overcome or prevent the development of warring factions including those between different groups of executives and blue collar workers. Perhaps even the British disease of demarcation disputes will eventually be cured by the correct application of the participative approach to the planning and control of an enterprise's operations.

Participation must be planned but it cannot be packaged into a general panacea. All corporations, departments, employees and jobs are different from each other and the true differences must be taken into account when participation is introduced. The form it takes will be different in every case as it must be tailored to suit these differences. The company must be willing to adapt its approach here also to keep abreast of changing opportunities and circumstances. It must be prepared too, to surrender some activities or opportunities which may otherwise optimise corporate activities to meet the expectations of employees. Yet executives must not succumb so much to the last point that they appear to be surrendering their responsibilities, effectively ceasing to perform the role of managers. Participation is not a substitute for good management but an essential aid to that achievement. (*See also* Section 8.3.5.)

2.2.4 Consentient management

A few short years ago, the points made above would have been seen by senior executives, at least, as managerial heresies. Today, in varying degrees, interest is being taken in what is implied by participation and earnest attempts are being made to apply it, in various modified forms, to practical situations. What is happening, in fact, is a gradual movement towards management by consent rather than by edict or order, the style of traditional hierarchical management.

In traditional management systems, the individual is in a job because of some special talent or ability required by the enterprise. In return for suitable remuneration and the excitement of participating in something that interests the executive, the executive lends or hires this personal resource to the company. If the compensatory mix is altered to something the executive does not want, problems arise. When the company no longer requires that special talent the executive may be moved or made redundant.

In consentient management the relationship takes on a more personal or individual slant. Each executive becomes a valuable resource which the organisation is expected to cherish, nurture and help to grow and develop. The chance of achieving higher levels of job satisfaction is enhanced. Deeper inter-personal relationships are created. Constructive discussions replace edicts and orders, leading to better decisions. Authority is granted by permission of subordinates because they respect the ability of, and consideration shown by, the senior executives. Subordinates will in fact have participated as fully as possible in decision-making and other executive actions. They feel themselves to be essential parts of the corporate whole and their cooperation and participation are thereby improved.

Once consentient management has been established, decisions flow just as rapidly as in hierarchical organisations. They are usually more soundly based, being decided by total consideration of all relevant and available facts and knowledge. Within their own specified spheres of responsibility, executives set up their own information systems to provide the data they need on which to base decisions taken by their departments. Each role is carefully defined. However, with important or superior decisions the team, or an appropriate part of it, comes together with other teams associated with the work concerned, to agree the necessary actions. Opportunities are given for the airing of dissent before the decisions are taken and implemented.

This is consultative management where ratification of authority is preceded by exposure to dissent and is the first, simplistic form of it. When it is working well, steps can be taken to move on to more sophisticated but workable forms leading eventually to fully consentient management. The essential extra ingredient required if this is to work constructively, is trust; especially trust of the subordinate by the senior that the former will perform as required. Then there is trust by the subordinate of the senior to provide the means needed for the former's tasks to be well performed and that decisions will be reached by common consent after due discussions. Of course, there will be times when some decisions will have to be imposed by the senior. However, when this is unavoidable the reasons will be stated clearly, and usually the subordinates accept the inevitability of this in special circumstances. In any event, if consentient management is working well, the reasons for such departure from normal practice will be patently obvious to all members of a team.

2.2.5 Delegation
The managerial approaches discussed earlier cannot be carried out successfully

if executives are unable, or unwilling, to delegate responsibility for discrete parcels of work. Executives often find the subject of delegation difficult to understand and implement. When they try to do it, it is often done imperfectly or inconsistently. This problem has been a long-standing one in the United Kingdom, yet at first consideration, delegation seems a relatively simple thing to do. It involves defining spheres of responsibility, parcelling the work accordingly and giving subordinates the responsibility of making decisions and implementing them. In most cases they are also responsible for proposing, if not actually introducing, modifications to activities when results obtained indicate these to be necessary. The subordinates are responsible to their bosses for the results they achieve. The bosses are themselves accountable to their superiors for what their subordinates do and for the overall results being obtained by their departments. They can never abrogate their responsibility and accountability for the work of their departments, no matter how they may delegate the detailed work.

However, many executives believe that just because their desks are clear of paper they have delegated the work correctly. Yet all it may mean is that the manager is not doing his subordinates' work for them. The manager may still be making all the decisions so that, in fact, true delegation has not been achieved. All that has, is that the hack work has been allocated to others, presumably but not necessarily, to subordinates best suited for the tasks in question. With proper delegation, subordinates have the right, but not the obligation, to consult their managers. The last are only involved in the decision-making-action process when matters superior to the subordinates' responsibilities (outside their job descriptions or terms of reference) arise. The tendency with managers, especially newly promoted ones, is to hang on to work with which the executive is familiar, usually what he or she was doing before promotion. In some cases the manager holds on to a lot more for fear of being winnowed out by a more brilliant, better educated and trained subordinate. Parts of the work considered vital to the executive's survival in the new management role may also be retained, regardless of relevance to the work and responsibility associated with the new managerial post.

In addition, some managers fear they will be blamed if their subordinates make the wrong decisions. If they make too many bad decisions then the manager is to blame for not keeping a good enough watch on what is happening. This will happen if an effective communication channel with subordinates does not exist. Or lethargy and oversight on the part of the manager will mean that he or she has effectively surrendered accountability and authority for the overall running of the department. Managers cannot be expected to be experts in all delegated fields of work but they must be kept informed of progress and developments at regular time intervals and not only at the end of each reporting period. In this way when subordinates have taken, or are contemplating, incorrect decisions, managers can ensure that remedial action is taken before things get too bad, through consensus discussion with subordinates. As stated, there may also be times when the manager has to step in fully and direct that certain action be taken to avoid disaster. However, whenever possible, effort must be made so to structure the discussions that subordinates discover what has to be done, apparently on their own initiative, not because of obvious imposition of orders by the superior.

Notwithstanding the difficulties, delegation is justified since it motivates subordinates, helps them to grow in the job and to develop for the future demands that changes in the work to be done and their future promotion will impose on them. It helps managers also to distinguish between what is urgent, important and relatively routine. The routine work is delegated to subordinates, the important or superior tasks are done by the manager and the urgent matters attended to by the manager and appropriate subordinate as necessary.

Happily progress is being made in the study and understanding of the entire subject. Organisations that have delegated work successfully have established some relatively simple ground rules for it. *First,* the manager must establish the limits and opportunities of the department's work and the vital, superior areas of it which should not be delegated but remain the direct responsibility of the manager. The job descriptions should indicate this, giving managers scope for initiative without undermining the position and areas of responsibility of subordinates or other colleagues of equal and senior status.

The *second* rule is that subordinates must know precisely what is expected of them and what their responsibilities and tasks are and must be given the means whereby they can carry them out successfully. Subordinates ideally, should be given their own job descriptions which have been agreed with them. Their responsibilities should extend to expenditure (up to specified limits) associated with and necessary to their assigned functions. As stated, their responsibilities extend also to the control of the work allocated to them.

The *third* rule is that the delegated responsibilities should be stated in quantitative terms, where relevant, and not only in qualitative ones. Thus targets, budgets and other statistics should be provided and once again, these should be agreed by mutual consent. Some may have to be imposed but if imposition is due to the stubborness of the subordinate the manager should consider if the right subordinate has been chosen or if the delegation of work parcels has been done correctly. The subordinate's resistance may be due to fear or ignorance of the assigned work, suggesting that it is superior to the subordinate's knowledge and experience.

The *fourth* rule, or implication, is that delegation requires managers to display negotiating skills under a consultative or consentient management approach. Subordinates may not always respond with enthusiasm to delegation of responsibilities and it will be the manager's skill in negotiations that will overcome any defensiveness or resistance that may be displayed by subordinates. Again, good communications establishing the right *rapport* is an essential ingredient for success. Often, encouraging subordinates to seek guidance from appropriate seniors, not just the immediate boss, helps to overcome any reluctance to cooperate which may at first be displayed. What managers need therefore is quite considerable skill in man management. (*See* Section 8.3.)

2.2.6 Mismanagement of promotions

Another problem negating efforts at management development lies in the mishandling of promotion. The most common fault is to promote executives beyond their capabilities and inclinations, for ill-conceived reasons. The oft-repeated example is the promotion of a good sales person to a marketing role, even marketing director (executive vice-president, marketing)! This occurs when top management fails to realise that quite different personalities and interests are required.

A good sales person or manager tends to be an extrovert, often dedicated to achieving results 'today', in the shape of making a sale. The long-term consequences of this and even the long-term plans and objectives of the company, seldom interest them or engage their attention. They are 'doers' rather than 'thinkers'. While some executives may have the dual personality that will allow them to perform well in either role, generally a good sales performer is not temperamentally, or even mentally, equipped for a marketing role. They can be made so with suitable training but they cannot be pitchforked into marketing without such training.

Happily, more corporations are becoming aware of this problem. They are taking greater care in the recruitment, training and promotion of their staff. Greater attention is being given to the personalities, attitudes and expectations of executives and not just to their technical qualifications, past experience and performance. However, too many corporations have still to learn this lesson.

Another perhaps more damaging problem, is where an executive is promoted only to find some or all of his or her orders, suggestions and advice are countermanded by senior executives. This occurs frequently when top management is afraid (say) of the trade unions. They do not wish to disturb the workforce and they 'buy' peace through appeasement without realising the trouble they are storing up for a later time. The true price paid for this will then be much greater than if the point in question was faced at the time it arose. If intervention of this nature is necessary the subordinate was obviously the wrong person to have promoted. Some other remedial action, which does not penalise the unfortunate executive, will have to be found.

The author suggests that senior managers who mispromote juniors should, in all conscience, resign themselves. They are guilty of dereliction of duty. They have failed to inform themselves fully and correctly on the executives considered for promotion, the tasks that have to be done and the difficulties that may be encountered. They have fallen down on their own responsibility to the board. Alas this seldom happens and the unfortunate executives have to bear responsibility for the mistakes and oversights of their senior management.

2.2.7 Management development in developing countries

Five fundamental, environmental problems are encountered in developing countries when management development is involved. A fundamental difference of approach is needed since the granting of independence does not lead automatically to the discovery of a competent cadre of managers. If independence is followed by the repatriation of foreign managers the problem is made worse. The need to fill the leadership ranks of government departments and other institutions, as well as industry puts a further strain on and depletes the small reservoir of potential managers that may exist. Nor can the universities, old or new, provide the necessary calibre of people in the required quantity instantly. It takes years.

The first of the five key environmental problems associated with this subject is thus the limited sources of management potential available. In developing countries these are the educated elite, ex-military officers, university graduates and high-school graduates. The educated elite provides a very small pool of candidates for professional management. They are usually well educated, reasonably intelligent and free-enterprise orientated. However, their numbers are very limited and, if they hold views at variance with their government's ideas (e.g. the development of a Socialist or even totalitarian state), they may be reluctant recruits to management. They may seek their futures outside their country, further aggravating the problem. Also the long-term opportunities in their countries may not be sufficiently substantial, or of sufficiently high quality, to attract them. The risks may also be too great when they seek security in government appointments, usually non-productive ones.

Ex-military officers provide only a very small potential. They can be hard-working, loyal, reliable and intelligent but they may not be able to adapt their military logic and methods to a business environment. If they have had several years in middle or high-ranking positions in a military sphere they may not be able to adapt to civilian conditions. If they are reluctant recruits to industry they may find the change even more difficult to take.

University graduates form a limited pool of potential but they may be inadequately trained for the tasks and challenges in business. They may be hostile to the concept of capital and profit and their education may have been so biased against business generally that their reasoning power may be too low for the task of business problem identification and solution. They may be wrongly motivated for decision-making or economic growth planning. However, they may possess a wide range of intellectual capabilities but often prefer government work on graduation. High school graduates form a larger but still limited pool for business purposes and, depending on the standard of education, only a few may have the intellectual development potential for business purposes. They too learn by memorising and drill and many seem reluctant to show any initiative. Although highly motivated, they make the transition to learning for problem-solving in a slow and tedious way.

The second problem arises since most developing countries suffer from educational and technological deprivation. Their nationals as a result may be deficient in aptitudes vital to management performance. These include serious deficiencies in reading speed and comprehension, basic scientific understanding and quantitative reasoning. Their symbolic and numerical reasoning and mechanical aptitudes tend to be on a par with sixteen-year-olds in developed countries. Their lack of practice in problem-solving leaves them unable to decide where and when various decisions should be taken.

The third problem springs from general hostility to the objectives of private enterprise. These are often considered to be foreign ideas, contrary to many of the values of their cultures and therefore to be resisted strongly. There is also lack of economic understanding and the role that profits, surpluses and savings can play in improving the country's wealth and its standard of living. This is often so with opinion leaders who from their base of misunderstanding, then fan the fires of hostility against business and management generally. Where Socialist principles are held strongly the economic attitude becomes pronouncedly anti-private enterprise, even anti-business with belittlement of the role of capital and profits. Then management development becomes a difficult task beset by political irrelevancies.

Another difficulty arises when the basic concepts of what an ideal manager should be, differ from the established ideas in developed nations. In defining the characteristics of such a person, great variations in ranking of them occurs in developing countries. For example, while western nations rank 'sensitivity to others' feelings' below decision-making, future planning and hard work, in developing countries it comes second only to the 'ability to develop new methods of management.' Or 'belief in subordinates' and 'respect for authority' may be ranked much lower than in industrialised countries. Decision-making is often well down the list of important characteristics the ideal manager must have, while support of or loyalty to the government may be considered the fourth or fifth most important attribute. Probably because of the poverty and limited resources of the developing countries, risk-taking is, however, ranked as more important in developing nations than in developed ones. In many cases, though, the practical manifestation of an executive's ability in risk management is its avoidance as much as possible and the pursuit of safer projects. Thus development and growth are further inhibited.

The fifth difficulty encountered results from the sensitivity of nationals of developing countries, and their politicians, to criticism. They resist the western approach which seeks face-to-face discussions of a critical nature. They are offended by this and do not realise that only through constructive criticism can performance standards be improved and serious mistakes of judgment and decision be avoided. The fact that they see business enterprises as providers of jobs and welfare and many do not appreciate that they must make a suitable contribution in return, via diligent endeavour, increases this difficulty. Once their 'dignity' is offended, as they see it, they can remain offended for a very long time during which they become even more convinced that the 'wrong people' own the company and that they are only profiteers bleeding the country dry. In such an atmosphere it is difficult to get executives to work hard for success and anyone to take a serious, positive view of management training and development.

The hard economic realities of the last decade or two have made many of them rethink their attitude to business and profit. Several of the larger, more industrialised countries have shaken off these misconceptions and moved nearer to the ideas and concepts of industrialised, developed nations. Nonetheless, if only because of the limited pool of potential executives available and lower educational standards or opportunities, management development is a long-term, tedious process. If the government or its officials remain anti-business in outlook, the task can be a very long one. The resultant programmes should then consist of more effort to recruit promising candidates, greater support of further formal education, better assessment of hostile attitudes and the dissemination of appropriate information that will help to overcome these attitudes. Thus management development must take into account the five special difficulties encountered in developing countries before successful programmes can be devised. Where other special, local problems exist these must be carefully assessed and the programmes tailored to take these into account also. Above all success will depend on identifying people with management potential accurately. This acknowledges that while bright, eager and informed people do not necessarily make good managers, those who are hostile, ignorant or stupid never will.

2.3 Social responsibility of management

Corporations and their managers are now being subjected to a heavy barrage of propaganda about the social responsibilities of business and management. Traditionally the major responsibility of executives has been to secure optimal return on the investment of the owners of the corporations (i.e. the investors). Profit alone is no longer seen as the sole objective and almost everywhere corporations are being exhorted to be good, responsible members of society. This is interpreted as having concern for ethical standards, preservation of the environment and ecology and something called the 'quality of life'. A better educated, more perceptive society is now making a variety of demands on its various institutions, including business, of which money is just one and not necessarily the main one. These demands cover all or some of the following.

1. Concern for the disadvantaged (whether due to lack of good health, educational and other opportunities) including the old.

2. Concern for developments (technological and other) which could damage the environment or ecology of a region.

3. Concern for production processes and even modes of transport that could do the same thing. This has led to more stringent controls and laws covering many aspects of industry and transportation.

4. Interest in the achievement of higher ethical standards and that these are not sacrificed on the altar of increased profits.

5. Concern about those who are solely interested in making money, regardless of the harm that their operations may do to society in general.

6. Concern about investments in countries whose political and racial policies offend the citizens of the enterprise's home country.

The outward manifestations of all this are increasing pressures to provide for public representation on boards of directors, to give financial and other support to 'worthwhile' projects, to withhold price increases that are really necessary to cover increased costs, and to provide special training and jobs for the disadvantaged. Other pressures on corporations include attempts to limit investment in equipment only to that known not to offer threats to the environment or ecology, to contribute generously to charitable, educational and artistic organisations or activities and, in the U.S.A. and Japan in particular, to refuse to solicit for defence and defence-related contracts. Worthy as all these aims are, like all do-good activities the problem is who defines what is good and what is bad? What may seem good to one will seem very bad to others. For example, what are 'worthwhile' projects? Also, sacrificing profit for the common good cannot be carried to extremes for without sufficient profit a company will go into bankruptcy. If several do then the economy of the nation is made poorer and less able to support good projects.

The arguments on these subjects can continue indefinitely along many lines. However, it is true that the indifference to the social responsibilities of business by many corporations and executives borders on cynical callousness. (Note the comments in Section 2.1.1.) There are far too many intent only on making money, often for themselves. Others continue to take advantage of the ignorance of their customers and a few still twist existing consumer protection laws, so-called, to their own advantage. They ignore the fact that by failing to abide by sensible codes of conduct they may well be jeopardising the future interests of their enterprises. Continuance of their operations may well result in more severe official and other constraints which inhibit the development and continued well-being of all business activity. The big social issues of today which will remain for a long time, centre on environmental pollution, wastage of resources especially those becoming scarce, bad labour relations, consumer protection and care for the less fortunate members of society. Business enterprises cannot ignore them and happily there are signs of growing awareness of this fact also.

The emergence of these non-economic values stem from a few basic considerations. The first is the result of the considerable and visible achievement of private enterprise; its success in applying science and technology, under skilled management, to resources to increase the wealth-creating power of industry. Concern is expressed at the way this power is not being used, especially in the eradication of poverty and the grosser inequalities of social and economic inequities. It is also argued that industrial development degrades not only the environment but also living conditions.

Next there is growing recognition that general affluence does not lead to a general improvement for society. It is not simply a question of producing more consumable products but whether the sum total of business activity helps to improve the quality of life, the non-economic values listed earlier. As a result there is emerging a demand for a better relationship between business, technology, government, non-economic organisations and individuals. Unless this is achieved, man's relationship with his fellows would reach a chaotic condition which would be unendurable. It may ultimately destroy western society.

All these points are reasonable in themselves and it is good that business enterprises are giving them greater consideration. However, there is a danger that taken to extremes they could produce results which are as bad as the unbridled operations of selfish enterprises. Private goals and initiative could be replaced by so-called public concepts which in practice would mean total dictation by governments. The dynamics arising from private initiative and consumer dominance of the markets would disappear. If the examples of Communist countries mean anything the free enterprise system, or mixed economy system, despite all their faults, would be replaced by dull subsistence and the elimination of personal freedom and political liberties. Alternatively, there would be wholesale transfer of economic activity from the private to the public sector with similar, dreary results.

In the awakening of managers to their true role and responsibilities, including a greater contribution to social aspects, much more study and thought is required before a balanced system can be evolved. Management must participate more actively in the redesign of what may be called a 'social contract' between business, individuals and the environment in which they must live. Imbalance, whether towards business or towards the small bands of hyper-critics, especially those motivated only by malevolence to the existing system, would be disastrous. Also, the much larger groups sincerely motivated by concern about existing social evils but handicapped by their ignorance of private enterprise, should learn more about the realities of the latter and then ensure that their voice is heard more loudly. Management should help these large groups to learn the facts about business activity so that their demands can be properly balanced ones which would achieve mutually acceptable goals.

2.4 Management diagnostics

If the management of an enterprise is to be successful the right organisation has to be diagnosed for it. This will depend on the type of business involved, the skills required and the individual personalities of the people who will staff the organisation. Unfortunately in many countries, management diagnostics is not yet a fully developed skill. Partly as a result of American influence on management practice (in the last few decades every utterance out of the U.S.A. was taken as gospel which could not be ignored, when in fact much of it was irrelevant to the different conditions obtaining in other lands) and the inherent laziness of managers, organisations were compressed into some set package depending on which gimmick was popular at the time. People and organisations were considered in isolation from the practical work situations in which they would have to operate.

Happily, more and more firms are realising that before anything effective can be done about setting up or remodelling an organisation the firm itself must be studied to identify or diagnose how it works and operates best. This includes study of the persons available, how they like to work, what their true talents are and how these can be linked to produce optimal results. Then the organisational structure, managerial methods and positioning of executives can be completed. Short- and long-term training and development programmes, certainly for key people, can then be devised with the agreement of the persons concerned.

Another major contributor to former stumblings on organisational matters was the many business schools that sprung into existence in the 1960s and 1970s. They taught management in pre-packaged concepts. Some MBA courses of that era in particular, tended to 'sell' pre-packaged solutions. Little emphasis was placed on the fact that every problem is likely to have some unique quality, according to the company, business and economic environments in which it is encountered. There were of course honourable exceptions, business schools which strove and are still striving, to get executives to understand the broader realities of business.

Problems are like microbes and bacteria. There can be many mutations and in business the mutations can occur rapidly and in confusing complexity. This requires executives to have good diagnostic ability if they are to have a chance of dealing with the problems quickly and effectively. They must also be aware that there is no real, simple or complete textbook solution to any problem. Textbooks may point the possible ways (note the plurality) but in the end executives have to discover and work out unique solutions for their own situations. The medicine needed will vary. While in one case applying shock therapy (sacking all the senior executives) might work, in another it might kill the patient (enforcing voluntary liquidation or leading to bankruptcy if the replacements are no better, or are worse than their predecessors!)

Much of management education in the last twenty-five years has been good and useful to executives. However there has been almost as much which made no real contribution to the improvement of management performance. Not so long ago, Management by Objectives was promoted as a panacea for management ills. Yet all successful companies were already diagnosing their objectives and working to them via consultation and mutual agreement between key employees. Formal Management by Objectives just contributed a plethora of forms and paper. Large organisations could perhaps handle this but for medium and small companies, the majority of industry in most countries, it proved too great an addition to their administrative load. Perhaps the only real contribution made by Management by Objectives was in making people aware of the need to bring planning and consultation much further down the organisational ladder than hitherto; but even this was not a practical proposition for many organisations. In many cases too, there was the danger that more time would be spent on planning than on doing. For all organisations the widest possible consultation is still advisable but this should be tied in with the minimum of paperwork. That is, the corporate and departmental operational plans should be as uncomplicated as the situation will permit. Job descriptions should be provided and these should be related to the strategy, policies, objectives and targets set out in the plans.

Some management educators, a small minority, have tended to make of 'management' a new 'god'. They created a number of myths, incantations and shibboleths (*see* Chapter 1) but failed to notice that successful organisations gave scant attention to them. In the process they managed to downgrade some of the jobs that really mattered. For example, it took a long time for executives to realise that the personnel function (with, later, 'manpower' planning) was a vital cog in the mechanism of management. It was overlooked that, without a successful personnel operation, finding the people with the right skills and temperament and helping to train and develop existing employees, all other facts of 'good management' would be negated. Happily this trend has been reversed and the importance of this management function is now better appreciated. (*See* Chapter 8.)

When marketing was the latest fad, the selling function was downgraded, yet selling is the key profit-making activity and the vital one in the total marketing function. This too has now been corrected and marketing is seen to enhance the selling role. By providing essential support activities (marketing research and information, promotional activities etc.) marketing helps selling to realise its potentials and achieve its targets more effectively. Nor does it matter whether 'sales' is under the marketing wing or is a co-equal independent activity. It all depends on the type, nature and extent of the sales task.

Production management was also downgraded in some minds, being as it were a lesser cousin to 'management'. Only in recent years has it regained its rightful status of co-equality. Then senior management often showed less concern about the financial and planning operations in management activity. The more removed executives were from the processes of manufacturing and selling, the less 'management' appeared to have to do with them. Also in Britain, the transition from these 'downgraded' tasks to 'management' was seen as a one-way system. The executives who made the transition never came back to assist the production or sales departments. The transition was as final as the common concept of death! So long as executives view 'management' as something other than running things properly and running corporations as a whole, efficiently, then the gap between management education and the needs of the country will continue to exist and may well grow.

2.4.1 Alarm systems

The main safeguard for managers is for them to construct warning systems so that when things are not going according to plan, appropriate 'alarm bells' ring. In ordinary operational activities this is fairly simple to do. The 'alarm system' is in fact the review and control procedures which monitor the results being obtained by the plans they support. However, plans are managerial concepts only; since they express intentions as they cannot express certainties. It is hazardous to assume blithely that the implementation of an agreed plan will necessarily produce the stated results. There are too many unknowns.

Results will deviate from target and corrections will be needed from time to time to the company's actions. The monitoring information and control systems, if correctly conceived, will sound warnings when remedial action has to be considered. The trick lies in being able to set the standards correctly (the 'trip contacts' which set off the alarm) by which performance will be measured so that remedial action can be initiated at the right time.

In organisational diagnostics the time scale tends to be too long to permit swift remedial action to be taken on defects in the organisation. Once it has been set up and launched it may be some time before it is realised that it is a hidden fault in the structure that is sending the company off course. For example the lines of communication and authority may be too long, involving delays in the decision-making process; or too many persons have to be consulted before a decision is made; or the location of the administrative units may be wrong in some respects; or the internal postal system may be too slow; or the information may be provided in presentations that unintentionally obscure the true import of the figures; and so on. Before any of this is realised, several adjustments to operational plans and activities may have been made. They may have further disguised the true fault, or have had no effect. Often they could have done untold and sometimes unseen, additional damage to the company's long-term aspirations. A simple diagnostic procedure is needed. Experience indicates that this could be as described below; but again, specific modifications of this general approach may be necessary to suit the special conditions of different organisations.

First, the diagnoser must be prepared to cut across the traditional boundaries of the different disciplines, especially the main ones, marketing, manufacturing, financial management and personnel. This stereotyped classification of work may in fact contain the seeds of the real problems and only a total study of the whole organisation might uncover them. However, this work is costly in terms of time and money. The alternative approach is to identify the more likely locations of the real cause of the trouble and then undertake a detailed analysis of the discipline considered the most likely of the possibilities. (The format of Chapters 5 to 8 has been devised to indicate the interrelationships involved and so facilitate this type of approach to problem solving.) Thus, if it is suspected that some failure in communication is the most likely cause of the problem, the operations of the board and the departments apparently involved would be the starting points for the study. As information from these studies flow in, the work can be expanded or moved to other departments that may also be contributing to the problem.

There are also four other aspects of management that may have to be considered in seeking out the true causes of problems. The first is the *historical aspect* of the business. The questions that need answering would then include the following. How was the organisation set up, and what was the original rationale for it? What were the objectives, who set them and how have they changed in the meantime? Are they all still relevant for the present and the future projected for the company (as embodied in any long-range corporate plan)? How has the business environment changed? How do executives view these changes and the opportunities and the problems they present? What changes have taken place in the ranks of the executives and have these changed the methods they like to use?

The next aspect concerns *inter-personal and inter-departmental relationships*. How are power and authority exercised? What was the rationale for this? Does it still suit current and future conditions? What are the special interests and responsibilities of the different work groups? How are cooperation and negotiations handled within the company, and externally?

The third area covers *resources*. What capital and other resources are used or needed? What are available? What relevance do they have to the company's future intentions? What contribution does the organisation make to transforming these resources into outputs? What is the output and how does this relate to original intentions and future needs? What attitudes do the executives have towards the question of resources and their acquisition and utilisation?

Finally there is the subject of *knowledge*. What knowledge, general and special, does the organisation have and does it need to perform well? What does it need for future activities? What technology is involved and how must it be applied to obtain good results? Is it relevant to future intentions? What special qualities are expected of the people in the organisation? What training and development do they need? What are the key factors or areas where accurate and correct knowledge is needed for successful operations? And so on.

Throughout, the investigators will be looking for the right degree of coherence measured in terms of effective communications, corporate cooperation and the existence and acknowledgment of a common purpose, reflected in mutually supporting concepts and policies. Members of the organisation should also display a degree of creativity with ability to control potentially chaotic conditions and to prevent them from developing. If these are not apparent the reasons for this should be sought and identified. How much incoherence (i.e. the existence of discontinuities, cross-purposes, jargon and gibberish) exists? However, it has to be acknowledged that some incoherent organisations can still be reasonably successful when market opportunities favour them. A limited amount of incoherence will help to initiate a review of concepts and beliefs and, if the right questions are asked, executives will be forced to reconsider the rationale for the company's operations and existence. The result should include the evolution of more appropriate concepts for the future and these should also be better understood and appreciated.

2.5 The multi-national corporation

The problems discussed so far apply equally to multi-national organisations, sometimes also referred to as trans-national corporations. Some problems may be much larger as a result of the idiosyncrasies of the different nationalities involved in a multi-national corporation. The permutations are many. However, this is not the only reason why management problems seem greater with multi-national corporations. Various other difficulties arise as a result of the ways a multi-national corporation or international enterprise may have grown and the personalities and prejudices of the senior executives of the home or parent company, the root from which the multi-national corporation has developed.

The world is comprised of different social structures and groupings in many countries whose nationals hold different religious, racial, political and business concepts. Their basic social attitudes are also changing in different ways and, as yet, there is no firm evidence that all will eventually gyrate towards, as it were, a dull, world-wide egalitarianism. Business executives also possess certain prejudices, weaknesses and rigidity of attitudes (in addition to their positive characteristics) the exact nature of which will vary according to the ethnic and social groups to which they belong. Yet despite all this, they must strive to make rational decisions based on economic considerations, even if the latter are tampered with by governments who support public rather than private enterprise. Also, these decisions must be implemented by executives of different nationalities and from different environments who are often conspicuous by the prejudices, habits and attitudes of their countries. If the home executives' decisions are influenced too greatly by their own prejudices, then conflict between the parent company and its subsidiaries in other countries will be that much greater.

The development of executives to date has not generally prepared them to resolve the many human and technical problems faced by international enterprises. They are considerably different from the human relations problems encountered in the home country. These problems are made worse also by the shortage of management development potential in developing countries (*see* Section 2.2.7) and the less fortunate developed ones, where the general ignorance of the purpose and concepts of business helps to breed biased or prejudiced views. Besides these personality problems, there is the difficulty of incorporating into the same organisation people who have to work at considerable distances from each other. Unless the decision-making process and communications system are very good all the time, operational difficulties arise frequently. It is also more difficult to arrive at their solutions quickly. Then political and other social prejuduces play a part, as does fear of the unknown, represented here by the foreign national who is an unknown quantity to the executives concerned. The parent company's executives might in fact believe all the prejudiced and incorrect information held or published about 'foreigners' in the popular media and elsewhere. The business personalities of the executives may also have effect. If they are risk-avoiders, seeking to take only minimal risk at every turn, then overseas operations will not rank highly with them since they involve greater risk than most home activities.

Then the extent and nature of any overseas experience of the chief executive and other senior managers may colour decisions on the internationalisation of their company. If these experiences were favourable, they will be enthusiastic, but in their enthusiasm they may overlook some real problems and so be disappointed when results fall far below their hopes. If past experiences have been bad, they will not be keen supporters of international operations. They may overlook reasonable opportunities abroad even when their own home markets are facing grave economic problems. This perhaps explains why one corporation will steadily expand its business in several overseas countries, building from agencies ultimately to fully autonomous manufacturing and marketing companies, while other similar ones stay at home, producing less spectacular or satisfying results. Thus it is not necessarily financial resources and other skills which differentiate one international company from another. It is rather the personalities, abilities and outlook of the executives making up the enterprise.

There is also little agreement on the way the objectives of a multi-national corporation should be viewed and formulated. Much research continues on this subject and no doubt, the associated arguments will ensue for many decades to come. However, the internationalisation of world business continues if at a slower pace than before. A growing number of executives are realising that the survival of western democracy and free enterprise, if not the world's economic system, depends ultimately on world cooperation and partnership in business enterprises of all kinds. The creation of political and trading blocs, such as the European Communities and others, also indicates the realisation that eventually, full cooperation at inter-governmental level is needed. (Admittedly when first formed, these 'blocs' really do seem to act as 'blocks' as they try to protect and encourage their own industries, but sooner or later they learn that the bloc's tariff barriers work counter to their intentions of increasing trade and economic activity.) This trend could spread in the next century into full cooperation between national public enterprises, especially those that private venture cannot or will not undertake.

An ideal solution may not be possible. However, the author believes that a reasonable solution will be found on how multi-national corporations should evolve their objectives and strategies through developments in the social sciences leading to better understanding of the realities of the social, economic and political necessities of nations. Of course personal attitudes and prejudices will never be eliminated given that human nature is what it is. Somehow basic economic reality will have to be impressed on prejudiced opinion and political leaders. However, the individual conditions affecting corporations will mean that the structure, strategy and concepts will vary between one corporation and another. Ultimately these variations will be products of the corporate personality of the enterprise and not of ill-conceived prejudices. Thus no simple or general pattern of growth will occur. Executives will have to diagnose the aims and needs of their enterprise and evolve their own growth strategies for their international operations as they do for home-based activities. In this instance though the needs of both the home and host countries must also be taken into account so that the narrower, selfish interests of the parent company do not have adverse effects on the well-being and development of host countries (the ones in which their overseas operations are based). Leaders of multi-national companies will eventually be judged by their ability to be fair in resolving conflicting economic, technical and human problems. At the moment also there are three distinct concepts of multi-national operations.

2.5.1 The ethnocentric world-wide enterprise

The ethnocentric enterprise is firmly based on its own country of origin. Often there is near-open suspicion of foreigners and the foreign countries in which it operates are considered less stable markets than the home base. While they employ foreign nationals in the latters' home countries, and may have to by law, they consider them worthy of little confidence. The senior executives usually have little experience of living and working abroad and this does little to eradicate their ill-conceived views and prejudices, especially that foreign nationals are inferior in performance to those of their own home country.

Whether such views are or are not true, they produce frustration and friction in the overseas organisations as the bias of the home executives is evident in the way they organise and control operations, especially restricting the promotional prospects of foreign nationals. The foreign executives feel restricted and that their latent talents are not being allowed to develop. Not surprisingly resentment soon develops throughout the overseas operations. If this becomes too widespread, or if the parent company ignores the economic and business interests of the host countries, the governments of the latter will one day take direct action, even appropriation. (These points are not peculiar or exclusive to American and British multi-nationals. As one travels the world complaints are heard about the multi-national corporations of most developed nations including Japan, Germany, Holland and Scandinavia. Also as the larger, older 'developing countries' have industrialised and spread their own operations overseas to newer nations, the latter find reasons to complain in like manner! The weakness or arrogance discussed above are common to humanity and not special to any one race or nation.)

A variation of the above is the multi-national corporation that no longer holds any distrust of foreign nationals employed by it but the parent organisation still holds the view that it can put into operation abroad, without any modifications and with assured success, the methods and techniques which have been so successful at home. However, the vital techniques, concepts and (responsibility for) decisions are withheld from overseas operations. 'Head office' is still taken to be the sole repository of wisdom and the overseas companies are expected to conform to the parent's plans and procedures as faithfully as they can. While this may generate less friction, the inherent problems are the same and will one day emerge as truly serious ones for the parent.

Both versions of this type of enterprise ignore the differences that exist in personality and character of the nationals who work for them. Frequently they assume that all races are very similar to their own when the former are as well educated or as sophisticated as the latter. They forget that national characteristics always modify actual behaviour and will break out strongly at times, especially when the person is under stress or pressure. The parent company's executives are surprised and hurt when this happens. They refuse to accept that what works well in say, an Anglo-Saxon community, need not do so in another environment. They fail to realise that organisations and techniques must be modified to suit the way in which individuals work best and which will provide the best way of developing latent talents.

2.5.2 World-wide polycentric enterprise

The polycentric enterprise is based on the host countries with the original parent just a co-equal partner in the total enterprise. This type developed as nationalism grew in newly independent nations and in old-established ones finally developing an industrial economy in addition to their original agricultural economy. The threat of expropriation by host governments, and not only Socialist ones, gave impetus to this development. The subsidiaries have greater autonomy and give priority, sometimes exclusively, to the needs of their host country. In as far as group strategies and policies are concerned, these are evolved by group discussions. The basic concepts might have common agreement and support but the versions used in each country may be so modified to meet that nation's needs that each may be almost unrecognisable from the agreed concepts. The subsidiaries merge more and more into the economic, social and political environments of their countries. With their growing importance to their nations, each subsidiary increases its independence with local institutions and moves further away from the parent company. They face the same problems as the parent company though these are modified by local ethnic and other factors.

The executives of the original parent company admit that situations abroad differ from each other, that each is unique to its country and requires individual approaches. The executives believe they cannot exercise effective control in these circumstances nor follow adequately all the changes occurring abroad. Local nationals are considered, progressively, to be more competent to handle situations in their own countries, especially the problems which will be encountered from time to time. Besides the initial provision of capital (some of it) and the special expertise that might be needed, efforts are concentrated on helping the overseas operations develop and grow. This includes adequate basic training in the skills required and assistance with the planning of individualised programmes to suit the different requirements of each country. Capital and expertise will still be provided but only on the request of the overseas company when these are not readily available locally.

2.5.3 The geocentric enterprise

This enterprise is orientated world-wide, takes notice of the interests of the host countries but not in the exclusive way of the polycentric organisation. It is acknowledged that each subsidiary will have special problems as a result of local conditions and its attempts to conform to local requirements. However, in addition, there will be common points of comparison with the parent company and some other subsidiaries. The enterprise seeks to form a cosmopolitan élite of senior executives drawn from all countries who are placed in positions of authority in the parent company. Decisions should therefore be free of nationalistic constraints but cannot ignore the demands or needs of the different geographical locations of the subsidiaries. It is hoped that by having a cosmopolitan élite at head office the multi-national corporation's decisions will themselves be more cosmopolitan, finding a balance between what will always be the conflicting needs of home and host countries. This ideal is not always realised.

In these organisations awareness is growing that nationals working in their own subsidiaries must also be given equal opportunities for development and be encouraged to develop their latent talents. Executives should not feel disadvantaged by the location in which they work. Those of value with great development potential must have near-equal chances of promotion, even into the élite of senior executives at the parent company.

The geocentric organisation has its own problems however. First, there are many who consider it too idealistic and that the other two types of organisation show more realism. Certainly ethnocentric organisations seem best for developing countries with polycentric ones being best for developing countries that have already achieved considerable industrial development. However, geocentric companies will have greatest possibilities in developed nations and could be the ultimate evolution of multi-national corporations as their host countries become more fully developed. Next, geocentric organisations are not immune from ethnic clashes, prejudiced views of leaders of host nations and all the problems inherent in major international businesses. Given the disparities in the rate of economic growth and many variations of local or regional conditions, the development of multi-national corporations will not be a smooth one. The geocentric enterprise will be just as affected by this fact as the others, but the polycentric multi-national corporations may well persist for a long time in many parts of the world.

Other multi-national human problems include the reluctance of some families to change their domicile. This is stronger in some nationals than others. In geocentric multi-national corporations the movement of staff can take on quite a nomadic nature. Families may then feel rootless and unsettled, in every meaning of those words. This problem will engage the attention of personnel executives for some time to come. So also should the problems arising from the persistence of racial, social and national prejudices.

2.5.4 More recent problems

More recent problems stem from the growth of hostility towards the multi-nationals. First, there is fear that the immense economic power of multi-national corporations somehow offers threats to national aspirations and economic needs. In this respect the case of I.T.T. of the U.S.A. is cited because the total activity of this world-wide group is greater than the gross national product of several smaller nations. In host countries especially, attitudes range from admiration to contempt. Then the home nationals do not always welcome the development of 'transnational' activities. The setting up of manufacturing operations overseas is often seen by trade unionists and others as draining off employment prospects in the home country. This is notwithstanding the view, substantiated by research, that overseas investments and the development of facilities overseas, in fact add to the nation's economic strength and create jobs at home. This concept has been harder to get across as unemployment in developed countries increased and these higher levels took on the appearance of becoming permanent.

The fear generated by the size of the multi-national corporations has led to growing demands for more legal constraints on their operations. Among the organisations studying this aspect are the United Nations, the O.E.C.D., the I.L.O. and other agencies. At the time of writing a U.N. Commission on Transnational Corporations, an inter-governmental subsidiary of the U.N. Economic and Social Council, is attempting to draw up a Code of Conduct as well as devise actions that could be taken against corrupt practices. Some progress has been made towards the formation of a new international regulatory framework, though much is not to the liking of the multi-national corporations. This work has been given greater impetus with the knowledge that during 1971–76, investment by multi-national corporations increased by 80 per cent and that 75 per cent of this capital investment was in developed countries. Even the 25 per cent invested in developing nations is increasingly being placed in the more industrialised of these countries.

Multi-national corporations have to realise that while the United Nations is usually ineffective in political matters, it can affect their future considerably. However if the multi-national corporations are to be asked to be more open in their activities and information, the United Nations also must do likewise. If the original proposals are implemented, the multi-national corporations will feel very vulnerable and exposed. There is particular concern that multi-national corporations will not be given the right to dispute the validity or accuracy of information once it has been passed to the United Nations and is published by them. The United Nations' argument is that it would be administratively impractical, but this does nothing to engender the trust that should be built up between the multi-national corporations and any controlling body to which they must answer.

While a code of conduct is demanded, the reciprocal obligations this would place on host and home governments are ignored. Indeed, many developing countries have appeared to be totally unwilling to accept corresponding limitations on their freedom of action. At the same time countries may not be prepared to wait for an agreed international policy and may enact laws that will permit them to monitor policies on employment, investment, prices, exports and so on. They should be concerned with safeguarding employment, the effects on their industries if any multi-national corporation becomes overpoweringly dominant and guarding against sudden divestment by multi-national corporations which, though done for sound economic reasons, could be disastrous to the affected country. The fear is that they may, however, end up by turning the multi-national corporation's operations in their countries into something little better than nationalised organisations through ill-considered legislation. Then the potential benefits that properly guided multi-national corporation could bring would be lost and the host country's economy would be the poorer.

2.5.5 Possible solutions

One of the main reasons for resentment of multi-national corporations is the feeling that all nationalities employed by them do not enjoy equal opportunities, whether in salary, status, responsibility or promotion. So a first solution is possibly to make it quite clear, and to prove it in practice, that all nationals have equal chances, subject only to qualifications and performance. Care should be taken that the methods used in measuring performance and assessing qualifications are equitable and do not appear to be slanted against local nationals. The latter should know that if they have the necessary abilities there is no barrier at all to achieving the highest office even at head office or with the parent company. Where suitably trained and experienced people do not exist locally, the necessary training and development programmes should be launched. The nature and content of the courses, who should attend them and the personal objectives of each executive attending them should be agreed with the local executives. This problem is encountered most frequently in developing countries, especially those with a racial or religious minority who feel oppressed or restricted.

Then there is the belief that multi-national corporations have little respect for, or give little thought to the host countries and their economic aspirations and needs. This can be overcome if the parent company ensures that full consultations take place regularly with the authorities in the host countries when any major decision regarding future development or change has to be considered. In other words integrated management and cooperation is extended to ministries and agencies directly concerned with the business and general economic activity. This is taking place in most developed nations so there is no reason why it should not be extended generally. Then the parent company should permit the sale of shares, of the parent and the subsidiary, to local nationals in their own countries. This should be allowed to take place as freely as sales of shares in the parent's country. Many non-American multi-national corporations do this with the shares of their subsidiaries in the U.S.A. but it is not yet a general practice. However, in Europe with the existence of the E.E.C., subsidiaries are being integrated with each other across national frontiers. Individual subsidiaries then become cogs in the machinery of the entire multi-national operation and to offer a satisfactory shareholding to local nationals of the local subsidiary would be difficult. It would prevent the total integration of all multi-national corporation's activities. The answer may be to allow the sale of shares of the corporation itself to be sold freely in all countries. Or the subsidiaries could be grouped into reasonable self-contained units whose shares could be on offer in all the countries in which each unit operates. However, until legal and financial aspects are fully harmonised even this solution can encounter insurmountable obstacles.

Perhaps a better solution is for multi-nationals to establish satisfactory relationships with the governments of the host countries. Where the company's operations have a substantial impact on the economies of their hosts, the company would be advised to consider the governments as part partner and part shareholder. Many countries now insist that specified amounts of the shares should be held by their nationals so that conditions exist for this solution to be achieved. There are many multi-national corporations which have achieved part if not all of this solution. Examples that spring to mind include the Anglo-Dutch Unilever Group, Britain's I.C.I. and Standard Oil of New Jersey (EXXON). Much more could still be done.

Another helpful step is to ensure that investment and development plans take into account the needs of the host country and not just the essential requirements of the parent company. Governments can lead here by encouraging international direct investment. However, this must be done in ways that will not allow the hosts to feel that their industries are being taken over by, or falling under the control of, foreign nationals. Full and frank explanations of the reasons and purpose of the development plans and the provision of equal opportunities to foreign nationals employed by the multi-national corporation should help to achieve this. There must also be conscious effort to ensure that no multi-national or its subsidiary avoids its obligations to its countries and governments. There should be agreed codes of conduct based on agreed international rules, similar to those already existing for export incentives. The basic objective is to stop multi-national corporations from playing off one country against another.

Finally, resentment is encountered in host countries that believe that multi-national corporations cloak their strategy, policies and operations in too much secrecy. They feel that even such statements that are made do not reveal all the facts or the whole truth. The solution is to maintain an information flow that is patently transparent in its honesty, truthfulness and the complete detail of information that it releases. This means that there will be a full and voluntary reporting system involving all matters within and outside the corporation, with all their resultant implications. Lack of information and comprehension on critical subjects, especially the intentions of the company, the role and purpose of prices and profits, the need for expansion or retrenchment, to mention just a few, exacerbate the hostility shown to multi-national corporations.

Companies seriously misjudge the situation if they wait until pressures force them to adopt more open communications strategies. Admittedly transparency of communications requires courage and can lead to awkward situations but the damage caused by secrecy is always much greater. The advantages of open communications include:—

a. complex issues are more easily understood by all and are, therefore, more manageable;

b. myths, emotions, prejudices, fears, conjecture and aggression are reduced;

c. credibility and confidence are increased both internally and externally; this also improves the image of the multi-national corporation;

d. better and brighter employees are attracted to the company; ethical behaviour is encouraged; and

e. the opening up of channels of communication, providing valuable feedback of information to the company.

In other words, a high degree of honesty should be maintained. It would be a good thing if these principles were adopted by all companies in all countries. Then many of the existing consumer protection laws and agencies would not be required. However, with human nature as it is, this may be too Utopian.

2.6 Leadership

Leadership is a personal quality that varies from individual to individual. Because executives are different persons in their attitudes, perceptions and behaviour, the style of leadership varies. Indeed it cannot be standardised. Each leader will have an individual style and this is not necessarily successful in every job situation. Care is needed therefore to see that executives are fitted into posts where their own style of leadership will prove successful. Too often they are fitted into the wrong jobs and when they fail to produce results, they are damned as failures for ever more. No thought is given to the fact that the environment in which they had to operate was the wrong one for their methods.

One common point is that leaders all have something unique or distinctive about them, which is what makes them stand out as leaders. It may be an air of assurance, a manner that generates respect or devotion, or they may just be able to draw the best out of people. They may also have certain individual idiosyncracies and (unfortunately) in many organisations, especially British ones, these personal traits are positively discouraged. While on the one hand the executive is encouraged to do his or her own thing, on the other personal idiosyncracies are frowned upon. They are in fact being discouraged from leadership by being compressed into a pattern of conformity that can only lead to mediocrity.

There are in most countries plenty of leaders in the business world. It is just that they have not been allowed to develop this flair by their employers who look on any behaviour they consider 'unusual' as something that has to be eradicated at all costs. These employers have just not realised that the value of personal leadership is a vital ingredient for the improvement of profitably, operational efficiency and productivity. Sometimes too the general atmosphere or environment does not encourage the use of such individualised talent. This is particularly the case in large organisations.

Thus leaders must be recognised and encouraged. They can build and hold together an efficient and happy team capable of achieving mutually agreed objectives. The leader usually tries to get to know each team member personally, not confining the relationship only to the work situation. This is important. If an executive can discreetly and genuinely help subordinates on personal as well as work matters, loyalty and cooperation will increase with resultant improvements in business activities. Another important quality, perhaps the leading one, is the ability to be decisive and to make sound decisions quickly after consultation with the team. The true leader seldom postpones decisions unless there is a very important reason for this. However, leaders generally have a clear idea of the right time to make any decision and will not be deflected for this because of lack of all the information that is ideally necessary or because of some feeling of indecision or fear. These last two are usually unknown to them.

In times of crisis the leader will not form a committee and so evade a difficult decision but will, with the team, seek ways in which the crisis may be overcome and will then decide what alternative course of action should be implemented. When any changes in the enterprise become necessary the leader will set about immediately to restore confidence in other executives so that the (new) team can settle down quickly and get on with the job of rebuilding the business. So the true leader is one who approaches problems with a genuine understanding of the feelings and responses of the people concerned, especially members of his or her team. Personal leadership is to do with humanity and human behaviour and so-called 'scientific management' may have nothing to do with personal leadership styles.

Again all these points are gaining greater awareness amongst executives. Personnel and manpower people in particular are giving considerable thought to it and conducting much interesting research into the subject. There is hope, therefore, that the shortcomings in this area will eventually be reduced if not eliminated. The former is practical, the latter may be too idealistic. (*See also* Section 1.9.2.)

2.7 Role of the board

It is outside the scope of this book to consider the minutiae of the activities of the board. This section is concerned only with the role the board should play in stimulating and encouraging subordinates, especially departmental heads, to perform correctly and well. That is, how should a board show interest and commitment in support of but not involvement in, the detailed work so that objectives, policies and plans are successfully implemented? This is apart from and in addition to the legal requirement of boards. These vary from country to country and in Britain in the mid-1970s much thought has been given to changes in the structure and function of them that seem to be necessary for current conditions and opinions. Much work has been done regarding the appointment of 'worker directors' and whether Britain should follow the systems in operation in other countries (e.g. the German 'two tier' approach). Also the E.E.C. is studying the subject and trying to find ways of harmonising the approach of its member countries. At the time of writing it is not known what the outcome of all this will be.

However, in general, a board's basic responsibilities can be defined as follows.

1. It must have complete responsibility to the owners of the company as prescribed by the laws of the land.

2. It must approve the strategy and objectives of the corporation, preferably in consultation and agreement with departmental heads or line managers. These should be re-examined at appropriate time intervals or when major changes in the business environment demand. (Sometimes it may have to do this on its own but this is usually when the corporation is in deep trouble, communication with line management has broken down or line management has become dispirited or disenchanted.)

3. It must approve or decide, in conjunction with line management, what policies should be followed, without losing sight of the quantitative targets enshrined in the corporate objectives.

4. It must keep a watching brief on and approve operational plans intended to implement the agreed policies and strategy, thus working towards the realisation of declared objectives.

5. It approves associated budgets, cash flows and operational targets.

6. It must exercise sufficient control of the operations, including the monitoring of results, approving (with line management) agreed modifications to plans which the results indicate to be essential. It must of course also ensure that these modifications are properly implemented.

The board should also review from time to time its own involvement in the business and the contributions it has made to assisting line managers to carry out their tasks successfully.

Thus the role of the board may be summarised as one of guidance, approval and control and the encouragement of innovation and leadership. As a body it must be interested in the company's organisation and operations but it should not interfere, except when things are going wrong very badly. The key therefore, is in obtaining the right balance between control and supervision of, and interest in, the work; providing encouragement to line executives. In some areas, e.g. finance, the board is responsible directly to the owners (shareholders) of the corporation for the correct deployment of resources and the securing of acceptable returns on their investment. Here more direct involvement with executives is unavoidable but the essential ingredient required is still encouragement.

2.8 In summary

The perceptive reader will be aware that these first two chapters are stating that what is needed to improve the performance of management is a better under-standing of the basic principles of management and the basic concepts which lead to successful management. The many techniques available all have their uses but executives should pause and think about their relevance to any situation before they commit themselves to them. During that pause it is worth considering what business is all about, what the aims and objectives of their own enterprise are or should be and then they will make a more relevant selection of the methods they should use. How these techniques interrelate is something else which should be considered and the chapters that follow will indicate the questions that should be considered in this connection, from the different standpoints of the four major disciplines which form the corporate quadrille group of an enterprise.

2.9 Questions

1. Discuss the development of management techniques since 1950 and show how these can both help and confuse managers in their efforts to increase profitability and efficiency in the management process.

2. What is your view of the 'gamesman'? Are his traits good or bad for business? How could this general attitude be used more positively and beneficially for a business?

3. What skills must an executive have to be sure of being successful and to warrant consideration for promotion?

4. What problems do management developers face these days? What are the common deficiencies in mental ability which undermine executive per-formance? How can these be remedied?

5. How can one prevent executives from 'rusting'? What is usually meant by this in executive terms?

6. What do we mean by 'executive participation'? How can this be achieved effectively? What roles do motivation and delegation play in achieving this?

7. What are the special problems facing management development work in developing countries? How can these be overcome?

8. What are the main social responsibilities of management? How can these be honoured without sacrificing the profit motive in private enterprise? What role should governments play?

9. What is meant by the phrase 'management diagnostics'? What do you consider are the most important parts of this work?

10. A company's operations will always tend to deviate from even the best laid plans? Why is this? What countermeasures should executives take to compensate for this?

11. What is a multi-national corporation? What advantages are said to accrue

from such operations to the corporation itself and the home and host countries?

12. Why do multi-national corporations face so much hostility from both their host and home countries? (What is meant by 'home' and 'host' here?) What can a multi-national do to counter this hostility?

13. What are the three basic approaches to the organisation of multi-national corporations? When would they be used to the best effect? Which form is likely to last longer and why?

14. What are the dangers for multi-national corporations of (i) concerted international legislation against them, and (ii) unilateral action by host countries? What role is the United Nations and other international agencies trying to play here? Are they important? Why?

15. What actions should multi-national corporations take to improve their image?

16. What distinguishes 'leaders' from the rest of the executive ranks?

17. What are the basic roles or responsibilities of a board of directors?

3 Integrated corporate management

The subject of management is bedevilled by the limitations of the English language as far as having suitable nametags is concerned. It has not helped that writers on the subject have ascribed different meanings to the same words. They have used words indiscriminately, sometimes without regard to the true Oxford English Dictionary (or Webster's) meaning for them. For example, 'operational management' has been used to describe the day-to-day activities of executives and thus has short-term implications while 'corporate management', when used, is given some other mysterious implication. Yet corporate management is really the total managerial activity involved in running a business enterprise and is concerned both with the short-term aspects as well as long-term objectives and intentions. The short-and long-term aspects of every business including objectives and strategy cannot really be divorced from each other especially in conceptual, planning and operational terms. Thus 'corporate management' is a more precise term than 'operational management' when management as a subject is being dealt with, though the latter is an alternative phrase to 'line management'. In that usage it differentiates between departmental executives, the decision-takers, and the specialists, (e.g. the economists, statisticians, operational research experts etc.) who may help the former to be more effective managers. These are the meanings used in this book.

Further, since sustained success in management demands continuous cooperation between all aspects of management activity, acknowledging the inter- and intra-dependence of all decisions and actions, then 'integrated corporate management' is the right term to describe the form of management required by every business enterprise. The use of this term also implies that a former concept of management has been abandoned. This was the containment of each discipline of management, as it were, in its own water-tight compartment with only minimal communications between them. Each department looked after its own interests and guarded them jealously. The discontinuities of the business world in the last three decades made the attainment of acceptable levels of corporate performance difficult under this concept. Hence the slow realisation that every department must be totally involved with corporate activity, especially those of related managerial responsibility. The first hesitant steps towards integrated corporate management concepts were taken in the 1960s.

Further, the severe discontinuities in business environments involved abrupt changes from past occurrences. This made the sole dependence on experienced-based methods of management impossible and inadvisable. There had to be the right mix between experience-based and research-based techniques. The executive team also had to be made up of people whose knowledge and strengths collectively covered both types. As always happens when two different concepts are involved, antagonism and rivalry between those who supported one approach against those of the other inclination developed and many arguments for and against both methods raged. Undoubtedly these arguments will continue for some time, if only because they are the stuff of which academic life is made. However, some academics and many executives in business are evolving a practical balance between the two concepts. This is noticeable in particular in the U.S.A. and to lesser extents in some European countries and Japan. In Britain the problems faced in the mid-1970s have given further impetus to a more rational approach to this question.

Experience-based methods are those which have evolved over a period of time as a result of knowledge and experience gained in the process. Initially intuitive methods of making decisions were formalised into rules, sometimes heuristic, from a vast wealth of data and results obtained by what were really, trial-and-error approaches. However, personal interpretation of these rules was often biased, according to the experience of the executive. For example, a pricing decision by an executive who came up through the sales department may tend to select the lowest price possible as that person's instinct is still to make a sale. An executive from the financial stream may try for the highest price possible for a given level of sales to maximise profit or return. Habits die hard! However, either approach could be right or wrong. For the best balance between short- and long-term needs of the enterprise, a more balanced and less biased pricing policy is needed. This should be capable of flexibility according to market and competitive conditions and could even include differentiated prices.

Research-based methods involve activities normally considered the responsibility of 'specialists' (frequently incorrectly referred to as 'staff functions'). These require research and consideration of appropriate sectors of the business environment and corporate activity and plans. Much gathering of data and information is required followed by detailed analyses of them. In this way indications are obtained of the various courses of action possible and their likely outcomes. This permits collective executive decisions on which possibility should be selected for use. These methods include all the standard forms of study in marketing research (economic, social, political and technological aspects), strategic planning, systems analysis, organisational development, econometrics, operations research and so on.

It is patently obvious that modern conditions ensure that these two different approaches are not mutually exclusive. If the choice of research-based methods is carefully made and kept to relevant techniques for a business, a correct mix of both methods will ensure that management effort is successful and will be so consistently. However, as stated already, adopting every new research-based technique, regardless of its real usefulness to an enterprise, is likely to ensure long-term failure, even if there is some short-term gain. It is the purpose of this book, and the main theme of the chapters that follow, to assist executives to obtain this right balance or mix so that they will optimise the activities, profitability and development of their companies. To do this there must be a thorough reconsideration of the first principles of management and what business activity is all about.

Research-based techniques can only be used successfully if executives have a sound education and understanding of management and all the techniques they might use. They need time also to be able to give full and careful consideration to this subject and the selection of the techniques they will employ. This is probably why executives responsible for this area of corporate work are kept free of normal line or decision-making operations which themselves require considerable time and effort if the right decisions are to be made. However, to exclude them entirely from the planning and decision-making work is wrong. They must take part in these activities even if they themselves are not responsible for making decisions, only having to guide and assist line managers so that the latter make better decisions. In this work time is of the essence; so consideration and study of which research-based techniques should be used should commence as early as possible, subject only to the cost constraints that may apply. If budgets are restricted, an even more careful selection of these methods is required.

As already stated, poorly conceived management education tends to concentrate on the details of the techniques themselves, giving little guidance on how to discern which methods are most relevant to any given business situation. Thus executives are not helped to make more correct choices from the many techniques available. It is only relatively recently that more emphasis has been given to the task of identifying the real problems of a situation and how executives may analyse and forecast the impact they may have on short- and long-term corporate aspirations. Yet until these are known, the correct selection of management techniques the company should use is not possible. Further, only one possible outcome of any situation is studied in many instances yet what is required is an all-round appraisal of all the possibilities that are posed.

How thoroughly this can be done will depend on the time and money available but even a quick, overall look at the situation is preferable to an in depth study of only one aspect of it. When management education is restructured to take these points into consideration it will be found to have greater relevance and value to the pressing needs of executives in business enterprises. Then perhaps private enterprises in particular, will not be so reluctant to send their executives on courses, or to run their own in-house programmes, and will not be dubious about the value of courses. They may change their attitudes to management education and follow up the efforts in countries like Britain to promote the benefits that accrue from regular executive training.

Thus, what is needed are executives who understand reasonably fully, what is happening around them so that they are not caught unawares by developments and changes in the organisation and its business environment. They will thus be in a better position to resolve any problems encountered in their work.

These problems arise from time to time in all aspects of their work, whether in the setting of short- and long-term objectives or in sales forecasting and control. They require experience- and research-based executives to work closely together at all times, maintaining a good communications network throughout the company. In addition, they must be aware that finding the serious problems is a relatively easy task but identifying the apparently less obvious ones is not; yet the latter can have considerable, if disproportionate, effects on a company's business. Second, they should remember that problems are more easily conceptualised, as are possible solutions, by those closest to them but the latter may not be able to discern the overall or long-term consequences of these. So they need advice and assistance from colleagues not so close to the problems and thus able to take a wider view of them. (For example, a marketing problem is easier for a marketing executive to understand and analyse, but only a production colleague can see what the manufacturing implications are likely to be.)

However, serious problems are rarely solved until some considerable time has elapsed from their recognition since much detailed study, work and reorganisation are usually required. In the meantime the problems themselves may have been altered by changing circumstances. Where investment in further resources are needed (e.g. executives, plant, skills) the time required to solve difficult problems may be further extended. So again time is a critical factor.

3.1 Depth of management

Failure to invest in management (recruitment and training) is an equal factor in the reason why serious problems remain serious for so long, and prove so difficult to resolve. Keeping management thin on the ground may be a false economy. So also is cutting the executive ranks when business times are difficult. When business becomes more competitive it may be wiser to increase staff, rather than thin it out, in critical areas. These are the ones from which salvation of the company could arise. For example, increased marketing effort may be needed so more executives and others may be required here. Or if the difficulties have a technological or manufacturing basis then more experts in the appropriate technical field, and possibly also manufacturing executives, may be advisable. There is a finite limit to the amount of work that one executive can do and when problems increase that workload it is wishful thinking to imagine that executives, already hard pressed, will always be able to find the solutions quickly.

More thought is being given to the depth of management by executives. In particular, the question is also raised: how much managerial skills should the company have on its full-time staff and what can be bought-in as and when required? The latter has the appeal that it helps to reduce fixed overheads, the cost of the bought-in help being paid for out of untaxed profits. Also, theoretically, the best 'experts' on any subject can be hired as needed; whereas to keep such experts on the permanent staff could be an expensive operation. The company may also have difficulty in keeping the experts fully employed so that dissatisfaction may arise and they eventually leave. Given the large number of competent consultancy organisations, covering every field of management, existing in several industrialised countries the temptation to depend on recourse to them is strong. However, a company should not be so dependent on consultants being called in to resolve problems that management for normal activities is very thin on the ground. Otherwise it will find itself in a very vulnerable position, unable to respond quickly to changes in its business environment, especially competitive activities.

The disadvantages of depending on 'hired help' include the fact that the best may not be available when wanted or may be difficult to identify. Then, good though consultants are in their chosen expertise, they lack the vital experience of working in client companies for a sufficient length of time to gain an intimate knowledge and feel of the company. (The counter-claim is that they are free of bias and the internal politics that rage in all companies.) Further, they do their investigations, make their recommendations (which may or may not be accepted) and then they usually leave. They are not responsible for, or committed to, the achievement of the results that should flow from their work. Thus they can lack commitment to the work! Also, there is no guarantee that the company will pick the right helpers since personal bias and prejudice will again influence executives' decisions here.

The author recalls a senior executive who would never call in a particular firm of consultants, even when all the evidence proved they were the right people for the task. This was because, many years before, when the executive was a young man on the junior rungs of the executive ladder, the personnel side of the consultants had judged him to be unsuitable for promotion. This judgement was subsequently proved to have been very wrong. Yet the staff of the personnel division of that consultancy had long since changed and the decision had no relevance to that division, whose help was not required. This is yet another example of the many irrational decisions that can undermine the progress of the company.

Another disadvantage is that the executives may stand aloof from the consultants and their work. They may consider the latter to be some type of whizz-kids, possessing some arcane knowledge that mere, humble executives do not have. This could create deep-seated, unconscious hostility to the consultants or an inferiority complex on the part of executives. Even if these do not occur, the executives will not learn anything new. If they worked with the consultants they would add valuable knowledge and experience to their armoury of skills. If executives are hostile to the thought of employing consultants, however, they may try to undermine their work. More frequently, when the report is received they may fail to implement it, even though they go through the motions of doing so. Thus when things get worse they blame the inadequacy of the consultants, and their report, somewhat unfairly. Thus, even when consultants are called in, an integrated management approach is needed in that the consultants and their work must be integrated with the discussions and work of the company's own executives. Thus the best form of consultancy is where only one or two consultants are involved and they form a team with some of the company's executives to study, consider and recommend possible solutions. The detailed work is done by the executives and the consultants act as catalysts to the work, providing the special expertise that may be missing in the company. The decisions and plans are then 'company' ones and more likely to be implemented and to gain the support of all employees.

One thing is certain. There will always be a shortage of executives with proved experience and the ability to maintain that reputation. Also, most dynamic organisations, and many less dynamic ones, will always have a backlog of projects with high potential return on investment. The oft-repeated cry from boardrooms is that there is so much to be done that many projects have to be shelved because the companies do not have the executive skills, or time and money to do them all. However, by remembering first principles, keeping eyes firmly on corporate objectives and aims, seeking to improve the management development work of the corporation, resisting the temptation to rush to every new technique that comes along without consideration of its usefulness, avoiding bias in thought or decision and achieving a high degree of integration in its management work and concepts, corporations can find the best solutions to the problems facing them. They will also be able to establish the right depth of management for their current and intended future activities. In unusual or exceptional instances they can have recourse to consultants to help ease the workload.

More thought is also being given to the development of human resources throughout companies and not only in executive ranks. There are several reasons for this, the reasons now being well recognised. First, alienation, job dissatisfaction and boredom must be avoided and this cannot be achieved if human resources are treated in an impersonal manner and little attempt is made to maintain positive and successful development plans. There will be little job satisfaction evident throughout the company. Second, in-house human resource development provides a low-cost, low-risk return on investment in people. If the remuneration policy is also seen to be reasonable, this will counter to some extent the poaching of newly developed staff by other corporations too lazy to embark on their own development programmes. This safeguard will be increased if promotional opportunities are also known to be good. Third, the impact of increasing expectations will prove to be a strong motivating factor leading to improved proficiency and performance. Fourth, therefore, it will overcome declining motivation and increasingly counter-productive behaviour by all personnel. Fifth, it balances the increasing apathy to further mechanisation of managerial procedures, an attitude described by some as 'the post-industrial age of anti-mechanisation'. That is, if executives are not nurtured and encouraged, they feel that they are becoming mere cogs in a vast mechanised system of management and will respond accordingly. (*See also* Section 8.2.2.)

3.2 Failure of management sciences

The failure in many countries of management sciences to achieve the high hopes once held for them can be traced to a number of reasons. First, a management scientist by definition, should be one who studies management scientifically in order to achieve a much more effective form of management. Unfortunately, many do not. They have come to be persons who create mathematical models and construct certain new, mechanistic concepts of business theory and operations. The most popular management sciences and the ones where the defect mentioned occurs frequently, are resource allocation and scheduling, physical distribution, queuing techniques, portfolio selection and the use of operational research techniques applied to more common management problems. Generally also, efforts in these areas have been aimed at heightening the academic knowledge of how business systems work, of pushing the frontiers of knowledge forward. Scant thought has been given, until fairly recently, to the operational aspects: how this new knowledge can be used to increase the effectiveness of management decisions and actions. Executives, on the other hand, need simple concepts which can be translated into relatively uncomplicated methods and techniques which will produce better results. The management scientist is primarily interested in the development and extension of theories; the executive is concerned with the practical realities of business. So far the twain have not met too often or successfully.

Thus the antipathy between 'doers' (executives) and 'thinkers' (management scientists) has been heightened. This is perhaps not a true analogy, but it will suffice. They have not worked together as well as they might have done had the scientists not been so technique-orientated (i.e. too theoretically inclined) and the executive too operationally intent. So there was a clash between these two 'cultures'. Thus executives tend to reject new ideas as not being of much practical use and the scientists are tempted to dismiss executives as the 'morons' responsible for all the company's problems. Perhaps the academics must take the greater blame for this? However, both attitudes are unfair assessments of the situation, representing extremes of the cases for both 'cultures'. Luckily, recent years have indicated that executives and management scientists are coming together more frequently and are beginning to understand the interests and needs of each other. The implication of an integrated management approach will help to improve the working relationships between these two types of employees to their mutual benefit and that of the company. Then both could work together to demonstrate the benefits their new knowledge would have on the practice of management.

Business executives are also reluctant to employ trained, specialist management scientists who have not had any practical experience of business. This is understandable. The reluctance was at its peak some years ago at the start of the management science craze. Since then there have been increasing attempts to give newcomers some practical experience before turning their expertise loose on corporations. A better balance is being achieved between experience-based and research-based executives and techniques. However, the failure of management scientists in the first flush of the youth of their science, due to the inexperience of the scientists and the untried and unproved nature of their techniques, has left far too many line executives with, at best, a reserved opinion of, or at worst a continuing hostility towards, management scientists.

Even closer cooperation between these two groups is still required as business conditions and activities become even more complex. The information flows are, as a result, increased and made more complicated and require more sophisticated collation and analysis. This cooperation can be improved if experience-based executives are sent to carefully selected and planned appreciation courses on appropriate management science subjects. These courses should emphasise what each technique can and cannot do and its appropriateness for different working conditions and problems. Science-based executives besides attending similar appreciation courses on the work of line managers must also have some practical experience working in a line department, preferably the one with which they will be concerned. Only then will they have a true understanding of the practical side of a corporation's activities. It must be remembered also that the greater the development of these techniques, the further apart in understanding the executives and the scientists will find themselves. The effort needed to improve communications and cooperation will itself become greater.

3.2.1 Business education

One of the major hurdles facing management and business education is the widely held belief of executives, even today, that management is an intuitive activity based on judgement which is acquired only after long years of struggle and experience. While carefully selected experience is an essential ingredient in the training and development of successful managers, it does not exclude the need to learn all that is appropriate of the techniques of management. This is especially necessary for the more scientifically based methods relevant to the executives' present and future responsibilities and businesses. However, experience measured only by the length of time spent in the same job may not add up to so many years' experience. It may only be one year's experience gained so many times! The attitude has been nurtured by the fact that too many entrants into the managerial ranks have taken degrees that are not related to business or management subjects. They can range from engineering, to law, sociology, science or the liberal arts, to name a few. Good as they are and sound subjects for study as they may be, being of use at some later stage of an executive's working life, for entry onto the bottom rungs of the executive ladder, persons must have a solid, generalised grounding of basic management and business subjects. Surveys made from time to time during the 1970s in the U.S.A. and Europe showed that over 60 per cent of newcomers did not have management/business related degrees. Of the remainder most were on business related specialisms but without the vital overview of the major disciplines of management.

However, in Britain, the development in the last quarter century or so, of general business studies degrees or their equivalent diploma or certificate, has proved more useful to young executives. These give an overall appreciation of the subjects of business and management. They do not aim to turn out specialists in any one subject. That stated, it should be pointed out that these courses can still be too greatly biased towards one aspect of a total subject, for example economics, finance or accounting, if the academic team responsible for them is particularly strong in that subject. If this is avoided, specialisation will follow almost naturally after the new executive has had sufficient general experience in business, when latent talents and *métiers* have had time to show through.

Another common failing is that formal educational programmes do not always teach executives what they must know to build successful careers. Further, there appears to be no attempt to correlate how well students do on their courses and their achievement in management. Such studies would help to evaluate the relevance of courses to practical needs. Not surprisingly there is often a high turnover rate of young executives due to their dissatisfaction with their progress. This frequent changing of jobs indicates that job dissatisfaction is high and perhaps, expectations have been exaggerated. Academics and employers must take the blame for this, for not pointing out what the true rate of progress might be, that the mere attainment of a degree does not automatically equip an executive with the right to the top job in a year or two and that considerable experience and further study would be needed before this can be realised. Until this is done regularly job performance by graduates is always likely to be lower than expected.

The major reason for these problems lies in the fact that too many graduates have developed finely tuned analytical abilities but are still under-developed when it comes to making decisions, taking action and getting things done expeditiously. They may also be short on some experience-based skills which are essential parts of an executive's armoury and which, unfortunately, cannot be taught except in general terms. These include the ability to make the right choice from several possibilities especially in conditions of uncertainty, leadership, motivation, knowing the right time to make any decision and when to change the company's course because external conditions indicate this might be advisable. Certain guidelines can be given on all these subjects but knowing when to take each step and taking it successfully, are things that can only come with suitable experience.

3.2.2 The all-rounder

What is becoming clear from the discussions taking place between educators and managers in business is that the truly successful executive is one who has reasonably all-round abilities. Only occasionally will the narrowly trained and narrowly experienced executive succeed at the top, and then only because the enterprise's activities are comprised mainly of things to do with the executive's specialism. (E.g. banking and accountancy, though even here reasonable general knowledge of business is required. Other examples include statisticians in computer bureaux and economists in economic research establishments.) The successful executive then is a person who can see the whole corporate picture, or take an all-round view of every situation, without bias, even towards his own original specialism or interests. Such executives know too, almost instinctively, what is the right mix of experience- and research-based methods needed for any situation so that it can be successfully resolved or implemented.

They can discard with certainty and firmness those techniques which are not particularly relevant to the task in hand or those which have mainly gimmick value, i.e. making no real contribution to the job of managing the enterprise. In an age when 'new' techniques are being spawned at frequent intervals, this ability and the freedom from dithering are vital assets. It was once believed that new techniques and their associated machinery would make individual managerial skills obsolete! Now it is realised that while mechanisation will relieve the executive from dull, routine work and speed up the processes, management and other human decisions will always need the intuitive and ingenious mental processes of mankind. Thus, another requirement is courses aimed to improve the mental abilities of executives, i.e. to teach them how to think through problems, not necessarily to provide them with stereotyped solutions. This involves posing the type of critical questions that arise in practice and considering how they might be analysed towards finding solutions, i.e. concentrating on the thought processes involved rather than possible answers. When this ability is linked to the speed of operation of routinely programmed machines, the looked-for improvement in proficiency and productivity may be realised.

In other words, this changed approach would concentrate on improving the ability to spot possible problems before they occur, analysing them accurately in practical terms, thinking through to the possible long-term effects of possible alternative solutions and then selecting the most appropriate action. A subsidiary, but equally important aim, should be to ensure that quality, not quantity, matters; that the decisions taken are of the highest quality and accuracy possible. Being able to make a whole lot of decisions in a day counts for nothing if they are the wrong ones, or ultimately do damage to the company. For example, dismissing an executive who is not performing well may seem to be a good decision; but if that person has some other skills the company could use with mutual benefit, then such a decision can be judged to be of low quality, bordering in fact on the criminal. The curricula of many courses still give the impression to inexperienced executives, especially newcomers, that management is simply a set of skills that can be reduced to standard formulae. Then, an appropriate formula is selected according to the defined or imagined situation being faced. This ignores the fact that the real problems may be quite different from those initially imagined or identified. Also, these curricula do not help students to conceptualise the problems that might be encountered, nor develop their abilities to analyse them correctly. Neither are they shown how to think through to the consequences of their decisions or of the alternatives which may be available.

In the situation of change that is currently being experienced, survival may require executives to specialise in one or two areas of management. That is, they must study them in depth and become familiar with at least the key aspects of them. However, this does not mean that it is done to the exclusion of all else. In addition they must have a good, if general, appreciation of all the other aspects of management, linked to a mind trained to think and consider without bias, every facet of the problem or business. This heightening of managerial awareness is vital for sustained success.

Line executives should also work as members of teams with appropriate specialists according to the problem or project in hand. They are often the most valuable members of such teams since, regardless of their background, they can develop a better, comprehensive understanding of what the problems are, which opportunities offer the best solutions and how the selected one should be implemented. Line executives should perceive this as the team works on the problems, not as often happens, sometime after the team has completed its task. In this case it will not be a team answer but the executive's own idea and, as such, may meet greater opposition than any mutually agreed team solution. Participation in the team work by line executives enhances the possibility that associated research-based work will be relevant and fruitful. They will also become aware of the strengths and weaknesses of research-based methods and will be able to guide the work so that it makes maximum use of the strengths while avoiding their weaknesses.

3.3 Integrated corporate management

If managements can achieve this type of cooperative working throughout their enterprises, then truly integrated corporate management will be in action. They will achieve a high degree of coordination, as well as full cooperation, between the *strategic planning*, *managerial action and control* and *organisational control* elements of management. The main areas of work under these three headings are listed in Figure 3.1. With this approach many of the recurring problems associated with resource allocation, personnel selection and development, cash flows, labour relations and managerial effectiveness should disappear or be overcome by a corporate team working together towards agreed goals. They will not be wasting time and effort in fighting each other over individual territorial imperatives. Territorial aggression between executives would be largely overcome but, of course, there is no system that can completely compensate for the failings of human nature!

Strategic planning	Managerial action and control	Organisational control
Appraisal of the business environment and changés taking place.	Investigation/appraisal of the company's present position and results.	Investigation of effectiveness of current organisation and training and development needs.
Selecting corporate objectives.	Checking relevance and feasibility of corporate objectives.	
Setting corporate strategy.	Helping to formulate, and agree, corporate strategy and policies for line activities.	Investigation of labour utilisation, turnover and general effectiveness of labour and other administrative policies and methods.
Agreeing strategy and policies for line activities (marketing, finance, manufacturing, personnel, research and development, etc.).		
	Agreeing departmental operational plans, targets and expenditure budgets, cash flows etc. Also production scheduling, quality control and credit control.	Health and social aspects of organisational control.
Resources audit and future planning, including fixed and working capital.		Estimating future needs and planning the longer-term development of the organisation.
Acquisitions and mergers. Disposals.	Agreeing performance standards to be met.	
Study of new horizons for the enterprise.	Study of new horizons for the enterprise.	Improving labour relations and motivation.
		Formation of management task forces and monitoring of their results/ achievements.

Fig 3.1 Integrated corporate management — key activity groups.

In the process, they will agree the kinds of specialisms which are needed or should be encouraged. This will be linked to a programme of personnel development while agreeing also the formal and informal information systems and organisational procedures which will be used. Figure 3.2 lists some of the more usual practices which will be needed by most management teams, grouped into those that are mainly experience-based and those that are research-based.

Experience-based	Research-based
Line management (marketing, finance, manufacturing, research and development, personnel)	Accounting Law Economics
Decision-making	Management science
Planning and control activities	Strategic planning
Administration and organisational planning and control	Data processing
	Organisational development

(Note that organisational planning, development and control, in particular, require both an experience-based and a research-based approach. The others are listed under the type of approach that is critical for them, or which makes the major contribution to their effectiveness. In practice experience-based activities need inputs from research-based activities for greatest effectiveness, and vice-versa.)

Fig 3.2 Management activities and specialisms common to most enterprises/organisations.

The integrated corporate team should also be promoting regular self-evaluations by individual executives, while monitoring the success and failure of the team itself. It should be checking also that the right degree of integration is being achieved and maintained throughout the enterprise's activities. In general, the greater the complexity of the operations, the larger the organisation and the faster the rate of change being encountered (in the industry, economy, technology etc.), the higher will be the performance standards required. Also achieving total integration at all times will demand greater effort on the part of all executives and other personnel. Fuller integration will be vital for success.

3.3.1 Task forces in management

The above stresses the need today, for the work of management to be packaged into appropriate task forces, each with the right mix of skills and executives for the problems that each group has to tackle. This is particularly essential for the research and development work of an enterprise. This is the area of work in most companies where resources seem to be most wasted. The creation of these task forces will initially be the responsibility of the chief executive who must bring together the right executives for each of them. He or she should also agree with each team what its terms of reference should be, but the teams should always have the option to suggest changes in these terms as work and subsequent information indicate these to be necessary.

Excessive rigidity in the formation of teams and decisions on their areas of work should be avoided but not to the extent that they receive no initial direction in launching them on their tasks. There are several corporations now following this task force approach. The basic aims of their task forces seem to be reasonably common. They include a high level of commitment to improving the overall effectiveness of management, a comprehensive approach to planning and subsequent actions and the full utilisation of all appropriate management procedures. Also, the task forces for mainstream management activities are of a permanent nature. Where they are temporary, i.e. formed to tackle a specific problem, the task force is seeking to inject some new innovation into management methods to overcome the special problem being tackled.

3.3.2 Planning's role

Misconceptions about planning still abound, so that it is worth restating here the role it should be allowed to play in management activity. First, there should be a systematic investigation and appraisal of the company's present position, of changes taking place in its business environment and the possible effects they may have on the business. This will indicate what has to be done to ensure future survival and so permit the setting of correct business (corporate) objectives for the enterprise. Having decided what the objectives should be, the most favourable strategy, one offering the best probability of success, can be selected to ensure the realisation of the objectives. This can only be done after critical examination of the strategies that are possible in principle, within the resources and capabilities of the corporation.

Next, the various plans of action, for the number of years of the planning period, can be decided. However, at this stage it may be necessary to reappraise or reconsider the objectives if it is found that the skills and capabilities of the enterprise are not sufficient to make the achievement of the original objectives possible. The whole planning process may have to start all over again. This may be necessary also when the performance of the company is found to be differing greatly from previous plans, or when some major environmental change has occurred, or if progress has to be speeded up to meet some change in shareholder expectations or requirements. Finally, the necessary information and control systems can be devised, or existing ones modified, so that the results can be checked and analysed speedily as they are received. Then any modifications of the plans that may be necessary can be selected and implemented.

While this work will produce a formal and carefully documented plan, company planning is more valuable than just the final piece of paper it produces. On its own it will produce nothing. In its formulation the entire operations of the company, its business rationale, how and why it works best in certain areas, the reasons for failures in others, why policy decisions have been taken, how correct they are proving to be and so on will come under intensive examination. Many myths will be laid bare and exploded. Several taboos will be identified (and hopefully discarded if found to be counter-productive). The executive team must be committed to the objectives and actions embodied in the plans. They must be willing and eager to implement them as successfully as they can, to the best of their abilities.

Planning is both an occasional and continuous task. It is occasional in the sense that formal planning takes place once, or perhaps twice a year at specified times, when the corporation's operational and corporate long-term plans are reviewed in the light of progress being made and fresh plans are agreed. It is continuous in the sense that continuous and regular monitoring of results and control of the operations should go on right through each and every year. It means that the planning activity is on a rolling-plan basis.

Most industrial companies find monthly checks adequate but industries with faster developing technologies or markets (e.g. electronic components, consumer goods) often find it advisable to use fortnightly or three-weekly checks. Some, like the big food chains and departmental stores, check progress at the end of each week. However, modifications to plans and actions are not usually made until two or three of these checking periods have passed. This is to make sure that major changes in plans are not made just for what may turn out to be a momentary faltering of the market. In other words, companies prefer to wait until it is reasonably clear that some major change, of a more or less permanent nature, has taken place before initiating alterations. If they responded too rapidly, before this fact was established, they would be changing course at every change in the wind. This would negate the whole object of planning, since they would effectively have no plan. They would be responding instantly, without careful thought, to every minor market or other fluctuation occurring in their business environment. On the other hand, when some major change is known to have taken place speedy consideration must be given to the implications of this on the company's plans, and adjustments should be made as quickly as is possible. In some instances modifications may have to be introduced in advance of, or in addition to, those that might be seen as necessary at pre-determined revision times. In other words, planning and the implementation and control of plans must have the necessary degree of flexibility built into them if they are to be successful.

Planning encounters special communications problems when it is not taken seriously by all executives and if it is treated only as an interesting theoretical exercise. The necessary attention will not be given to it and the important information and data will not flow to those involved in planning. Alternatively, little effort may be given to ensuring that the information provided is as accurate as possible. Approximations, amounting to little more than rough 'guesses', might be all that is provided, 'to get this nonsense of planning' out of the way. It will be seen as getting in the way of getting on with the job; and executives will not be aware of the short- and long-term difficulties they may be leading their company into by the ill-considered decisions they take. Further, when the planning has been completed it may not be implemented in full or at all.

Planning must also be realistic and in being so, communicate to all its importance. Top executives must also be convinced if they have any reservations about it. The best way of achieving full commitment of all concerned is to involve them in the planning process as and when it is right and proper for them to be involved. This does not mean keeping the entire executive team immersed in planning, to the detriment of their day-to-day tasks and responsibilities. The planning itself must be carefully planned so that the right teams are involved during its various stages. The basic integrated corporate management planning process is illustrated by Figure 3.3.

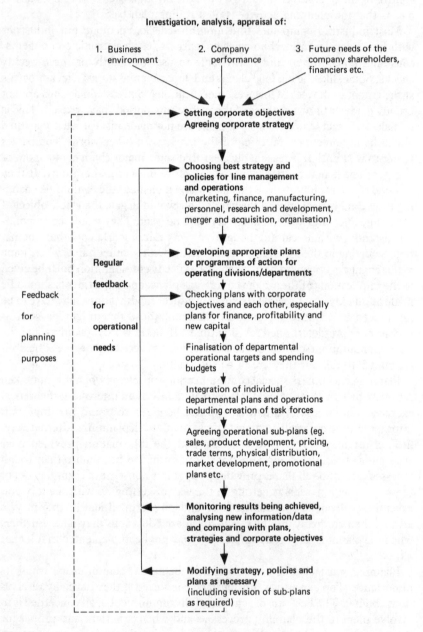

Fig 3.3

3.3.3 The key

The key to success in planning lies in what has been described as the major corporate quadrille, the close and constant cooperation that must exist between marketing, manufacturing, finance and personnel departments and their main supporting activities (*see* Figure 1.5). If their individual departmental plans are not carefully devised and fully integrated with each other, success with their implementation cannot be assured. It follows that there must also be mutual agreement on all decisions and targets set. The reasons should be obvious but they will be stated here briefly.

First, the market, or market demand, decides what the corporation should try to provide in terms of products or services. It indicates also whether there is sufficient total demand to provide the volume of business (market share) required by the enterprise and which would give manufacturing satisfactory loadings on its plant. It will also show what competition is likely to be met, the nature of that competition and perhaps, how it might be contained or overcome. The market may also suggest by any growth or decline taking place, what changes in demand are likely to occur in the foreseeable future and the problems and opportunities that this will provide for the company. Ruling market prices will provide basic data on which the company could forecast its own price ranges and pricing policies with estimates of the unit costs required for these to be implemented. Manufacturing could then estimate if the quality, volume and price indications are within their capabilities. Only when the above marketing information and indications are known can manufacturing begin to finalise their interpretation of what all these mean to them and present this in terms of manufacturing plans.

In this process of course, manufacturing will be finalising all other aspects of their possible activities. They will be working closely with the personnel department who are responsible for finding and obtaining the necessary skilled and unskilled labour, and also the executives, needed. Personnel, in conjunction with other departments, will also have to decide what skills are available within and outside the company, the costs of these skills and whether those outside the company are available in sufficient quantity to let the enterprise have a sufficient supply. They will also be studying the possibility of improving the in-company skills and developing some of the additional ones required from internal sources. They can then begin to finalise recruitment, training and remuneration plans. Other aspects of personnel management, such as labour utilisation and turnover, labour relations and the health, safety and social aspects will also be engaging their attention.

In the meanwhile the finance department will have been considering the possible capital needs, capital utilisation, cash flows and funds management aspects of the business. However, it will be only when the other departments have gone some way towards preparation of their own possible departmental plans that finance can begin to finalise their own plans. These will also take in all the other financial, accounting and budgetary control factors for which they are responsible. High on their priority list of studies will be those connected with under-utilised assets. Can these be put to better use? Can they be cashed and the funds released re-employed more profitably elsewhere? What is the cost of capital and can this be improved? What new capital is needed and what would be the best way of raising this? What would be the cash flow and liquidity positions given the intended marketing and manufacturing operations? Are the profit projections of marketing and the estimated corporate overheads acceptable? And so on. Then they can join with colleagues from other departments to arrive at a final, mutually agreed, corporate operational plan for the next period, from which they can forecast the implications for the shareholders and other providers of finance. They will also be able to gauge the possible impact on future recourse to the money markets for additional capital, if the company can realise its agreed plan. Financial plans can then be finalised.

It is worth saying again, that if all these details and some others (described more fully in later chapters) are not properly assessed, agreed and integrated then the right resources will not be made available in the right quantities and at the right times. Nor will results be optimised if there is poor coordination and cooperation between all the company's departments. Then all the familiar problems of management will arise, regardless of how sophisticated the individual, operational techniques may be, or how much effort is put into the operations. Finally, as also stated previously, in achieving a high quality, integrated approach to management, executives will have considered both the short- and the long-term requirements, obstacles and implications for their activities.

3.4 Company appraisal

Company appraisal as implied by Figure 3.3 is the essential starting point for integrated corporate planning and management. Mistakes and omissions at this stage will undermine the entire planning and operational activities of the enterprise. Appraisal should not be restricted to a few, critical internal operations but should cover all aspects plus markets, products, customers, competitors, technology and the economic, political and social factors that have bearing, or are likely to have bearing, on the company and its business. Figure 3.4 indicates some of the key questions that need answering by any appraisal. These have been grouped under short-term and long-term considerations. The chapters that follow spell this out in greater detail and include other points which may have to be added to a comprehensive list, as special circumstances may demand.

Obviously, the appraisal should give special attention to the problem areas. In this the forecasted or possible future difficulties should not be overlooked, or left until they actually strike the company. Under this heading the more common factors requiring study include the capability and effectiveness of the sales and promotional organisations and their activities. Then there are the difficulties thrown up in the development or decline of markets, the effects of

Short-term	Long-term
Markets	
In which markets are our products selling?	How are markets or market demand changing or likely to change?
Size of total markets — home and overseas?	What factors are causing these changes — technological, economic, political, social, ethical?
What are the company's market shares for the different market segments? (sub-classify by nature and age of the segments and sales channels used).	What will be their effect on total demand and thus possible market shares for the corporation?
What factors influence customer choice of products? (Price, technical aspects, quality, performance etc.)?	What factors are likely to influence customer choice in the future? How will these change in the future?
Any other critical factors?	Any other critical factors? (Any possible new suppliers entering the business)?
Products	
How effective are the products, product range and product mix, in satisfying demand?	What changes are needed (i.e. product modification or new products) or will be needed to meet future demand?
What resources and skills are being used?	How relevant are these resources and skills to future needs?
How do customers appraise our products *v.* competitors'?	How will our present and projected product mix stand up to competition, especially from new entrants?
What quality/performance changes needed?	How should quality and performance change?
Are the pricing, discount and trade term policies right?	How will prices, discounts and trade terms have to change?
Who are our competitors, where and how do they compete?	How will the competitive picture change in the future?
What are competitors' strengths and weaknesses?	How will competitors' strengths and weaknesses alter in the future?
The corporation	
What are our resources, skills, strengths and weaknesses?	What resources, skills etc. will we need in the future and how can these be developed, attained?
What is the company's image?	What should be our image?

Short-term	Long-term
Are our financial resources adequate for the present?	What financial resources will be needed in the future?
How are we performing? (i.e. in all areas of activity)	What performance standards will be needed in future?
Is our manufacturing facility adequate?	What manufacturing facilities will be needed in future?
	See Figure 3.2

Fig 3.4 Company appraisal.

other environmental changes and product obsolescence and development. The last should cover also the need to adapt products to changes in the markets and of consumer requirements and expectations. Study of production matters, especially with regard to technical and economic changes, are needed. Where political and social changes require alterations to product formulation, technological and manufacturing processes, marketing and production executives should consider the implications for their operations. Changes in safety rules and regulations, for the workforce and for society at large, also need to feature in corporate appraisals, especially for the future.

In comparing the company's present performance note must also be taken not only of performance related to past achievements but also the performance of the industry as a whole and especially competitors. The judgment, attitude and expectation of customers cannot be ignored. Product and market appraisals will hinge on how customer demand is likely to change and how customer attitudes are changing towards competitors and their products. Alterations to the composition and structure of markets (consumer/customer) should also be considered. The basic question to be kept in mind is: how will present products or services satisfy customer demand under changing market and economic conditions?

Market changes offer both opportunities and dangers. Their correct assessment and containment will depend on how well the company assesses the impact of technological and economic change. Also important could be changes in the composition of the corporation's customer profile. This in turn may be affected by changes in price levels, sales, distribution channels, competition, government regulations and controls and new laws. All these points affect both large and small enterprises.

3.5 Setting objectives

The objectives selected by company executives depend on the position achieved so far by the corporation, market opportunities, the company's willingness to take risks, technological developments and the improvements required in return on investments and growth. The task of setting objectives poses a number of critical questions that must be answered before correct decisions can be taken. While it should be a process involving purely rational thought, in reality several irrational factors may have a disproportionate influence.

For example, if growth is required should this be obtained in the short- or long-term? There may be irrational support for one or other of these possibilities. Should the rate of growth be a rapid one, producing quick and substantial results, or be at a steadier, less spectacular rate, over a longer period of time? Again, executives may support one or other concept for quite spurious reasons. They may feel that winning the day with one or other proposition, regardless of its appropriateness to the company's interests, will enhance or underline their reputation or future prospects in some way or other. Or they may not have considered the consequences of their contention, or may believe that it is easier to obtain short-term growth and that the company can continue to do so regardless of what is happening in its industry, markets or with its competitors. They do not seem to realise that rapid growth can bring advantages and disadvantages. (In economic and business conditions in 1980 it may not be possible to achieve immediate growth. It will be too costly and market conditions, e.g. declining demand, rising prices, may generally be against such an achievement.)

The advantages of rapid growth include the possibility of lowering unit production costs and thus prices, and so strengthening the company's competitive capabilities. The resultant bulk purchases that can be made for bought-in materials could also reduce unit costs through better quantity discounts etc. If the products could be sold, i.e. demand existed and was not being satisfied by competitors, the unit cost of sales and promotional activities could also be reduced, leading to further cost savings. Rapid growth could also give a company a dynamic image which may or may not be justified. Nonetheless this tends to attract executives with sound experience or those who are results- or achievement-orientated and not content to lead a quiet life. Younger executives on the payroll can be offered promotion and more challenging jobs as the company expands. Also, the financial world sees sustained growth as a sure sign of successful management (which need not be true; growth could be obtained by acquisitions and mergers, not by hard work in eradicating deep-rooted problems of the original business). Access to capital markets may become easier if the inherent problems of the business, which may one day cause serious troubles for it, are successfully hidden from prying, outside eyes. There are other arguments in favour of going for short-term growth, especially if the company has been in a static position on profits for the last few years.

The disadvantages include the fact that short-term growth may not increase profits sufficiently. Too much effort and money may be needed so that the consequential increase in profit for every increase in sales is too small. Overall profitability may in fact decline, although profit in money terms may be up. If growth depends on reduced prices, customers who judged assured quality as the important factor may be turned away. They may believe that quality must be cut in some way to achieve price reductions and they will turn to competitive or substitute products. Alert and experienced executives might not be misled by short-term growth and, with a little probing, might discover the real problems facing the company. They would then be less eager to join the enterprise. Prudent financiers may also be turned away.

Then in striving to achieve rapid and quick growth, the company could over-reach its capabilities and resources and the enterprise could go out of control. It may commit so much of its resources to quick growth that it does not have enough to proceed with the essential long-term growth and development that market and other circumstances indicate to be prudent. The quality of products may decline and costs rise, through trying to do too much with limited resources and working excessive overtime to obtain the necessary output. Plant breakdowns may increase through overworking equipment and not being able to maintain a high standard of maintenance through lack of time and having to skimp the work. Output could fluctuate widely and be unable to cope with sales demand leading to out-of-stock positions arising and the company losing its customers and their goodwill. Customer service generally may deteriorate, either for these reasons or because the relevant teams are not large enough to deal with the expanded business and the increasing problems. Facilities may be over-stretched.

Cash flow problems may also arise. This could be either because delays in effecting deliveries hold up payments (cash inflows) while total operating costs (i.e. outflow) rise. The resultant imbalance could lead to serious liquidity and creditor problems. If unforeseen developments occur such as economic recessions, a sudden increase in competitive action to counter the company's moves, or the arrival in the market of a new, major competitor, the company may not achieve its expanded market shares and be left with considerable inventory of unsold goods. This could put the financial position out of balance. Then increasing counter-activity by competitors could trigger a price war, again worsening the financial situation if the company cannot meet the price reductions without selling at a loss. If the short-term growth is powered mainly by price reductions then it is certain the company would not have the margins to survive an intensive or long-term price war. If major new customers are slow payers, the debtor position might become untenable. If this is experienced with cash flow and creditor problems then the company is in serious trouble. Voluntary or compulsory liquidation or a take-over may be the only solution.

Even if the company could sit out adverse conditions for some time, an executive team born and bred on achieving substantial growth over short periods does not have the character to play a waiting game. Dissatisfaction, friction and dissension could arise. Executives could leave for more dynamic opportunities elsewhere. The arguments for and against can be continued; but these show the inherent dangers of committing a company almost entirely to short-term growth. Arguments for and against long-term growth can be similarly marshalled. The real answer lies in developing a rational policy that is the right mix of the attainment of both short- and long-term growth based on a soundly devised corporate plan.

So in setting objectives, executives have a double balancing act to perform. First they must balance short- and long-term objectives and needs. Then they must arrive at decisions which will balance the different rates of growth possible for its various activities. This is similar to the dilemma facing marketing executives. Should they adopt the shorter-term skimming price policy, or the longer-term market penetration pricing policy? The objectives themselves must be stated precisely, positively and (preferably) briefly so that ambiguities and uncertainties do not arise. Yet they should not be so precise that they feed rigidity into management thinking and activity. Modifications should be made to them as changing circumstances dictate.

3.5.1 Attitudes to growth

It is worth discussing attitudes to growth a little more, especially as economic conditions prevailing in 1979 suggest that growth in future will be much harder to achieve. The author does not hold the view that all types of growth will not be possible. The point is that deciding what growth could be achieved and how it should be realised, requires more precise application of the associated techniques and rigorous monitoring of the results obtained. Then, with the growing acceptance of the social responsibilities of business, growth and personal gains at the expense of other responsibilities is no longer tolerable. Society at large and some governments in particular, will not accept or permit them. Modern concepts of man management principles and the need for improved labour relations also act against the practice of promoting one or two activities (or executives) to an extent where it is possible to make workers redundant. This was always a short-sighted policy which tended to waste resource potential or the potential for future development.

Next, apparent growth where the sole, disguised purpose is the stripping of the assets of the acquired company, is also no longer acceptable to the public of some western countries. In these countries the people object to activities which just increase the private wealth of one or two people in favoured positions. While the more blatant activities have ceased, asset-stripping and the pursuit of personal gain regardless of the cost to others, still goes on unabated behind the scenes. From time to time the media learns of a new case and publicises it. Where the uninformed see these activities as the main part of 'corporate growth activities', they obtain an unfortunate image of the subject of growth. Ammunition is provided for the several anti-establishment and anti-business organisations existing in most western nations to use indiscriminately. The public are impressed and further impetus is given to the idea of 'nil growth' in future for industry and business.

Yet no-one has given any serious, comprehensive thought to what this means for western economies. Given that modern economic systems, after the Second World War, are based on business growth, expansion and allied developments and that high levels of employment, prosperity and standards of living resulted from such growth, it is likely that nil growth for industry would mean that unemployment would rise to quite high levels leading to declining economic activity and prosperity and substantial falls in the standard of living. A brief glimpse of these possibilities was obtained in Britain during the second half of the 1970s as that country attempted to get its economic and fiscal policies into order and struggled with problems associated with the rapidly rising price of oil. For managers and executives it would mean a much harder fight for the survival of their enterprises and probably considerable retrenchment or contraction of activities. Then gimmicky techniques would have to be abandoned and a much wider and deeper understanding of basic management principles and their application would be absolutely mandatory for survival.

Growth through the acquisition of competitors purely to stifle or reduce competition, thereby allowing the acquiring company to dominate markets is viewed with disfavour in most free enterprise and mixed economy countries. Several of them (especially the U.S.A. and Britain) now have laws and regulations to prevent the emergence of harmful monopolies. As usually happens, some monopolistic situations (e.g. where considerable capital and other resources are needed to run a viable operation) which would not be harmful to consumers have also suffered under these new rules. Thus only growth strategies offering beneficial effects (e.g. increasing employment and economic well-being, improving international trade and so on) are acceptable to governments and society opinion leaders. This again stresses the need for executives to reconsider their attitudes to growth along more positive lines as suggested in this book.

So growth that will allow a company to survive profitably, offering advantages to customers and not disadvantaging them in any way, should generally be acceptable. Growth that will even out seasonal or cyclical fluctuations in a business, or the demand fluctuations of different countries should be acceptable especially if this leads to greater overall corporate efficiency and stability. Indeed such growth is desirable if the economy of a nation is itself to grow and prosper and be in a position to provide ever-increasing help for the disadvantaged. Further, growth through the acquisition of suppliers of raw materials and components in short supply, to safeguard user companies would also be understood, especially if the beneficial end-results mentioned above are obtained. However, if growth is to be achieved only by diversification, then it should not be forgotten that mastery of the new technologies and techniques that would be involved would be essential for success.

There is, too, another form of growth: growth in operational efficiency and proficiency, usually measured by increased profitability and return on investments. This would be generally acceptable to all informed people and opinion leaders. In modern terms this requires more efficient management and extending the automation and mechanisation used by an enterprise. However, increased mechanisation has to be kept within viable limits, not only in terms of a company's abilities but also in regard to its social responsibilities. For example, automation in countries with a large pool of unskilled labour and high unemployment would lead only to increasing the unemployment levels of the unskilled. A more responsible growth strategy would then be one that does not involve further mechanisation but utilises more unskilled labour. Automated production is more capital-intensive than labour-intensive activities. In countries with a high level of unemployment of unskilled workers it is usual also to find a shortage of investment capital. Many such nations in fact discourage capital-intensive schemes and look with favour on, if they do not actually encourage, alternative labour-intensive ones. However, if the alternative to further mechanisation is the prospect of an enterprise going out of business, then mechanisation may be unavoidable.

At the same time it is appreciated that production and other operational costs can be reduced when increased automation replaces out-of-date systems. This assumes that the increased mechanisation is correctly used and not just installed to keep pace with current trends and thought. Further, improved technology may lead to the creation and need for new machinery and methods. Replacement of existing plant may then have to be judged not on the remaining life of existing equipment but rather on its technical obsolescence. Modernisation of plant may thus place further pressures on the need for growth strategies that will absorb the additional capacity profitably. As stated, the capital cost will be increased and the effect of this on short- and long-term profitability and profit margins must be gauged accurately.

3.5.2 What objectives?

The more commonly used quantitative objectives are discussed in Chapter 4. These are not the only criteria that should guide an enterprise. There are qualitative objectives also, as illustrated in Figure 3.5. It is probably the newer ones, stemming from the persistent call for businesses to acknowledge their social responsibilities, that prove the most troublesome to implement. Executives have little experience of them and they are usually not easy to quantify in any useful way. Getting a right balance of all these is not easy and the art develops only over a longish period of experience of trying to achieve this.

Even the relatively simple objective of reaching a stated profit figure is not as straightforward as it appears. This has to be related to the rate of growth of profit to be achieved and what rate should a company follow? The answer to this question will vary according to the economic conditions that are expected to prevail over the period being planned, what the corporation has to do in that time, the other targets to be attained, what the anticipated competitive activity is likely to be, what the enterprise's long-term objectives or intentions are and what the cost of capital is likely to be. Then the company's social standing and thus, the socially defensible positions it can sustain, will also help to decide this apparently straightforward question. In addition, the rate of growth of profit selected must be compatible with the company's need to balance profits earned with sustained growth of the business and reasonable stability. These could be illustrated by three vectors (lines) pulling from a centre point at an angle of 120° from each other. Make one too strong or important and it will pull the

̱tive	Qualitative
Short-term profits	Market leadership
Long-term profits	Market standing
Market shares	Corporate image
Turnover/volume	Prestige
Return on investment	Responsibilities to the public
Annual rates of growth	(shareholders and society in general)
Financial resources and their utilisation	Executive performance, morale and development
Other resources and skills and their utilisation	Workers' performance, morale and development
Productivity	Innovation
Cash flows and liquidity (if not included in 'financial resources' above)	Productivity and quality
	Labour relations and welfare
Growth	Stability with flexibility

(Not necessarily in order of importance: *see* text of Section 3.5.3.)

Fig 3.5 Business objectives.

centre spot in its direction and away from the other two. In managerial terms, make one vector (profit or stability or growth) too important, taking too much of the company's time and effort then the other two items would be much harder to achieve and keep in balance. Finally, this balance between these three objectives must also take into account both the short- and long-term aims and needs of the corporation.

3.5.3 Magnitude of objectives

Figure 3.5 has listed the various objectives towards which all enterprises should be working. Objectives are needed in every area where performance and results affect the prosperity and survival of the company in some vital aspect. For most corporations this is every facet of their business! The spread therefore is quite considerable but the magnitude and importance of individual objectives varies. For example, the key corporate objectives discussed in Chapter 4, profit, return on capital, sales volume, turnover, market shares and annual rates of growth, are important to all businesses. They are the prime targets for all executive planning, thinking and effort. They are the basic rationale on which everything else is based. On the other hand, for some corporations, prestige and image might be rated as supremely important and may take some precedence over the ones mentioned earlier, even profit. Then other enterprises may consider market leadership and standing more impor-

ant, and may be prepared to sacrifice some profit, market sha
and return in order to safeguard their position in these res₊
In practice, executives must also strive to balance such conti.
tives. They must make sure that, say, profit is not sacrificed too n.
prestige, image or market standing. They should also make sure that
company's cherished views of qualitative matters such as the last three mentioned, match reality! Frequently a company thinks that its growth and the
defence of its present position against competitors hinge on the good image
that customers have of the company. It can just as frequently be shocked to
find that this is not true and consumers only support it because its prices are
within acceptable limits. Then sacrificing profit, or volume, or market shares,
might just be wasting money and opportunities. Thus the magnitude of
objectives, in terms of their relative importance to the firm, will vary from
company to company. It will require sound judgment by executives on past
experience and knowledge of their business and markets and accurate forecasts
of the changes expected in some stated future period.

In addition, publicly quoted companies will be interested in securing satisfactory returns on investors' capital for the many reasons already discussed
earlier. This will have to be balanced with growth and stability, but flexibility
of approach and security for the investors' money are also important. State-
owned enterprises should, however, attempt to keep unit costs down to the
lowest levels possible, consistent with any re-financing which they are required
to achieve through their own efforts, that is the earnings of the business. This
does not mean, however, that other objectives similar to those required of
industry in general, should be ignored. In this case also, as with all businesses,
the standard and quality of the service provided, with its dependability, will
influence the importance placed on any one objective. For both types of
enterprise, social goals are now looming larger and may in many instances
impose restrictions on the magnitude that can be given to any objectives.

Finally, some objectives can be quantified and these will form the major
yardsticks by which progress and success are measured. Others will be qualitative in nature (*see* Figure 3.5). Though difficult to use as measures of success,
they provide essential guidance to executives on how the quantitative targets
and operations generally should be seen and judged. They help executives in
the difficult task of obtaining the right balance to their activities and decisions.
Qualitative objectives can be said to set the tone, nature, quality and philosophy of managerial activities.

3.6 Risk management

Most of the literature published in Britain and some other countries in recent
years has concentrated on the risks involved in portfolio management and in
cover for the things normally the business of insurance companies. However,
for managers the subject of risk covers a much wider field; though even here,
emphasis has been placed on the risks inherent in new ventures or projects. In

roject appraisal, the financial and general business risks involved in launching out into something new are estimated and assessed. In many instances the risks are not assessed particularly accurately. Hunch, opinion and the cherished hopes of the executives involved are allowed to influence the study and decisions too much. (Alas, also, many companies do not do them at all.)

For example, in the early 1960s a major British manufacturing group was committed to launch a new technological operation of a complex, difficult nature. The risk and opportunities involved were estimated by the engineer who first devised the new product and operation. His knowledge of marketing matters was non-existent and his market research on which his projections for future demand were based, was (at best) rudimentary. He also ignored what was going on in the U.S.A., at the time the acknowledged world leader on the technology. The project was launched and then a marketing executive was called in. His studies, which he made a condition of his acceptance of the job, showed that demand had probably been overstated by a factor of ten. When new developments from the U.S.A. reached the market here these further reduced the demand for the new product in European markets.

However, risk management should involve much more than just trying to assess the business risks of a venture in order to minimise or avert taking risks. The following list is a summary of the different types of risks which executives should take positive steps to manage or control.

1. *Speculative risks* arising from operations such as—
   (a) marketing; (b) manufacturing; (c) financial matters;
   and associated factors such as—
   (i) innovation; (ii) political developments; (iii) social changes; (iv) technological developments; and changes.

2. *Static or pure risks* arising from—
   (a) physical damage to assets (especially by fire, explosion and similar hazards);
   (b) injury to third parties whether caused by (a) or by other means;
   (c) death or disability of employees, owners or third parties, whether due to (a) or not;
   (d) fraud on the part of employees or third parties;
   (e) criminal violence by employees or third parties;
   (f) adverse legal judgments; and
   (g) damage to third party property.

3.6.1 Speculative risks

These, if tallied, would add up to a frightening number and might deter the timid from ever having anything to do with business! As more consumer protection and other liability laws are enacted in different countries, so the range of risks that have to be faced are increased. To deal with the subject of risk management in its entirety — not just the glamorous bit about the risks involved in portfolio management — requires a substantial and comprehensive book. It is beyond the purpose of this work. However, the range of subjects to be considered under this heading can be indicated.

For example, in marketing the risks can include death, injury or damage to third parties. This could be due to normal accidents, such as a person being run over by a staff member in a company car to damage caused by badly designed products, items that do not make sufficient allowance for human safety or the ingredients in consumable products subsequently found to have harmful effects on humans, animals and the countryside or seas and rivers in general. It is impossible to test the latter group for safety conclusively. With additives in foods, for example, normal laboratory tests may show that a particular additive should not be harmful when consumed in small quantities. Without samples of people subjected to tests for 60 years or more, it is impossible to prove conclusively whether there are any long-term cumulative harmful effects. This is not a practical proposition. Cases that spring to mind include a very successful pain killer, recommended and used for years, but only recently found to be a cumulative poison in that it damaged some internal organs, because the body does not discharge it completely. Over a number of years sufficient amounts can build up in the body until dangerous concentrations are reached.

Then there is the question of safety standards. These are always subject to change and new information can show that standards previously thought to be adequate are in fact not so. In addition, new concepts on businesses' social responsibilities are adding new standards, laws and regulations. These all involve various possibilities of new risks arising. Executives have to try to take all these into account, including keeping abreast or ahead of new knowledge and information on the subject. While existing knowledge on these sorts of risks can be dealt with in many cases in the product development stage, monitoring of developments is vital if future reformulations are to be made to avoid newly discovered inherent risks. Apart from the humanitarian aspects, the financial liabilities for the company could be severe.

There are also the risks involved when products or services fail to perform as claimed. A product failing to produce the results expected of it can lead to impairment of customers' own business activities. This may range from a loss of production and thus loss of sales and customer goodwill to health and other hazards in their own plant or organisations. To these must be added any new liabilities resulting from new legislation on product liability. In Britain, this is now being extended to involve organisations that finance the purchase of products, for example, through hire purchase agreements or purchases made via credit or bank cards. Even major clearing banks with their own credit cards can now be held responsible for the replacement of faulty products. This results in yet further financial liabilities and risks for both the banks and the manufacturers.

On the manufacturing side the more usual risks involve breakdown in the production process leading to loss of output, sales and goodwill to injury, damage or death to the company's own personnel and to users of the finished products. Then there are the liabilities and risks to the community arising from the inherently hazardous nature of the manufacturing processes needed. On top of that is the risk of any carelessness in controlling operations or in ignoring elementary or complex safety rules. The storage, handling and usage of potentially dangerous raw materials involve yet another bag of risks for the company. Even here, new knowledge is being acquired to show that some items, hitherto considered as safe, may involve long-term hazards. The example that springs to mind is the process of vulcanising rubber, where some vulcanising agents were found to expose operatives to long-term hazards connected with cancer. Others are the recently established hazards associated with the dust of certain materials, e.g. some forms of asbestos.

Also, there are the various risks to the company from financial and personnel activities, especially those associated with carelessness, or insufficient attention to the less obvious possibilities. Some are the result of deliberate or criminal omissions. Others, probably most, stem from harassed or overworked executives not having the time to give proper consideration to them. This is of course no excuse. No matter how hard-pressed executives may be, they must make the time to give proper consideration to all the risks that might arise. The examples are legion but perhaps the few stated here will suffice to show that risk management is a far wider and more complex job for executives than they may have considered it to be in the past. Thus the boards of companies need to take the lead by insisting that risk management is accorded a more important and prominent role than hitherto and give impetus to a more thorough management of all risks.

3.6.2 Management of risk

Readers may dismiss many of these points as being in the realm of insurance and assume that the company's insurance cover is adequate for these needs. It never is. Apart from the fact that many of the risks may not be known as applying to a company, those that are are seldom sufficiently covered. The question of establishing what is the right amount of cover is not easily answered. To start with, what risks or activities should be covered? How much risk can or should a company carry itself? If the probability of a risk arising seems small, then not insuring against it (i.e. the company is prepared to pay out from its own resources should the risk occur) may seem a sensible cost-saving decision. However, if the risk does arise and heavy liabilities are involved the company could be in serious trouble and voluntary liquidation of the business might be the only answer.

Then consider fire risk. Obviously areas with the greatest fire risk or hazard should be insured; but, again, to what extent? Obviously the personnel who work in that area will be covered, but what about those in adjacent areas or who have to walk through or visit the hazardous area from time to time in the course of their work? What about third parties who can range from visitors on legitimate business (delivering materials, calling to see production executives to arrange orders or deliveries etc.) to those who live nearby? The last may be endangered by fire or explosions and their property (homes etc.) may also be at risk. What cover should there be for third-party liability, and how extensive or comprehensive should this be?

Accident insurance for marketing employees, especially those on the road and truck drivers is an obvious and necessary cover that is needed. However, what about those who may travel occasionally on company business either in company or their own cars? What about those who have to travel overseas, or by air? On overseas business travel, should employees be covered just for accident, or should illness and other possible hazards be covered also? What about third-party liabilities? Also if a person overseas is killed or lost while on company business, what cover should there be for compensatory payments to surviving dependants? What cover should there be also for the company? The loss of a key person might be a very serious loss to the company.

As Drucker has written, it is impossible or futile to try to eliminate all risk in a business enterprise. Risks are inherent in the mere existence of businesses and people. Even trying to minimise all risks can produce irrational, unbearable conditions. They may inject an even greater risk into the business, that of rigidity in the conduct of the business and its operations.

The fire risk is an obvious one that should be covered. Damage to and destruction of, plant and other assets can destroy the company's production and earning capacity. Business and goodwill can be lost, never to return. If the company does not have sufficient financial reserves to survive the period before rebuilding or to pay for it, then closing down might be the only answer. Political risks are not always obvious. They include drastic reductions in earnings or earning potential due to new financial policies by governments that suddenly impose levies or other payments on corporations. Government intervention leading to nationalisation or confiscation of the business involves a further set of risks. There are social aspects of political risks also. The public could force a government or local authority to close plants if the effluent discharged can be proved to be a serious hazard or danger to health or public safety, or if the products made are considered in the same light.

Labour risks to the company include the loss of opportunities arising from a difficulty in getting the right skilled personnel or from vulnerability to dissatisfaction amongst personnel. Strikes lose business, can be very destructive and lead to long-term developments which are very harmful to the profitability and future prosperity of the company. Technical risks are caused by a company's ability or inability to handle its technology correctly and expeditiously. Or they can arise because the company fails to keep up with developments in its own technical field or because some competitors have developed new processes which make the company's products obsolescent. These risks are manifested by loss of business.

Risks in marketing arise because customers suddenly change their requirements or attitudes. Gradual changes which go unnoticed until it is too late can have the same effects. A move to competitors' products due to changes of taste or preference offer further marketing risks. Changes in customer locations, by major moves to other locations, pose many marketing and distribution problems and so present further inherent risks. Then there are all the other types of risk mentioned earlier.

How should a company cover all these risks? The problem is made worse by the fact that not all these risks are insurable. For insurable risks the exact amount of cover needed should be carefully assessed by executives drawing on their experience and knowledge of the business. This will include forecasts of the probability of the risks arising, how frequently they might arise and the financial and other consequences of their occurrence. Then they can decide what part of these total risks the company should carry and the effect on the business if all these probabilities occur at the same time or in some likely combinations. For non-insurable risks, the company has to fall back on careful planning, with flexibility in the plans, of its activities and a monitoring system that will give early warning when trouble is looming. Then executives can implement corrective or evasive actions to minimise the risk or its consequences.

Executives' work in the area of risk management might be made easier if they would keep the following questions in mind.

1. What are the insurable risks affecting the business?
2. What losses are likely to arise, and how frequently, as a result of these risks? What would be the extent of their effects on the business?
3. What are the effective costs to the business of these risks and how do these compare with the cost of cover?
4. What is the cost/benefit situation for these risks if (i) cover of some kind is arranged, and (ii) no cover is provided?
5. What proportion of total loss can the company afford to cover itself? What other risks are inherent in this?
6. How serious might the consequential losses be to the company's business and survival?
7. What alternative plans or actions are possible to contain these risks or their consequences for the company?
8. What speculative risks are inherent in the company's business? What are their probabilities of occurrence?
9. What can be done to minimise these risks or at least their effects should they arise?
10. Are plans, policies and strategies correctly conceived not only to suit corporate aims but also to minimise consequential and static or pure risks?

The executives will then stand a better chance of reaching the right decisions on this subject. However, they should never hesitate to call in acknowledged experts to help them to resolve this very important and potentially dangerous aspect of their business. Saving the cost of having expert advice may prove to be a false economy.

3.7 More case histories

It is perhaps helpful to end this chapter with a few more brief case histories. Readers will no doubt judge them to be examples of more successful management approaches. Of course not all of them have employed the managerial methods or techniques precisely as discussed in this and preceding chapters. However, they have all found that the simpler tenets of management worked in their situations. They are worth considering when executives find their companies staggering from difficulty to difficulty.

3.7.1 G.E.C. Ltd.

This is one of several cases of companies that faced most of the problems mentioned in the cases in Chapter 1 which, by sensible and hard-headed management and business concepts, found the right solutions that ensured their continuing success. The British General Electric Co. Ltd. (G.E.C.) was by the end of the Second World War, Britain's largest electrical manufacturing group. It had held this position from about the 1930s when its proud slogan was 'Everything Electrical'. Until the late 1940s this was a fact and market, competitive, financial and cost aspects were such as to make it possible to honour this concept profitably and efficiently on a world-wide basis.

However, after the war, competition increased at home. Industrialisation abroad and the internationalisation of business accentuated the effects of this. Labour and material costs began to rise, though by the rates of the 1970s the increases seem almost negligible. Capital was getting more expensive, profit margins were being eroded and it soon became clear that the extensive empire of G.E.C. could not be continued. An extensive reappraisal of the company's markets, products and operations was launched. The resultant reorganisation and rationalisation was not painless and was seen at the time to have been drastic. However, it did meet the needs resulting from the changes taking place in the company's business environment, especially those of the electrical engineering industry. G.E.C. believed that it had to take a leading role in the rationalisation of that industry and did so by taking over other well-known British companies such as Associated Electrical Industries (A.E.I.) and English Electric.

The philosophy of its present chairman, Sir Arnold Weinstock, also helps to maintain the successful impetus of the rationalisation. First, there is no complacency. Sir Arnold and his senior colleagues and managers acknowledge that nothing is perfect and it is always possible to do better, provided the right standards have been set to serve as guidelines for further improvement. Then the importance of customers and their requirements gain continual acceptance. The executives realise that the justification for the company's continued existence, and theirs in their jobs, depends on how effectively the needs of their customers are met, on an expanding scale. In a competitive society, it is realised, companies survive by giving people what they want.

Next, there is the belief that the company must employ the right people in every job ('first class people' as described by Sir Arnold) who are as self-sufficient and self-contained as regards their work as is possible. Head office's role is to provide the stimulus and specialist aid to operating companies when this is too expensive and scarce to be provided at operational levels. The subsidiaries or operating divisions are left to get on with managing their businesses and achieving mutually agreed targets. The persons in charge of them are accepted as people who are competent and know their own businesses best. Resources are disposed to the right places and financial controls are mutually agreed, becoming the standards by which the efficiency of the operation and its expansion are measured. Managers commit themselves to agreed objectives and targets and must honour obligations to customers, employees and the group.

When things are not going right with a subsidiary, speedy remedial action is taken. In this respect it is worth recording the experience of one group operation, that of G.E.C. Measurements located at Stafford, England. The company makes electricity meters, relays and other companies' electrical switchgear. Until about 1975 performance was slipping and an almost endemic problem was its apparent inability to keep delivery dates and promises. Though no worse than competitors' delivery, the operation was consistently failing to satisfy its customers. (This is also an appalling insight into the inefficiency of British industry, or far too much of it.) The delivery period for domestic-type meters should have been three months but in fact stretched to twelve or more. For some products delivery was up to two years behind schedule. Customers of protective devices and electrical relays were even more inconvenienced. One customer reported that he was driven to distraction trying to find alternative overseas suppliers because of G.E.C.'s delays in delivery which could then range from six to eighteen months.

It was not Sir Arnold Weinstock who stepped in to sort out the problems. Instead the group selected a qualified engineer whose initial experience had been gained at English Electric, who had left school at fifteen years of age and obtained his qualifications by night school and sandwich courses whilst working at English Electric. He was appointed managing director in 1945 at the age of forty-one. The only brief he received from head office was to get things right, especially getting back to an earlier level of profitability. Otherwise he had a free hand in the factory. His chief priority was getting rid of production and other bottlenecks, which meant they had first to be identified. It was found that half the overdue orders were for export, a far higher percentage than the amount of export business undertaken warranted. They had been pushed to the rear of the queue because it is easier to ignore a telex message from overseas than an irate telephone call from a home customer.

The new managing director launched a crusade to cutback on the length of the order book. When he took over the company had an order book worth about £10 million. In 1978 this was still its value but it represents four months' work and not fourteen. This speeding up was not the result of new production planning methods. What was needed was a blitz on improving the supply of components that made up the finished goods. One of the main reasons for their problems was the fact that the company was made up of three different businesses which used very few common components, but which for historical reasons had been lumped into one factory. They had 18,000 component bins with availability of any one component being around 86 per cent. In three years this had been raised to 96 per cent. Another part of the solution was to move the meter production to a new factory at Stonefield. More investment was made on improving the manufacture and supply of components as this would reduce the amount of work-in-progress held at different stages of production, a much more expensive operation. Finally, there was the problem of building up morale. The company did not follow the traditional British approach of management by criticism, epitomised by questions on why something is not being done. Instead employees and executives were asked what should be done to achieve specified results. This encouraged all the workforce to be positive, not defensive. This open management style affected everyone not just executives and gave back to the enterprise its confidence in its own abilities.

Because of the essential decentralisation of control throughout the G.E.C. group, rapid and efficient communications and control systems usually operate. Friction and in-fighting are at a minimum and amount to nothing more than momentary irritations. The chairman-chief executive relationship is good, each fulfilling the role he should play. The chief executive makes the decisions with senior colleagues, and the chairman is the check and watchdog, who also encourages and sustains the senior executives in their work. With good communications, major battles just do not develop.

As a result, the reorganised G.E.C. had grown substantially in the decade to 1975, before the horrific economic conditions of that and subsequent years hit Britain. Even then progress has continued. The company remains hungry for improvements and keen for the development of new business. The impetus is maintained not only as a result of the general philosophy outlined but also by recruiting competent young executives and encouraging them to do better. Part of this encouragement includes the provision of carefully thought out management education courses that have very practical meaning for the group.

3.7.2 The Bestobell Group

This approximately £65 million ($130 million) group is active in a large number of industries ranging from engineering to chemicals, consumer goods and physical distribution, but has managed nonetheless to maintain a good performance. During the first half of the 1970s, pre-tax profits rose annually by about 27 per cent with a very satisfying growth of 40 per cent in the year ended December 1974. Its pre-tax return on capital, on an historic basis, exceeded 20 per cent during the same period.

It used to be a much cherished maxim, now realised to be a fallacy, that management principles were totally interchangeable between industries. Business education taught these principles on the assumption that all executives had to do, was apply the principles in their work situations and success would be guaranteed. As stated in this book already, this took no account of the individualities of corporations and their employees. Nor did it take notice of the flexibility of their mental attitudes, nor the managerial methods used or sensitivity to market, technological and competitive conditions. Neither was their speed of action and reaction to any situation taken into account. All of these factors vary from industry to industry and company to company.

A highly diversified corporation, for example, cannot remain finely tuned to every market sector or technology in which it is operating. It cannot respond correctly or rapidly to the changes occurring in all these activities. Nor will all facets of such a business contribute equally or evenly to corporate performance, nor develop or grow at a uniform pace. The executives, therefore, have to strive to keep things in reasonable balance so that a momentary set-back in one area never endangers the whole. They should also try to counterbalance this set-back in one area with an upsurge in another. Bestobell is a good British example of a group that seems to have mastered the necessary skills to do this and maintain a good record.

One of the main contributory factors to this success is the fact that they operate strongly overseas. In the mid-1970s their overseas activities began to make significant contributions to corporate targets, advancing significantly faster than business in home markets. This was perhaps predictable as the United Kingdom economy was then heading for another recurrence of its economic and financial problems. A down-turn in business activity was easily foreseeable and the up-surge in overseas business was fortunately timed since it permitted overall balance and stability to be maintained. By 1975 overseas business contributed more than 60 per cent of the group's total results.

The group's geographical spread, involving more than fifty distribution points in over twenty countries means that the average sales or merchandising branch is relatively small, turning over on average about £200,000 ($400,000) a year. Yet given the group's extensive product range it means also that each branch can specialise in its inventories according to the types of industry it supplies. This allows considerable flexibility to be maintained in the business. For example the Johannesburg branch in 1978 served the mining industry while the Natal branch is designed to serve packers and canners. The specialisms can also be evolved to suit the local characteristics of markets. Thus, in 1977, the Malaysian company was the only group operation fabricating pressure vessels while the rest of the South African company was the only one that could design hydraulic systems in their entirety. This variety also permits a considerable degree of autonomy which in turn promotes high level motivation of the employees in each location. The group's management realises that only by encouraging this autonomy can it be run successfully, yet decentralisation was not a conscious aim of original management policy, but rather the result of the historical development of individual industrial activities.

The group is also marketing orientated in that it recognises the only way to make money is to sell products not necessarily to make them. Over one third of the group's turnover is in the distribution of products which it does not make in its own factories. A further 20 per cent or more come from engineering contracting. The former in times of inflation makes an inflated contribution to profits. (Perhaps one of the few ways of safeguarding profitability during times of high inflation?)

The group's origins go back to the development by John Bell of a process for producing spun asbestos while owning an asbestos mine in Canada. The asbestos production was eventually sold to Turner & Newall. After its incorporation as Bell's Asbestos and Engineering Supplies at the end of the 1920s, it continued to sell asbestos, but this was being made for it by Turner & Newall. In the late 1940s it acquired a small company making valves and pipeline fittings in Rotherham. This was followed by the acquisition of Ronald Trist, a more substantial manufacturer of similar products, including also boilers, heating and ventilating equipment. The purchase was made more because the surviving owner of Trist, a near-neighbour on the Slough Trading Estate, wished to sell out. This purchase brought with it a number of overseas outlets, especially in Europe, which added to Bell's own subsidiaries in Australia, Canada and some Commonwealth countries in Africa.

In the early 1950s Bell's set up a Danish entrepreneur in the manufacture of Venetian blinds made from aluminium strip. In the 1960s this venture into consumer goods was buttressed by a move into paints through the acquisition of Carson & Son and later, Paripan. In 1969 they purchased a further major paint manufacturer, Hadfields, to increase their volume of business in this market. Paripan also made chemical cleaning products. While the former Continental subsidiaries of Trist existed mainly on the sales of group-made fluid controls and valves, the bigger overseas subsidiaries in Australia and South Africa had manufacturing operations of their own. They also sold other locally made goods to about 20 or 30 per cent of turnover and acted as distributors for foreign manufacturers, not necessarily British or Bestobell. Bestobell Engineering Products Ltd., the merchandising arm of the group in the United Kingdom, while selling the group's valves also sold the products of other manufacturers. Finally, asbestos now accounts for less than 5 per cent of total sales.

Various internal reorganisations and name changes were also carried through after the Second World War. Sometimes resistance to this was encountered as when the Trist name (thought to have important meaning in the fluidics industries) and to a lesser extent Bell, were dropped and replaced by the group name Bestobell and its derivates. By 1969 four United Kingdom divisions had been created, each under a general manager, controlling a handful of (vaguely) related companies. It was thought that this would form a good basis for future development and acquisitions. These activities involved the incorporation of the industrial seals business based on Slough, the eventual hiving off of aircraft parts (engine and test bed seals) and flexible ventilation ducts. The Slough valve operation was merged with Rotherham and the heating business was sold off. The seals, valves and controls division was enlarged by two smaller purchases, one making butterfly valves (from Bovis) and the other making fluid controls (from Guest Keen & Nettlefold Ltd.). An overseas acquisition, intended to open up the American aircraft industry to the products of Slough involved the take-over of a small Californian manufacturer of aircraft ducting equipment.

The Australian subsidiary was the largest and most diversified in the group. Its performance had declined badly in the early 1970s but by the injection of new products and managerial changes it staged a spectacular recovery with profits 60 to 90 per cent up on previous years. This subsidiary has since been granted divisional status in its own right. Other changes were made in the group's various divisions or subsidiaries and the manufacturing base was enlarged by further, minor acquisitions. Also there have been moves to build up the merchanting side and not just the manufacturing facilities in the United Kingdom. More factored goods are being sold side by side with group manufactured items, into a wider spread of industries. This case shows how careful application of simple principles and concepts, applied with considerable common sense can help a company to develop and grow even in tough economic times.

3.7.3 Sony Corporation of Japan

In its 30-odd year existence Sony, building on the brilliance of its engineering team which developed magnetic tape and transistors, through careful innovation, has gone on to become one of the world's leading electronics manufacturers, particularly in consumer products (radios, record players, hi-fi equipment of all kinds etc.). The early innovative drive has not slowed noticeably in recent years. The company still leads the world in the fields of solid state and transistor research. Indeed, one of their scientists won a Nobel Prize.

In the second half of the 1970s, although Sony was making only about one third of its own needs for transistors and integrated circuits at its plant at Atsugi, just outside Tokyo, it has the resources and skills to make everything for audio, radio and television equipment. Such is the corporation's technical strength that it is prepared to be late with the development of new products (e.g. colour T.V.) rather than depend on major purchases of important equipment or components from outside suppliers. The company believes it can produce items to its own high standards to such an extent that any disadvantage due to loss of time in launching a new product is more than offset by the high quality and reliability of the Sony-made product. Experiences with some foreign suppliers of components have not been very happy or successful ones. Thus the company's purchases from other suppliers tend to be limited to simple low value items. However, like the British company Marks & Spencer Ltd., in a totally different field, Sony's policy towards sub-contractors is to guide and foster them in ways that will help them to expand and so strengthen the pattern of mutual help.

The corporation believes that factories should be built close to their markets, where local political and trade union attitudes permit. If there is major opposition it does not force through its ideas but finds an alternative site. This is even though the company believes that exports of items made in foreign countries prove a net benefit to the host country's balance of payments. The company believes also in the importance of the internationalisation of its activities and the internationalising of the products to achieve widespread market acceptance. This leads, it contends, to the maximisation of the benefits from the economies of mass production on a very substantial scale.

There is a genuine desire to make Sony investments real benefits to the overseas regions in which they are made. Often promises are made (and can be kept because of the world-wide nature of the company's marketing) that even when sales slump in some areas in difficult times, there would be no lay-off of employees. Also, management and workers are expected to integrate day-to-day operations and resolve problems by continuous joint cooperation. A truly integrated management operation results. Motivation and job satisfaction are therefore high, as are labour relations and utilisation. However, not all overseas ventures are successful.

For example, the Irish venture at Shannon had to be closed down because it could not compete in making radios to match good cheap products from Hong Kong and other eastern countries. The company insists in the maintenance of its policy that the company will make and sell at high prices, products which can demonstrate a technical advantage or superior quality. This sometimes means that abrupt changes of course are necessary. The company does not hesitate to do this. It withdrew quickly, for example, from transistorised clocks and electronic calculators when it was clear that competitors could offer equally good products at cheaper prices.

However, when new product ideas are held to be important to the company and to have importance for future survival and growth, despite initial teething and other problems, Sony will stick with them until success is assured through the application of its considerable abilities in the technical and marketing fields. In an industry renowned for its rapid changes in technology and end-products, Sony is prepared to do whatever is necessary to keep up with, or preferably ahead of, competition. It always strives to surpass whatever competitors have achieved.

Few Japanese companies are more international in their outlook than Sony. Few also depend on a continuance of the post-war climate of international free trade. To silence growing criticisms of Japanese industry's success in international markets, Sony formed a separate division to handle imports of western products into the Japanese market. Unfortunately, variations in quality and delivery have hindered this venture. A major investment programme was also launched for the manufacture of electrical goods and television overseas, although this has had mixed results. In creating the new division, Sony invited foreign manufacturers to link with one of the more sophisticated marketing networks in Japan. The foreign imports which have proved unsuccessful, failed for technical, quality, delivery and cost reasons. They could not maintain the high standards demanded by Japanese markets. Sony continues to enjoy long-term business success by clearly envisaged policies and decisions which are fully supported by the company's employees and operations. They are also quickly modified when major changes in market and other conditions demand.

3.7.4 The Leiner Group

The Leiner group has been described as the leading private company in the world league. The group celebrated its bi-cententary in 1977 and has prospered through a careful mix of family commitment and pride in their achievements, world-wide connections and operations, and tight management methods. The last work effectively despite rather a long line of communications, unavoidable with truly internationalised ventures. In the United Kingdom it has won the Queen's Award for Industry three times; in 1974 for quadrupling exports of encapsulated products; in 1975 for having doubled exports of pharmaceutical, photographic and edible gelatin products; and in 1976 for continuing to increase exports of encapsulated pharmaceutical, cosmetic and health food products. The group's exports exceeded £12 million ($24 million) a year to over 70 countries.

The group's North American companies were formed in the 1950s. Its factories processing raw materials or manufacturing gelatin and capsules have since been set up in Brazil, Ethiopia, India, Italy, Nigeria and Pakistan. The group is vertically integrated, from collecting and pre-processing raw materials for high grade gelatin production to the manufacture of soft-shelled capsules of gelatin for the health food and pharmaceutical industries. While believing in tradition, Leiner is not afraid of innovation and is actually concerned to develop products with good future prospects. In a highly competitive business, the group is ready and able to move quickly, reacting speedily to market and technological changes.

The group believes in growth and product diversification, especially in the challenging times of the 1970s. An export orientated private company simply cannot stand still or be content to rest on its laurels. The story of how the group created its exporting success is a classic and worth study by other executives.

First, there was the decision to set up marketing subsidiaries in the U.S.A. and Canada. Next, the board realised that diversification into other overseas markets was essential. This required more investment and effort at their home base in Wales. Then, when one of their biggest American customers decided in the early 1960s to discontinue the purchase of soft gelatin from them, Leiner made what proved to be one of its most momentous decisions. This was to sell its own machines to new outlets, risking entry into the difficult technical field of capsule manufacture. This was in addition to the continued expansion of the sales of gelatin. It pushed its way into American chain stores and supermarkets with completed capsules. This required expansion of the marketing organisation and thus further investment in people, so the marketing overheads in the U.S.A. rose by $500,000 a year.

In Brazil, Germany and Japan, the group has continued investing in people by having representatives in all key markets, well supported by home-based technical and other experts. The group's directors travel the world extensively searching for new business and maintaining or reinforcing existing contacts. There is a touch of the old merchant-venturer in all this, but they do not lose sight of simple, down-to-earth management concepts. One important part of this is the ability of senior executives to contact each other regardless of where in the world they may happen to be. The trade union leaders are also able to contact the chairman regardless of where ever he happens to be on his travels.

Further, top management is not introspective, nor does it exude any cosiness, nor does it preen itself over its success and remain content to enjoy its obvious success. As one of the joint chief executives (managing directors) has stated, it is visible management requiring the involvement of all the staff, as far as possible, in the process of making management decisions. Internal and external communications are good. Not surprisingly, the group enjoys equally good industrial relations. Staff can find out with whom to discuss specific problems and how to contact them. They can find out what is going on and know the aims, objectives and purposes of the group. They help executives to decide what should be achieved and how best this might be done. Though the coming years may prove a test of the company's ability to preserve its entre-preneurial flair and warm human relations, as the need for capital and technological skills become more demanding, the executives are excited by the opportunities and challenges.

In the first half of the 1970s the manufacture of gelatin has grown from nil to 30 per cent of total turnover with the penetration of new markets in North America, South-east Asia and Europe. There has also been the creation of new markets for new products (e.g. cider vinegar capsules) and new speciality markets in the pharmaceutical and photographic fields. All their products have interesting prospects in Easten European countries. Their example should be an inspiration even to the smaller companies.

3.7.5 A.H. Williams of Coventry, England

The early part of the 1970s saw the decimation of Britain's construction industry due to the economic recession and government expenditure cut-backs that highlighted that period. It was a time of many bankruptcies. However, the executives of this company were determined not to be numbered amongst the victims. Their activities were mainly in aluminium window frames and demand during this period fell substantially. They resolved to win orders through the development of a bold and imaginative scheme.

To do this they had, initially, to subjugate to second place, the immediate interests of the company's shareholders, existing customers and employees. They formed a marketing consortium (called 'Unit 6') with five other companies in related areas of the construction industry. Its simple aim was to find new markets abroad through the integrated offer of various related products. For small companies with limited resources and manpower (Williams employed just one hundred and thirty people at the time) it was impractical to send a sufficiently large marketing team abroad for this purpose. The vulnerability of companies with a handful of key executives was underlined shortly before the consortium was formed when Williams's sales manager was killed in a car crash in Saudi Arabia shortly after his arrival there. However, this was after reports had been sent home about sales prospects. These showed that developers in the Middle East had strong preferences for packaged deals which allowed the contracting-out of all aspects of supply, finishing and fitting of construction products. It was then that the company was approached by a marketing specialist with the idea of the formation of a marketing consortium.

For the new joint venture the Middle East was an attractive market with its expanding economies based on increasing oil revenues, especially after the hefty price increases for oil. With a shortage of local expertise the markets were open to foreign experts. In addition the company was able to draw upon its association with Warwick University. For each of five years, MSc. students, under their professor, carried out projects that evaluated market opportunities in the Middle East. The reports identified the most promising prospects and what type of effort would prove most appropriate for each of them.

The most crucial part of the exercise was the design and costing of projects since the markets were competitive and offered margins lower than would be acceptable in the United Kingdom in normal circumstances. Accuracy was important and the technical director's contributions were the most critical. While prospects were alluring, in the Middle East they are not easily won. Time delays in fulfilling contracts can also upset pricing calculations.

The company achieved considerable success and by the beginning of 1978 was unwilling to rely solely on United Kingdom contracts for continued success. It continued to look for other export possibilities while at the same time, following up its own sales leads through agents. It also used its contacts in international construction and in other developing countries. This case shows that even small companies with limited resources can win and hold substantial overseas orders and business if they are sufficiently determined to do so and can apply simple management and marketing concepts correctly to their special situations.

3.7.6 The M.A.N. Group of Bavaria, Germany

A few comments about this group would make a useful ending to this chapter for it is one of several German firms which follow concepts completely opposed to what is now held to be the American approach to management theory. It does not hold to the modern cult that tends to over-stress the contributions that management consultants and business schools can make to individualised company situations. Nor does it follow general U.S. practice of recruiting inexperienced graduates of these schools, putting them into jobs and then relying on management development activities to turn them into successful executives. It follows the opposite course, the traditional German approach, based on the belief that managers learn by doing, by facing real problems in real work situations. It believes the best on-the-job training starts at the bottom of the enterprise with the executive working up through the organisation, thereby acquiring as varied an experience as possible as a result. Outsiders, regardless of their qualifications and talents may well be handicapped in German enterprises practising this concept.

M.A.N. is a highly diversified group in its two main areas of activity, commercial vehicles and engineering products. Each accounts for roughly half the turn-over, though the exact proportion varies from year to year depending on the business cycles of these products. The company is organised into four separate divisions, with the commercial vehicle one having its own marketing department. The other three are served by a single marketing organisation. This is necessary as buses, trucks, other public service vehicles, diesel engines and power units have highly specialised markets differing in many respects to those for the engineering products. The last covers a wide range from gas engines, exhaust gas turbo-chargers, oil and gas burners to mechanical handling equipment, railway rolling stock, hydraulic presses, lifts, escalators, pumps and steel structures. The third division builds plants and equipment for the iron, steel and mining industries, sea-going and river ships, floating drydocks, compressors, turbines and forgings. The group has been doing reasonably well despite the recession which has been severe in the capital goods industries. In the year 1976–77 net profits were about £8.75 million ($16 million). This was more or less similar to performance the preceding year but since group turn-over had increased by about 6 per cent, there has obviously been a squeeze on profit margins. Increases in taxation and wages have also contributed to this deadline in profitability. The group has attempted to counter rising labour costs by large-scale rationalisation backed by investment. The five-year rationalisation programme in the commercial vehicle division began to show results by 1977 and the same approach is being tried in the other divisions. Productivity has improved. In the four years from 1972–73 the workforce declined by about 1,000 to a total of 39,000 but turnover rose by over 60 per cent.

The second half of the 1970s has been a challenging time for German industry. It has had to deal with recession, inflation, labour difficulties, technological challenges and currency appreciation, all at the same time. The way M.A.N. tackled the problem is typical of many traditional German companies. Its strategy was to seek further technological advantages and wider geographical penetration by direct exports and acquisition of foreign interests. It is a strategy founded on an old belief that close knowledge of the business can still be maintained in a complex, multi-product-market group, despite many current difficulties. It is a strategy that seems to work in this instance. This case is interesting as it supports for the contention that there is no one, text-book solution to every management problem and that every organisation must modify the theory to suit its own special, practical situations and needs. In some cases, entirely new or opposed solutions will work provided these suit the mentality or philosophy of management and how it works best, or how it wishes to operate. Blind application of the fads of the moment can often prove to be disastrous for a company. It is worth pondering the concepts used by the M.A.N. group.

3.8 Questions

1. What is involved in the subject of risk management? What additional complications arise due to the inter-relationships of the various 'risks' that have to be 'managed'? How can executives go about solving these problems?

2. What is meant by 'management sciences'? What situations or applications are more likely to lead to failure of these activities when used to improve corporate performance? What role can business education play, and how should current practice be modified to increase its usefulness?

3. What is involved in the work of company appraisal? What are the more common failings and how can these be avoided?

4. What is implied by integrated corporate management? What role does planning play here and why are management task forces useful?

5. Why are corporate objectives helpful to managers? What factors influence their inter-relationships and help to decide the priorities that should be given to some of them?

6. Growth, survival and stability are all important to corporate activity. What is necessary to obtain a reasonable balance between these objectives?

7. What changes in attitudes to growth have taken place in recent years? How will these affect the strategy and plans of corporations?

8. What factors will decide whether a company needs specialists or all-rounders in the executive team? How may the former operate most effectively? What are the advantages offered to a company by the latter?

4 Corporate planning

This chapter will not be discussing the components and details of corporate planning in any depth. For those who need such a text, recourse can be made to the many good books on the subject. (*See* the Bibliography for one or two suggestions.) This chapter will concentrate on the conceptual aspects of corporate planning as they relate to integrated management. It will, however, dwell for a while on those parts of corporate planning which are quite often not done well and are sometimes completely overlooked. The basic aim is to show how and where corporate planning slips into the 'quadrille' concept of the book.

Corporate planning is a process wherby an organisation achieves, for the entire business, the systematic development of a comprehensive range of action programmes to reach selected business objectives. It involves detailed analyses, evaluations and forecasts to permit the selection of the optimal opportunities for a corporation from a usually substantial range of possibilities. However, while forecasting is a very important part of the process, it is not itself corporate planning.

Planning has been described as an exercise in foresight, helping an enterprise to decide on the direction it should follow, the pace at which it should proceed and the goals or objectives to be reached in some specified period of time. Logical methods of assessment and analysis are used, but this does not exclude the use, also, of intuition and experience. Intuition is after all the stuff that motivates the true entrepreneur and there is a modicum of entrepreneurship in most executives. Initially, planning is an inaccurate exercise but practice over several years and the build-up of relevant data and information will increase executive skills and thus lead to improved accuracy of forecasts, actions and results obtained. Also, the methods used should be within the capabilities of the executive team and, ideally, should be kept as simple as possible. The greater the sophistication and proficiency of the executive team, the more sophisticated the techniques used could be; but even then simplicity should still be the guiding word.

Forecasting is the cornerstone of planning but forecasts are subject to error for many reasons. First, changes in the business environment will alter the value or impact of some variables. They can also change the inter-relationships between variables and constants. Then the pattern of the past may not be repeated and the time elements of the forecasts may themselves change or have been inaccurate. (When will forecasted events occur? Have some a very low probability of realisation? What are the correct time scales that should be used?) The more distant the future being forecast, the less accurate will be the predictions. There are too many uncertainties and unknowns. Forecasting cannot eliminate all these uncertainties and risks but it can help to reduce the probabilities of major, adverse effects occurring. Forecasting, then, helps the resultant planning to minimise risk and reduce the degree of uncertainty.

Even when there appears to be only one possible course of action planning is still advisable. If done properly, it forces executives to re-examine the rationale, techniques, axioms, beliefs (or myths) on which the company's operations have been based and is thus a soul-searching, purifying process. Corporate planning leads to the proper coordination of all the facets and operations of the business, exposing fallacies, permitting the more efficient use of all resources and indicating alternative courses of action which may not have been known to exist before. In these and other ways, corporate planning helps to avoid the waste of resources, skills and time.

Flexibility in planning and the resultant plans is essential. Executives will respond more positively if they have room to manoeuvre within stated objectives (which are perhaps better written in maximum and minimum terms rather than in single figures). Most do not like being forced to follow a rigid process or system. Humanity responds to the expectations placed on it and planning should place expectations on executives that can be attained with a little extra effort. Giving them objectives that are easily reached may in fact lead only to sloth and over-confidence. A lazy attitude could creep in and executives are then vulnerable to unexpected moves by competitors, changes in customer requirements and technology etc. They will not be mentally tuned to see these problems arising nor to respond quickly enough to them when they have occured. Thus planning must also be based, in part, on foresight and knowledge of the personalities forming the executive team. The last will indicate how the team works best and therefore the best way of presenting the plans and their facts to the executives for maximum, positive response.

The corporate plan is the basic instrument or document that guides corporate management action and ensures the correct and successful application of the integrated management approach, the 'quadrilles' of this book. It is an important link in a continuous and successful communications system, providing all the important information and data to those who need to have them for use, or control purposes. However, all this would only be achieved if corporate planning can emerge from the oft-held belief that it is just a once-a-year gimmicky exercise, which nonetheless is endowed with the miraculous ability to solve all an enterprise's problems at a stroke. While the main planning work must be done at some specified time each year, regular monitoring of results and the introduction of modifications to the plans as necessary, should go on right through each and every trading year. It is thus a continuous process.

Like all so-called 'new' management techniques, corporate planning has suffered from several misconceptions. It has also suffered from the behaviour patterns sometimes encountered with management teams, of which the one mentioned above is perhaps the most damaging. Another is that there can be strong resistance to it. The result may be that some of its supporters will feel bound to 'sell it' strongly to its opponents, leading to 'over-sell'. In this case, the technique is endowed with capabilities it never had and could never realise. Over-selling usually occurs when executives do not really understand the technique and its limitations. When it fails to realise its expectations, the technique is condemned as being of no value, as its opponents had always contended! Other common misconceptions include the belief that corporate planning is just budgetary control extended to cover every activity and it is something that is used when a major diversification programme is required. It suffers also from conceptual misunderstanding when its true purpose and value are hidden in a fog of jargonised semantics.

So again, balance is needed in the mental approach accorded to corporate planning, as it is for all management techniques. A clear understanding is needed of what it can and cannot do, how it may be best applied to an enterprise's operations and how its basic concepts have to be modified to fit the unique conditions that face most corporations from time to time. It is also important to know the common pitfalls that can arise in its use and how these may be avoided. These are discussed fully in books on corporate planning. So executives must not only know the techniques thoroughly but also how to identify and analyse the associated problems.

Further, it is not a one-year process concerned only with making plans for the next trading year. It should cover a period of consecutive years, the exact number depending on the general gestation period of the enterprise. The latter depends on the speed of innovation in the industry and company, how long the company takes to do or achieve targets and aims, the evolution rate of its markets and technologies and the mental abilities of the executives, measured by the speed at which they can work or appreciate problems and propositions put to them. The complexity of the business and the number of technologies in which the enterprise is involved, the resources available, market, economic and competitive situations will also determine the time scale to be used. This means that corporate planning periods are usually not less than three years long, more usually about five years, and normally do not exceed seven to ten years because of the difficulty of forecasting so far ahead. Whatever the period, the planning is done on a rolling plan basis. The periods used to review and revise plans are important. Again, these will vary from company to company but it is usual to review progress at the end of each reporting period (weekly for fast moving consumer goods, monthly for most other products) with revisions to plans made every three periods. This gives time to ascertain if any change that has occurred in the business environment is temporary or permanent in nature.

4.1 Effective management

Since the phrase 'effective management' is mentioned from time to time in this book, a few words on the subject are appropriate. People have misconceptions on what 'effective management' (or 'managerial effectiveness') means. It is not some peculiar quality that executives bring with them to their jobs. Nor is it the same as 'efficient management', though efficiency in management cannot be achieved without effectiveness. Effectiveness is more an input into management tasks, whereas efficiency can be measured by the various outputs that result. It is more the extent or manner by which executives achieve the output requirements placed on them. Effectiveness is something that is achieved in any situation by managing it properly. It is the manager's chief task, some say only job, to be effective.

Managers who are effective think in terms of performance, not personality. It is not so much what is done but what is achieved that matters. Thus it is something more than leadership. Some leaders are more effective than others! So every management job has effectiveness standards associated with it, even if these are not known or appreciated. It is suggested that job specifications should be so written as to state clearly what these effectiveness standards are. The difference between efficiency and effectiveness can be illustrated by the following comparisons:

—doing things right, rather than doing right things;
—solving problems, rather than producing creative alternatives;
—producing lower costs, rather than increasing profits;
—safeguarding resources, rather than optimising the utilisation of resources;
—carrying out assigned duties, rather than obtaining agreed results.

Thus while a leader is a person seen by others as one primarily responsible for motivating people to achieve objectives, *leader effectiveness* measures the extent to which a leader succeeds in influencing subordinates to achieve their group's objectives. *Apparent effectiveness* is the extent to which a leader appears to be effective, while *managerial effectiveness* is the extent to which managers achieve the output requirements of their jobs. *Personal effectiveness* is the extent to which an executive or other person, achieves private objectives. Integrated corporate management is primarily concerned with achieving high standards of managerial and leadership effectiveness.

4.1.1 Principles of managerial effectiveness

The basic principles involved are quite simple and can be learnt from an appropriate book. The approach needed is summarised here.

First, executives must decide what has to be put into practice if they wish to be more effective. This requires obtaining a clear understanding of their potential contribution to the enterprise and what improvements are necessary. Next, executives must know what effectiveness standards apply to them and their jobs, especially the objectives or outputs that have to be achieved. The next logical step is to decide what is required to make the executives more effective, especially vital changes in attitudes and actions needed to bring this about. This should be considered in the light of the company's business philosophy and strategy. Are they conducive to these changes? If they are not, then the company must consider a much bigger task: reviewing whether philosophy and strategy should be changed. This is not easy to do unless the whole company team is interested in improving its collective and individual effectiveness.

There are other considerations. For example, how can the effectiveness of superiors, colleagues and subordinates be improved? This, too, will take time to achieve and presents all sorts of inter-personal and operational difficulties but is still worth doing. Next, does any change in technology seem essential? This requires a hard and long look at the future prospects of the company and its executives. It may well be that, at the end of all this, the executives will have to decide whether to change their jobs within or outside the enterprise. Many job changes have been influenced by such considerations. Executives find other jobs because they are dissatisfied with their effectiveness in their present positions — not only for simple advancement — and feel that the necessary corporate changes cannot be affected. So this is a cautionary tale for top managers. If they wish to improve the effectiveness of their subordinates, their own attitudes and expectations may have to be changed also. They may even have to alter the corporate philosophy and objectives.

How does a corporation improve its organisational effectiveness? First, it must be prepared to make adaptations to suit changing business conditions and, above all, maintain flexibility in its planning and operations. Next, it must mentally unfreeze the organisation and thereby revitalise managers. To do this, discussion meetings, formal seminars and conferences may be all that are required. The chief executive, acting for the board, would have to present proposals or suggestions on how the philosophy, strategy and methods of operation could be altered to improve executive effectiveness and talk them through at various meetings until mutually acceptable ideas are agreed. Usually these will represent some considerable compromises by all parties. Then the strategy and objectives will have to be re-examined and re-stated with the implementation of any modifications to operational plans that might be necessary. The main reorganisation will usually be in the structure of the enterprise and the communications network if this has not been operating well enough. Then the management teams will be reformed.

4.2 Problems

Companies fail for many reasons, ranging from over-centralisation to decentralisation ineffectively carried out, incorrect diversification or merger, poor cash flow positions, resistance or inability to change and the many others discussed in Chapter 1. The main cause of failure depends on the type of company in question. These have been defined by some management theorists as Types I, II and III.

Type I organisations are those that are launched but never manage to get off the ground or become firmly established. They fail within a few years. This type comprises some 60 per cent of all company failures in the western industrialised world. Failure is due to the sales level never reaching the point where survival is assured. This could be due to initial marketing research being faulty and wrongly estimating total demand, market shares and competition. Or the formulation might not meet customers' approval, or faults and delays in manufacturing undermine prospects. Lack of finance, leading to insufficient plant and limited production can also be contributing factors to failure. If the company has obtained substantial loans from the banks it will find, when sales levels are not realised, that it has made the fatal mistake of having given the banks excessive leverage.

Type II companies are those launched by so-called entrepreneurs in a blaze of publicity. Partly as a result of this and the (possibly inflated) reputation of their initiators the companies soar to quite fantastic levels of prosperity in a very short space of time, only to collapse in an equal blaze of (adverse) publicity! These are relatively rare cases and the real cause of failure is that they are based on little substance; business houses built on business quicksands. However, they give few outward signs of impending trouble and the various reasons for their failure are difficult to identify. The reasons may include over-optimism on the part of the proprietors, the products or services may be short-term gimmicks, there may have been an under-estimation of the capital needed and unit costs of production and an over-estimation of the prices they could command. They may also have overlooked better, cheaper substitute products and thus under-scored the competition they would meet. Or customers may just not be interested. Even though they change and adapt quickly to economic conditions, all their other problems prove too great for them to overcome.

Another reason may be the autocratic entrepreneurship of the founder(s) whose knowledge of sound business practice is negligible. Thus when the company reaches a size that makes it impossible for the entrepreneur to control it by intuitive effort, the whole edifice collapses. The rate of growth of Type II companies, if it could be maintained, would mean that in a few years they would outstrip the largest corporations in the world. The improbability and absurdity of this escapes the attention of observers at least in the early years. If they paused to think about the implications of what was happening to these companies, their ultimate collapse would be no surprise. Only a few of these cases arise in the western world. The average seems to be about one a year. In developing countries they hardly occur since there is no scope there for this type of company.

Type III companies are the mature, well-established ones that last for decades and centuries. There are no signs of impending disaster as far as the observer is concerned but employees may know that some seeds of future disaster exist. These include all the ones discussed in Chapter 1. Sometimes they do not have a finance director or equivalent to provide the company with expert advice, or the chief accountant's budgetary control methods and reports are hardly ever studied in depth and understood.

Common to most companies is the fact that failure takes some time to happen. Collapse is never really an overnight affair. All or some of the symptoms are present in some form long before the failure is evident but they are ignored, or not understood, until the trauma of disaster occurs. Two recent examples of warning signs not being noticed were the British merchant bank that bought £1 million of the equity of a Japanese company in 1975, just two weeks before it failed; and the collapse of Court Line whose bankers realised that 'a new dimension of risk' existed, just thirteen days before the company went into liquidation.

Other common threads include poor response to change which is usually linked with failure to have any form of corporate or forward planning. The latter and its work will make it clear that the need to forecast possible changes, and the preparation for such changes should they occur, are essential if the company's long-term survival is to be assured. Then, there is the failure to keep abreast of technical developments or to keep the plant up-to-date and capable of producing the quality and quantity of product expected by customers. Another is allowing the company to over-trade and as a result, stretching already limited financial resources beyond reasonable bounds. Finally, probably because of the last point, there may be savage cost reduction programmes which so effectively reduce operating costs that the company can hardly handle its current business, never mind find the resources to develop and grow. These are the sorts of problems that assail different types of companies but the three most serious, indeed fatal, mistakes, undoubtedly, are high leverage, over-ambitious projects and over-trading. Corporate planners should always be on the look-out for these early signs of impending danger and, by and large, they handle this side of the work well. However, there is always the question of bad luck which can arise to upset even the best plans, but good planners are prepared for this. They include plans to counter bad luck with those for remedial actions which would be necessary if the warning signs mentioned are discovered.

4.2.1 Pitfalls

Common pitfalls associated with corporate planning include mistaken belief that corporate planners necessarily have better information and conduct better analyses than line executives. They do not, but they have the time and detachment to be more watchful for the more critical mistakes getting through the analyses. The greatest effectiveness is achieved when corporate planners and line executives work together on a continual basis. The corporate planners' main contribution springs from their more objective approach to the work of the company. It is mostly devoid of the bias, prejudices and politics that usually assail line executives at every turn.

There is a belief that corporate planning can be introduced regardless of the state of the existing budgetary and control systems. It cannot. If these systems are inadequate for the company's historical way of doing things, they will be even more so when corporate planning is introduced. Corporate planning (and integrated corporate management for that matter) is a much bigger, more detailed, and in that sense complex, activity and poor budgetary and control systems would not be able to sustain them to the high standards that are needed.

Another misconception is that corporate planning is a centralised activity. It may be physically convenient so to locate the section dealing with this work but it is only successful when there is a sufficient degree of involvement and participation in corporate planning by all executives and in all corporate activities. How this is actually organised and structured will again depend on how the enterprise likes to do things and operates best. Nor is it true that even committed executives will adapt rapidly to the longer time horizons involved in corporate planning. Practice has shown that they will need time to adapt and adjust their thinking and actions to the new requirements. Cases show that from one to two years may be needed for this. It is a psychological adjustment and like most such, cannot be rushed. Attempting to force the pace usually leads only to failure of the corporate planning process or, far worse, strong resistance to its concepts.

Some senior executives use the corporate planning operation as an excuse to push through a complex set of changes, some of which may have little to do with corporate planning but have been managerial necessities in any event. If changes are needed, regardless of corporate planning, they should be introduced in their own right. Also, some think that a good response to a crisis is to introduce corporate planning. This is not so. Any crisis needs special diagnosis in some depth and the careful selection and application of the necessary therapy. This action should be taken first, before corporate planning can be introduced effectively.

Further, there is the belief that the corporate planner's role is best done by a person highly trained in all modern management techniques. While reasonable knowledge of economics, financial skill, and an ability to handle and interpret statistics are essential, the best planner is one able to take an all-round (corporate) view. The person should also be a respected member of the executive team whose reputation, based on past performance, gives the planner the necessary senior stature. In other words, a person who is accepted by colleagues as one who knows the work and is able and willing to help line executives be better operators.

Finally, there are the misconceptions that arose in the early years of corporate planning and still persist in places. These include the view that corporate planning is just normal strategic planning stretched over a longer time scale; that it is the usual budgetary system also stretched over a longer period; or it is a method for dealing with a specific, isolated problem. It is of course none of these things. However, they all feature from time to time in the corporate planning process and the resultant plans.

4.2.2 Corporate life cycles

Everything in the world has a finite life span. What it is varies according to the subject concerned and the ability of mankind to change and to adapt to new circumstances. How well all this is done will determine how long the life cycle of the subject may be extended. So, not only products and markets have life cycles, but also corporations and enterprises. They pass through the similar stages of introduction, growth, maturity, saturation of demand and decline. In the case of corporations, technological change can accelerate the decline stage. Identifying where in its life cycle a corporation is at any time is vital if forward planning is to be effective. For some, however, it may be a difficult and not fully understood art. It is nonetheless an interesting and challenging task. Some academics have been formulating theories on this subject. Some of them are interesting but all have yet to be proved in practice.

Most of these theories are based on analyses of the different managerial motivations, problems and priorities which arise as an enterprise grows from a small company to a medium-sized one and, finally, to a large corporation. These aspects are also influenced by the countries in which the companies are based and how those nations develop. The more mature the economy the more it will change from one that is export-orientated (usually of primary products) to one that is based on a mixture of industry and agriculture. The companies themselves will then alter from importers of foreign-made products eventually to manufacturers of these same products in their host countries. The corporate life cycles will be altered accordingly, usually extended. However, the main cause of changes in motivations, problems and priorities arise from the fact that the larger a company the more complex are its operations and the greater the demands made on the capabilities of the executives. Whether the life of the company will be extended or shortened as a result depends on how well executives can cope with the challenges.

The problems are greatest at the thresholds, where a company is moving say, from being a medium-sized one for many years, to a large corporation. This 'threshold' is in fact quite wide in terms of years, since it takes some time to grow to this extent. However, the threshold where a small company passes over to being a medium-sized one is much more quickly passed and can represent an abrupt or rude awakening or shock to the executives. Often they do not realise or notice that this important change is occurring and that a total reappraisal of the company's organisations and methods is needed. This transition is often the most painful part of a company's history. New experts may be recruited in a hurry and if the corporate appraisal has not been well done, the unfortunates may soon have to be dismissed. The wrong people may have been recruited or the new requirements of the company may turn out to be quite different from the forecasts. These are usually stressful times for executives, especially if they try to adapt too quickly to the new circumstances. The threshold where a large corporation is moving to a multi-national condition is less traumatic as the development is usually planned in advance or has evolved slowly as the overseas business developed and the host countries became more industrialised. (*See also* Section 2.5.)

A metamorphosis of management is necessary at each transition and this cannot be successful if it is hurried or carried out on some piecemeal basis. It needs the coordinated and balanced approach of integrated corporate management and corporate planning. With the former the necessary degree of cooperation and understanding is in existence. With the latter, the forecasts and predictions for the future will indicate in ample time, what has to be done and the correct timing for all the work. One of the main points on which more thought will have to be given is whether businesses and academic institutions should continue to train and develop narrowly-based specialists or concentrate more on the development of internationally orientated potential general managers, i.e. the all-rounder. If the success of major corporations which have been able to transform themselves into truly international operations is anything to go by, it would seem that the right emphasis would be the latter.

4.2.3 Forecasting the future

Since corporate planning has an immediate and futuristic element to it, forecasting future trends and developments is necessary. It is also one of the more difficult things to do successfully. This forecasting has to take into account not only the changes in the usual environmental factors (economic, technological, political, legal and social) but also the status of the enterprise itself, its industry's conditions and likely trends, similar aspects of present and future customers' technologies and industries, the national business scene and international aspects. The last is important when there is likelihood of a move to international operations. The work is not easy because of the inherent uncertainties and unknowns that would be involved. Hence the assumptions on which long-term forecasts are based will contain a certain element of inaccuracy and vagueness, and this cannot be avoided. Forecasting must try to take into account, also, the probable effects of the problems and difficulties that will be encountered when a corporation is making a major change in size or in the scope of its operations.

Thus, executives have to consider not only the tangible points (things that can be measured or are known in some way) but also intangibles such as the company's reputation, image and knowledge of new product-market situations, especially the local condition of new overseas markets. They must differentiate between what they can control and what are beyond their control (e.g. foreign government decisions, laws and regulations). Finally, the factors under study should be divided between those that are reasonably forseeable and those that are not. Of all these, government policies and technological developments prove to be the most difficult things to forecast. The former requires sound knowledge of political history and political science, with indepth knowledge of the people, country and its politicians, particularly their behaviour patterns. Even then the forecasts may appear to approximate to 'inspired guesses'. Technological forecasting requires the necessary technical knowledge, foresight and luck. All need considerable information and data to help the forecasters and this calls for really well-integrated marketing and other research programmes seeking knowledge on questions of immediate importance and likely future events.

Thus marketing research attains far greater importance in integrated corporate management than it would have if restricted to meeting relatively simple and shorter-term marketing needs. Technological forecasting is an extensive and complicated subject. It and its techniques form the texts of many good books and readers wishing to learn more about this subject should have recourse to them. Its importance became clear as corporate planning became more widely accepted. Since corporate planning is a strategic concept, with present and futuristic components, executives could no longer sit and await the next relevant technological happening. They had to try to perceive what developments they needed to make the future happen for their corporations. They had to attempt to foretell what was likely to occur so that they could be ready to exploit events when the anticipated developments took place. In attempting to bring potential future developments into focus, technological forecasting aimed at targets which differed qualitatively from whatever was the current state of activity of the enterprise. Originally, forecasting followed the principles of linearity and sequentiality. This extrapolative forecasting meant that long-term intentions were adapted to match the changes. The present tendency is to forecast, through the corporate plans, future needs and required technologies and then to see if technological developments can be matched to produce the desired results. Therefore, technological forecasting must provide much of the material on which the new enterprise system is to be built.

In practice, successful executives also continue to plan to exploit the results of on-going technological developments. Thus this forecasting should be done on three different levels: that of strategic planning, policy planning and operational planning. In the first, the aim is the recognition and comparative evaluation of alternative technology options. In the second, it must determine the future boundaries for corporate development. In the last, it is concerned with the probabilistic assessment of future technology transfers. Corporate planning here aims to determine the good strategies to be followed, selected from a broad base of alternatives. Technological forecasting at the strategic level is required to enrich the basis of this selection.

However, executives must keep their eyes wide open of they wish to avoid the mistakes commonly made, even today, when they try to forecast future trends and development. There are a number of points they must keep in mind. First, purchases will not be made in the same business context as in the present. Various things will have changed including the nature and technologies of industries and nations. Then, demand for different products will alter as will the patterns of demand for individual products. Next, prices and pricing structures will also change, dependent upon changes in the general economic, technological, political and social environments. These changes will also affect demand patterns, potential for growth and business in general.

Next, customers' order of priority for the purchase or consumption of different items do not follow any set patterns for long and whatever pattern exists could change gradually or suddenly for no discernible reason. Many of the changes in purchasing patterns may be due to rational reasons but there will also be some irrationality. The actual mix of rational/irrational reasons that is encountered will usually depend on the importance and cost of the purchase and whether potential customers see the products bought as being essentials for them or just frivolities.

Then some competitors in every industry will change their attitudes on, or ideas for, certain products, technologies, raw materials and even markets or consumers which are important to their current and future business. So they may initiate product-market and manufacturing changes which may have a profound effect on general demand and expectations for different products or services. These may trigger off a new family of products which change the entire business picture for certain industries. This may or may not be brought about by successful new products such as Xerography, which completely altered the needs and processes in most offices for reprographic purposes, or computers which have revolutionised data processing and other procedures for most companies. Or some entrepreneurial marketing person may get a bright idea that fires the imagination of potential customers and reveals an unsatisfied need. (E.g. Britain's Sir Freddie Laker and his 'Skytrain' air service, introduced in 1977 which, if the idea is extended, could revolutionise the whole of long distance air travel. In 1978 the first moves to extend this idea were made by scheduled airlines, led by the big national companies.) Demand in these markets will never be the same as in previous years.

Alternatively, consumers may change their ideas on what may be ideal about any product. For example in the 1950s and 1960s, the trend for cars seemed to be towards bigger and bigger models offering great comfort and associated status symbols. By the 1970s, with oil prices rising, leading to substantial increases in petrol prices, growing awareness of the need to conserve fuel supplies in some cases backed by government pressure and economic pressures reducing everyone's net discretionary incomes, the trend seems to be reversed. Interest is growing in the smaller cars offering fuel economies.

Then sudden interest in the possible side-effects of some drugs or food additives could change demand patterns. In Britain and some other countries, when the possible dangerous effects of cyclamate sweeteners were publicised, the government moved swiftly to ban their usage. (Some said the speed was close to that of a panic!) Demand for these products evaporated while demand for alternatives increased. And so one could go on. The warning therefore is not to assume that projections of current conditions, however modified to suit forseeable economic and other logical trends, will be enough. Much thought is needed from corporate planners and executives generally on all aspects of changes that could occur, especially in the most difficult area, that of technology.

4.2.4 *Ecology and environment*

In many countries today, society is growing increasingly concerned about the damage that is being done to the world's ecology and the environment generally. While much of this deterioration and destruction can be traced back to population growth and the unthinking or selfish habits of individuals, industry and the business community are not without their share of the blame. Thoughtless or selfish actions ranging from the discharge of harmful effluents and vapours to the development of products that are thrown away after use, adding to the waste disposal problems, feature frequently in critical articles in the media and on television and radio programmes. These are increasing the social pressures on companies to raise their values and standards regarding the polluting effects of their activities. A similar improvement is expected of individuals but industry is expected to lead in this.

Executives should therefore give more thought and attention to these aspects and incorporate appropriate actions into their operational plans. No longer is the mere pursuit of profit an exclusive criterion of management. Maintaining the right balance of nature is vital for the survival of the world. The basic resources of land, water, air and minerals are finite and their correct use and conservation are vital to survival of all concerned, including industry. Profligate use of them can no longer be tolerated and corporations must economise on the use of all scarce resources. This is despite the increasing demands being made on resources and manufactured products by a growing population that is demanding ever higher standards of living, reflected in product and service demands. This is another aspect of social responsibility that should be included in future corporate plans.

Attempts to correct the situation have often been fragmentary and even then only concerned with short-term aspects. Very little has been done to achieve a coordinated approach that also takes into account long-term considerations. Executives must therefore evolve more comprehensive solutions to the problems of damage to the environment and ecology and the conservation of resources. Perhaps adding the following principles to corporate objectives might prove helpful.

1. Conservation of all resources is the responsibility not only of individuals but also of enterprises.

2. Natural resources must not be wasted, damaged or seriously depleted for purely short-term or local, selfish purposes.

3. While each nation should assume responsibility for adherence to these guidelines and enterprises must honour the laws and regulations that exist, in countries where there are no such laws, corporations should follow the best precepts of other nations.

While progress will depend on nations' ability to stabilise population growth, the full answer will only be found when enterprises ensure that resources are used with discretion and economy and all harmful practices are stopped. It may mean that several tenets on which modern economic activity is based may have to be changed. People may no longer be able to have what they want, but only what is best for society! It will mean that a new dimension, strange to corporations and corporate planners, will have to be added to their planning and decision-making processes. This is embodied in a new question for planners to ponder: 'Are our plans beneficial to society?' If the answer is negative then the associated actions should be rejected. Irksome though this may be and reminiscent of the Age of Big Brother, it seems unavoidable if the world's survival and high standards of living are to be sustained, with less fortunate people given a chance to improve their lot.

4.2.5 The spoilers

Corporate planning points the way for the future development and business of a company. Corporate appraisals try to measure whether a company has the right resources and skills to get there, what additional skills are required, whether the company will go off target along the way, why this might happen and what remedial actions would then be necessary. To do this well, the exercise cannot ignore the people making up the organisation. It must recognise that companies are people whose attitudes and opinions must be taken into account and whose support must be won.

However, there will always be some people who doubt whether what is proposed will be possible, or are resistant to every change, or simply are antagonistic to all proposals from certain quarters. Corporate planning that concentrates on products, techniques and customers but ignores the people employed by the company will run into difficulties. Resultant plans will fail to achieve targets. So it must be remembered that evaluation of the workforce is an essential element of corporate planning. This must go as far as understanding the jealousies that exist. For example, there will be some executives who are determined to undermine the standing of others, regardless of the damage done to the company. They have no interest in achieving planned results. The corporate plans must take this into account, especially if senior management is reluctant to take the only remedy: dismiss such spoilers.

Then there may be a department that has a rapid staff turnover. The manager may be energetic, able, highly regarded by superiors and be a person who works very hard. However, the manager's fault and the reason for this turnover, may be refusal to delegate the work correctly. Somehow this problem must be overcome, even if replacing the manager is the only solution. Perhaps he or she could be moved to another job where this trait is no longer important and does not have adverse effects. Otherwise this type of manager will become yet another 'spoiler of plans'.

Feelings and subjective reactions have considerable impact on the course of every business and can undermine the success of even the best corporate plans. If persons are temperamentally unsuited to their roles, this will be reflected in their performance. Then the ways in which executives achieve a high level of performance must be understood. Some respond to impossible challenges. Others prefer calmer, more harmonious working conditions and these form the majority of a workforce. Some work best on a tight rein, while others prefer freedom of action within clearly specified terms of reference. Assessment of inter-personal relationships is also advisable and it should be remembered that some otherwise good executives will turn into spoilers themselves in retaliation for the destructive attitudes and actions of natural-born spoilers. (These points are discussed further in Chapter 8.)

4.3 Objectives

The quantitative objectives that should feature in corporate plans include:

—profit or profitability
—return (on capital, or investment)
—turnover and volume of business
—market shares, and
—annual rates of growth for the above,

plus any other management ratios that help to achieve greater efficiency in management activities. However, there are over 300 known ratios, but not all are relevant to a business or have much value. Indeed it has been claimed, that only about twenty of these ratios have any real useful purpose for managers. So care is needed in selecting the ratios to be used. The contributions they can make to improving management need to be queried very closely.

Besides these quantitative standards, there should be others such as targets for cash flows and the creditor/debtor positions. Then some aiming marks should be set, for such considerations as utilisation of capital, price/earnings ratio, liquidity, risk reduction and acceptable levels of wastage in the manufacturing process. Targets can be set similarly for other activities in manufacturing, marketing and personnel including such key items as standard of labour utilisation, labour turnover and cost reductions.

Then there should be qualitative objectives. These help to set the rationale or philosophy of the business. For example, there may be a statement that no new idea will be contemplated unless it can provide £x profit and £y turnover by the end of the 'z−th' year. What values are given to 'x', 'y' and 'z' will depend on the industry, markets and technology concerned and how quickly the company can react or respond to opportunities. Or there may be a statement that the company will only enter into new fields where it has the strength and resources to compete successfully and achieve specified market share targets in a stated period of time. Or there may be a further statement that acquisitions will only be contemplated in industries or with companies, whose poor performance is due to the lack of certain skills or expertise which happen to be plentiful in the acquiring firm. The company's prestige and image may also be featured. In specifying and implementing qualitative objectives there is the same need to maintain flexibility as with planning and the other considerations mentioned in Section 3.5.

Setting objectives is not an easy task (*see* Section 3.5). With growing awareness of a corporation's social responsibilities, the task of setting objectives becomes more difficult each year. Pressures from new lobbies also add to the difficulties. Increasing government involvement and control of business further restricts a company's freedom of action and so the corporate objectives it could be aiming for in future years. It is unlikely that the tasks of executives will get any easier in the foreseeable future. There is no alternative to the fact that executives must get down to obtaining a thorough understanding of the basic principles and theories of management, forsaking the less relevant, more gimmicky, so-called modern techniques.

4.3.1 Validity

When the objectives have been provisionally selected, it is worth checking their validity. For example, are the corporate objectives compatible with the developments and aims of the national economy? If it is a multi-national corporation, are all the objectives (of parent and subsidiaries) compatible with the national economies of the home and host countries? How do they fit host governments' aims and aspirations and the other points mentioned in Section 2.5? How would the objectives ensure long-term survival and the degree of stability and flexibility required? Can the corporation develop internally, or obtain from external sources, all the skills and resources required to achieve the objectives? Would their cost meet the financial parameters set by the corporate objectives? Do they balance the conflicting claims of shareholders, government, suppliers, customers and all employees? Finally, will the intended unit profit margins and the estimated sales volume of all the company's products produce the corporate profit that has been set as an objective for each of the years in the corporate plans? This is the one that is most overlooked, yet executives are surprised when the sum of the year's efforts does not meet the (after-tax) profit target. Given the amount of time spent in setting pricing policies, in costing and pricing and then marketing the products, it is a pity if this small but vital calculation is not made. With pocket calculators and computers available it is now no longer a tedious and time-consuming task to carry out this verification.

In checking the validity of objectives it may also be helpful to try to obtain the answers to the following questions. Given the known and forecasted constraints likely to be encountered, is it true to believe they would not impair the chances of success? What is the risk factor? Do the objectives balance the claims of marketing, manufacturing, finance and personnel departments and the technical operations of the company? Is the management structure strong enough to handle the implications of the plans and objectives? What resistance to change is likely to be encountered? What training and development needs are indicated and can these be attained? Are the objectives sufficiently challenging and stimulating to bring out the best in all members of the company, or at least the key people? It is also worth checking if the objectives and targets are feasible by reference to interim comparison.

4.3.2 Attitudes to shareholders/stockholders

In the corporate planning process, executives must also consider what their attitude and policy will be regarding the shareholders and their dividend expectations, since this will have some effect on the objectives selected and the ability of the company to obtain the necessary financial support. How far should the company be run for the benefit of shareholders/stockholders and how should their interests be balanced with those of other equally important groups and the long-term aims of the corporation? In many cases the p/e ratio will be the one objective influenced by these considerations. What levels are expected by shareholders and what levels will make the company an attractive investment prospect to them and other sources of finance? How will decisions here affect the raising of future capital on advantageous terms? What growth in earnings per share would satisfy shareholders and others? What sort of image, market standing, market leadership or reputation do they expect the enterprise to gain and hold? Companies must comply with the laws of the lands in which they operate, but how do shareholders expect the company to honour the spirit as well as the letter of the law? This is a crucial point for multi-nationals.

Shareholders do not generally judge a company solely by its financial growth. Their attitudes are also influenced by the company's overall reputation and its readiness at all times to honour the spirit of the laws that govern it. Institutional shareholders appear to be committed to long-term holdings. They face the problem of having a very substantial inflow of funds at regular intervals, all of which must be invested as advantageously as possible. Pension fund managers face this problem most acutely as the size of the funds swells very substantially with each passing year. At the same time, they have a limited choice of acceptable outlets and so face the task of having to dispose of massive funds in ventures which offer good long-term prospects, especially growth in capital worth and dividends, and security. The private investors, according to their needs, will be seeking income, security or long-term capital appreciation or any combination of these three. So in all events, pressures will continue to be placed on executives to improve the performance of their companies not only in financial terms but also sociological ones, if they wish to keep their shareholders content.

4.3.3 Corporate strategy

Strategy is concerned with the question of choice from the alternative opportunities open to the corporation. Selection of the corporate strategy to be followed involves the identification of these alternatives, the collection and evaluation of relevant information, and the selection of the better alternatives and decisions on the strategy that could then be followed. This requires disciplined thinking, including the ability to assess the associated problems that are involved.

However, operations planning is concerned primarily with optimal achievement of what has to be done as a result of strategy decisions; yet strategy decisions cannot be divorced from operational intentions (and vice versa). For example, what should the company's strategy be regarding performance improvement of existing products in current markets? What effects would such improvement have on the strategy possibilities open to the company? Also, what new products should be developed for existing and new markets? What new markets should be opened up to existing products? What product modifications and rationalisation would be required over the life of the corporate plan?

Then there is the question of the diversification strategy to be followed which should cover acquisitions, mergers and divestments. Associated with this are questions concerned with whether, and to what extent, the company will vary its organisational structure and administrative arrangements. Next, decisions are required on the growth targets that should be achieved, the competitive advantages that are expected and whether the firm will expand its own manufacturing facilities. The last is dependent on the growth that is required in the product range and sales and decisions whether to make everything or to buy in components, leaving the company only final assembly work. In other words, before strategy decisions can be taken, the entire corporate entity and its activities must be studied in depth, i.e. corporate appraisal is necessary.

As with objectives, it makes sense to test the validity of the intended strategy. How consistent will it be internally and in the company's business environment, especially in current and future markets? What risks are involved? How will future constraints prevent the achievment of the strategy's goals? How satisfactory is the allowance for business and other changes? What would be the outcome if these changes were greater or smaller than implied by the allowances made for them? Is the time period of the strategy adequate for its fulfilment? Is the strategy workable? What in fact will be its impact on future growth prospects? Will it inhibit long-term growth through over-stimulating short-term developments?

4.3.4 Short- v. long-term needs

This is a common conundrum for executives and has come up in various discussions already in this book. Suprisingly however, this dichotomy sometimes gets forgotten in the rush of the corporate planning stage. Also, over-emphasis on short-term needs continues to predominate because of the intense pressures on executives to achieve what is described as 'present profits'. However, this preoccupation with immediate profit can so absorb resources of all kinds that it prevents long-term development and possibly the survival of the company. Often also, the personalities of the chief executive, or other senior executives, unknown to them, may produce powerful demands or hints for immediate results. If the corporate planning team's personality is not strong enough to counter these pressures and keep a right balance between short- and long-term needs, then the over-emphasis on present profits and other short-term requirements will continue. The team should also consider the longer term consequences of actions taken, correctly, to satisfy short-term needs.

On the other hand, if the senior executives are too enthusiastic about corporate and long-range planning, it is possible for over-emphasis to be given to long-term aspects of the business, to the detriment of the need for some immediate results, especially profit. There is sometimes the tendency, when business conditions are difficult for executives to try to escape, ostrich fashion, from the hard realities of the present by evolving spectacular long-range growth and development plans.

However, if the root causes of their present problems are not solved then, at worst, their chances of surviving into that 'golden future' are slight and at best, they would encounter growing difficulties in trying to implement their plans and achieve their long-term goals. So that once again, it is clear that successful executives are those who can maintain a calm balance in their approach to, and resolution of, inherent conflicts between short- and long-term needs of their business enterprise.

4.3.5 Growth

Decisions on the growth that a company should aim for cannot be reached solely from consideration of marketing factors. Financial strategies and capabilities are equally important determinants of what can be done. While marketing and survival aspects will state what ideal growth is needed, financial considerations will indicate what is practical. Thus, if financial executives default in any way on their responsibilities they can have a disastrous effect on growth achievement.

For example, if too rigid quantification (e.g. discounted cash flow) is used in evaluating the deployment of assets, the alternative paths to growth can be obscured or distorted. Leaving factors which cannot be quantified easily to intuition or hunches can have similarly disastrous effects. Insistence on all projects achieving 'black figures' as soon as possible (i.e. too early achievement of profit through the elimination of avoidance of all risk; an impossibility anyway) denies the unavoidable need to take calculated risks from time to time for the sake of better long-term growth and profitability.

This lack of creative financial planning leads to conflicting objectives and policies for financial parameters, especially growth, liquidity and the return on shareholders' investments. The enforcement of uniform or minimum rates of return criteria, regardless of the different conditions that may apply to each project, is another manifestation of restricted creativity in financial management. The reluctance, or the refusal, to accept the need to balance risk against return limits the corporation's growth prospects and strategic choices. It will also limit decisions on long-term acquisitions and the development of future financial resources and the best methods of financing future growth. The sustainable rate of growth depends partly on the rate at which the company can generate funds for commitment to the attainment of growth targets and partly on the effect that resultant divided policies and turnover of capital will have on the ability of the company to raise new capital.

Flexibility and creativity in debtor policy is also needed. Relatively liberal use of debt enables a company to accept lower profit margins, overcoming short-term cost disadvantages and allowing capture of a greater share of markets. Thus, a higher rate of growth than the industry's norm may be possible. The company could also pay more for assets such as capacity. Of course there may be valid reasons why such debtor policies should or should not be followed. However, a flexible, open mind should be kept until all the relevant facts are known when more appropriate decisions on this and other financial policies, can be taken. The decisions will have bearing on the credit control and gearing policies that should be followed.

Thus decisions on growth depend on many inter-related aspects. First, there are the financial policies and objectives which must be considered, with the debt and risk elements involved. Next pricing policies and the competitive cost/price situations must be considered. Also important are forecasts of the growth of the industries in which the company operates and of customers' industries. Finally, the question of dividend policy must be considered. When these are linked with other marketing, manufacturing, personnel and long-term corporate objectives, the right growth decisions for the company can be taken.

4.4 Diversification

Executives will need from time to time to consider moves to diversify the company's operations if they are to ensure long-term growth and development of the firm. To most executives, diversification means developing new products for new markets, obtaining manufacturing and marketing licences and company acquisition and merger. However, there is also the question of divestment and company reorganisation. The last will be necessary to some degree or other whichever aspect of diversification is involved. Failure to appreciate this and to see that sufficient reorganisation has been carried through is often the reason why efforts at diversification of all kinds fail, or prove disappointing in terms of the results accruing to the parent organisation.

4.4.1 Reorganisation

Reorganising an enterprise is a tough mental exercise for executives. It calls for detailed and unbiased or unprejudiced investigations of every facet of the business and of what is required or implied by the proposed diversification. These studies must cover the rationale, principles and techniques being used and their relevance to the future. It entails investigations in depth into the organisational structure currently in use, how and why it developed, the inter-relationship between its various components and whether all this will be relevant or adequate for the new organisation required after the acquisition, merger of divestment. Questions such as whether the management function should be further centralised, or decentralised, are just relatively small parts of the total reorganisation task that has to be done. Without this thorough company reappraisal, optimal results from diversification may be the result only of pure luck. Senior management is, therefore, responsible for choosing the form of organisation that will afford effective, efficient, overall, coordinated control of the operations, resulting in optimal results. The reorganisation must be congruent for the new business which the company will be handling after diversification. (*See also* Section 8.1.2.)

4.4.2 Mergers and acquisitions

No matter how well or correctly conceived, mergers and acquisitions will not produce the expected results unless the acquired company is fully incorporated and integrated with the parent or acquiring company. That is, the merger or acquisition must be seen through to a complete conclusion. Many companies start off well enough but somewhere along the way they run out of steam or determination. Either they have not thought through the requirements carefully enough or in sufficient detail, or have run into insurmountable obstacles that compel executives to give up in exhaustion, or some sections of both parties are totally opposed to the acquisition or merger. Where the acquiring company has weak or excessively kind senior management, these problems are never likely to be resolved. The merger efforts peter out and the full benefits of the diversification are never realised.

In the early 1970s it was discovered by a survey in the United Kingdom that something like 30 per cent of all merger and acquisition attempts could be considered to be failures in that the objectives of the moves were not realised. Perhaps to the surprise of some readers, the equivalent failure rates for Continental Europe and the U.S.A. were reported as being appreciably higher. (The 'myth' of American managerial efficiency being shown up again?) In addition, another 20 per cent were considered not worth repeating. The equivalent waste of shareholders' funds was put at about £1 billion. Mergers and acquisitions would seem to be a form of managerial gambling, but is this really true or is it due to shortsightedness or lack of resolution on the part of the management teams? How can the risks be reduced?

First and obviously, thoroughness and care are needed with the investigations made prior to decisions being taken. However, these investigations should go further than just going through exhaustive checklists on assets, liabilities, management and the business performance of the intended acquisition. The relationship of these to the would-be purchaser's activities and methods is also necessary. In addition other questions have to be considered.

These include consideration of whether the purchaser should diversify or whether concentration (with or without divestment) would be better for the forecasted future conditions that might be met? Then comes the question of size.How big should the purchasing enterprise aim to be, and how diversified? The final size and complexity may be beyond the capabilities of the new management team if these questions are not considered. Further, if the final size of the company is allowed to become too big it will be unmanageable, no matter how large or good the executive structure may be.

If diversification is necessary much more careful thought is needed on which industries, countries or markets should be featured as possibilities. Too often it is all done in a rather *ad hoc*, hit-or-miss manner. The decisions here will again depend on the skills and resources existing in the company and the additional ones that could be obtained at acceptable cost levels. Then realistic assessments should be made of the acquisition and future running costs that would be incurred and the (most pessimistic?) additional profit that would be achieved. Finally, how should the diversification be financed? What would be the best way in the long term? Often this last question is answered only on the basis of existing conditions, yet future changes may make what was initially a cheap way of financing the project a most expensive method when long-term developments are taken into consideration.

In considering the profit question, thought must be given to the size of the current profit of the would-be acquisition. Should one buy a very profitable operation which could prove expensive? Or should one buy a company making losses? In the latter case, if the purchaser believes that the losses are due to lack of managerial depth, or for some other reason, and the purchaser can easily remedy such short-falls, then buying a loser might be the better proposition. The timing of the move is also important. Is the attractive profit-earner at the peak of its performance, or is its market at a peak and likely to go downhill shortly? This could mean that performance of the acquisition will decline fairly soon, creating problems for the purchaser. Or is the would-be acquisition and its business on a rising curve, i.e. about to take off in profit terms, and thus prove to be a very good buy for the bidder?

Thus, besides the usual study of financial aspects, pre-acquisition and pre-merger studies should cover also, current and forecasted future performance of both parties, with estimates of how the merged operations will prove beneficial. Finally, a detailed study of the product ranges is advisable. So is consideration of how all this will integrate with the purchaser's activities. Then the reorganisation and other developments that would be necessary have to be considered.

4.4.3 Turnround

When an organisation needs to be turned round, with or without diversification, the problems faced are very similar to those for mergers and acquisitions. The studies required are also similar. Apart from hiring temporary help to achieve immediate improvements in performance, the studies follow similar lines and must be to similar depth as mentioned in the previous Section. In both cases a degree of ruthlessness is unavoidable. The 'internal politics' of the company have to be ignored, i.e. should not be pandered to in any way. Many 'sacred cows' (e.g. inventory levels, method and extent of entertainment, personal cars, foreign travel, labour policies etc.) may have to be killed off.

The aim is to make the most effective use of human and material resources. This requires detailed understanding of what is happening in the company and its business environment and the major problems that are preventing greater effectiveness and profitability. Then decisions can be taken on what needs urgent attention, what urgent action would be least expensive and most profitable and what can be phased over a longer period, perhaps after further detailed study. Included in this will be decisions on tasks and operations that could or should be eliminated immediately, the degree of temporary help needed and the highlighting of major problem areas. Finally, there should be early indication of what is not being done that needs to be introduced quickly and urgently for short- and long-term success in the turnround.

4.4.4 Divestment

This is probably one of the most difficult things to ask long-serving executives to do; recommend those products, markets or operations that should be sold off or terminated. Executives become attached to activities they have known for years and, for various irrational reasons, they cherish. They hate to give them up even when market, consumer and other business conditions have altered so much that these items are now obsolete. Where the affected product has been a former big profit-earner, or a prestige product, the resistance to this change can be considerable.

In current conditions it is no longer possible to humour such attachments. An equally ruthless policy on divestments, as with turnround and acquisition, must be implemented. When activities are known, or are proved reasonably, not to have viable profit performance or other benefits, they must be axed. However, the timing of divestments is also crucial. Ideally divestment should take place before the activity has 'gone over the hill'. While it is still making profits it is easiest to sell. Provided that one knows the crest of the hill is only a year or two away, any loss in profit due to divestment would be more than made up by the better sale price that should be attainable.

Also, some candidates for divestment may in fact be continuing to help the sales of other more profitable products. In those cases it may be advisable to continue with them, provided the gain in profit from the supported products is much greater than the losses incurred by the item that would otherwise have been divested. Ultimately, even for these products, changes in technology, economics, markets and other factors will indicate that divestment, or closing down of the activity, can no longer be delayed. Then it should be done with determination and in the time span planned for the operation.

4.5 Corporate planning

Figure 3.3 gave a simplified explanation of what is involved in the corporate planning process. Figure 4.1 is a more detailed *schema* of how the process works in a fully integrated corporate management approach.

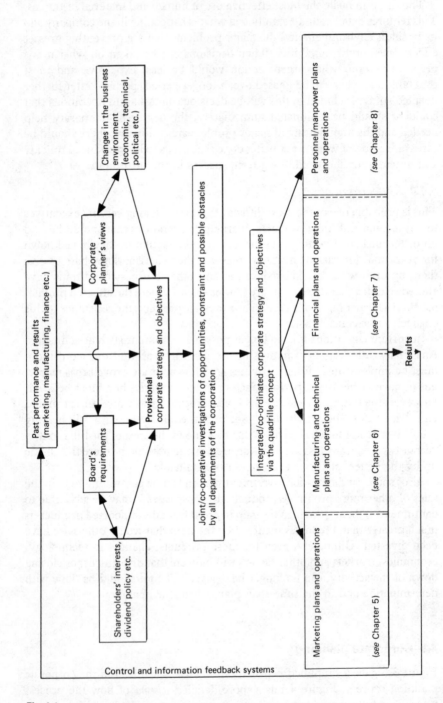

Fig 4.1

4.5.1 The process

The initial inputs leading to a statement of *provisional* corporated objectives and strategies are the previous performance and results of the company, the board's requirements for future growth and development, the corporate planner's view of what is possible after study of economic and other relevant factors, the changes forecasted in the business environment and the dividend policy and other interests of the shareholders. When the provisional objectives have been outlined, the operational (or 'line') departments investigate what can be achieved given existing and forecasted future conditions. This is done with a high degree of interdepartmental discussion and cooperation. Some trade-off between departments will be unavoidable and there must be give-and-take regarding their conflicting objectives and targets. This is the 'quadrille' concept in action. As a result the operating departments will be able to recommend what seems to be the best possibilities and will have mutually agreed these amongst themselves. The more acceptable alternatives will also have been agreed. With some horse-trading between the departments, the corporate planner and the board, final corporate objectives and strategies can be agreed. The departments can then proceed to finalise their own operational plans and targets but will still maintain close cooperation and discussions with each other.

As Figure 4.2 illustrates, there will always be some disagreement and mismatching between what line departments say can be done, what the corporate planner thinks should be done and what the board wants to be done for their own short- and long-term purposes. The relatively close match shown in

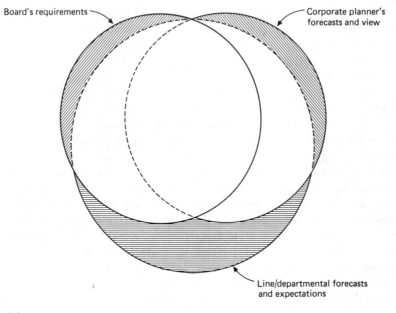

Board's requirements ⌐ Corporate planner's forecasts and view

Line/departmental forecasts and expectations

Fig 4.2

the figure would be encountered only in firms that have been using corporate planning for some time. They have got to know how the system works. For those new to corporate planning, the mis-matching would be far greater. This then, is why there is need for the three groups to try to reconcile their conflicting views between themselves until the best strategy and objectives they could follow become apparent. They will depend on the skills, resources and knowledge of the company. If a satisfactory compromise is not possible either some drastic change has taken place in the business environment and not been allowed for, or the original objectives have been too ambitious or contain some fundamental error or misunderstanding. It may then be necessary for all three parties to return to their desks and start the process all over again, trying to identify the reason for their inability to arrive at mutually acceptable decisions.

It is often believed that corporate or strategic planning is done by the chief executive and his senior executive colleagues (board members and executive vice-presidents) while tactical or operational planning and the implementation of strategy is undertaken by line or departmental executives. True, the board is responsible for evolving the broad business concepts of the company and indicates the provisional objectives and strategies that appear necessary. True also, that they have the task of finding, providing and allocating the resources that have to be used. So in these senses it is true that boards lead in, and are responsible for, evolving broad strategy. However, if companies stick rigidly to these demarcations, operations will not work as smoothly and profitably as when a totally integrated and cooperative approach is used throughout the executive ranks.

Thus line executives and others will advise and guide the board on strategy possibilities. Through discussions with line executives, the board will reach agreement on strategy and objectives to be followed by the company. On the operational side, it has already been stated, board members must be more involved with line executives by showing interest and encouraging and guiding the executives to achieve better results. Line executives, in their turn, will keep their directors or executive vice-presidents informed of progress, opportunities and obstacles being encountered. Thus each person by contributing his or her portion of thought and activity, without usurping those of others, can collectively sustain more efficient and profitable operations.

The basic difference and inter-relationships between strategic and operations management is nicely illustrated by David Hussey in his book *Corporate Planning, Theory and Practice* (Fig. 2, page 25). However this author prefers to consider administrative plans and the control functions as part of the inner ring, with finance and the personnel function, around the central core of the strategic plan. This revised concept is shown in Figure 4.3. The inter-relationship between the corporate plans and other company plans is shown in Figure 4.4.

The corporate planning process should also cover forecasts on factors such as the following:

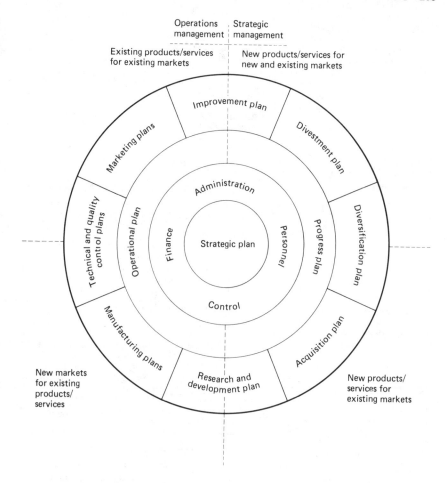

Adapted from: Fig.2, Hussey, D. *Corporate Planning, Theory and Practice* (Pergamon Press 1974).

Fig 4.3

—rate of economic growth or decline of the home country and the host nations in which the enterprise is operating, or plans to operate in the future period of the plan;

—effects of competitive activity from large, medium and small competitors at home and from foreign countries;

—capital investment requirements and the availability and cost of alternative sources of raw materials (including new materials that would be required);

—effects of changing technology on product obsolescence and development; also the effects on plant, equipment, methods of manufacture, quality control etc.;

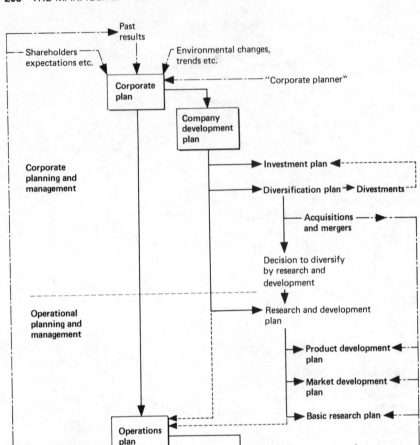

Fig 4.4

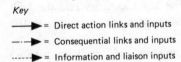

Key

⟶ = Direct action links and inputs

---▶ = Consequential links and inputs

·····▶ = Information and liaison inputs

—total industry demand and changes thereof for products or services (both existing and possible new ones);

—segmentation of total demand, and how this may alter in future, especially during the period of the plan;

—selling prices and the quality of products or services currently on offer;

—general availability of funds; cash flow; debtor, creditor and dividend policies.

These approaches and concepts apply both to the private and public sectors of industry. They apply in modified form also, to national and local government planning. In plans for the development of a national economy, for example, the equivalent critical parameters have to be identified and assessed before accurate forecasts can be made on how the products, services and capital goods required for the basic infrastructure of the economy can be generated, increased or decreased. These must be done for specified periods of time also. Otherwise economic growth and development necessary to match economic, social and political expectations will not be possible except by sheer good luck. The fact that the world's economy appears in the second half of the 1970s, to be heading into a time of upheaval and great change makes it even more essential for national planning to return to a more realistic basis. Political fantasy is a luxury that countries can no longer afford. Thus corporate planning is a far more comprehensive, all-pervading exercise than has been recognised so far. It is the vital starting point for an integrated management approach, or as described in this book, the 'management quadrille' concept.

As Figure 4.3 implies, financial and personnel planning are two important elements in any successful business enterprise. They provide fuels on which the company works. Financial aspects have long been given their just attention (sometimes overdone perhaps) but the personnel function has still to be acknowledged as an equally important activity. The control and product-market development activities are also being raised to their just levels of importance in the corporate scheme of things. However, it should not be forgotten that every sphere of corporate activity should have contingency plans to cover the occurrence of least likely events, or the unforseeable which is nevertheless suspected of lurking around the corner. There should be provision also for the totally unexpected thing happening, even if this is just setting aside from budgets a small 'contingency allowance' for such an event.

4.5.2 The corporate planner

The role of the corporate planner is often misunderstood and this is a contributory factor to the failure of corporate planning. First, the planner is not a line executive. He or she does not issue orders, instructions and directives to line executives, but assists and advises them on the choice of opportunities or decisions available and the ones most likely to prove the best if optimal corporate results are to be obtained. The planner thus helps line executives to be better managers. The planner is a specialist, offering specialist knowledge and ability to those who need or ask for it. (The planners are sometimes mistakenly called 'staff' persons. The only 'staff jobs' in business are positions described as 'personal assistant to . . . .'. True, staff people have no executive authority or responsibility in their own right. They assume responsibility only for tasks assigned to them by their superiors and only for the specific time period in which the work is done. Once the work has been completed and the results handed in this temporary responsibility ceases. It is then the staff person's boss who makes the final decisions and issues the necessary orders or directives.)

When a corporate planner assumes or is given line authority all sorts of conflicts arise. First there is the hostility of existing line executives who feel their authority has been usurped in some part. Then there is conflict of interest for the planners themselves. If corporate planning is to be done well, the planner must have the time for this work, must be free from the internal politics involved and be able to study in depth relevant economic and other aspects of the business. Current business activities of the firm also come under close scrutiny. This is not possible if the planner also has executive authority and therefore loyalties and bias. Unknowingly, the planner may then be favouring, or pushing hard for, a solution that would be beneficial to his department and its work but not necessarily be in the best interests of the company. If the line authority includes some major aspect of management, e.g. marketing, the planner may have difficulty in preventing some critical aspects of marketing or corporate planning from becoming submerged or overlooked, Or one responsibility may be given ascendancy over the other and the planning will not be a balanced, unbiased activity.

While the corporate planner is not the sole arbiter, he or she must be involved in the work of setting objectives and maintaining the necessary intelligence systems on the business environment (current and possible future ones). The planner helps with the development of planning systems and has an important part to play in diversification planning (divestment and acquisition or mergers as well as new product-market planning). The planner will also help in the planning of the necessary budgetary and control systems and in organisational planning and development. The planner will, from time to time, act as mediator, helping line executives to reconcile conflicting requirements and departmental objectives. However, the reconciled decisions must come from the line executives, not the planner, even if the planner has had to implant the idea in the heads of line executives in such a way as to make them believe the idea was theirs! (This management politicking, some claim, is an essential part of a planner's armoury!) Finally, the planner has the responsibility to report to line and senior executives when results are diverging from planned targets and should recommend the modifications that should be made to existing plans to pull the company back on course.

4.6 Company appraisal and corporate planning

In Section 3.4 brief comments were made about company appraisal but these were summaries of what had to be considered in normal day-to-day management. Here, the 'who', 'why' and 'when' of the subject will be studied with particular reference to the needs of corporate planning. Corporate appraisal is the starting point for corporate planning. Until the strategies, policies, operations and philosophies of the company as it exists are re-examined in the light of changing conditions, effective corporate planning is not possible.

Company appraisals expose the strengths and weaknesses of the enterprise and re-examine the rationale for its continuing existence into some future specified time period. It is probably one of the most difficult parts of a planner's work. It strikes at established practices and beliefs. It forces executives to face up to unpleasant facts. It tears away any protective wall of complacency behind which many executives like to hide. It forces a total re-examination of a company's very being and existence. It can too easily be seen as criticism of managers and executives, yet that is not its intention. Its aim is to establish correctly, how the enterprise is working, how good the results are, what it is doing well and what badly, what remedial action may be necessary and to check their relevance to the needs of the future planning period. Nor should it overlook such, perhaps, mundane, things as seeking ways of achieving cost reductions and improvement in profit performance. Especially at times of regularly increasing costs, executives should always be seeking ways of keeping operational costs under control. New ways of doing things, if they save money and do not compromise quality or the company's reputation are worth consideration in any corporate appraisal exercise.

Regardless of the size of the company, when a decision has been taken to embark on regular corporate appraisals, the big question concerns how best this could be done and who should be responsible for the work. The first and most preferred way is to call in a consultant. While companies may be short of appropriate executives to do this work, or cannot afford to employ them, when the only recourse is to consultants, too many executives still hide behind consultants when faced with what they think is unpleasent work. (Company appraisal is not and need not be, unpleasant. It all depends on the mental attitudes of the executives doing the work.) The executives wish to avoid all the crunches and do not wish to be seen as the ones causing all the aggravation and ructions. Appointing consultants to do their dirty work is management's 'Pontius Pilate act', keeping their hands clean while letting the consultants wield their axe on all the deadwood that must be pruned from the corporate trunk. The blood is on the consultants' hands! Yet, no matter how good and experienced consultants may be they cannot in the time permitted, absorb all the vital nuances pervading an organisation. They cannot have the intimate knowledge of and contact with the company that its own executives possess. Their findings and recommendations will exude a certain academic coldness or remoteness from reality. Their reports may not appear to have the human touch or appreciate the intricate human relations on which the successful progress of the company will depend.

The next possibility is for the chief executive, or some assigned senior executive (main board director or executive vice-president), to do the work. Well, if they have their usual responsibilities in addition, it is most likely that they will not have the free time that should be given to this important work. Or they may not be able to afford sufficient, uninterrupted time. The ability of one person to deal expeditiously with this work depends on the size of the enterprise. If it is a big one, a single person will not be able to do it with the speed that would be essential. It is not the sort of work that can be done piecemeal, as and when the persons responsible have the time to spare for it.

It cannot be gainsaid; relevant line executives with the corporate planner, if one exists, and other appropriate experts or 'specialists' have to be formed into a team to do this work. There can be more than one team when each will be assigned to a particular part of the company's operations. All teams will have to make depth studies of their areas of responsibility, finding out how these really work, why they obtain the results they do, the speed at which they do and can work, their suitability and adaptability for the future, their shortcomings and failings, how and when they prefer to work, how they work best, and so on. Then the teams come together to appraise all the findings collectively before making recommendations to the board. Ideally, each team leader should report directly to the chief executive or some assigned senior executive, though the latter is really a second-best arrangement.

The work depends for its success also on the self-analysis of the work of the departments by the people who staff them. They might be helped if they could be given a checklist of the important questions that need answering at the time and encouraged to face them bravely and give unbiased answers! Then personal self-appraisals of the executives themselves are also necessary, since these will be required in the personnel side of the corporate appraisal. Terms of reference for the work should be prepared since middle and junior ranks will need guidance on what should be done and what results or findings are expected or required. Properly handled, this can lead to better job motivation of individuals and working groups or departments.

How the findings are classified can vary, but usually they should be grouped under such headings as 'strong' (or 'strengths') 'satisfactory', 'poor' (when this is due to operational faults rather than lack of resources) and 'weaknesses' (when this is due to lack of resources and skills). It may also be useful to have other classifications such as 'opportunities' (areas that seem to offer interesting development possibilities, now or in the future) and 'threats' (where some internal or external factor may be seen as a future threat to the continuing success or even survival of the company). Obviously, the work is done in a manner orientated to the future, that is too much attention is not given to the present day. For consistency, the period considered by the appraisals should be the same as the length of the corporate planning period or some multiple of it, e.g. double.

The teams would consist of at least one appropriately experienced and senior representative of each major department. More may be necessary if any department has a major contribution to make to the appraisal or has a complex arrangement of inter-dependent activities with other departments. For example, the manufacturing department of a large organisation may also need in their team experts from research and development, quality control and production planning and control. The marketing team from a similar organisation may include a marketing researcher, sales expert, physical distribution executive and someone knowledgeable on promotional activities and/or pricing. Although the work is a depth study of the company it should not be introspective. The relevant external factors and their inter-relationships (between themselves and the company) must be examined. Nor is it an isolated occurrence. Each factor hangs or depends on others so they must not be studied in isolation.

The work may also be classified according to the type of team member required to do it, i.e. the expertise needed to investigate the subject properly. Amongst the various 'positions' that have to be investigated and therefore the types of teams wanted are the marketing, manufacturing, financial and personnel positions, the operational, organisational and competitive positions and the research and development, executive and shopfloor (blue collar) positions. Of course any one of these can be sub-divided into smaller areas for study, if they are considered to be of special importance or to contain some intractable problem.

The investigation of the company's results should be broken down into those of subsidiaries, operating divisions, departments or even more specific areas of work. It will be hampered from time to time for lack of information which may not exist or may prove too costly in time and money to obtain. Gaps therefore will exist, as will information imperfections and uncertainties. However, as corporate appraisals are continued over several years, these gaps, imperfections and uncertainties will be closed.

Another area that has to be studied for corporate planning and normal management purposes is the profit-earning ability of the company, particularly the main sources of profit for the company's current activities. Then consideration should be given to those areas which could be the company's source of future profits. Many myths exist in executive minds of where and how the company makes its profits. Corporate appraisals will often explode these myths and executives will be surprised and startled to find where the profits are generated. This side of the study may well highlight the shortcomings, inconsistencies or errors of the financial department's work and reporting systems. Better reporting and control systems could result.

There is also the question of risk (*see* Section 3.6). Too many assumptions are made on this subject mainly based on hunches or 'experience'. What is needed is more detailed knowledge of where and how risks arise and the degree of risk inherent in the major activities of the company. Included in this appraisal should be an assessment of risk in the purchasing function, i.e. what risks are incurred in assuming that bought-in materials and goods will always be available in the right quantities and quality at reasonable cost? What risks are inherent in sources of supply drying-up, whether for natural or political reasons? What risks are involved in switching to alternative materials or sources of supply? Market risks must also be studied. This should cover the individual market positions of products (especially key ones) and the risks resulting from competitive activity. How will these change in the future and what new competition may arise? What competition will cease as a result of some company withdrawal from the market? What new competitors are emerging? Technological risks must also be appraised not only because of current technical difficulties but also due to new developments making the company's operations obsolete. Manufacturing risks for the same reason must be studied as must those arising from raw materials difficulties, plant limitations, labour problems, lack of suitable skills etc.

The studies on the manufacturing side will be just as detailed as for any other department. Particular interest will lie in checking the suitability of present methods for future needs and what changes must be made to make them more appropriate, countering or taking maximum benefit from, future developments. Then the resources needed and the efficiency of their utilisation must be assessed, together with the ability of the company to handle future resources, especially new ones. Similar detailed study would be made of financial matters. This would cover cash flows, expenditure budgets, capital requirements and utilisation, cost of capital, disposition of surpluses, cost reductions, dividend policy, management of funds, budgetary control systems and so on. Finally, the organisation, management structure and methods would be appraised and this must include what would be a check of the efficacy of the communications system being used, particularly that part that links blue collar workers with various levels of the executive ranks. Then the company can judge its ability to face the future and achieve its long-term aims. The corporate planning team would then possess most of the information and data it would need to proceed, in partnership with other executives, in the formulation of corporate plans.

4.7 Some legal notes

Until about the middle of the 20th century, the legal requirements that businesses had to meet, in the United Kingdom and other industrialised nations, were fairly straightforward. The laws and regulations were designed to safeguard the money and interests of investors, to prevent fraud and fraudulent conversions, protect against embezzlement or executives absconding with the company's cash and generally ensure that businesses were correctly and properly managed in an orderly fashion. Some of the legal facts with which company directors and secretaries had to be familiar are shown in section A of the list below. Although there are many facts and the list is not comprehensive, it was within the abilities of senior executives to know the important aspects of all these points. They knew where to go if they needed to look up the details. Recourse to a legal adviser was a rare thing. It only arose when the company had got itself into difficulties or when it was contemplating something new of which the executives had had no experience.

Major legal aspects of business

A. Historical or long-established

Accounts and balance sheets
Agreements
Allotment of shares
Alteration of capital
Annual general meetings
Annual returns
Applications for shares and debentures
Articles of association
Auditorship

Balance sheet
Books and registers
Borrowings

Certificates of incorporation
Certificates of shares, stocks
Certification of transfers of shares and debentures
Change of name
Charges on the company
Commissions
Copies of documents

Debentures
Directors — appointments; compensation for loss of office; disclosures of
    remuneration, shareholdings, interests; loans to; meetings of; names and
    register; removal of; reports

Extraordinary general meetings
Exchange control

Group accounts

Increase of capital
Inspection of registers

Members resolutions and statements
Memorandum of association
Minutes
Mortgages, registration of

Name of company
Notes to accounts

Offences and penalties

Power of attorney
Prevention of fraud
Profit and loss account
Prospectus
Purchase of shares, financial assistance for

Quorum

Receivership
Registered office
Register of directors and secretary
Register of directors' shareholdings and interests
Register of members
Register of substantial individual interests
Resolutions
Responsibilities of officers

Special notices and resolutions
Statutory meetings

Transfer of shares
Transmission of shares

B. Some more recent developments (United Kingdom)

Agency
Creation and authority of — ratification — breach of implied warrant of authority — effect of contracts made by agents — rights — duties — termination of agreement.

Contracts
Formation — form of — capacity to contract — conditions affecting enforceability, voidability — illegal contracts — discharge of contracts — breach of contract — privity, assignment and interpretation of contract — injunctions and limitations of actions. Misrepresentations.

Contract of employment
Terms of employment — job protection — termination of employment — industrial tribunals — duties of employer — duties of worker — wages — safety and health at work.

Consumer credit
Agreements — licensing — seeking business — rights and obligations of partners and parties — enforcement of agreements. Misrepresentations. Consumer Credit Act 1974.

Liabilities
For wrongful acts — criminal liability — negligence — employer's liabilities — compensation.

Monopolies, restrictive trade practices and resale prices
Monopolies and mergers — restrictive trade practices — resale price maintenance — E.E.C. Treaty rules of competition — various guarantees. Misrepresentations.

Partnership
Creation — dissolution — relationship of partners — change of partners — limited partnerships.

Sale of goods
Form of contract — conditions and warranties — transfer of property — performance of contract — rights of buyer and seller — sales by auction — Unsolicited Goods and Services Act 1971 — Fair Trading Act 1973 — Trades Description Acts (1968 and 1972) — product liability — advertising controls.

Hire purchase agreements
Hire purchase transactions — Hire Purchase Act — door step sales — cooling-off period. Misrepresentations.

Bankruptcies and company liquidations

C. Some United Kingdom statutes relevant to business activity

Arbitration Act

Bankruptcy Act
Banking and Financial Dealings Act
Bills of Exchange Act
Bills of Lading Act
Bills of Sale Act

Carriers' Act
Carriage by Air Act
Companies Acts
Contracts of Employment Act
Consumer Credit Act

Employment Protection (Consolidation) Act
Equal Opportunities Act
Exchange Control Acts

Factories Acts
Fair Trading Act
Finance Acts (various)

Health and Safety at Work Acts
Hire Purchase Act

Insolvency Act

Marine Insurance Act
Mercantile Law and amendments
Merchant Shipping Act
Misrepresentations Acts

Race Relations Act
Resale Prices Act
Restrictive Trade Practices Act

Sale of Goods Act
Statute of Frauds
Supply of Goods (Implies Terms) Act

Trades Descriptions Act
Transport Act

Unsolicited Goods and Services Act.

(This is by no means a complete list. Other countries have equally complex laws to negotiate in the normal course of business.)

In the last two decades in particular, so many new laws have been enacted, especially in Britain, that they have changed the nature of business quite substantially. Increasing government involvement and regulations have further complicated the legal side of business. Now large companies are finding it necessary to have on their full-time staff, a suitably qualified and experienced lawyer to guide them through the labyrinth of legal requirements facing all corporations and especially multi-national ones. Some medium-sized companies will also soon be needing their own full-time lawyer while the executives of small firms will find themselves spending much more time consulting their legal advisers. The wealth of new legislation arises from increasing interest in consumerism, the protection of the consumer from nefarious actions by smart businessmen and the protection of consumer's health and safety.

The first, protecting the consumer from sharp practices, was necessary as greed seemed more and more to enter into some business considerations in this materialistic age. The second became important because of the increasing use of additives and other materials or processes which were found to be potentially dangerous to life. The legislation has sometimes been too sweeping in its attempts to catch all and this has only increased the difficulties facing business people. In addition there has been growing interest in improving labour relations, providing job security and various attempts to help the individual or consumer. The last ranged from the Sale of Goods Act, to product liability and sales descriptions of products and services on offer, including clearly marked and displayed prices. Then there was the Monopolies Commission to prevent monopolies springing up and controlling markets (there are equivalents in other lands, e.g. anti-trust legislation), the Prices and Incomes Board (where governments attempted to control, artificially, prices, salaries and wages). Finally, there was new legislation for safeguarding things like fair trading, equal opportunities and the abolition of resale price maintenance. The United Kingdom Race Relations Act also has many implications for the business world.

All have spawned their various laws or regulations. Then there have been regulations and rules to try to control insurance practice, financial loan operations, banking generally and the overseas activities of multi-national corporations. With Britain now a member of the European Communities there are the further additions and changes which 'harmonisation' with European practice will bring. The legal aspects of business have now reached frightening proportions. It is all beyond the comprehension of many executives, most of whom just do not have the time to delve deeply into every side of it. Hence the growing need for specialist help. The list on pp. 213-16 indicates the complexity of the position today. Section B shows the main areas where new laws or amendments, or regulations have been introduced in the United Kingdom. Section C lists the main statutes (laws) which have effect on business activities. The list illustrates the legal load on executives at the moment and more can be expected from the governments of most nations in the future.

4.8 A few more case histories

It is worth recording here a few more cases. The wisdom contained in them, as in those of Chapter 3, might then be imparted to others.

4.8.1 Crow Hamilton of Scotland

This company, formerly part of the Associated Engineering Group before the conglomerate decided to divest itself of a number of small companies, is one of an increasing number of companies in Britain that have made a success of exporting. It exports a considerable proportion of its output at acceptable levels of profitability. (This is a great and vital change for the better for Britain where for so long 80 per cent of the nation's exports came from fifteen or twenty companies, usually the big ones. 'Export' was a dirty word, despite official exhortations. It was something that was indulged in only when the home market was in trouble. As soon as the home market picked up, overseas markets were forgotten, in fact abandoned in mid-stride as it were. A growing number of *Queen's Awards* to industry, particularly those given for export achievement, have been going to the smaller companies in the second half of the 1970s.) The company's products include coal slurry piston pumps for the coal-mining industry, pneumatic concrete pumps for the construction industry and scaffold straightening machines.

When Associated Engineering decided to divest itself of Crow Hamilton, its then chief executive (John Fordham), convinced of the future in concrete pumps and not wishing to be tied for ever to large organisations, persuaded a friend to join him in buying the company. That was in 1973. Once independent, the small executive team (seventeen persons strong in 1978) established a 'get-up-and-go' attitude to their working life. This was vital in 1974 when the slump in the British construction industry hit the country, especially small suppliers to the industry. A determined drive for export sales was necessary if the company was to survive. The prime product for this effort was the pneumatic concrete pump. It looks like a giant spinning top and was based on techniques originating from the U.S.A. and Germany. It replaced a wheelbarrow or bucket on a crane for the spreading of concrete. Competition is still fierce from Germany and the U.S.A., but few competitors interested themselves in the Middle Eastern markets. Crow Hamilton made a deliberate drive for these, starting in 1974.

By 1976 overseas sales accounted for half the company's total turnover. This was quite a turnround in its own right for a company which in 1973 had registered sales of £218,000-odd with exports of £78,000. By 1977 exports accounted for some £397,000 of production.

Originally, Associated Engineering had bought Crow Hamilton because of its know-how in the production of turbine blades. Its eventual emergence into the field of this pump illustrates the value of being resilient and prepared to back knowledge on future opportunites and their resultant products. For, when Associated Engineering moved turbine blade production to another factory in the group, Crow Hamilton's survival depended on the entrepreneurial skills and determination of the chief executive who was recruited to find ways of filling the resultant production gap. Since its independence, many if not all of the senior executives are likely to be found visiting its Middle East markets rather than sitting in the United Kingdom. Iran, Saudi Arabia and Egypt, for example, are well known to this intrepid team of executives.

Creating interest for this pump in the construction industry was not an easy task. It was such a simple idea that it was difficult to persuade potential customers that it would do what was claimed of it, despite its considerable price advantage over its American and German competitors. (In 1977 Crow Hamilton's price was about £4,000 while competitive products started at £18,000.) There are no moving parts to go wrong and its maintenance involves just keeping it clean. However, the technology is not so simple. Because the quality of sand can vary so much, the actual mix used on any site has to be adjusted to allow for this variation. As the mix used has to be softer (wetter) than construction engineers are normally used to, so that it can be pumped down a pipe, construction engineers had to be convinced that it would not crack as it set. Then if the pump is moved to another site using different sand, it may not work as originally set. A Crow Hamilton engineer is needed to show how it is done and ensure the right mix is used. Thus after-sales technical service and advice of a high order are essential ingredients for success with this product.

The success of the company has also depended on close cooperation between executives that has been maintained despite their extensive travelling. Besides getting on well with each other, they work as a closely knit, integrated team prepared to help each other at all times. Being small also means that no-one need be confined to a narrow specialisation. While life is not always easy for the company, these attitudes have helped it to prosper and grow. It is an ideal example of the benefits that accrue with a totally integrated and cooperative management approach. It is one that can be copied even by bigger companies with their more complex problems. Indeed, because of these complexities, larger companies need an integrated management approach to survive, never mind grow.

4.8.2 Porsche of West Germany

It was generally believed in 1974 that the era of the sports car manufacturer, especially high performance cars, was over. The substantial increase in the price of oil and petrol (gas) and the changed political situation in the Middle East, with countries prepared to use their oil resources as both an economic and political weapon, seemed to indicate this. Given that Porsche had decided at that time to launch two very expensive new models, it seemed like a determined move towards major problems of survival. By 1975, specialist car manufacturers were going into liquidation (voluntary and compulsory) in substantial numbers. Stocks of unsold cars were building up considerably and even Porsche had to slash its labour force by about a quarter.

Nonetheless the company took its two key product decisions to launch the 924 and 928 models and maintained its faith in the company's sports car traditions. It also launched its policy designed to triple the size of the business in a few years. By 1978 the gamble appeared to have come off. Survival and growth resulted from the belief that the sports car is a reincarnation of the class automobile (differentiated from the modern motorised tin cans called cars) and would always have an appeal. This is a different attitude to that of Volkswagen the original partner in the 924 project which, faced with cost problems in its own model development, saw the 924 as a 'doubtful' car. It was not prepared to take the risk while Porsche considered the risk worth taking and succeeded.

The risk was not just about the new model. Going it alone without Volkswagen, forced Porsche into a different, larger scale of business than previously. This posed several risks for the company. Until 1964 Porsche had never made more than about 14,700 cars a year. Investing in the 924 meant planning for a volume of 24,000 units a year for that model alone. It would obviously stretch management, marketing and financial resources. With the sanctioning of the 928 model as well these problems were increased, especially as the V-8 engined sports car contained many innovative ideas. It cost the company DM 100 million (about £25 million) to develop these ideas.

Such headlong expansion in troubled times may read like managerial recklessness, but considerable commercial logic lay behind what otherwise might seem mere intuition. The company took the view that the scare on oil prices was temporary. (By 1978 the upward trend had been stemmed and in fact reversed as far as retail prices were concerned. But what of the rapidly escalating prices of 1979?) Porsche continued to believe that the world's demand for specialist cars which were well engineered, designed and conceived would continue in a volume in keeping with their limited production plans. (The company had no intention of moving into the mass or volume markets bedevilled by all their troubles.) The withdrawal of Volkswagen from the 924 project, though it exposed Porsche to greater risks at first would nevertheless permit the company to establish a wider base for its business. A deal was struck whereby Porsche bought Volkwagen's share in the project for DM 120 million while Volkswagen financed this with a loan of a similar amount at a fair rate of interest.

The deal was extended to cover marketing arrangements. When the 924 project was initiated, the two companies formed a joint marketing company with both partners injecting staff and appropriate expertise. Porsche, except in Britain and France, where it had its own companies, had always marketed its cars through the Volkswagen network. When Volkswagen withdrew from the 924, Porsche simply took over this organisation. The results of these determined management moves included an increase in the company's business. While in 1974-75 Porsche hit its low point with production of only 8,000 cars, by 1977 they had reached 37,000. Turnover rose from DM 350 million to DM 1,000 million. Excluding the Volkswagen loan, borrowings throughout that period remained fairly constant while at the end of 1977 only DM 70 million of the Volkswagen loan was outstanding.

However, in the profit side performance was not comparably impressive. In 1975-76 the return achieved was only 1.2 per cent on turnover and in 1977 was estimated to be 1.7 per cent. However, this figure was in line with the targets projected when the schemes were planned. Being a company still tightly controlled by the Porsche and related families, it is not subjected to the pressure for immediate profits of other publicly owned or quoted organisations. It does not need to attract equity capital through a high profits record and the families are more concerned with the image of solidity and as manufacturers of assured quality vehicles. Growth has been largely self-financed. The resultant investment has been high for a company of its size. In the five years from 1973 the company has ploughed back DM 310 million. Its plans for 1978 called for investment of DM 80 million covered largely by a depreciation charge on the outstanding Volkswagen loan of DM 70 million. However, the talented family members now have seats on the holding board only and the company could attract public funds if it wished. So far, this has not appeared to have been needed.

The threat to small manufacturers of vehicles is no longer production methods and their associated costs. It is the cost of meeting government legislation on safety, fuel economy and anti-pollution aspects. This will probably be the reason why many of the small specialist car makers will have to close down. Porsche is seeking to overcome this by obtaining contract work in similar fields. Thus its greatly expanded technical centre served practically every major motor manufacturer in the world.

Another principle that has helped the company to be successful is to design cars capable of considerable development. The major manufacturers aim to design cars which will have substantial demand for several years without needing further large investment in development costs. Porsche follows the other approach, the development of a car which can be built for fifteen years or so and with the injection of new ideas and further slabs of investment every two or three years, can be assured of sustained, if not growing, demand, for that period. Total investment and the investment needs of any year are kept within bounds. Machine tools are built to last twenty-five years and not, say, five. An example is the 911 model now in its fifteenth year, but with quite different performance with the addition of a turbo-charged power unit version into its range. On the other hand the 928 is designed to be quieter and smoother than previous Porsche cars even if it lacks the shattering acceleration and speed of its predecessors. With nations introducing relatively low top speeds on their roads for safety and fuel economy reasons, these limitations may no longer be important.

4.8.3 Waterford Glass of Ireland

This company is in fact a conglomerate which besides making lead, hand-made crystal is in retailing, bone china manufacturing, high quality printing and garage and car franchising. Handcut crystal was made in Waterford in the early 1700s but with the heavy export levies on lead glass the industry shrank and in 1851 production ceased at Waterford. For about a century no glass was made there but a small pilot plant was reopened after the Second World War. In 1951 it was incorporated into the Irish Glass Bottle Company. By the beginning of the 1960s the crystal manufacturing activity was outstripping the production of bottles. In 1966 Waterford Glass was floated off as a separate company. By the mid-1970s the company employed about 2,500 persons on two modern sites. Ninety per cent of its production is exported, mainly to the U.S.A., where Waterford sells more glass than all the other European manufacturers put together. Total production is pre-sold a year in advance and the waiting list for some individual pieces has been as long as two years.

The buoyancy of market demand is reflected by an uninterrupted record of profit growth over the last twenty years or so. Between 1967 and 1970 profits rose from £444,000 to £1.3 million. This was despite substantial investment in the major development of a new factory on a 45-acre site. With the exception of 1973 when growth was a mere 7 per cent, the average rate of profit growth has been in excess of 30 per cent a year. In 1976 on a turnover of £80 million profits were £6.75 million (8.4 per cent). This growth was boosted by a series of acquisitions between 1970 and 1974. This included the purchase of the English Aynsley China Group and a 60 per cent stake in the Switzer Group, a chain of department stores in Ireland whose other 40 per cent is held by the House of Fraser. Purchases also included the small quality printer, John Hinde, and the Smith Group which holds the Renault franchise in Ireland and operates a chain of garages and some light engineering and vehicle assembly subsidiaries.

Waterford's purchases were prompted by the realisation that diversification was essential and that long-term survival and growth should not depend on a one-product operation. In addition, the success of the lead crystal business depends on the goodwill of a highly skilled labour force and is an operation in which labour costs are about 70 per cent of total costs. Expansion of this business by the mid-1970s depended on the ability to expand the labour force and the building of a new multi-pot factory. Nor in this business can the company afford to flood the market. Demand for high quality, high cost products requires the maintenance of an element of scarcity value.

The chief advantage of the acquisition of John Hinde was that this business is reasonably independent of fluctuations in consumer demand which affects the other division of the conglomerate. The acquisition of the Switzer Group and its retailing operations has shown the need for closer attention to cash flow aspects. The lessons learned here have been applied to the other activities. The acquisition of the Smith Group provided other lessons. They were importers while Waterford's experience prior to diversification was almost all orientated to exporting. This acquisition also taught Waterford that its reserves of human resources, especially management, was limited. It did not have sufficient to place its own management into a newly-acquired business unless the rest of the business was so healthy as to be capable of being left to tick over more or less on its own while the new managers of the acquired business restructured the latter's organisation.

While in the mid-1970s conglomerates had somewhat passed out of favour, Waterford has shown that with care and learning from experience, it is possible to turnround even a relatively small company with a one-product base for its operations. Properly done, it can become a well-balanced and profitable conglomerate, or at least a multi-product company with a stable base. In Waterford's case the diversification has also evened out the problems brought about by fluctuating currencies. This case shows that even a relatively small company with limited product-market activites can, with care and common sense, apply simple management concepts so that growth and stability are achieved.

4.9 Questions

1. Why is it important and necessary to conduct corporate appraisals from time to time? What contribution do these make in corporate planning?

2. What is corporate planning? What role does it play in successful integrated corporate management?

3. What role does the corporate planner have?

4. Describe the corporate planning process. How do the board, line executives and corporate planner work together here? What is the key to success?

5. What is meant by 'diversification'? What work is involved? How is it done? What problems might arise?

6. What are corporate objectives? Why are they needed? How are short- and long-term needs reconciled? What points must be covered by the objectives and why should they be checked for validity?

7. What problems are commonly met in corporate planning? What are the pitfalls? Who are the 'spoilers'?

5 Marketing—
manufacturing—finance—
personnel

This chapter studies the more common problems, difficulties and failures encountered in marketing, especially those that have inter-dependence with the other major disciplines of management. That is, it will show the quadrille concept of integrated management in action. It will not be involved in detailed discussion of the various components of marketing. Readers are expected to know these or be prepared to study specialist books on marketing. (The same approach is used in subsequent chapters from the starting point of one of the other three major disciplines.) The chapter will concentrate on the things which seem to have been misunderstood or forgotten about critical areas of work in the rush to adopt gimmicky techniques, or because the literature to date has ignored detailed discussion of them. The aim continues to be, as before, to get managers to rethink from first principles what constitutes successful management. In particular, these chapters will re-emphasise the links of inter-departmental cooperation and coordination that are the essential ingredients for this often elusive success.

5.1 The marketing quadrille

It has been stated that management activities and responsibilities work in groups of four; four activities that depend very much on each other for them, singly and collectively, to be successful. These quadrilles at management levels also group themselves together in four to form the *basic management quadrille*. This was illustrated by Figure 1.5 while Figure 1.6 (The Quadrilles of Integrated Management) showed how the quadrilles of each line department come together to achieve close coordination and cooperation, thus forming a fully integrated management team. Each departmental quadrille group is subdivided into a major quadrille of its four main activities (shown in the smaller circles of the illustrations) and four important support activities (shown in the segments of the major circle around the main activities). The axle is the management of that department.

Thus the *marketing quadrille* can be represented by Figure 5.1. The main partnership here is between *marketing research and information — personal selling and after-sales service — promotional activities — physical distribution.*

However, these come to nothing without their key support activities, forming another quadrille between *market development and management — product development and management — pricing — packaging/merchandising*. The axle here is marketing management. These two foursomes are themselves intimately inter-related and inter-dependent, hence the form of Figure 5.1. Without good product-market planning development and management, pricing strategy and sound pricing, appropriate packaging and merchandising, the other activities of marketing would be hindered or frustrated.

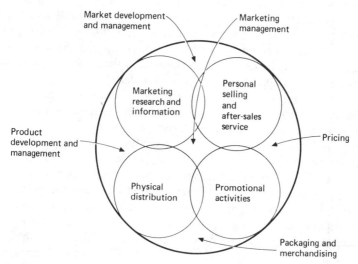

Fig 5.1

The placing of the components of the second quadrille around the central group of four is also meant to be indicative of the communication and coordination links that are of prime importance to the department. Thus, product development influences the work of, and is influenced by, marketing research and information. Product development also determines the size of the product mix and market development is also dependent on this mix. Between them they influence the personal selling, after-sales service and physical distribution needs and preferred operations. Or conversely, the company's abilities and capacity for personal selling, after-sales service and physical distribution, and their past record in these two activities, influence what is practical in product-market development. Promotional activities will be influenced by the amount and scale of personal selling it has to support (including here the range of product-market situations) and the pricing and physical distribution aspects. Alternatively, pricing decisions influence what can be done in promotional activities, personal selling, after-sales service, physical distribution and, if relevant, packaging/merchandising. Distribution itself is influenced by the packaging/merchandising and promotional and selling efforts since they will influence the flow of goods through the system.

Pricing decisions and the resultant cash flow determine the extent of the promotions, packaging/merchandising and selling effort that could be used. While pricing affects the degree and nature of personal selling permitted, the selling needed to fulfil targets will in turn influence decisions on pricing policy and price levels. Then personal selling, after-sales service, market management and development, marketing research and product management and development are all inter-related and inter-dependent. Decisions on one of them cannot be made successfully unless the effect on the others, and on each other, is known. Research will indicate how and what product and market development is needed and, according to the development undertaken, the extent and nature of the selling work required to support these activities. Or, the need to undertake specified market development will indicate what marketing research may be necessary and eventually the personal selling and promotional roles the department will have to undertake.

These inter-relationships must also be extended to relevant sections of the other major departments of the company. For example, anything to do with pricing must involve the manufacturing department (on costs and quality and their control) and the financial department (regarding cash flow, profit plans, capital needed and utilised, return etc.). Product-market development work will involve manufacturing (regarding specifications, quality and quality control, materials to be used, skilled labour required etc.) and the personnel department (who have the task of finding the skilled labour and planning, and running associated training and development courses that may be needed). The financial department will also be involved, for the subjects of cash flow, profit plans, capital utilisation, funding of additional capital etc. will arise. These inter- and intra-departmental links are important. Any reasonably competent executive, knowing the work that has to be done can, before it begins, jot down on paper all the other company departments that should be consulted and note what should be discussed with them and when in the development process this might come. Then the communication system will be well used and maintained. Yet how often, for example, in product-market development does the marketing department fail to contact (say) the financial department, or does so only at the end of the exercise when most of the work has been done? It is too late for financial executives to bring their expertise to help in the work. They can only oppose the proposals strongly (when friction will be increased) or let them go and run the risk of having 'sponsored' a disastrous project or plan. Or they could insist that all the work be done again; but this will not improve relationships between executives!

5.1.1 Marketing concept reviewed

Thus it will be seen that marketing effort is not simply a homogeneous input in management activity but a composite of many different types of activities, themselves influenced by several factors. It is also affected by events and developments in other management areas. For example, price decisions depend on cost decisions of manufacturing and cash-flow requirements of the financial department, with all three playing equal roles in profit-planning. Market response to variations of the input level of any one marketing activity will also be dependent on the level of input of other related marketing and management activities. Thus the market response to (say) a change in product specification will depend on the nature and implications of that change, plus the promotional activity (how well is the change put across?), the selling effort (are the right decision-makers at customer firms being influenced?) and the ability of the distribution department to handle this changed product. Further, markets comprise a wide variety of customers or buyers, both professionals and individual consumers. Their awareness of the product or service on offer, their interest in or preference for, and intentions regarding the use of it (hence their need for it) vary. Their attitudes will also be influenced by the conditions prevailing in their own companies, industries and/or markets, if bought for corporate use; or their standard and quality of life, economic circumstances and expectations, if bought for personal use. Thus the propensity of segments of any market to buy will also vary widely.

The basic challenge then is to derive the optimal mix of marketing activities and associated activities from other management areas that will best match the needs of acceptable segments of a market (potential demand) believed to exist for the product or service on offer. This is the simple, basic, original *marketing concept* which required all the corporation's activities to be orientated towards its customers and their needs; outwardly that is, rather than inwardly to their plant, equipment or assumed technical excellence. The original concept concerned all the activities of a company but unfortunately, too often, it was interpreted to mean all the marketing activities of the firm. Whether the other departments participated directly depended on the relationships between executives, the communications network and how the executives felt at the time! It was perhaps with the original meaning in mind that the British Institute of Marketing issued a new authoritative definition in 1976:

'Marketing is the management process responsible for identifying, anticipating and satisfying customer requirements *profitably*.' (Author's italics)

Yet, as with all definitions, it can be criticised as being too limited and, in trying to be concise, it has perhaps made several serious omissions. First, it does not stress or make clear that all management disciplines, at some time or other are involved in making marketing activities profitable. The opening phrase of the definition can be read to mean reference to marketing only, and be so interpreted by those (too many) who do not really understand what marketing is all about. Next, it is admitted that marketing has to give the lead in time, because until marketing research has indicated what market demand exists the company cannot plan its activities with precision. Third, it does not stress that 'customer requirements' centre on something more than just the products or services offered. Finally, it could be construed that profitability is the only goal; but in fact marketing has to balance a lot of conflicting things, especially profit, growth and stability of results. The 1976 definition makes no reference to this vital fact.

The newer concept acknowledges that customer needs are something more than just the products they buy, or the apparent reasons why they buy them. The real motivating forces may be customers' ideas on the standard and quality of life they should lead, other personal expectations and attitudes and more generalised opinions on conservation and so on. Improving the quality of life ranges from more labour-saving devices in the home, to more active interest in the arts, reading and music, to more extensive travel to see and learn at first hand about peoples and cultures of other lands. These and other expectations have played a part in the developments of past decades leading to the horse and buggy being replaced by the motor vehicle, jet aircraft replacing the luxurious ocean-going liner, modern electronics replacing the crystal 'wireless' set, earth satellites replacing cable telegraph systems and processed, preserved, frozen convenience foods replacing raw, unwashed, untreated foods. Not all these 'advances' are considered to be beneficial by all the world's inhabitants, but they illustrate how customer expectations, with their attitudes and interest, can lead to major changes in product needs and hence opportunities for businesses and industries. When customer needs are more accurately defined and their true motivations identified, the selling and merchandising efforts of a company can be more effectively planned and executed.

In more recent times it has also been acknowledged that the marketing concept allows corporations to bring their own interests into greater harmony with those of the society in which they must operate. Thus, if marketing is used properly, companies can relate their activities to the support of the customers' growing interest and concern in consumerism, conservation and other aspects of a business's social responsibilities. Thus, the need to earn profits, essential for long-term survival of a company, can be harmonised with the goodwill of society towards the enterprise. This will be despite the selfish, thoughtless activities of a greedy few who use marketing solely to advance their own self-interests.

The marketing concept today acknowledges that man is not only an economic being, responding simply to economic and economic-based pressures. There are complex, non-economic reasons behind every buying decision. Modern societies around the world have grown, or are in the process of growing to a more adult, mature stage. In addition, fundamental changes have taken place in the political, cultural and social attitudes adopted by people; and this has affected their lives, often altering them beyond recognition. These are changes over and above those resulting from economic developments. Individuals' greater knowledge of life in general, stemming from more widespread (if not better!) education has fuelled this interest in improving the quality of life. Live TV transmission around the world by satellite has enhanced this, as events halfway around the world are now instantly made known in almost every home.

Shortages of raw materials have increased costs and prices and place different responsibilities on executives in control of companies. In addition to their normal work, they must consider how best to conserve supplies by better utilisation of scarce commodities and how to use acceptable substitutes. New activities or products have also to be planned from the same basic consideration. Will they help or aggravate the problems over supplies?

Political developments have brought new pressures to bear on corporate strategies especially those for development. In both developed and developing nations, growing government involvement in the business and industrial communities has restricted their choice and freedom of action. In many cases the authorities have issued orders or regulations, or given instructions, that a firm must proceed in a certain way or risk being nationalised or closed down. New strong challenges have been presented to marketing since all these changes eventually alter the individual and collective needs of customers. Even if direct government control restricts consumer choice, ultimately they will accept this limitation and exercise their choice within it, quite often moving to alternative products or services.

Thus human behavioural factors are increasingly becoming significant in the buying decisions of people. This in turn will affect the marketing activities, from planning to implementation, of corporations. Notice must be taken not only of the stark economic facts of a business and its markets but also of the other factors, generally called 'environmental factors'. Planning must now cover the cultural, psychological, sociological and political influences on buyers, Given that the last-named spring from political expediency not from economic or financial realities, it will prove the hardest to interpret or forecast. The growing importance of these four new influences on the buying situation is very subtle in nature and not always easy to identify. Their effects significantly alter the consumption habits and buying preferences of buyers. They call for thorough knowledge of marketing and its techniques by executives and the ability to assess and interpret the implications mentioned above with subtlety and great sensitivity.

5.1.2 The many faces and perspectives of marketing

So, today, there are many faces and perspectives to marketing. These depend on the aims or purpose of each marketing operation and the business, economic and political environments in which it has to operate. Therefore it is no longer simply a question of transferring a highly successful marketing plan and programme from the home country to a host country, even if the latter is economically and financially very similar. If politically, racially and even religiously the host country is different then there will be subtly different nuances at play and the transferred programme probably will not work. Indeed, it could even give offence to the local nationals. As stated in an earlier chapter, a multi-national corporation must take into account the special needs of each national society and then organise its activities to suit the conditions locally. In its home country, a developed nation, straightforward business activity and approaches may suffice. In poorer, developing nations, the pure business role may have to be subdued to allow the organisation to make a positive, worthwhile contribution to the development of those nations. This will include accommodating other aspirations the government or the people may have and see as having a vital role to play in securing the nation's future well-being.

The true role of marketing depends on a myriad of influences and needs, some of which are at times in conflict with each other. Besides the points mentioned above, the influencing factors includes the company's structure and how it does things best, the geographical spread and the industries, technologies and products with which it is involved. Then consideration must be given to customers and the technologies in which they are involved. Finally, there is the time dimension and scale and the initial or basic rationale on which the business was founded.

Marketing also has many perspectives and these determine the nature of the marketing programme required. Again the perspectives vary from company to company and nation to nation. They depend on the type of business and technology involved and the various local conditions and attitudes encountered in foreign countries. Further, where a company is highly diversified and has several decentralised or divisionalised activities, the perspectives for each division may also be different. For example, marketing heavy chemicals requires a different approach and mental attitudes to the marketing of (say) ethical pharmaceuticals. The information and knowledge needed will both be substantial and quite different. The marketing of desks and chairs which can be used in offices, commercial buildings and the home has a different perspective to the task of marketing specialised built-in furniture in the kitchen or bathrooms of new houses. Even the marketing of a Rolls-Royce car has a totally different perspective to that of marketing a small, mass-market vehicle like the 'Mini'. Thus each operation should identify the perspective that applies to it and plan the correct marketing programme for it. However, this should be done in such a way that each sub-unit maintains an integrated management approach based on total and constant coordination and cooperation with colleague activities and the corporation as a whole. Otherwise, sustained, long-term success will be difficult to achieve.

Studies in the U.S.A. (cf. Carlton P.McNamara: 'The present status of the marketing concept', *Journal of Marketing*, American Marketing Assn. Vol. 36 No.1, Jan. 1972) and less specific research in Europe show, however, that while the concept has been more or less fully applied in consumer goods companies and most consumer durables manufacturers, firms making industrial products have been much slower in adopting it. While most batch production companies and mass producers of these products use marketing in part, in various ways, it is not yet totally accepted. This is because they have not found how to adapt the basic techniques to their own unique requirements. In the case of capital goods, marketing is hardly used at all though it could be argued that marketing research, promotional activities and personal selling are required to some extent by everyone in this sector of industry. The situation has not changed to any measurable extent in the second half of the 1970s.

The fundamental differences between consumer goods and capital equipment operations explain the reason for the slower development of the concept in the latter case. The purchase of capital goods calls for considerable technical and professional skills on the part of those making the decision. (*See* Foster, *Planning for Products and Markets*, Section 8.7.3: A basic model for industrial purchasing process.) All these factors need careful consideration and are of greater importance than the question of price on its own. Customers' needs and the problems that create these involve many technical points, many more than in the case of a consumer deciding what food to buy or what clothing to purchase. The technical factors have to be considered carefully and might themselves involve some very complex or difficult technology or technical questions. The future well-being of the customer's business may well depend on a correct interpretation of them and thus of their equipment requirements. Further, a capital goods enterprise has fewer customers to deal with at a given time than an equivalent consumer goods manufacturer. The former can give every customer a highly individualised, personalised service and attention. Indeed, the technical aspects mentioned make it imperative that this is so. The consumer goods manufacturer finds it impossible to do likewise and would be mad to try it. Finally, the larger the enterprise in U.S.A., Japan and Germany the more willing has it been to accept the marketing concept fully. This has not been the case in Britain and other countries.

The question is still asked if the marketing concept can be applied to public services and goods. The argument goes that as marketing is geared to improving profit or profitability and public services at any rate are not required to earn profits (in some cases they are specifically barred from doing so by regulations) the marketing concept fails. This is a superficial argument. If it is accepted that marketing adds value (another way of considering profitability) in various ways, including holding down or reducing costs by increasing demand and efficiency of selling, then marketing, suitably adapted has relevance to public services and goods. Given that these operations all over the world are having the same objectives and constraints placed on them as those for manufacturing and service industries (e.g. to be self-sufficient, equivalent to 'break even' in industry; or earn sufficient surpluses (i.e. profits) to raise at least some of their future capital) then the marketing concept is even more applicable. Only by satisfying consumer needs and by convincing would-be customers that the utility or service being offered represents value for money and is necessary for their well-being can these new objectives for public services be realised.

Even in non-profit making areas such as (in Britain) education, health services, the police, consumer advice bureaux and similar pure service operations, marketing has a role to play. With the exception of the police, all these services have still to be sold to the public. Consumers have still to be made aware that the services exist to help them and how they are designed to do this. The public has also to be made aware of the role of the police in society, the help the police can give the public and the assistance the public can give to the police. All have to be made known, or 'sold'. Then there is the need to attract recruits to the police force and this cannot be done without use of at least one part of marketing-advertising.

For private non-profit-making organisations there are three major marketing tasks to be undertaken. First, there is the one of resource attraction. This means getting all the resources needed for the organisation's work through marketing the name, aims and intentions of the body to those who would be interested in supporting the work. Then there is the task of resource allocation which is akin to product policy in manufacturing industry. How should the funds be allocated, in what amounts, to which beneficiaries? The groundwork is similar to considerations of product policy such as: what products should we offer, in what quantities and to whom (markets)? Third, is the task of persuasion: persuading non-donors to do or support something that the organisation desires and that is part of its aims, e.g. anti-pollution, consumerism of all kinds, equal opportunities etc. The task of selling an idea is basically no different to that of selling a product, except it may be harder to do. It requires promotional activities and personal selling. If much literature has to be distributed then some professionalism in the physical distribution of the material is advantageous.

So the marketing concept is applicable not only to the wealth-creating sector of any mixed economy but also to the wealth-consuming parts, even in the public service sector. This is so even if in effect, the 'products' of the last named are given away rather than sold, in the sense that there is no direct payment for them by their consumers. Payment may be effected by direct or indirect taxation (or rates in the United Kingdom) imposed either nationally or locally. So consumers still have to be convinced ('sold') that the taxes they paid that went partially to cover the cost of these services, represented good value for money. (In some cases this is an arguable point admittedly!) In the case of nationalised utilities (as in Britain: electricity, gas, water, rail transport etc.) consumers make direct payments for their use of these services, but again have to be convinced that the products and services are good and worth the prices paid.

There remain the cases concerned with raw materials or skills in short supply, especially in instances when demand far exceeds the possibility of supply. Philip Kotler and others have coined the word 'demarketing' (an ugly, if correct, explanation of the process) to describe the use of marketing to limit demand within the bounds of resource availability. 'Demarketing' is an ugly word that is also open to misunderstanding, especially by junior academics with limited knowledge of marketing or limited intelligence. (They see it as justification for the removal of marketing as a subject from management courses!) In fact, with important raw materials entering a state of scarcity, stressing the need for conservation and avoidance of unnecessary wastage, marketing has come of age as it is adapted to reduce or restrict demand to clearly specified limits. Marketing would then stress the importance of efficient use of the resultant products or services (as has already happened in

Britain in 1978 regarding the use of North Sea gas) and the need to limit use to when there is no acceptable substitute product or service. Thus a better phrase to describe this part of marketing's work could be 'economical marketing'. The fact that it could also mean the economical use of marketing techniques themselves would be no bad thing. Too often they are over-employed, squandered perhaps, as witnessed by the mass of useless paper exorting everyone to buy or use some item which most people could do without and which has no intrinsic value except that imagined by the mailshots, or which would acrue to the promoters. Thus the application of revised concepts on marketing call for planning ability. The marketing executive must now be that rare combination of planner and doer. Or at least a team of marketing planners must work intimately and well with a team of marketing doers. (The teams can be any size from one each, upwards, depending on the amount of work that has to be done.) Given the many aspects of economics, politics, technologies, sociological perspectives and marketing that are involved, integrated management approaches as suggested by the *quadrille concept,* seem to be unavoidable for the foreseeable future.

5.2 Marketing planning

Marketing's aim is the realisation of agreed corporate objectives through the attainment of marketing targets derived from these objectives and the corporate plan. It involves reaching agreement with all other departments on each department's targets and policies, usually during the corporate planning work. To do this, marketing executives must analyse and understand the reasons for the results obtained during the previous planning period, the changes taking place in the business environment and then be able to extrapolate these inputs for the planning period under consideration. They also have to estimate implications and the effects of these changes and future requirements on the marketing operation, the results it should achieve and so make whatever modifications may seem necessary to give the company a better chance of achieving its objectives. In other words, the company is not content to be dictated to by external events occurring around it but will try to forecast their implications in advance and be ready to exploit these events for the maximum benefit of the company. This 'benefit' should include benefits for the customer. The work calls for good understanding of present and likely future business conditions and the activities and plans of competitors, as well as a sound grounding in the subject of marketing.

5.2.1 The quadrille effects on relationships in marketing planning

If the fully integrated efforts implied by the *quadrille concept* are in operation, there will be various effects during the work of marketing planning. This is illustrated in a generalised form by Figure 5.2 which has been limited to showing the main activity groups. Space prevents a more detailed illustration. The main activities in marketing are shown in the 'box' formed by the

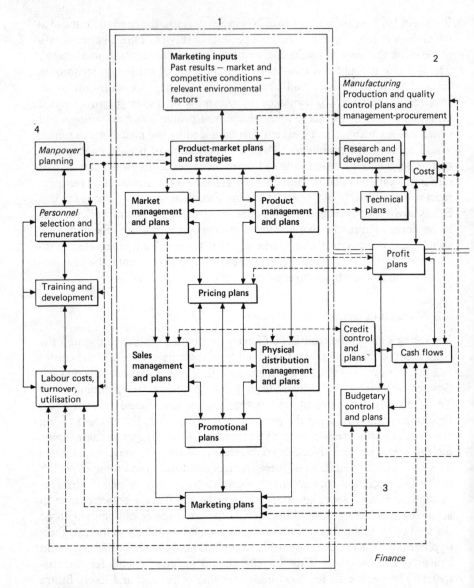

1 = Marketing planning — major activities
2 = Manufacturing — associated activities
3 = Finance — associated activities
4 = Manpower/personnel — associated activities
◀──▶ = Main departmental planning, action and communication channels
◀--▶ = Main *inter-departmental* planning, action and communication channels

Fig 5.2

broken-and-dotted-double lines and numbered '1'. The main sections of manufacturing activity that are involved in arriving at agreed plans with marketing planning work are shown in summary in the group of activities marked '2'. Similarly interested sections of the finance department are shown in the group marked '3' and personnel/manpower are summarised in the group marked '4'.

The normal internal negotiations, planning, communications and monitoring networks are shown by the full, double-headed arrows. For example, product-market planning and strategy decisions lead to formulation of new or revised product and market strategies and plans which themselves take into account and influence the pricing plans and decisions. The reverse is also true. What happens in the market regarding prices will affect the product-market strategy and plans that can be implemented. Decisions taken on product-market-pricing matters will also help to determine what can happen on the sales side, depending on competitive activity. If any of the original targets formulated from the corporate plan prove to be unattainable for any reason, the executives will have to rethink the matter, amend marketing strategy and policy and even have to amend the corporate strategy and objectives. Physical distribution requirements depend on the product-market-sales-promotional strategy and plans that will be implemented. Also promotional activities are determined by the sales-distribution plans and targets and the product-market mix that are required. In every case there is regular feedback of information and results. Hence the use of double-headed arrowed lines.

Remedial action will also be needed when results exceed targets. This has many possible meanings. In marketing planning, competition may have been over-estimated and the company's abilities under-estimated. Then should the expenditure on marketing be reduced, or increased to allow the company to drive on for a bigger market share etc.? The effects on other departments have also to be considered. Can manufacturing handle the increased volume if the market share is increased? What will be the effects on purchasing (procurement) requirements? Can the additional raw materials and skilled labour needed be obtained? What will be the effect on costs and cash flow? How will the profit plan be affected? How will future development plans be hindered or enhanced? Etc.

Thus there is need for continuous cooperation with and feedback from manufacturing, finance and personnel departments. This is implied by the broken-lined, double-headed arrows used in Figure 5.2. For example, decisions on pricing interest not only product, market and sales management but also executives in manufacturing (dealing with costs, production and quality control), purchasing and, where new products are involved, research and development and other technical executives. Financial colleagues responsible for overseeing the profit plans, cash flows and budgetary control activities should also be involved with pricing work. Similarly, sales management must maintain contact with financial colleagues responsible for the agreed credit control activities. The marketing plans should be checked, and the results obtained monitored, against plans and targets for budgetary control, cash flows, labour costs and utilisation, production and quality control aspects, manpower and personnel plans and whatever training and development is needed for marketing department. Personnel will also check how the last fits in with the company's overall training and development plans and budgets. (For simplicity these essential links have been shown as existing at the product-market strategy stage of marketing planning but they will also exist at other levels if integrated management is being used effectively.) Careful study of Figure 5.2 will show what the important integrated management links should be and that a complex network of cooperation is needed. Planning and control systems used have to take this into account. Executives must decide what precise links are required, to keep things as simple as possible. Then they must agree the frequency of contact and formal reporting and the critical points where contact must be almost continuous, and so on. Then they can devise an integrated marketing, planning and communication system that is right for their situation and preferred method of doing things.

5.2.2 In times of scarcity

The integrated approach to management is important at all times but is especially so in times of scarcity, whether of raw materials, demand, productive capacity or skills, or finance. In these circumstances the planning and resultant actions have to be evolved more precisely. Control of the operations must also be more precise. Integrated management and marketing aimed at reducing if not eliminating waste and profligate use of resources, will be particularly important, especially if the forecasted energy shortages and crises occur. However, while these scarcities will produce problems for society and business organisations, they will also offer executives new opportunities to devise novel marketing strategies to meet the situation, or challenges.

These challenges may be described simply as those arising from the need to balance off the profitability and other objectives of the business (e.g. market shares, market standing, reputation or image, cash flow requirements and return on capital — especially where this influences future capital availability) with the social and economic responsibilities that will be thrust onto executives by situations of scarcity. Many questions will be posed. These will range from the relatively simple (what alternative resources are available?) to the more difficult (e.g. what should be the future strategies and policies of the company if nil growth is an unavoidable fact of future life?) Should some defensive diversification be planned (since growth — offensive-orientated diversification will not be possible or will be very costly and difficult to achieve)? How should the much increased competition for a share of a considerably reduced total demand be handled? And so on. In general, the strategies that could be followed will depend on demand availability, how it holds up despite scarcities, how it will alter as a result of scarcities and the resources available.

The generalised nature of the strategies possible under three conditions of demand and resource availability are shown in Figure 5.3. When demand is increasing and resources are unlimited the unrestricted growth strategies of past years can be followed. Of course, greater attention should now be given to

Demand availability	Resource availability		
	Unlimited	Adequate	Scarce
Increasing	Unlimited growth strategy	Selective growth strategy	Nil growth—market retention and increased efficiency strategies
Static	Market development strategies	Selective market development strategies	Market retention or limited market divestment strategies
Decreasing	Diversification strategies	Highly selective diversification	Divestment with balancing and realigning of strategies — for optimal profit *and* social responsibilities

Fig 5.3 Alternative strategies.

the general social responsibilities of business such as the protection of the environment and the ecology, anti-pollution and the other general safeguards for humanity at large. Where resources are adequate, but not unlimited, more selective choices of strategies would be required to ensure that resources are not wasted and are husbanded for as long as possible. When resources are scarce, nil growth strategies will be essential. Emphasis will be placed on market retention (holding on to existing markets and market shares despite increasing competition) and the more efficient use of available resources. The search for alternatives (resources, production methods and products or services) will also feature strongly. Where demand is static and resources unlimited, the usual market development strategies can be followed. However, greater selectivity of strategies will be required because of the restrictions imposed by static demand. Where resources are scarce, more emphasis will be needed on market retention and limited or selective diversification into new activities. These should be where resources are not in short supply. It could mean an early withdrawal from established or historic businesses into quite new fields of activity. Selective market development strategies are needed when demand is static and resources are adequate but not plentiful. Resource husbandry is vital.

With decreasing demand and unlimited resources, normal diversification strategies can be applied. This becomes a highly selective operation if resources are adequated but limited. When scarcities exist, divestment of some activities will be necessary to make the scarce resources available for more profitable and worthy activities. In this last situation, considerably more attention will be given to the profitability aspect of all businesses. Executives will be seeking to maximise efficiency and profitability and should be running a more tightly controlled, stringent organisation than is the general practice today. The general aim will be to balance and realign strategies to achieve this with better resource utilisation, while taking full account of the growing social responsibilities that will face management teams. It will no longer be a simple question of what maximum profit can be made but what level of profit is in the best interest of society while keeping the company viable and capable of long-term survival at acceptable levels of return. The latter may have to be very different from today. Executives, investors and the public may have to readjust their thinking to accept lower return figures if this means operations that husband scarce resources effectively.

It will involve balancing the immediate needs of cost-revenue relationships while other activities that permit survival are evolved. For example, with unlimited fuel and the development of private transport, public transport demand has declined. If oil products become permanently scarce and expensive, the first development might be the revival of public transport and more efficient transport systems. An impetus might also be given to the development of alternative motive power sources, especially electric battery-powered vehicles, with serious attempts to develop lighter, more efficient batteries. Development of an automated sailing ship to replace fossil-fuelled ones had started on the drawing board in Britain in 1978. It would have remote control facilities and could complete most long-distance voyages in only a few days more than the average ship plying the routes. It would be able to move substantial loads at competitive capital and running costs to existing ships of the same size.

In general also, executives would have to alter their practices to meet changing social expectations and environments. This will place greater emphasis on the need for strategic or long-term planning and identification of opportunities, since these changes tend to take place over long periods of time. Of course, some may occur very rapidly and executives will have to rely on the flexibility of their operations for an equally rapid change of course to match. Market analyses will set the priorities for marketing strategy. Inability to satisfy several market segments that would otherwise have been, will focus attention on the identification of the more important segments. These will be the ones that the company will continue to exploit because of their long-term potential and lower demand for scarce resources. Products and services will be expected to make positive contributions to life, i.e. will not be just gimmicks. Executives who continue to indulge themselves by marketing the latter will probably be ostracised by consumers. These market analyses would have to identify the most promising market segments offering the best economic and strategic advantages in accord with developing resource scarcities and identifying those with the best opportunities for future, long-term, growth. They will also be searching for new product-market possibilities in accord with prevailing conditions. The forecasts from these studies should also indicate whether the resource shortage will be short-term in nature, or long-term, or permanent. Then the appropriate strategies (*see* Figure 5.3) can be selected.

Studies of the marketing environment will range from standard assessments of changes taking place, as normally, in the market environment to the identification of permanent changes in customer satisfactions as a result of their attitudes to shortages of resources. The public's increasing interest in consumerism, anti-pollution measures and similar matters will also bring about a change in the products and services they will support with their purchases. Companies may then be faced with major, if not wholesale, changes in their product ranges. As this will be costly, the earliest possible warning, from market studies, will be vital to survival in any age of scarcity.

The strategy opportunities that will be identified by these studies may then be classified in various ways. First, are those that take account of economical use of scarce resources and the conservation of those approaching exhaustion. Second, would be those that maintain satisfactory levels of return and profit, with or without market development but with the elimination of products or markets that waste scarce resources. The third would be those that offer by-product possibilities from the utilisation of former waste material. Finally, there would be those that reduce capital requirements and make better use of funds, marketing and other effort.

5.2.3 Marketing research

Executives cannot be certain that they have made the right or best decisions unless they have had trustworthy and relevant information and data on the problems requiring solutions. The information will range widely over market and product facts, economic, technological, political, social, demand and customer profile details. In addition, verification may be needed on the effectiveness of the sales and promotional activities and even the marketing research methods themselves. The chief constraints are the cost of the research and the time that can be allowed for them. There is never enough time or money for research and even if a company could afford all the money and time needed to gather and analyse everything about a problem, the situation would have changed by the time such a comprehensive study had been completed. Thus considerable selectivity is needed in the management of marketing research. When is the right time for certain things to be done? How can a big study be broken up into more manageable parcels which can be timed for optimum benefits to flow to the company, without destroying the total value of the whole study because of the time lags between each sub-study?

The usual sources of information are of course published material from all organisations (industry, government, research establishments, foreign embassies, the press, technical publications) and interviews of experts, users, appropriate technical staff of companies, etc. The first group, published material, is secondary data while the latter, gleaned from field work and not known or published before, is primary data. However, many companies forget sources of information within their own companies. These are the company's

documentation of past business, ranging from sales invoices and correspondence, delivery notes, records of complaints, manufacturing's records of
rejects, returned goods and finance department's data on credit control and
other relevant factors. These are not often consulted and when they are it is
usually done superficially. Properly analysed, they could save a company
considerable time and money that would otherwise be spent on marketing
research.

There are several ways in which research can be conducted. First, there is
the mailed questionnaire. This is the cheapest method but obtains a low
response. People usually do not like answering mailed questionnaires,
especially as the modern trend has seen profligate use of this method. Then
there is the personal interview conducted over the telephone. This is more
expensive than the first but the interviewer has a chance of instant recall, or
requestioning, of the respondent at the time of the interview. It has to be
carefully planned if it is not to become too expensive per call. The response is
higher but there is no chance for the interviewer to gain additional information
by observation; actually seeing what is happening in the respondent's work
situations. Then there are personal interviews against a carefully planned
questionnaire. The respondent's answers may be sought at the first meeting
with the interviewer asking the questions and filling in the form for respondents, or the form could be left with them. Agreement would be reached as to
when the interviewer would return to collect the completed form. This is an
expensive method.

Then there is the in-depth personal interview that does not use a questionnaire. The most time-consuming and expensive, it permits detailed study of
particular points. The interviewer may have a few notes to hand and will
skilfully guide the unrestricted discussion along pre-conceived lines or let the
discussion flow freely thus avoiding the injection of bias into the results. In
both the personal interview methods the interviewer can often learn a lot more
about the subject being discussed, or the points being made, by just using his
or her eyes to observe what is happening around them. This can help with ideas
on supplementary questions or on which replies need further clarification or
explanation. The in-depth interview is the most difficult to quantify and
assess, depending as it does on the interpretation of words and statements.
Given that people use words differently, it is sometimes hard to 'translate' the
meanings applied to the same phrase by different people. This is why this
method is used sparingly and usually as a qualitative follow-up of studies based
on more limited or precise methods, e.g. structured questionnaires.

The main thing to remember, and it is not often, is that it is very easy to
inject bias into research. The tone of voice of the interviewer, or the way a
question is put may be taken by respondents as a hint of what answer should be
given, or is expected. This is a particular hazard in in-depth personal interviews when the interviewer's interest in the subject or apparent attitude to it
may push respondents down pathways of discussion that are not relevant, were
never intended to be covered by the study, or are just misleading when read

with all the other information gathered. If a questionnaire is used, the design of the document, including the type and nature of the questions asked, the number of questions to be answered, the choice of answers available etc. must be very carefully prepared. Otherwise bias can be injected. For example, if a question is ambiguous, respondents will have difficulty in understanding the question and so in giving the right answer. If there are carelessly-worded questions, the respondents may be confused or may believe that the wording hints at the answer required. If answers to questions give respondents too wide a choice or range of answers by which to express their opinions, they may become confused and may just tick the first one that seems right, without any careful thought. If there are too few choices, the same confusion and problem may arise or there will be too high a proportion answering 'don't know'. Or if the respondent is a nice, helpful person there is always the danger that he or she will strive to discern what answer the interviewer would like and then give that one. These are just some of the points that have to be watched when planning and conducting marketing research and in devising questionnaires. Both are highly specialised and skilled jobs. Even long-experienced marketing executives are not experts on marketing research or questionnaire design. It is advisable always, therefore, to call in recognised experts to help with this work if there are not some already on a company's full-time staff.

It must be remembered also that customers or potential users have difficulty in anticipating their response to any new product idea. They cannot visualise it precisely and are uncertain about its relevance to and usage in their situations. Where a product exists they can see, measure, weigh and otherwise test it, or can deduce what the specification would mean in practical situations. Thus research for new products is the most difficult to do. Innovations which call for a change in mental attitude of a buyer to the purchase and use of the innovation are also hard to research with any certainty.

Finally, there is the subject of sources of information. It is important that all useful sources of information should be tapped where time and money permit; but it is even more critical that their trustworthiness is known, i.e. the degree of reliance than can be placed on the information and data received from each source. Also, known 'experts' tend to provide information which support their expert opinion or status, i.e. it is biased that way and the degree to which this might occur should be checked. They are useful in that the other non-experts they suggest should be contacted are less likely to give biased data and might provide the information that allows the experts' views to be checked for impartiality.

It goes without saying that marketing research cannot be done in isolation from other activities of the company. Obviously those in charge of research will be in regular consultation with other marketing and sales colleagues, especially those who have requested or commissioned certain studies. However, they should also ensure that relevant colleagues from manufacturing, finance and personnel are also involved. For example, in market studies on a new product, contact with production and quality controllers will be needed also. Then if prices are involved, marketing and sales executives will be consulted but so should production people (for verification on matters such as costs, quality, capacity) and finance colleagues (to verify cost-volume-price factors, estimated profit plan etc.). Where new skills are needed, personnel people will also need to be consulted from time to time.

5.2.4 Marketing strategy

Marketing strategies establish the set of principles by which marketing programmes are planned and adjusted to meet changing conditions in a company's business environment. They can be grouped into three basic kinds. These are undifferentiated strategies, differentiated and concentrated marketing.

Undifferentiated marketing strategies treat the market as an aggregate, focusing attention on what is common to the needs of customers rather than what is different. Products are produced and marketing programmes devised that appeal to the broadest and largest number of people. It calls for 'mass marketing', the use of wide or comprehensive channels of marketing and distribution, mass, national advertising and selling and the use of universal themes or appeals. A good example was the original Coca-Cola operation. Its main advantage was that it provided economies of scale and thus of costs although actual costs were of a substantial order. Where several corporations in the same industry follow this strategy, hyper-competition results. Also, the more adventurous small competitor can erode a company's market share by following a *differentiated strategy*.

With this strategy the corporation decides to operate in all or most markets but will design separate products and marketing programmes that appeal to some need or preference specific to each market. This enhances the appeal of each product and should lead to higher market penetration and the strengthening of the company's product-market reputation. The result is multiple product and brand offering as with toiletries, cars and the later operations of Coca-Cola covering different can sizes and drink products. Finally, there are *concentrated marketing strategies* where the enterprise concentrates on a limited number of total markets, offering products and programmes designed specifically for these limited ventures. They appeal to corporations of relatively limited means.

There are several variations on this basic theme. First, there is the *time-dependent strategy* where pre-planned changes in the marketing and product mixes take place. Then there is the *competitively adaptive strategy* where the marketing mix is altered to match, or improve on, changes made by competitors. Next there is the most used, the *sales-responsive strategy* where adjustments are made according to the sales response obtained. One gaining interest is the *profit-maximisation strategy* which is designed to maximise the profits of the company. A variation is the *profit-responsive strategy* which involves adjustments to plans according to the profit being earned by the operation. Finally, there is the *diagnostic strategy*, the one in increasing use, where changes are made only when the causes for current developments have been identified and analysed and the changes advisable have been diagnosed.

The basic problem is that in too many instances, companies just happen to fall into following one or other strategy. That is, the strategy is not a result of a logical decision based on a detailed study of the business, its markets, competitors and so on. Events just push the company in one direction or other. Also, the 'chosen' strategy may lend itself to such frequent changes that in fact the company has no long-term, consistent planning or control. The sales-responsive strategy is most likely to be abused this way as is its partner, the profit-responsive strategy. However, the decision on marketing strategy cannot be taken by the marketing department alone. The capabilities and cooperation of manufacturing, finance and personnel colleagues must be known and obtained. For example, if the plant, or technical skills, or research and development resources, or financial and manpower resources are inadequate (in any combination possible) for the intended strategy, then the latter should not be implemented. To do so would be to invite disaster.

5.2.5 Control

It should be obvious that the most sophisticated planning is of little use unless the results are properly monitored against plans and the operations correctly controlled. This is true for marketing; some say vitally true since marketing is the profit-earning department of a company. Yet many marketing control systems leave much to be desired. The problems range from systems that do not respond quickly or accurately enough to ones that are too fast in response, beyond the capabilities of the executives to react as quickly. Or in attempting to control everything strictly, a very rigid control system is devised which defeats the objectives of its existence.

The control system should cover, of course, every aspect of marketing. It should also permit the assessment from time to time, of demand variables, strategy and mix, effort and its effectiveness, market response and all budgets. In addition, marketing control systems should concern themselves not only with total marketing effort but also should feed information to and receive data from, other company departments whose activities are directly relevant to marketing operations.

5.3 Product-market management and strategy

Product-market management, for those who have not met it before, is a phrase used to describe all the work involved in managing and controlling all the marketing activities associated with looking after products and markets and as represented by the 'boxed' activities in Figure 5.4. The hyphen is to indicate the close and intimate relationship that exists between products and markets. It stresses that final decisions on one partner of the pair should not be made until the effects on the other partner have been estimated. Thus, if product strategy, range or mix is altered in any way, the market potential for the company and market mix possibilities might be altered considerably. Similarly, any change in market strategy or mix could seriously affect the opportunities for some or all the products.

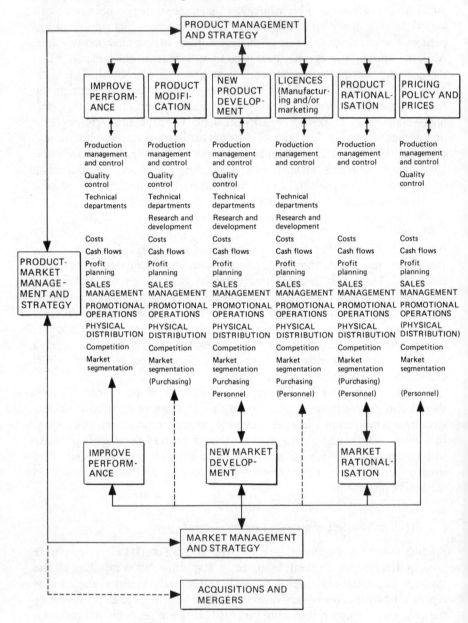

( ) = Limited or possible involvement

Fig 5.4

More precisely, product-market strategy seeks to exploit the concept, talent or orientation identified by a company as its own. It is the thing that gives the company its unique competitive edge. This strategy can be devised only after the company has correctly identified the business it is in, that is its true or real skills, capabilities and experience, not those imagined incorrectly by executives. These assessments must extend also to the plant available and its practical capabilities. Then the product-market strategy will indicate how the company intends to develop products and markets together, in an integrated approach. The work involves continuous effort to improve the performance of products and markets, to regain lost markets as well as to uncover forgotten markets, ones that somehow got overlooked. Then there are the tasks of rationalisation of and modification to products and markets, and the finding of new ones. Searching for licences (for products) and pricing work also normally come under this heading.

One part of the work that is overlooked is the development of peripheral markets, i.e. those that have very similar characteristics but vary in one or two details. Yet these are relatively simple to develop to worthwhile levels and can add quickly and considerably to the profits and sales of the company.

Then there is the subject of market modification. While markets cannot be modified in the same way as products (i.e. by change of formulation) the composition of the market segments that the company will develop can be changed to give improved, or more favourable, business potential to the company. Finally, another weak aspect of product-market management is the timing of product and market rationalisation. This ideally, should coincide with the introduction of new products and markets so that the new ones take over the overhead and other contributions of the ones that will be cut from the range of activities. If this is not well synchronised (and it is admitted that the ideal is difficult to achieve, there will always be some time delay or overlap) then the cash flow situation of the company can be adversely affected. If the introduction of new products and markets is too long delayed it can lead to very serious difficulties for the company, including liquidity problems.

In the quadrille concept of integrated management emphasis is put on the need for close cooperation in all the work done, and marketing is no exception. So in product-market management, all the work mentioned above must be related to the activities and responsibilities of other departments. Figure 5.4 shows what this implies. Every part of product-market management involves a number of different departments or sections. Activities or sections that are part of marketing are shown in capitals, while the contributions of others are shown in upper- and lower-case letters. Where a contribution is necessary only at intermittent times or in special instances, it has been shown in brackets. Though on the market management side there is no direct equivalent of product modifications and the acquisition of licences, market executives should still be consulted, if not involved in detail, in the planning and progress of these areas of work. They will then be able to check that these plans support the agreed market strategy of the company and that no imbalance or damage is imparted through failing to consider short- and long-term effects of the decisions taken in these areas.

Acquisitions (of companies or divisions) and merger are more the responsibility of the board than product-market management, but these should also be integrated with, or be relevant to, agreed product-market strategy. Board members and product-market executives should maintain contact of an advisory nature over this subject also. This is why this activity is shown in Figure 5.4 connected with a broken line. The acquisition of *licences*, however, is a product-market management responsibility and are spin-offs from decisions for future product-market growth and strategy. For example, if long-term plans showed that the company would be moving away from steel as a raw material to plastics, then a licence to manufacture and market equivalent products in plastic would be a first step in that direction. It is an easy, less costly and painful way of gaining expertise.

So that readers can link this book with other specialist ones on marketing, it should be stated that product and market improvements are part of what other books describe as 'market penetration', i.e. increasing the sales of existing and new products into existing markets. Product modification and new product development comprise what is called 'product development', while new market development and finding new customers is obviously 'market development'. Where the company is developing or acquiring new products involving technology and other skills new to the company, is acquiring licences or is involved in acquisitions and mergers, the work is known as 'diversification'. Figure 5.5 taken from the author's book *Planning for Products and Markets* shows the planning and integration involved in developing and launching a product-market strategy. The actual timing and time required will vary from company to company, industry to industry and even country to country.

As with all managerial activity, the objectives of product-market strategy should be clearly stated in writing. Besides incorporating the quantitative marketing targets (profit, sales, market share etc.) in their assessments, other qualitative objectives should be covered. For example, the company may wish to avoid over-dependence on one type or group of customers, or one type of technology or product. Then there is need to balance the requirements for future growth, stability and profits and the decision to move into a new technology over a given time scale. All these should be stated in the written strategy document. Further, in current conditions, the strategy should also take into account the resources position and the need for conservation. It may well be that when this is taken into review it will be found that some part of the original strategy may not be possible. Then some rethinking and replanning may be necessary.

5.3.1 Some common pitfalls

In new product-market development certain common pitfalls prevail. First, the contemplation, investigation and development of new ideas are frequently

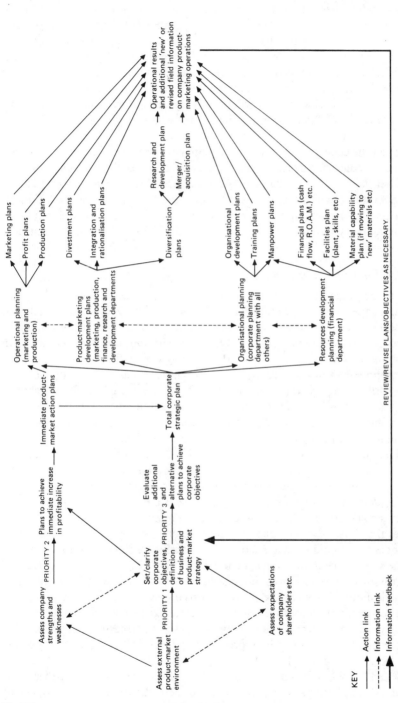

Fig 5.5

KEY

→ Action link

---→ Information link

⟹ Information feedback

Source: Foster, D.W. *Planning for Products and Markets* (Longman 1972)

based on hunch or 'feel', rather than hard facts. Or insufficient consideration is given to both the short- and long-term implications of the strategy proposed. The emphasis may be too strongly on immediate or present profits. Then there is the crippling liability resulting from looking at this work as a part-time activity, embarked upon only when the company is heading for trouble. In fact the work is time-consuming, and if it is left to the last moment, its benefits will not accrue at times when they will be most needed. They will occur some time later, often much later, assuming the company has not gone into liquidation in the meantime.

Then the concept of a new idea may not have been fully tested or analysed. Where a radical departure or change is involved the result often is a product or market failure. Or the company produces a product which offers no advantages or attractions over existing, well-established competitive ones. Finally, and perhaps surprisingly, research reports may not be studied carefully or their contents are misunderstood or misread. Often unfavourable points will be missed or glossed over.

5.3.2 Customers and competition

Customer orientation and the satisfaction of customer needs are important cornerstones of the marketing concept. However, they should not be allowed to obscure the other cornerstones of corporate survival and the need to make adequate profit. Executives should therefore consider how far they can go in meeting customer requirements and increasing sales without excessive erosion of profits. It is not an easy question to answer and is also influenced by competitive activity. If a corporation limits its sales to safeguard profitability, in present times it is almost certain that some competitor will try to meet that unsatisfied demand. In doing so, the competitor may gain some considerable economic, marketing or other advantage or strength and thus become a very serious challenger to the company. Thus the objective of customer satisfaction has to be balanced with many other considerations and all this should be embodied in the written marketing strategy that has been agreed.

In addition, customer or market response is a function not only of a company's marketing effort but also those of competitors and the product advantages they have. The company has no control over the moves made by competitors but should be in a position, after careful consideration, to respond in some way. Since in many instances delayed market response is unavoidable, the timing of counter moves should also be carefully considered. The problem is made more complex by the fact that most corporations operate today in many markets, with numerous products and technologies. They also have multiple goals or targets. Over all this is superimposed the question concerning the uncertain, sometimes totally unpredictable, developments in the many external factors that affect the company's business environment.

When considering competition it is usual for executives to consider competitors' marketing, sales, promotional and distribution activities and product-market strategy. This does not go far enough. Information on and analyses of competitors' finances should be studied through their balance sheets and published reports or other commentaries. Besides covering the obvious things like declared turnover and profit, return, the earnings per share, assets and net worth should also be analysed. This could give an insight into their strengths and weaknesses and indicate what counter-measures are likely to be most successful. Similar analyses of their product range and mix, manufacturing performance and plant could indicate further strengths and weaknesses in their manufacturing department. Counter-moves can then be planned to put particular pressure on their production facilities where they are weakest, e.g. encounter delivery delays, quality problems or inability to produce sufficient volume of goods. Finally, an analysis of customer mix, goodwill, market standing, labour relations and known operational problems will also help in the assessment of competitor's strengths and weaknesses prior to counter-moves being planned and launched.

5.3.3 New products

Something between one-half and two-thirds of new product ideas (depending on the industry and country) can be classified as failures. Either they have failed to achieve their commercial objectives, or have only partly achieved them, or have failed totally to emerge as viable products. Intended new markets may also have failed to come up to expectations. Many failures do not become apparent until considerable expenditure of money and effort has been made. In Britain, also, the poor management of expenditure on research and development has not improved new product development effort.

Among the many reasons why new ideas fail are the more common ones, such as the formulation or specification of the new product does not meet customer requirements. Or the cost, and hence selling price, may be more than customers will pay. Then the performance of the product, its frequent failure or breakdown and need for maintenance may also deter potential buyers. The dimensions may not be right, or the weight may be too heavy or too light. Its expected life may also not be realised in practice. It may offer no particular benefit over competitive or substitute products. Then the company may be unable to produce it in sufficient quantities and of the right quality at the right time. The product may seem to customers to be more of a gimmick than one they really need to improve their work performance or personal lives. Market demand may have been over-estimated and/or competitive activity under-estimated. These and many more reasons can be the cause for new product failure.

While closer and more effective management of research and development work is necessary, economic developments of the 1970s demand that new product development should be based on true innovation that has been carefully researched (market and technical). Then the product ideas selected for development should be ones that have specific appeal to selected, potential markets. This is necessary also because of the growing scepticism of the majority of customers of all kinds. They have become aware and fed up with sham innovations. Gimmicks are no longer popular. Greater attention to product design management and product reliability will also be necessary. Finally the sort of simple, but common, mistakes mentioned earlier must be avoided. Yet again, in this area of their work, the marketing department must work closely with manufacturing, research and development, technical, financial and personnel executives according to the important contribution they can make to the work. Product design is a particularly neglected part of the work and much more attention should be given to this, if only to improve product acceptance by customers, hence sales and profits.

5.3.4 Market shares

All marketing operations rightly aim to achieve various specified shares of their markets. For every activity there is a minimum market share which must be held if the operation is to remain viable over a reasonable period of time. What that level of share is will depend on the industry, products, markets, total demand, prices, profit margins and competition at any time. Then there is also a maximum share which most companies try not to exceed. Their operations may then be vulnerable to small operators able to nibble small bits out of their market share. Or the cost of obtaining each increase in market share may exceed the incremental gain in profit. Thus profitability overall will decline. It is preferable to use the extra effort that would be needed to push market shares beyond reasonable limits, to develop other, newer markets or products that had not yet been fully exploited. The return for individual operations and the company as a whole would be better.

Thus it is not a question of maximising market shares but of optimising them. That is, executives must aim to get the right balance of market shares for all the company's activities. At the same time they should balance the conflicting needs of short- and long-term requirements, obtaining sufficient immediate profit without jeopardising long-term survival and development. Again, full integration between at least the four major divisions of management is essential. While marketing are asking themselves various questions on what market shares they should aim for and why, they with colleagues should be considering the following also. Can the manufacturing department produce the range of products in the right quantities at the right times? Can distribution handle them? Will quality and specifications be assured? Can the intended prices and cost be realised? What will be the cash flow position? Etc.

When setting objectives and making policy decisions it can be dangerous to place too much importance on the subject of market shares. It is an important criterion but only one of many; and going for the largest market share possible may be self-defeating. Indeed, recent developments emphasise that the cost/benefit to the consumer/customer is perhaps the criterion that matters and permits markets to be more accurately identified with customer needs. Thus a product which costs more than a competitive item, if it has a longer useful life and lower maintenance costs would have a greater cost/benefit relationship for the buyer. Total costs and annual running costs might both be less also. This cost/benefit aspect may well be the key to the selling and promotional strategies and policies. Also it will avoid the disastrous adherence to some arbitrary advertising/sales ratio to achieve some unexplained market share. The ratio and market share may have been right for that industry, market and product some time ago but conditions may have changed so that they are just irrelevancies that succeed only in eroding profits.

There is no substitute for market (i.e. customer) orientation as the ultimate source of profitable growth. It was the overriding business concept of the 1960s. So it is surprising that in the 1970s there are many companies which still organise themselves in divisionalised structures based on regions or organised around products, a special technological skill or, sometimes even, just a company name. The only way to be market-orientated is to base the organisational structure around major markets. Thus these markets become the centres around which the divisions are built. Put another way, the corporation is decentralised by markets, when each market centre forms a natural profit centre.

Some example of market-centred organisations include IBM whose data processing operations are segmented according to their key markets of retail establishments, supermarkets and hospitals. The General Foods Corporation is organised on what it calls 'strategic business units' defined in terms of markets or customer groups. General Electric of America uses strategic business groups which are defined by the types of customer they must serve. Monsanto has organised its fire safety products according to the markets they serve: building and construction; transport; furnishings and apparel.

Market centering in this way requires markets to be defined as a system of closely-related needs which allow a diversified package of products or services to be sold to it. The package should combine a number of closely-related benefits for customers. Because these centres are operated as profit centres it is better to have a person with entrepreneurial tendencies in charge of each of them. It is too much to hope that there will be a sufficient number of real entrepreneurs about to take charge, but this is the ideal. Meanwhile, executives with a touch of entrepreneurial flair will have to suffice. They are certainly not product managers or brand managers but, as market managers, they are fully responsible for the profit earned in their area and in its development. All important decisions are within the terms of reference of these market managers. They are line executives in the corporation's marketing organisation.

Once established, these centres soon build a valuable bank of detailed information on their market. Thus growth is achieved through basing future expansion on detailed and accurate knowledge. The information can be held by the centres or at some central corporate location so that all market-centred divisions have ready access to all available information. Finally, the role of the board then becomes similar to that of a holding company with a group of independent subsidiaries. Within marketing terms, the centres are independent operators though they may draw their supplies from the same group of factories. They could of course buy in other manufacturers' products if these would be useful additions to the fully integrated package of products the centre is selling. (*See* Section 3.7.2.)

Market-centering may involve a company in extra costs. There is the expense of setting up an information system for each market. Each centre will require its own sales force, specially trained for the package they must sell and the information they must help to gather. Other operating costs may also increase in total, corporately, as each centre requires its own support services, from marketing research to documentation. However, if the market potential is big enough, the increased business (market shares) that could flow as a result of centering should more than off-set extra costs.

5.3.5 Joint ventures

Since joint ventures are still open to misunderstanding, a few comments here might prove helpful. Joint ventures are of particular, potential importance to the medium and small firm. They can be the means of providing mutually beneficial growth and diversification. The greatest benefits seem to arise when smaller, highly technically expert companies join forces with larger corporations with the necessary marketing power. Also, large companies unable to market a new product because the potential market share is too small can combine with a smaller company able to market it profitably at the indicated market share. Through royalties and other financial arrangements the large company can recoup its development costs and eventually show a profit on the idea. The smaller partner adds innovative muscle to its marketing and improves its profit-making ability.

Also two small companies with complementary skills and/or products and market knowledge could combine to launch a mutually profitable joint venture. (*See* Section 3.7.5 for a case illustrating this point.) Provided care is taken to make sure that skills, products and markets are a good match and that the two companies combined will be capable of achieving more than twice what any one partner could do, success should be assured. There are, however, other steps that must be taken for all types of joint ventures.

First, the participants should be quite clear in their own minds that a joint venture is the most appropriate strategy given the findings of candid analyses of each other's business, especially their strengths and weaknesses. Ideally, the strengths of one should cancel out the weakness of the other; but so long as this happens on key issues it will suffice. The second step is to examine the legal and financial arrangements that would be mutually acceptable and the manufacturing and marketing activities that would be required. These will then permit the third step, working out the modus operandi that would offer the best opportunities to both parties.

If the joint venture is not viable or seems doubtful an alternative is to have a straight licensing agreement. Or one partner can divest himself of the operation considered for a joint venture and sell it to the other erstwhile partner. Whatever the decision, there must be complete trust between the partners with the realisation that success depends on the combined efforts of both parties given freely on a continuous basis. It follows that choosing the right partner is a very important consideration when decisions on joint ventures have to be contemplated. Both should also be keen to achieve and maintain the respect of customers and competitors and they should be prepared to reveal frankly, all the information relevant to the planning and creation of the joint venture. Then, when the venture is operative, the technically expert partner should brief the marketing people of the partner firm (the one with marketing strength) on all technical aspects and provide the necessary technical backup that may be required. Similarly, the marketing partner should keep the technical partner fully informed of what is happening in the market and the results being obtained. Also, any problems that are encountered should be reported back quickly and joint discussions held regularly to deal with them. Then success for the joint venture becomes more probable.

5.4 Pricing and profit plans

Much has been published and there have been many discussions and studies on the subject of pricing. Pricing techniques and methods have been analysed in depth in every conceivable way and much is known about the subject, today. All this effort has probably made some contribution to improvements in pricing procedures and policies. However, the biggest gain in the effectiveness of the management of pricing will not necessarily come from additional knowledge of the various aspects of pricing work. It will come from a more rational and consistent application of established first principles of pricing. In Britain in the 1970s price fixing was bedevilled by government control of prices, which was linked for political reasons, with control of incomes, and wages and, by other legislative means, corporate dividend payments. Basically all price increases had to be justified to the Price Commission (formerly to the Prices and Incomes Board) prior to their implementation. That is, applications had to be made in advance. The reason most likely to be accepted was a genuine increase in costs; but even then, the company was expected to carry some of these extra costs (sometimes quite a substantial proportion) through improving efficiency and productivity. (In 1979 the new Conservative Government in Britain abolished price control. The immediate result was substantial increases in the price of many items.) Those readers interested in discussing pricing in the light of government price policies (and there are several governments other than the British which excercise some form of price control) should read Dr. Joan Mitchell's book *Price Determination and Prices Policy* published by George Allen & Unwin Ltd. (1978).

5.4.1 Pricing plans

The first principle is that pricing plans and objectives should be consistent with, and related to, corporate and marketing objectives. This means that using these 'higher objectives' as guides, objectives for pricing must also be agreed by all interested parties in a corporation (marketing, manufacturing and financial executives) before pricing policies and price structures can be formulated. Further, the pricing plan must relate to the company's profit plan as well as other marketing plans. This is a simple check when the estimated unit volume of sales of each product is multiplied by the planned profit margins expected from the proposed pricing plans to see if it comes up to the corporate profit target for each year of the plan. Simple and obvious though it is many companies throughout the world do not do this simple exercise as a matter of course.

There are also other considerations. For example, if the corporate objectives include the maximisation of short-term profit, then the pricing objectives must reflect this need and the price structure should permit the maximisation of total cash flow in the present or next immediate planning period. Alternatively, it can aim to maximise total contribution. The company could opt for skimming prices, those which have substantial profit margins at the outset so that sufficient profit can be recouped quickly. Then, as competition or sales resistance increase, the prices can be reduced and smaller profit margins would operate. If optimisation of long-term profit is the aim, that is the product is expected to have a long life and the intention is to earn the highest total profit over a number of years, penetration pricing may be used. This gives prices with reasonable, but not large, profit margins that will allow the product to build up a substantial market share, that is to achieve a high degree of market penetration. Or the pricing could be a combination of both; starting with a skimming price and then descending to market penetration prices when competition increases. Finally, of course, the company could determine what were the ruling market prices for their products and aim to price on or close to those levels, or that of the market leader, to improve its own market position without attracting too much competition.

Another marketing consideration is that of competitive activity. If competitors are altering their prices, the company should try to find out the reasons for this before planning a response. For example, if they are just trying to clear old stock or inventories then the right response is to do nothing and let them get on with it. It will help the industry if they can clear accumulated goods quickly. Then markets will return to more normal conditions. If competitors are raising or lowering prices, the company should try to find out the objectives or policies behind these moves, even though this is a difficult piece of research. (Talking to distributors and customers might help here.) Just rushing off to match competitors' price changes is not good enough. Especially with price reductions, if the company panics and cuts its prices below those of its competitors' all that might happen is a price war from which no-one really benefits.

Then total demand, sales volume, market shares to be obtained, physical distribution aspects and general activities of competitors have all to be considered before pricing plans and policies can be decided. For example, will the proposed prices win the company the sales volume (or market shares) specified in the corporate targets? How will competitors respond? What counter-measure would then be necessary? What would be customers' reactions? Are they price sensitive and are the markets price elastic? Then the legal, social and political implications and reactions have to be taken into account. What constraints have to be met? Does the proposed price policy meet or contravene any legal or political regulations? Or does it just offend against the attitudes and opinions of customers to price levels generally? Obviously also, customer requirements and expectations must be taken into account, including their view of quality and what importance, if any, they place on assured product quality and the reputation of the manufacturer.

Then major financial aspects must be considered. How do the proposed prices affect cash flows and the liquidity position of the company? What effects will the proposed pricing plan have on credit control and budgetary control plans? How does the pricing plan fit the profit plan? In addition the manufac-turing aspects have to be contemplated. Will the prices proposed result in a substantial number of orders to produce capacity or output problems for manufacturing? Can they sustain the quality with near-continuous and sub-stantial outputs? Will the prices of the different products lead to an optimal mix of loadings on the plant? Are the quantities sufficient for economical machine loadings? Etc. The personnel side may also need to be consulted if the pricing policy leads to a considerably increased volume of business. Can the extra skilled labour needed, probably in all divisions, be found? What would be the cost? If new products are involved, and the pricing policy anticipates strong demand, can the extra skills be found in the quantities and at the cost that can be afforded? Etc.

Thus there is more in pricing than just deciding what the prices and discounts should be! Many other departments and divisions are involved in the discussion and planning stage. Figure 5.6 is a simplified schematic diagram to illustrate this point. It stresses also the importance of costing work in the pricing mechanism. This is patently obvious, readers will think, but too many firms still operate costing and pricing at arm's length from each other. Even when marketing is correctly in charge of deciding price levels, they find it difficult sometimes to obtain full and frank cost information from whoever in manufacturing is responsible for this. Worse, pricing and costing may be left to some manufacturing employee who has not the slightest knowledge or idea of marketing and market conditions. This person then arrives at a price by adding a specified percentage to the estimated unit cost figure! Not surprisingly, the company may find it difficult to sell its products or to realise its profit targets. Another point is that unit costs should be changed to match as exactly as possible, any changes in the cost of the raw materials and the components used and other manufacturing expenses. Yet very frequently they are not. Costs are adjusted by some arbitrary percentage figure, the result of someone's lazy guess as to what these manufacturing increases might mean to the products' final unit costs. Then prices are incorrectly adjusted on these cost 'guesses' and the company is surprised at the end of a trading year, that while its sales volume

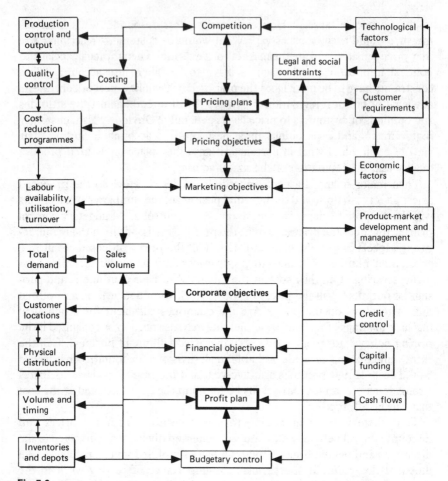

Fig 5.6

is on target, its profit target has not been achieved. The top management goes on a witch-hunt in the marketing department when the real culprit is hiding away in the manufacturing department or elsewhere.

The work on pricing should also indicate if corporate objectives can be achieved. If these objectives include both maintaining profit and market shares, it may be that owing to several prevailing conditions (market etc.) it is impossible to set a price structure that would achieve both. Either market shares can be maintained with some sacrifice of profit, or profit levels can be held with some sacrifice of the market share. There may then be a rethink of corporate and marketing objectives and strategies. Or it may be decided that the policy should be to get the best prices possible that will give an acceptable balance between maintaining the market share and safeguarding profits. However, a better solution may be to adjust the selling and promotional programmes and activities to ensure that sufficient volume is obtained to maintain the market share and profits at whatever level of prices may be dictated by competition and other market and manufacturing factors.

The company's market profile will be another criterion bearing on pricing decisions. An established company will have a certain standing in its markets and it will wish to maintain or improve this reputation. Pricing decisions which will erode it, putting the corporation in a poorer light, as far as customers are concerned, will be avoided. The effect of such pricing decisions should then be checked through for their effects on the profit plan, cash flows and other marketing, financial and manufacturing plans and policies. It may be that in order to nurture the company's reputation, considerable replanning of corporate and other strategies, policies and plans may be needed.

It should be remembered also that pricing decisions can affect the life of products. By increasing prices for any reason a corporation can shorten some product's life cycle because demand for it decreases substantially. Price reductions might extend the life of it. However, if quality is an important criterion and customers believe that the price reduction was achieved through some reduction in quality, they may stop buying the product. There are other reasons why price reductions may not lead to increased sales. If the product is an important one, say some major piece of capital equipment, customers may think that a higher-priced product must be better quality and offer better reliability than a cheaper one. They will not buy the latter. Then there are others who believe that a higher-priced article will always have a longer useful working life than a cheaper one. They can be so wrong!

5.4.2 Pricing guidelines

Pricing is therefore an intricate activity for marketing executives, as illustrated by Figure 5.6. Many things have to be considered and it may be useful for the following summarised guidelines to be listed here.

1. Pricing analysis should begin as early as possible in the product development stage. It should be continued at regular intervals (as reviews) during the life of the product so that allowances can be made for increasing costs and changes in competitive and other market conditions.

2. Thinking about prices for a product long after the initial design work has been completed and the first trial quantities are produced, is far too late. Price should be seen as an integral component of a product specification. So pricing should feature right from the start of new product planning.

3. Costs are a good indication of what might be the floor price, but should not be the sole criterion. Other market, technological and economic factors should be considered both for immediate and long-term profit and sales needs.

4. A broad view should be taken of pricing and its implications. It should be remembered that every facet of the business is involved and has some contribution to make at some time or other. Figure 5.6 summarises this point.

5. In the initial stages of the work it is not possible to be precise on any major aspect because of the unknowns and uncertainties then existing. Work has to

proceed from approximation to approximation until sufficient data and experience have been gained and more precision is possible. Continuing the work over a number of years allows improvements in the precision obtained to be realised.

6. Judgement, based on past experience and knowledge, will be required. In pricing it is advisable for judgement to be exercised in small rather than large steps.

7. It is necessary to collate and keep up-to-date information on all things relevant to pricing. These must cover competition, market conditions, ruling market prices, itemised costs and, ideally, most if not all the items shown in Figure 5.6. The sales department, it should be remembered, with promotional executives (or the agency if agencies are used) is a very good source of marketing information.

8. It is also advisable to ensure that product-market strategies, policies and plans are in line with corporate, marketing and financial objectives. Then pricing decisions will be more straightforward in that it is easier to make a choice from apparent alternatives. Difficulties arise when the product-market situation has been allowed to drift away from its objectives. It will then be difficult to arrive at prices which will obtain the right sales volume, optimal production levels and earned profit and satisfy other product-market objectives.

Where the *pricing of new products* is concerned the following additional points should be kept in mind.

9. The product must be fully described not only in terms of its manufacture and composition but also in marketing terms — its purpose, the tasks it performs, durability, maintenance, etc. and the technologies, end-use or customers for which it is intended.

10. Its application must be known (it should generally be designed for a purpose), especially anything unusual about the product's characteristics or market usage. Any advantages it offers different types of customers should also be stated as these may indicate if differential pricing could be possible.

11. The alternative or substitute products to the new product and their prices should also be known. Some estimate is also advisable of the strength of the competition that might be encountered.

12. Estimates of the reactions that might be met (price reductions? If so, by how much? More intensified marketing? etc.) should also be to hand.

13. The performance intended for the new product should be checked against the known performances of the alternative or substitute products. The effect of any price differentials should also be calculated.

14. Finally, a check should be made to see how far the proposed performance of the new product meets the performance requirements of potential customers.

After all this it will then be possible to estimate the threshold price for the new product, i.e. the price that will engage the interest of potential customers in the new idea. This is a measure of the premium customers might pay for the advantages offered over existing products. Then, taking corporate and marketing objectives into consideration, an effective pricing structure and level for the new product can be established.

5.4.3 Quadrille pricing

Pricing under the 'quadrille' or 'integrated management' concept is particularly dependent on various information flows between departments of the enterprise, if the correct prices are to be set. These information flows are summarised below.

MARKETING PLANNING   Programmed marketing costs for all activities for existing and projected new products and markets; sales volume and profit targets; market shares; competitive situation; customer needs and locations; physical distribution aspects especially costs, volume, timing and channels of distribution; field sales forecasts including volume probabilities.

MANUFACTURING   Output forecasts; unit costs; quality standards and effects on costs of variations therefrom; forecasted effects of cost reduction programmes; additional labour costs when special skills are required; plant loadings and effect on output of alternative choices; indications of optimal mix of output.

FINANCE   Reports on costs, profitability and performance being obtained compared with targets and thus indicating the profit and return gaps to be filled; investment plans and allocations to new activities; investment requirements and investment turnover; cash flow; liquidity; funds utilisation.

PERSONNEL   When special, additional skills required, their availability and cost; effects on production output and unit costs; effects of training etc. on labour turnover and utilisation, and hence costs; special risks involved and resultant effect on costs.

The detailed work for executives involved in pricing will include the following.

1. Pricing to meet profit targets and checking on the viability of the latter, e.g.—
   (i) prices for stated volumes and profit goals;
   (ii) volume required at stated prices to achieve profit goals;
   (iii) volume required at different prices to achieve profit goals.
2. Determining breakeven volume and minimum volume to cover variable costs.
3. Constructing discount schedules.
4. Estimating effect of meeting competitors' prices and effect of not matching prices or offering more competitive ones.

5. Estimating comparative safety margins of alternative pricing decisions.

6. Selecting price/volumes required if production output is limited (or when bottlenecks exist).

7. Pricing on conversion costs and pricing for individual bids or tenders.

8. Estimating effects of expansion and decisions whether to make or buy components.

Throughout, attention must be given to achieving the correct cost-volume-price-profit situation for each product and to estimating this relationship for new ones. (Further comments on cost and prices are given in Section 6.6.)

5.4.4 Profit planning

Every enterprise should have a profit plan as part of its operational plans. It is an essential complement to marketing, manufacturing and financial plans of a company. It is the important central nub of the control activities of managers, setting the vital standards (profit and return) by which their progress is measured. If the pricing procedures discussed previously are followed, it will be easier to reconcile profit and profit needs with pricing and pricing objectives. The close relationship existing between profit planning and pricing work is illustrated by Figure 5.6.

Like pricing, profit planning cannot be done in isolation from the rest of the corporation's activities and the external factors that have bearing on its business environment. Like pricing also, profit planning requires objectives to be set for it if the plans are to be sound and viable. These objectives must also be properly related to the other corporate objectives, strategies and policies. Thus consideration has to be given especially to the volume of sales, its supporting promotional and distribution activities, the prices that are operative, output, quality standards and unit costs, cash flow needs, credit and budgetary control, to mention just a few. Competitive activity will again be critical as this sets an upper limit to prices and according to unit costs, to the profit that can be earned by any product. Cost reduction programmes are also relevant since the results accruing from them could mean reduced unit costs and improved profit margins. Marketing may also wish to use these savings to lower their prices to hold the market share or volume. Then profit planning will have to ensure that this does not pull profits down (if sales volume is increased this will be so) or will not be reduced beyond acceptable limits (if volume does not rise). It is pointless, for example, to set profit targets that cannot be attained because the output, prices and sales volume that could be won are too low to achieve this. The resultant cash flow would also be too limited.

The important role of profit to a business cannot be denied. It is necessary to attract new capital at advantageous terms and is a useful measure of performance. However, it is not the sole criterion and if used as such, it may provide disappointing long-term results. For example, pressing indiscriminately for improved profit may upset the general stability of the company, its earnings and performance. Its long-term growth may also be jeopardised as too much emphasis may be placed on immediate profit-earners, to the detriment of products which currently are not earning much profit but have considerable potential for the future. Profit, therefore, is not the over-riding purpose of a business. Satisfying customer needs more effectively and efficiently is gaining acceptance as the prime purpose of business management. So if these two concepts are combined in executives' minds when the subject of profit is under discussion, they will appreciate the correct perspective for profit planning. Thus in Figure 5.6 'customer requirements' and 'legal constraints' are shown prominently as being relevant to the process of profit planning, as well as other management tasks.

Thus the financial objectives set should include objectives for the profit plan. It is not just a question of how much; but also of why, and for what purpose? The profit targets should not be so high as to require high prices which customers will not accept for then the company will not be effectively satisfying customer requirements. It will lose business and eventually good-will. With proper objectives, carefully reasoned from the aims and purpose of the profit to be made, more effective profit plans are possible.

An alternative approach is to consider the added-value involved in the marketing/manufacturing operation. The creation and improvement of added-value is in reality another acceptable corporate objective. Sales turnover of itself has no merit, and added value may be the best available measure of the worth customers assign to the products or services provided by an organisation. Added-value is the difference between the value of goods produced and marketed and the costs of materials etc. consumed in their manufacture. It discounts the effect of material cost variations. This concept cannot completely replace the profit motive as a spur for innovation and productivity. However, while the return on capital for any company can vary enormously depending upon the accountancy conventions used and their interpretation of 'capital' and 'profit', the added-value figures are less liable to misinterpretation and distortion. As a means of measuring the use of all resources — i.e. productivity — it has advantages over other techniques and replaces esoteric financial manipulations with a realistic, down-to-earth philosophy.

5.4.5 Profit centres

The concept of profit centres depends on the assumption that it is possible to separate the operations of an integrated corporation into separate divisions. Also, that it will be possible to measure the profitability of each division separately and correctly. Where the divisions are inter-dependent it is difficult to obtain the necessary clearcut allocation of profit accountability that the profit centre concept requires. In addition the amount of management talent may not be sufficient for such divisionalisation, and some products may not have a large enough profit margin to allow it to work. Since each division must be viable in its own right, procedures must be established for all activities and especially transfer pricing and the allocation of common services costs.

Thus, before profit centres are established, a number of questions have to be answered.

1. Are they feasible, and will there be real distinctions between the resultant divisions to give realistic operations?
2. Can there be real profit responsibility without the necessity of highly inefficient forms of organisation?
3. Can a financial control system be devised, and on what should it be based?
4. What central services and staff are needed? How would they operate and what authority should they have?
5. What areas of interest would be common to all centres? Should these be organised on a central or divisional basis? What costs would be incurred and would these be greater or less than those for existing methods?
6. If technology is common to some divisions, how would the specialised skills and advice be provided? What would be the cost?
7. Would any additional management control systems and procedures be needed? What would be their cost?

The creation of separate profit centres usually leads to increased operating costs and attempts to reduce them just erode the concept of profit centres. A larger workforce and more elaborate information flows will be needed. The assumption that these increased costs will be more than offset by increased sales and better performance and profit, is not always borne out by events. Further regular reviews of the decentralised organisation and its operations will be needed as the structure evolves and external business environment conditions change. The divisional structure may need alteration from time to time, involving more costs and unsettling operations while the restructuring is in hand. Changing business conditions may also require modifications to the methods being used, further unsettling the executive teams.

The benefits include the freeing of top management from routine work, allowing them more time for strategic thinking and planning. Decision-making is brought down to divisional level and closer to executives who are better informed and aware of the conditions applying to their products and markets. They become more accountable for their decisions and actions and are more committed, being able to identify easily with localised objectives. However, where divisions have business interactions, unless a good communication system exists, the adverse effect on one division by decisions taken in another may not be known until too late. If management talent is limited, lacks sophistication or the intellectuality to design and administer the new organisation, the results may be more disappointing than with the previous integrated organisation.

There is also the tendency for top management to retain some of the features of the old organisation, adding to any friction that may already exist. Thus decisions to set up separate profit centres need considerably more thought than is usually given to them. It can be argued that with a properly integrated management team, profit centres in their full sense, cannot be operated efficiently. All that may be needed is a division into operating units that split executive tasks into manageable workloads, controlled by integrated plans, targets, budgets and objectives. (*See also* Section 7.2.)

5.5 Sales management

Sales management is responsible for the planning, direction and control of the field selling activities, the selection and training of staff, the selection and organisation of distribution (in conjunction with physical distribution management if it exists), the definition of the communications and sales tasks to be performed and the organisation and administration of the means with which to do this (i.e. the department and its work). Sales managers should establish procedures for sales reporting, statistical sales analyses, standards of performance for all sales staff, the setting of sales quota or targets for each member of the sales force, and analysing competition and the results being obtained and comparing these with planned targets. They should also recommend changes to the sales plans when these seem necessary. A sales manager must also decide how, and when, all this information should flow through the department and to other divisions (e.g. other marketing colleagues and manufacturing and finance divisions) by consultation with the recipients, and how the department should be administered. In a properly integrated management team, the sales manager is the company's expert on all sales aspects of the business and acts as adviser on these things to other colleagues, especially in the marketing division.

The important relationship is that between sales management and physical distribution management. If this is not good, deliveries will breakdown or customers' requirements on delivery will not be met. Business and goodwill will be lost. Figure 5.7 illustrates this relationship and shows how these two activities link with other relevant marketing activities. In recent years 'consumerism' has grown into a force that corporations and their executives cannot ignore. Designed initially as a movement interested in getting enterprises to do a better job of producing goods and services, it has developed into one insisting that the interests of consumers, as a group, be taken into account by corporations, even if this acts against the latter's interests or even those of some individuals. Seen originally as hinderances to the pursuit of corporate goals, this and other similar movements have brought fundamental changes in the marketing and manufacturing policies and actions of corporations. The sales manager and the sales department, being in contact with customers or consumers, have additional responsibilities to bear in this connection.

In sales terms, certain former common but less desirable or more dubious practices have been either banned by law or by common rejection by society. If the general public turn against some activity or product the result for the company is as damaging as if the government had passed a law prohibiting it. Thus more care has to be taken to ensure that sales plans and activities do not

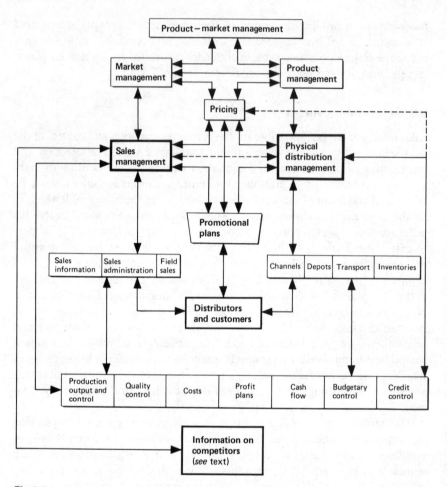

Fig 5.7

offend against the public good and comply with existing laws, regulations and current attitudes to selling and sales persons generally. The operation of the sales staff, especially door-to-door salespeople in Britain, and adherence to things like the statutory cooling-off periods for hire purchase and across-the-threshold sales now need to be controlled more effectively.

The consumer and the business executive are not natural enemies. The latter believes that success is obtained by seeking out and satisfying consumer needs and was generally proud of how well this job was done (though in most cases considerable improvement was possible). The new attitudes of consumers came about from a dramatic change in consumer values and priorities. Consumer segments split off and became polarised so that in serving one segment the corporation could easily antagonise others. However, most of the problems can be contained or avoided if executives, particularly in the sales department, recognise that consumers have—

— the right to safety;
— the right to choose;
— the right to be kept fully informed; and
— the right to be heard.

5.5.1 Sales planning and control

Sales plans and activities must be fully integrated and coordinated with corporate, marketing and other relevant strategies, policies and plans. Without this, the sales activities will not provide optimal returns for the corporation. The plans must also take into account market and competitive conditions and the capabilities of the company's physical distribution facilities.

Accurate sales forecasting is an essential element of successful planning. The greater the known inaccuracies of forecasting, the greater will be the need for contingency plans. These will either increase total costs, or in making provision for contingencies from limited funds, reduce the amount available for normal activities. One way of improving the accuracy of forecasting is to draw information from all relevant sources (subject to the time and money available), including the internal records of the company. These, linked with other desk research and field studies can provide a wealth of information and data on which to base sound sales forecasts. The main internal sources and the information they provide are summarised below.

INVOICES AND OTHER SALES DOCUMENTS   Name etc. of customers; products and services sold; volume of sales; monetary value of sales; industries and technologies served; end-usage of products; salesperson responsible for obtaining orders; location of customers and geographical spread of the business; terms of sale; transportation and method of delivery used; delivery or frequency of delivery required; potential demand for company's products (in total, and by customer or other groupings).

REPORTS BY THE SALES FORCE   Customers and prospects called on; lost accounts and attempts to regain them; new accounts opened; orders obtained; products sold or discussed; customer needs and usage of products; other relevant sales/marketing/competitive information.

SALES EXPENSES DOCUMENT   Expenses incurred by sales force in selling; direct selling costs; and when related to records of orders received, the cost of sales per item or order; amount of travelling done; cost and effectiveness of this; amount and effect of entertaining done.

FINANCIAL DOCUMENTS   Sales revenue (by product, area, customer, salesperson, industry or end-use); direct sales costs; profits (classified as for sales revenue); credit control standards and actual credit/returns/allowances; warranty aspects; cost of customer services.

MANUFACTURING DOCUMENTS   The main interest for sales forecasting purposes centres around capacity and output data and information on quality standards and actual quality levels achievable.

REPORTS FROM DISTRIBUTORS, DEALERS ETC. (if separate from sales documents) The roles played by the different channels of distribution used, i.e. their effectiveness, relative importance, costs; attempts to improve performance and past results of these, i.e. degree of success obtained; sales into channels by type of channel, product, area etc.

This is all important information for the preparation of business and market forecasts, especially sales forecasts. The above information is also important when the company sales and expenditure budgets, the quota to be applied to each salesperson (or area, product and customer) and similar targets has to be compiled. It is also helpful when decisions on distribution matters are necessary. The major end-products of this work should include forecasts on—

— sales volume and gross sales revenue;
— total cost of sales and estimated selling expenses;
— estimated gross margins before promotions;
— estimated general and administrative expenses;
— estimated net profit before tax.

Sales control requires the use of standard documents such as invoices, records of complaints and replacement, sales force call report forms, logging of enquiries/quotations/orders received (in total and classified by customer, area etc. as necessary) and so on. Where a large sales force is operated, journey planning is also advisable (as it is to most companies). It saves time wasted in travelling and makes more of the working hours available for 'selling' calls as apart from sheer social uses. Where company cars are provided, a note must be kept of maintenance, repairs and replacement; and these activities and expenses must also be properly controlled. The following ratios, individually and collectively in various combinations, have been found useful in the control function.

TOTAL SALES
/ total quotation and/or enquiries
/ total orders
/ quota or sales targets
/ total expenses
/ total calls
/ potential (in total or per salesperson,
   customer, area, industry etc.)

REGAINED ACCOUNTS
/ total sales
/ total calls

NEW ACCOUNTS
/ total sales
/ total calls
/ new accounts quotations

NEW PRODUCT SALES
/ existing accounts
/ regained accounts
/ new accounts
/ new product quotations

TOTAL ORDERS
/ salesperson
/ day
/ total sales revenue
/ total profit
/ total expenses (also possibly by area, salesperson,
  customer, industry, etc.)

To be effective, targets have to be set for the selected ratios when performance can then be checked against them. Something is wrong with the selling
activity or some marketing assumptions, if actual sales diverge consistently
from targets. Or it may be due to sales activities lacking selectivity, precision,
purpose or drive. In any event full-scale investigations and analyses are
required. It is no good executives merely hoping that things will improve.
They will not, especially in highly competitive markets. The problem has to be
found and the necessary solution or remedy applied. When trouble threatens,
sales managers all too often go to a remote area and stay there until the trouble
has blown over. Needless to say all these analyses and investigations must be
done in conjunction with colleagues from related or affected departments.

5.5.2 Competition

Most corporations acknowledge the importance of maintaining adequate
information on competitors' strategies, plans and activities, but only the larger
ones appear to make an organised attempt to be more than superficially
informed on this critical subject. Sometimes the expense of appropriate marketing research deters them. More often than not it is simple dereliction of
duty, or because executives think this part of their work is too difficult for them
to do, or raises too many problems.

However, the sales department is in contact with customers and distributors
and only too aware of what competitors are doing. It makes sense to ensure that
field sales staff are fully briefed on the sort, nature and type of information they
should obtain and report back on to other colleagues (not just in marketing). In
general terms, the things they should keep an ear open for include developments concerning pricing, product improvements and developments, important product and market rationalisation by competitors, and any change in
their strategies, channels of distribution, selling methods, tactics or promotional activities. The sales force should also be shown how to report back on
what are the strengths and weaknesses of competitors and the views held by
customers and distributors on their own company's strengths and failings.

They should realise that the company is trying to build up an accurate and detailed picture of who is competing against it, how this competition manifests itself, with what products, where competition is strongest, and when and why it peaks at certain times of a trading year.

In more detail, information is required where possible, on the following.

MANAGEMENT Reputation, age, structure and methods; outstanding executives, resourcefulness, aggressiveness; willingness to innovate; changes taking place in all these areas.

PERFORMANCE Market shares, sales volume and turnover; profits; earnings per share; return on assets; reserve capacity. (Not all this will be available to sales staff — some will have to be deduced from analyses of published accounts, reports etc. over the previous five or ten years.)

PRODUCTS Historical information on record for new product development and product improvement; pricing policies and trends; margins and trading terms; life of products; quality; style; rationalisation; inventory levels.

SALES Organisation; type of salesperson used; effectiveness of activities; territories covered and efficiency of cover; selling methods and back-up services; acceptance by customers and distributors.

MARKETS Type of markets and customers covered; areas where competitors are strong and weak; customer strategies; amount and nature of government contracts; industries served or applications of products; markets offering competitors greatest volume or share; market shares; ruling market prices.

PRODUCTION Facilities, equipment, locations; product made at each plant; condition of plants; ex-works or other unit costs as available; labour situation; management, engineering and technical resources, talents, capabilities, failings; material and other resources and skills.

DISTRIBUTION Methods and effectiveness of; present and possible future strategies; intermediaries used; acceptance of present methods by channels used and the customers; pressure for changes; estimated costs and delivery times; inventory levels and problems; obsolescence of finished goods stocks; methods of moving unsold items.

5.5.3 The sales force

The quality of performance by a sales force is of considerable importance and relevance to the degree of success achieved by the rest of the marketing operation. Much more care and attention should be given, therefore, to the recruitment, training, motivation and remuneration of persons in this force. In Britain particularly, the attitude prevails that a person is 'put into sales' as a last resort when appointments to all other departments have proved to be failures. This always results in low performance in sales activities. People must be selected because they are suitably qualified and experienced for each post, not because they are *not* disqualified to hold it.

Sales activities and performance are capable of considerable variation from company to company. As the sales force is the main instrument whereby companies achieve their quantitative targets (sales, profit etc.), it is variance of performance here that accounts for significant competitive differences between otherwise similar marketing operations and management. The variances exist because in every decision a value judgement has to be made, despite statistical methods which have been evolved based on logical analyses. So the personalities and attitudes of the persons making the judgement will colour the decisions and so the eventual performance of the sales force. Another contributory factor is the speed of response to any situation by the sales force and the rest of the company's organisation. Also, when information is scanty, recourse to hunch may be unavoidable.

Sales executives should spend most of their time trying to make the selling operation more effective. Various simple steps are needed. First, the planning and forecasting must obviously be of a high order. Next, salespeople must be thoroughly briefed on the objectives and purpose of the exercise and their important role in it. Third, they should be assigned workloads which they can manage in the time available. This requires consideration of and agreement on what is a reasonable selling call rate to apply and the level of call required, with the frequency of repeat calls. These will depend on the importance of the customer to the company in terms of potential business, important connections, prestige, reputation etc. This, in turn, means that potential customers should be classified accordingly and also by the potential business they could give the company. Next their geographical locations should be noted and sales areas drawn to give each member of the sales team an area of approximately equal potential, preferably without the necessity to travel long distances between customers. The latter is difficult to achieve in countries with large tracts of sparsely populated territory or with little industrial and commercial activity.

In drawing sales territories, a knowledge of the effective road and transportation systems is advisable, especially where, when and why traffic bottlenecks exist on certain routes. These points may require territorial boundaries to be drawn in what an uninformed onlooker might consider to be an odd way. The real criterion here is the time taken in travelling between calls and the aim is to keep this as low as possible. The actual size of the sales force will depend on the number of sales calls to be made in a working year. The working year for selling, or number of sales days available, is 365 less allowances for weekends and statutory holidays, annual leave, days set aside for conferences and routine reporting, time that has to be spent in the sales office and any other requirements such as training and development meetings. The average is about 200 days per year and this should be divided also between time spent on obtaining orders from existing customers to allowance for the finding and development of new accounts and for regaining lost ones. Some time should also be allocated to additional calls required to settle some question or problem with existing customers. Knowing the number of days available, the number of customers to be covered, how frequently they should be visited (i.e. total number of calls needed in a year) the theoretical size of the sales force can be calculated. The actual size will then depend on what can be afforded and other corporate reasons and will always be some compromise from the ideal.

Time wasting is a common problem encountered with sales forces. Surveys in North America and Europe on the way salespeople spend their working day produce consistent results. For example, most distributors consider that sales staff calling on them spend too much time in idle talk and other timewasting ploys (average 70 per cent of call time in North America and 65 per cent in Europe). Then time is wasted also because no attempt is made to find out customers' real problems (North America 55 per cent; Europe 65 per cent). Then the salespeople may not know their products or understand the technical aspects that relate to the products or the customers' technologies (North America 40 per cent; Europe 55 per cent). Also, many salespersons seem unable to present an effective sales message (North America 35 per cent; Europe 55 per cent). Then there are sales force who believe that stepping up their rate of calling means their efficiency is improving. If this does not lead to increased sales — the extra calls are more 'social' than 'selling' calls — then their efficiency can be judged to have declined. They are just wasting time and money.

The figures above from different surveys, indicate where sales executives should concentrate their attention to improve operations. There is also the problem of lack of enthusiasm. This may be due to poor motivation, or communications, or briefing on the marketing support being given, or statement on the important role that sales department plays in marketing operations. Lack of enthusiasm is also manifested by unpunctuality. This will cure itself if salespersons can be motivated to a high level of enthusiasm. Finally, there are those who rely too heavily on friendship with the buyer to sell their products. They think they can buy the business by buying the purchasing decision-maker a lunch or dinner.

The role of sales management, the sales department and its sales force and the inter-relationships with physical distribution management are illustrated by Figure 5.7. In addition it should be stated that the sales manager's role splits into clearcut groupings each with a different purpose. First, the sales tasks to be performed have to be analysed and the problems that may arise on the way should be identified or forecast. Then targets and quotas, agreed with each salesperson, can be set; their areas having also been agreed with them. The work must then be supervised, motivated and controlled. Special attention should be given to the support activities to ensure that they occur in the right manner and time in the right places. Then there is the recruitment, development and training of staff. In addition, the sales manager provides continuity and representation for the sales department in the management team.

It should be remembered also that the sales task can often be routine and boring for the people involved. Motivating them should therefore be given high priority amongst all the other work that sales managers have to do. It is not always easy to define accurately the personal characteristics and abilities which will be required. Skill in interviewing and selecting staff is needed and is not easy to develop. However, it would help if sales executives knew the way people actually do their work, the tasks they find easy and difficult, their background and record and their attitudes to the job and the organisation. The chief aim of sales executives is sales revenue maximisation, consistent with other corporate objectives. This cannot be achieved without close integration with relevant operations in marketing, manufacturing, finance and personnel divisions. This is especially true for physical distribution. Thus the selling function cannot be relegated to a minor role but should be seen at all times as the most important activity of marketing, if not of management as a whole.

5.5.4 After-sales service

After-sales service (of whatever kind) is often considered a separate operation from the actual selling work. It is in fact a very important part of the selling function, especially for companies making or selling technical products. The quality and trustworthiness of the after-sales service will often influence potential customers in their buying decisions. Bad after-sales service, or a totally unreliable one, will turn away business.

This is why this service should be considered as an important, integrated section of what is normally called personal selling. When the product-market and sales policies and plans are being considered and decided, full consideration must also be given to the extent and nature of the after-sales service required and the expectations and needs of customers in this respect. The cost, expertise and technical complications which may be required by the servicing needs might require revision of original ideas on the product-market and selling activities. Conversely, sales policies and plans, with even pricing, may have to be adjusted to match the servicing capabilities of the company.

There is little point in launching ambitious product-market and sales plans if the after-sales service cannot meet the necessary (implied) standards. Nor is there any point in fixing price levels which do not generate enough revenue to pay for the after-sales service while leaving acceptable amounts for pre-tax profits. Here again is another area of management activity which requires more careful thought and closer integration with related activities than is normally given to it. Whether the service manager reports to the sales manager or head of marketing depends upon how each company works best but usually a sales manager – service manager relationship seems to be the better idea.

5.6 Physical distribution management

As stated and as indicated by Figure 5.7 physical distribution is a close partner of the sales activity. The relationship is very similar to that between products and markets. The broken double-headed arrow linking these two functions in Figure 5.7 is meant to emphasise this point and is akin to the meaning of the hyphen in the phrase 'product-market . . .'. Coordination between sales and distribution is vital. Failure to achieve this at a high level will frustrate sales, marketing and corporate plans. Yet, despite the growing acceptance that success in business hinges on satisfying customers' requirements, few corporations around the world are giving sufficient thought and attention to the problems associated with physical distribution. Most bemoan the cost of distribution but do little to plan and control it more effectively for greater efficiency.

The magnitude of the problem of physical distribution is often obscured by the way distribution (and marketing, sometimes) is defined by different enterprises. For example, confusion can arise if it is seen as part of a customer relations operation only. Even in these instances the various activities of physical distribution are often assigned in haphazard fashion to different departments of the corporation, according to which seems to have the spare time to see to them! Then while inventories (finished goods and work-in-progress), depots and the actual distribution of products from company to distributors and customers may be assigned to the manufacturing division ('because they make the products'!), customer requests, servicing and the subjects of allowances and returned/replacement goods may be assigned to marketing and financial departments. In these cases, no attempt is made to coordinate the various activities of physical distribution and no-one is formally responsible for managing them in an integrated or coordinated programme. Nor are regular contact and cooperation maintained with other interested sections of the business (*see* Figure 5.7). Little thought is given also to the different distribution needs of the different types of customer being served. Yet examples have existed (e.g. Coca-Cola, motor and motor component manufacturers etc.) to show that a properly coordinated and managed physical distribution system, linked to the special needs of major customer groups, reaps rewards greater than the effort demanded by such an approach.

A channel of distribution has been defined as an organised network of agencies, distributors and others which in combination, perform all the necessary activities to link producers with users, and vice versa, to give an efficient and profitable marketing operation. Nor are these networks, once formed, static in nature. As the product-market mix changes for any reason, so the distribution network may have to be modified. Further, new intermediaries and networks develop from time to time as new techniques and new customers with their own special requirements become available. Developments in the last quarter of a century include the introduction of computers, automation, improved mechanical handling and the growth of franchising which have all helped to hold down costs or improve the service that could be provided. New channels may be created because both buyers and sellers need them to improve the total effectiveness of marketing activities. Thus conventional thinking, or a rigid approach may be counter-productive in physical distribution. Finally, it should be understood that the type of physical distribution system required will depend on the characteristics and usages of the products handled and, when these change, the system may need to be changed also.

The complexity of the physical distribution task and its inter-relationships with other corporate activities demand that the entire physical distribution activity be properly coordinated and managed by a team carrying responsibility for all this. Whether physical distribution is a separate department in its own right (advisable if it is the key or sole activity of an enterprise or very much work is involved) or a department within the marketing division (but a coordinated and properly managed one) is not of prime importance. The decision depends on which form of organisation would work best, providing the greatest customer satisfaction. Nor does the success of a system depend entirely on the manufacturer. The needs, preferences and requirements of distributors must also be taken into account. So the manufacturer does not construct the physical distribution system in isolation, but should seek the advice and cooperation of those third parties who will be involved and who play important roles in the distribution activity. Thus in planning the system note should be taken of the following.

1. The company's need for a physical distribution system and the tasks which it must accomplish successfully.

2. The needs and responses of each unit or agency within the system.

3. A proper evaluation, of each channel used, its ability to handle the variety of products and volumes which would be assigned to it, its ability to handle expanding business and to satisfy customers' distribution needs.

4. Regular consideration of the adjustments and modifications needed in the light of changes in relevant factors should not be forgotten.

The above requires detailed study of the following areas.

1. The physical flow of the products through the system — how they flow, their routes and volumes, the timing of these flows — the facilities required (depots, depot locations, size, routes, transportation), storage factors including insurance, protection of finished goods, and the agencies/distributors through which the goods will pass.

2. What can be described as the flow of ownership or control of the products, i.e. how ownership responsibilities and rights change as the products move through the various parties in the network.

3. The cash flows and how payments are made, the terms of trade and deferred payments and how capital for distribution purposes is assembled and used, including the fixed capital for the buildings and equipment needed for physical distribution.

4. Information flows, i.e. how producers advise distributors and how agencies/distributors advise each other and customers about the products, their availability, methods of distribution etc.

Where the distribution channel uses independent agencies the manufacturer is unable to order or instruct them to do anything, even that which looks to the latter like the best for mutual benefit. Such agencies are jealous of their independence and will do what they think best in their own interest. Thus products which are easy to sell and bring in the agent's best profits will always get the greatest share of their attention. Less favoured products, or those requiring more intensive selling, or technical knowledge, will be relegated to minor positions in the agent's operations. Only when manufacturer's and agent's self-interests coincide will the network act in ways the manufacturer thinks are best for the distribution and sale of its products. Thus physical distribution involves executives in considerable public relations work on distributors. Executives must create and maintain the interest and support of distributors and ensure that the latter are aware of the mutual benefits that would flow if the two parties can work together at all times. Even the use of effective advertising to stimulate customer interest and bring a pull-through type pressure on distributors to stock and handle the goods efficiently, will not be successful if the willing cooperation of distributors has not first been obtained. Thus more attention should be given to the aims, needs and interest of intermediaries if this cooperation is to be won. It may even require an adjustment to the entire marketing programme.

5.6.1 Decisions and costs

Physical distribution costs are substantial in any business, so the total cost aspects must be known and be well controlled. (*See* the Author's chapter, 'Distribution: The Achilles Heel' in *Modern Marketing Thought*, 3rd Edn. edited by Westing and Albaum; Macmillan, N.Y., 1975.) These costs include that involved in the task of sorting finished products from bulk packs to smaller packets or groups meaningful to the type of distribution that has to be done. The size and nature of these assortments will vary from party to party in the network and the smaller the package the greater will be the total cost of breaking bulk. Customers may also require an assortment of sizes and the more there are the greater, again, will be the total cost. Thus the sorting methods will have to be carefully considered before decisions on the method to be used, the size of the final packages and the variety of sizes available can be made. These will depend also on the range of customers to be served, the likely size of deliveries to, or calls-off by, customers and the handling aspects involved. Even at this level of decision, it is advisable for agreement to be reached between the manufacturer and the distributor on all points; thus carrying even further the integration of decision-making and actions between these two parties.

While it is now generally accepted that physical distribution and its costs cover not only inventories but also depots, their locations, size, the handling, sorting and storage of goods, packaging and packing, rents, heating, lighting, insurance of goods and local taxes (or rates) it is not widely appreciated that demand aspects and other marketing objectives have bearing on physical distribution decisions and their resultant costs. For example, depot locations besides playing a vital role in physical distribution also have a public relations function. Customers within easy range of depots have greater confidence in the company and the availability of its products locally. They know delivery can be relatively fast. It may also prompt customers to hold smaller inventories themselves, moving the burden of carrying stock on to their supplier and thereby saving some of their own costs. The advantage to the supplier is that the customer may then be tempted to place more business his way. There is, however, a limit beyond which this ploy should not be taken, as it will place dangerous, additional financial burdens on the company and might lead eventually to disaster. Thus the design of physical distribution systems must take the widest possible marketing view, assessing the various important factors that must be considered and, at the end, be prepared to trade-off some of the benefits that would accrue in order to optimise the physical distribution operations in terms of service to customers and minimal, controlled costs (and other problems) for the manufacturer. The main activities involved in the physical distribution process are shown in Figure 5.8.

Where several major customers or groups are involved, from large manufacturers with various delivery points to supermarket and other chains, it is useful to allocate distribution costs and profitability on a customer basis. The impact of distribution costs on the net profitability of individual customers can then be gauged. This is an important consideration where retail outlets have to be served. To do this effectively an equitable allocation of distribution and related costs must be achieved. The starting point is the establishment of the real gross margins of each account. Thus physical distribution and financial executives will have to work together on this with appropriate contributions from time to time by manufacturing and other marketing colleagues.

The gross margin is simply the revenue earned less the total of manufacturing, marketing and physical distribution costs, which includes the cost of selling and promoting the products. In practice this can only be achieved if these costs are precisely apportioned according to the effort and time taken to service each customer. They cannot be allocated roughly on some heuristically established percentage basis. A study of the relevant invoices and terms of trade, with the ex-works cost of each product is, therefore, required.

An analysis of performance will further establish the main elements of delivery costs. These include such items as fixed vehicle costs, outbound, inbound and inter-call travelling costs and other actual expenses incurred in effecting delivery to major outlets. Allocating a general overhead charge to give blanket cover to total delivery costs will not be sufficient for this purpose. It is possible to establish a high degree of refinement in making such a physical distribution cost breakdown. Time standards can also be established for the loading and unloading of goods, delivery to specimen outlets, driving times and so on. Appropriate weightings can be used to allow for road and traffic conditions and delays. While the selling and merchandising operations will be carried out independently, an analysis of the call patterns and selling and merchandising costs will establish the call frequency for each customer, the

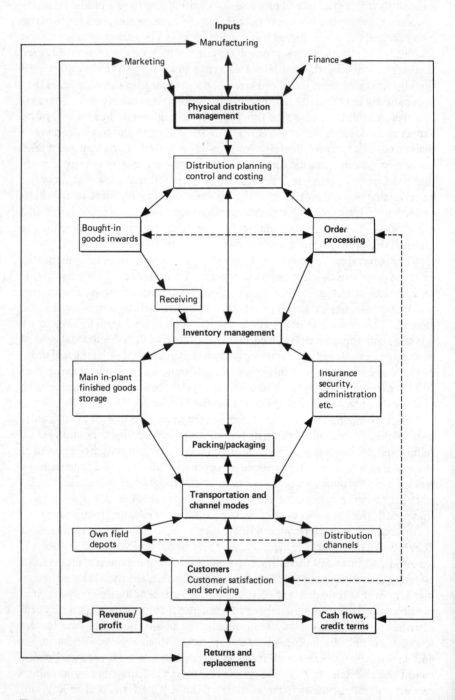

Fig 5.8

type of calls made and their related costs. Administrative costs are either product- or type-of-transaction-related but they can be attributed more precisely to customers' orders.

Finally, the status of the customer has to be assessed. This shows whether the account is profitable or not and in the latter case, whether the revenue covers just variable costs or variable and some fixed costs. The degree of profitability in terms of gross margins can also be established. This work will also increase awareness of the relative attractions of different customers in terms of their effect on overall corporate profitability. So, while a lot of work is required to set up this approach, the benefits, for the company could be considerable and worth the effort.

The work will also help executives to make better decisions on physical distribution matters. It will help also to resolve certain common conflicts, including deciding the best level of service to provide within cost and time constraints and the maintenance of such levels. The level of inventories matched against the risk of being out-of-stock for any given sales pattern or peak demand period will also be easier to resolve. So will the questions of which form of transportation and channels of distribution should be used.

5.7 Promotional activities

Promotional activities in Britain and Europe are usually taken to be advertising, sales promotions and public relations (including press relations). In the U.S.A. and some other countries, personal selling is also judged to be a promotional activity. (These four activities are usually referred to as the *Communications mix.*) The most usual argument that arises in this area is the size of the promotional budget that should be operated. How much money should be allocated to this work? Especially in Britain, the tendency is to cut the budget when hard economic times befall the business community. Yet when times are difficult competition increases and perhaps increased expenditure in promotional and marketing activities will be the only thing that would ensure survival. Certainly, companies will be fighting harder to maintain the same volume of business which means they will be trying to get, a larger share of a smaller total market.

Some promotional activities are essential while others are less so. In the first category fall activities aimed at creating and sustaining customer interest in the products and awareness of the continued existence of the company and its goods, especially new products. Selected techniques that ensure that the company obtains its share of any peak sales period are also in this category. What is less useful is corporate image advertising, or vague general promotional activity which seems to have no aim, objective or purpose. While corporate image advertising can help to keep the company's name and reputation in the minds of customers it can be overdone. There has never been any conclusive proof that the vast amounts spent on this advertising brought any tangible results. Thus it is important for executives in charge of this work to get the objectives and purpose of their exercises clearly established. Then they can pick the right activities and campaigns and will spend the promotional budget most effectively. They should aim for the right mix of the different activities open to them and for the right timing for each one used.

Effective promotional campaigns are really integrated communications programmes, involving the techniques in their most effective manner to get across to customers the most effective messages about the company and its products. The messages have to be designed so that they are received and interpreted in the way intended. Nor is it a case of one technique having supremacy over all others. It is not, for example, a question of advertising v. public relations. Each has different purposes and effects or varying aims and objectives; and each is indeed complementary to the other. The only determinant in decisions on the promotional mix that should be used is the overall promotional objective: what has to be achieved and when? Some requirements may involve major expenditure on advertising, others may need more public relations and some others still might need equal expenditure on advertising, sales promotions and public relations. It's a case of 'horses for courses'. Sales promotions will obviously be used where they will be most effective in supporting and enhancing the sales operations.

Outside the U.S.A., sales promotion is an undermanaged, underdeveloped area of marketing. This is so in Britain. It is also under-researched, despite the substantial sums of money spent on it. Few users have a clear idea of the purpose and effect of sales promotion and of the response of customers to various campaigns. The fact that this is true in the United Kingdom in the late 1970s, despite the growing interest in the search for goods that represent value for money, indicates the need for executives to give greater attention to this useful but neglected marketing tool.

Studies have shown that less than half of all shoppers could name one product that was on special offer in the supermarkets they usually used. Less than 10 per cent knew what the normal price of that product was. Appreciation of the benefits of larger packs, money-off coupons and other sales promotions has grown; but only at a very slow rate. Yet manufacturers continue to spend large amounts of money on these activities without checking whether the expenditure will be worthwhile. Especially in a prolonged recession, the well-planned use of sales promotions can help to maintain, and even build, sales volume, boost stock returns, improve liquidity and maintain production volumes. In this way the effects of the recession would be minimised. With a better appreciation of sales promotion, executives will obtain a better, more successful, integrated promotional campaign and better operational results.

Like everything else the planning and control of promotional activities cannot be done by an executive in isolation from other marketing colleagues and appropriate executives from manufacturing, finance and even sometimes, personnel divisions. Manufacturing will have to confirm output and quality so that the advertisements will not accidentally be misleading; and financial executives will have to check costs, prices, profit margins and expenditures proposed to make sure they all fall within the targets set by the corporate plan. Jointly, but especially with marketing executives, they will decide what the objectives of the campaigns will be, the impact they wish to achieve and hence the frequency and size of the advertisement, colours and the media to be used. The trouble that has arisen in the past stemmed from the few sharp operators who, for their own benefit, were prepared to ignore the laws or regulations applying to advertising, especially the ones prohibiting misleading advertisements. The planning team should, therefore, make a special check to ensure that they are not unknowingly finding ways over, under or around any legal limitations that may apply. The public is much more aware of this point and any corporation found guilty of any slip-up could pay quite heavily in the form of lost business and goodwill. (In the U.K. advertisements should also comply with the code of practice laid down by the Advertising Authority. With commercial T.V., compliance with the code of the Independent Broadcasting Authority is also necessary.)

5.8 International marketing

Confusion still exists about the difference between 'exporting', 'international marketing', 'international company' and 'multi-national corporation'. Exporting is simply selling goods made in the home country through the home organisation and agents appointed in foreign markets. The goods can be finished products, part assembled ones or unassembled components and a variety of agents and terms of trade can be used. International marketing is normally taken to mean not only direct exporting but also sales in foreign countries through the company's own marketing organisations abroad. They may work side by side with the agents originally appointed for exports. There may also be a small assembly workshop which puts together the imported components. Some items of simple design and material could also be made in the foreign country and used in the company's assembly works.

The international company is one that has marketing and manufacturing operations in some foreign countries. These are usually wholly-owned subsidiaries, though nowadays local nationals are usually expected to hold the majority of any shares issued. They serve the countries they are in and possibly also near neighbours where communication facilities permit. Sales to other countries where this facility does not exist would come through the direct exporting operation of the home company. The multi-national corporation (see Section 2.5) has full-scale operations (subsidiaries) in several countries. They may or may not be fully autonomous and usually, now, the parent company holds only a minority of the issued shares.

International marketing is thus not some new, different management technique. The marketing involved is basically no different from that used in the home country. Only the facts about the market and the general conditions will be different. When the ground rules applied by the local government, limitations of the area, market and competitive conditions vary and are taken into account, the actual marketing campaign used may be quite different from the home programme. But the techniques and methods will be basically the same. Marketing opportunities will also vary from country to country and the programme should take this into consideration. More detailed study should be given to the possibility of a company becoming involved in international marketing.

For example, how many companies consider investment in marketing and manufacturing facilities overseas rather than just 'exporting' from the home base? How many have considered combining the benefits of lower labour costs in the host countries with the technical and other know-how from the home base? What about the benefits of transfer pricing on an international scale? How often do make-or-buy decisions take into account the availability of acceptable but lower cost components from abroad? How many companies have considered reaping the benefits of their research by granting licences to suitable foreign manufacturers? How many have sold licences without the benefit of adequate market research beforehand on the markets the licensee would be serving? How disappointed are they when they find they have under-guessed demand and so not charged the higher terms that could have been obtained? These, and other points, need study if marketing overseas is to be successful and if costly mistakes are to be avoided. There is no reason why this should be left to the large corporations.

5.8.1 Strategies

The product, promotional and marketing strategies that can be used depend on several things. First, there are the products or services to be marketed, defined in terms of the need they satisfy or the function they perform. Then consideration must be given to the market conditions under which the products have to be sold and used and the cost involved in adapting the product to local needs and in marketing and promoting them. Included in consideration of market conditions should be a study of the preferences, attitudes and other behavioural aspects of the local nationals and their ability to purchase the goods, i.e. the income levels and patterns. Included in the studies must also be a thorough assessment of competition. Thus there is need for product-market studies similar to those for the home market. Only the parameters or standards against which the measurements are made may have to be modified to suit local conditions.

There are five basic strategies from which various permutations or modifications can be made. *First*, the company may just sell to another country the same, unchanged products with the same marketing and promotional message as used at home. This will work if the products satisfy the same functions or needs as in the home country, while the conditions under which the products will be used are also the same. Exporting to another developed country with similar ethnic background, economic and other conditions should respond to this simple strategy. Or it may be a product that has universal appeal, is low in unit price and where, if the local nationals do not buy it, they have no suitable alternative (e.g. Coca-Cola). This is a low-cost strategy; but if product-market conditions are incorrectly judged the result could be disaster.

Second, is the strategy that involves marketing the same products but with a different promotional message because the need to be satisfied or the function to be performed are different. The conditions, under which the products would be used, are, however, the same as in the home country. Again, the local nationals should have the ability to buy the products. Bicycles and motor-scooters are examples of products that could respond well to this strategy. While in more affluent countries they satisfy recreational or sporting needs, in poor countries the former supplies basic personal transportation and the latter a more expensive and sophisticated form for the 'better off' citizens. Marketing costs are low for this strategy, especially if the promotional and marketing campaigns can ride along with those of the home country. Additional costs for research and development, manufacturing and inventories are avoided. The only substantial additional costs would be incurred by having sound market and product research conducted in the foreign markets. These would be to establish market conditions and verify that the product to be offered would meet the specifications required in the foreign countries. However, if the product and market evaluations are wrong then a disaster similar to that which could arise with the first strategy, would result.

The *third* possibility is to offer different products, more suited to, or specifically designed for, foreign market conditions. However, if the need to be satisfied or the function to be performed is similar to that in the home country, the same marketing and promotional programmes could be followed. Adaptation of the home product will be necessary when climatic conditions, or conditions of use, vary greatly from the home market. Petrol (gasoline) is a good example. Its formulation has to be varied to meet different climatic conditions. Also, in poorer countries the cheapest grade is required so high octane fuels may not be marketed. Household appliances are other examples where modifications are needed because of different usage in different conditions, or environments and the electricity supply system may be different from the home country's. Protection against corrosion or contamination would be essential in humid, tropical climates. Extra manufacturing costs are involved. However, as the product has been almost custom-modified for the foreign markets, acceptance is more assured and the product should sell more readily than the unadapted one. Again, the consumers must be able to afford to buy the products.

The *fourth* strategy is that necessary when market indications are that both the product formulation and the marketing and promotional messages have all to be altered. Instant coffee is an example of such a product. Different nationals have varying tastes and, because their expectations and needs are different, the product formulation and marketing and promotional messages must reflect this. Television sets are another example. Apart from the obvious cases of poorer countries where black and white sets are in demand (there may be no colour transmissions anyway), smaller sets may be needed (to keep purchasing costs down) or they may require simplified controls and circuits. This may be because the sets will be used in unsophisticated, probably remote, areas of the country where maintenance facilities will be rudimentary. Sets may need to be robust and may require extra protection against humidity, excessive heat, fine dust and so on. A sufficient number of potential customers should be able to afford the product. This strategy involves extra costs in manufacturing and marketing but the products being custom built for their markets and supported by promotional programmes tailored to local conditions, success should be reasonably assured.

However, conditions do vary greatly in overseas markets so that straightforward adaptations and adjustments to the product and the supporting marketing activities may not always be sufficient. In these cases, the development of entirely new products and marketing/promotional programmes will be unavoidable. So this *fifth* strategy is needed when new foreign markets with unique conditions and needs are to be exploited. This involves the greatest additional costs and risks, especially the fact that there may not be sufficient potential customers who could afford the new product. Yet many opportunities remain to be exploited profitably. For example, many millions of women around the world still handwash clothes. They may not be able to afford the western world's washing machines or there may be no reliable electricity supplies. This suggests that simple, manually operated washing machines, made from locally manufactured components, similar to some Victorian basic designs, but benefiting from modern materials and technology for lightness and ease of operation, could have considerable marketing potential. Yet to date, too few companies have risen to this sort of challenge. They have been reluctant to develop an 'intermediate technology' employing present knowledge and abilities in less sophisticated ways, as suggested above.

The choice of strategy will depend on which one optimises company profits over the longest period, under conditions prevailing in the overseas market. It, and the resultant profits, should not offend the propensities of local nationals and their government. The answer will also depend on the particular product-market-company mix the potential international operator wishes to have. In deciding this, consideration should also be given to several points such as, whether there will be local manufacture, or part component manufacture and eventual evolution to a multi-national corporation? Whether the host country has the necessary infrastructure to handle the proposition? Are there sufficient resources for the (limited) new skills that would be introduced? Are the potential markets ready to accept the products and their concepts or will extensive and costly promotional and selling operations be necessary? How difficult will it be to achieve the necessary market penetration or market shares? What potential competition is there? For example, would the Japanese be able to do something better at less cost and more quickly? What after-sales services are needed and can they be provided? Tackled in this way, many more companies should be able to afford and benefit from, more international marketing activities. It is obvious, too, that the right decisions about it cannot be made without close cooperation and planning between all the corporation's departments.

5.9 Questions

1. What effect does the application of the 'quadrille' concept have on marketing activities?

2. Why is it necessary to reconsider the meaning of the marketing concept? What are the implications?

3. What is product-market strategy? How is it evolved by any company?

4. What are the more common mistakes made in marketing planning? How can these be avoided?

5. Why is the formulation of marketing strategy so important? How is it done?

6. What steps have to be taken when marketing planning is done during times of scarcity?

7. Why are joint ventures beneficial? What conditions must exist for this? How should a venture be planned?

8. Why does pricing seem to be so difficult to do? What principles should be followed? How does the 'quadrille' apply here?

9. What are the usual difficulties about profit centres? What rules should be followed in setting them up? Does the 'quadrille' concept have any relevance here?

10. What are the salient points to be remembered about sales planning and control?

11. What is international marketing? What strategies could be followed? Under what conditions would each operate the best?

6 Manufacturing —
marketing — finance — personnel

Again, this chapter is not concerned with detailed descriptions of the many activities of a manufacturing division. It concentrates instead on the interdependence of key areas with the other divisions or departments of a company, without which there cannot be effective integrated management. Thus some well-loved aspects of manufacturing may get only a mention, regardless of their relative importance to the division, or the fact that they may have spawned a considerable amount of literature. Issues that are internal to manufacturing will be played down.

Also, the discussions will be based on manufacturing industry but in fact the points apply to all industries, including services. In the latter case the manufacturing department's equivalents are those departments or people who are responsible for providing the components that make up the services offered to consumers. For example, in *Tourism* these would be the persons responsible for making the forward block bookings of accommodation, transport and the other support services. In *Insurance* it would be the actuaries and others involved in devising the policies that will be underwritten. In *Banking* it is the executives who plan and organise the services that will be offered to customers. In *Hotels* the team would be drawn from such departments as food and beverage, banqueting, housekeeping and the front desk. Each contributes an essential element of the services provided by hotels. Thus with a little thought, readers from most businesses can derive guidance from this chapter.

6.1 The manufacturing quadrille

Figure 6.1 is a simplified illustration of the two main groups of activities that form the *manufacturing quadrille*, the subject of this chapter. They are the vital activities that must be efficiently managed and which must maintain regular contact with other disciplines of the company if the manufacturing operation is to be successful and provide marketing with the right products, quantities and costs when they are required. The first quadrille here is made up of *production planning and control — manufacturing — quality control — costs*. The supporting quadrille is comprised of *technical services — research and development — procurement or purchasing — labour and plant utilisation*. The hub around which

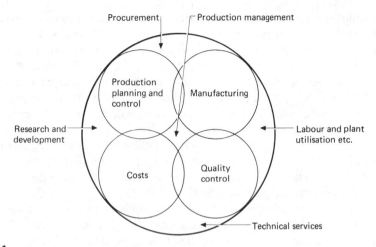

Fig 6.1

all these revolve is the production management team. Other, much-loved activities such as machine loadings, operations, maintenance, repair and replacement would, for the purpose of this book, be part of manufacturing and production management. Operations research, time and motion study and industrial engineering are considered part of technical services or production planning and control or quality control as circumstances, or how a company likes to operate, may dictate. They will be mentioned from time to time in the Sections that follow where they can or do make a contribution to more effective integrated management.

6.1.1 Old and new attitudes

Prior to the Second World War and for some time after, depending on the industry and country, manufacturing or production was considered the key activity, having absolute supremacy over all other management disciplines. Included in 'manufacturing' were all the technical services that supported production. So it was, too often, a case of the company producing what it wanted to make, to its own standards of excellence devoid of consideration of market needs. The products made were often not wanted by customers or were too highly priced for the consumer to afford them. The poor sales staff were just responsible for trying to sell them, frequently without planned and related support from promotional activities and technical backup services. Indeed, often the manufacturing staff who were supposed to provide the technical support to sales despised the selling role and staff. The support they gave was reluctantly provided and frequently was not made available promptly and efficiently. Quality standards tended to be much higher than was necessary or than customers could afford; but this was seen to be an essential part of maintaining the company's name and reputation in its industry!

With the relatively static conditions of the inter-war years this worked more or less but at much lower profit levels than would have been the case if more dynamic concepts were used. The degree of success depended on how close the company's product ideas were to actual consumer needs and pockets. A high correlation was often due to pure coincidence. Some sort of success was assured for a company if all its competitors were blundering along the same path. However, if one enterprising corporation set out to provide what the market wanted, it prospered and the others suffered to varying degrees. The names that were to become big after the Second World War usually made their big breakthrough in this manner before the war. However, with national economies not changing much and high unemployment, most companies managed to survive or were saved just in time by the war and the resultant high demand for all kinds of war goods. Most customers had to make do with what was available, often a poor substitute to what they really needed.

Since the war and especially in the last decade or two, the emphasis has changed, though in some countries slowly and after many hard defensive battles by production, defending the status quo! The marketing concept gained acceptance. Executives began to realise that sustained success and long-term growth depended on satisfying customer needs as closely as possible. Executives had to swallow their pride and not be intent on producing the best product (to the satisfaction of their own technical ego) but concentrate on producing the best products that met market requirements. Those who learnt the lesson more slowly than others suffered much pain and distress until, finally, the truth broke through to them. There are still some corporations which claim that they have not embraced the marketing concept. In reality, an analysis of what they do and how they do it, shows that they are following the major precepts of marketing and probably do not know it!

In financial terms, the old approach was to produce and sell products so that at the end of the day, black figures would appear in the profit and loss or trading account. Anything suggesting risk was avoided and if red (i.e. loss) figures appeared there was widespread consternation. A witch-hunt would be started to find the culprit. Accountants were primarily interested in strict observance of the laws applying to business (as they still are, mainly, today). They gave little thought to future growth as opportunities at that time were limited and restricted. They frowned on anything that would ruffle their figures at the end of a trading year. Accountants were just 'figures factories' interested in producing neat and tidy accounts and profit and loss statements which showed no losses! This was despite the fact that Pitmans published T. G. Rose's classic *Higher Management Control* in 1934, pointing the way to active partnership in the quadrille for accountants. Now it is realised that future growth cannot be attained without the acceptance of some risk ('calculated risk') because risk is inherent in all new ventures, whether products, markets or whole divisions or departments. The emphasis now is on risk minimisation and avoidance, but not to the complete exclusion of development and growth. It is also accepted that the bigger the opportunity the greater the risk is likely to be. Hence the change to calculating or estimating what the risk might be and then deciding whether the gains possible make it worth taking on the risk (cost/benefit studies). Thus experimentation is more readily accepted now and this has affected the philosophy and attitude of manufacturing, marketing and finance departments, if not the whole corporation.

On the personnel side, pre-war organisations just took what labour they needed from a large pool of unemployed and with minimal training (really just showing them how a machine was operated) turned them into semi-skilled machinists or 'trades'. If the people could not perform to satisfactory standards they were sacked and replaced by others. After all, there were almost two unemployed people for every job that was going, even the most menial and unskilled. Management did little to find out the causes of these failures. Was it the fault of the person or due to lack of training and experience or some executive failing? Since the war, with skilled labour in short supply, management has been forced to give more thought to the recruitment, training and development of all personnel it needs, including the blue collar workers. They are assessed and receive appropriate training from time to time. Key personnel receive more detailed and long-term training and their development is planned along lines that follow the planned, integrated development of the company and the additional skills it would require.

The personnel department has also become something more than just a group of people who hire a workforce for the manufacturing department on the basis of rough 'man' specifications issued by the latter. They now work with manufacturing executives to evolve personnel development plans consistent with manufacturing's changing needs, as spelt out by the corporate plan or long-term objectives. They help to measure labour utilisation and keep watch over labour turnover figures. They devise training programmes for groups and individuals to meet the needs expressed by manufacturing executives. They maintain a watch on all aspects of remuneration, changes taking place in the availability of skilled labour, wage structures and the social, health and trade union (industrial relations) sides of manufacturing. Thus personnel executives are essential members of the team working with manufacturing, marketing and financial executives in the planning and controlling of a company's operations. Only then will a company have reasonable chance of survival and growth at acceptable levels of profitability and productivity, especially in the difficult times of the early 1980s.

6.1.2 Myths and fables

Under today's difficult economic conditions, new technologies and new and insistent social demands on business, the old systems and mental approaches of conventional plant have become anachronistic. People can no longer be treated just as numbers of small cogs in a big machine; nor can their interests be totally submerged to those of the corporation. The problem lies in changing the time-hardened image of the factory as an undesirable place to work for resourceful, intelligent and independently-minded people. Many of the assumptions and values on which factory productivity has depended have come under considerable questioning. Conventional methods of making decisions and managing the manufacturing process have also got out of touch with the changing attitudes, beliefs and expectations of society. This has led to greater worker dissatisfaction and union/management conflicts, with low utilisation of expensive equipment. Whether they like it or not, executives are under increasing pressure to review the wisdom and appropriateness of conventional methods of workforce management, the job of foremen and supervisors, product design and liability, programming or scheduling of work and inventories. Views of the factory as a social and technological institution are being subjected to radical, even innovative, changes.

The factors affecting the pressures that have been brought to bear on manufacturing may be summarised as follows.

ECONOMIC
Increasing international competition.

Shorter product life.

Smaller production runs with more customers demanding special products for their own needs.

Narrowing profit margins.

Increased inflation resulting in higher labour and material costs.

Increased cost of equipment and capital.

For individuals:
more interesting jobs outside the factories, with better pay and opportunities in service industries or government.

TECHNOLOGICAL
New equipment, processes, controls, materials, products.

New and faster information systems.

Development and use of computers.

Advancing technology generally leading to more involved or complex technologies.

Corporations become involved in more than one advanced technology.

SOCIAL
Distrust of large corporations, especially multi-national corporations.

Less interest in or emphasis on, value of work, responsibility, obligations, quality of work.

Increased interest in or emphasis on, freedom, social hours, leisure, rapid advancement without appropriate personal effort, individuality, instant change (often for change's sake only).

The typical reactions as the result of the above are as follows.

ECONOMIC
Low return on investment because of low productivity and efficiency.

Shortage of skilled labour and trained and competent executives.

High employee turnover and absenteeism, giving low labour utilisations.

Union and other conflicts and friction.

MANAGEMENT

Tendency to become hesitant, or even paralysed in the sense of seeming to be unable to solve problems as they are presented.

Overconcern about most things especially about not upsetting unions or labour relations.

Overreaction and inability to handle crises efficiently and effectively.

Tackling all tasks on a piecemeal basis rather than in a comprehensive, constructive way.

EMPLOYEE

Lack will-to-work.

Declining interest in the factory as a place of work.

Growing conflicts between older and younger personnel, management and labour, as well as inter-union (demarcation) squabbles.

Reduced involvement in company objectives.

To remedy the situation changes had to occur in the conventional concepts on how to manage manufacturing operations and in acknowledging and meeting human needs in careers in manufacturing. However, before changes could be successfully introduced some long-held myths and fables had to be exploded. First, there was the belief that the management of factories is essentially a task of engineers; the implication being that only they knew enough about a manufacturing process to be able to handle it. Believed blindly since the start of the 20th century, it became an even more seductive attitude with the great advances in technology and the introduction of sophisticated machinery. It seemed to underline the fact that factory managers had to be mechanically minded. This attitude ignored the fact that this type of employee was often deficient in training, knowledge and experience of other important factors in plant management, human and social aspects, financial and marketing problems and the markets and strategy of the company. They might have been excellent engineers but it was more than likely they could not handle people equally efficiently. Frictions and conflicts abounded.

Second, it was thought that a well-run factory could simultaneously accomplish high quality, with low costs, minimum investment, short production cycles, rapid introduction of new products and high flexibility! It is impossible to design a factory system to be able to do all of these things together. Some criteria have to be given preference according to the corporate objectives and some trade-offs with the others are unavoidable. The diametrically opposed opposites must always be reconciled according to current corporate strategy, but this can be modified if or when corporate strategy has to be changed also.

Third, there was the view that the main criteria for evaluating factory performance was efficiency and cost. This is not so. Even when a factory is relatively inefficient it can still be a potent competitive weapon against other firms if it is highly flexible in executing product changes, can manage the usual fluctuations in output, introduce new products quickly while providing for and meeting short delivery promises with minimum investment in fixed assets and inventories. Depending on the context of the corporate strategy in force, many other criteria, not just efficiency and cost, may be vastly more important.

Fourth, was the belief that economics always favours machines! This ignores the abilities of humans to plan, remember and use judgement, wisdom and intelligence to expand far beyond the capabilities of machines, even computers. Humans are clever, intelligent and intuitive but slow. Machines are ignorant, repetitive, lack intelligence but are fast. Attempts to substitute machines for humans proved expensive and usually disastrous. Replacing a human with a machine involves substantial expenditure relative to the cost of employing the human. Thus, in fact, economics often favours the use of humans.

Finally, there was the myth that the systems approach and a high level of conceptualisation are substitutes for experience and knowledge. This fallacy is encountered most in highly theoretical planning exercises that have failed to produce worthwhile results. Instead they spawned a multitude of errors of judgement that proved very costly. There is no substitute for knowledge and experience. Everything else in management supports these two and helps to extend the capabilities that spring naturally from them.

6.2 Conflicting objectives

The objectives of the manufacturing division include producing specified outputs of different products and quality at agreed unit costs. The executives also aim to keep costs down by making sure that machine loadings are at levels which will give optimal efficiences. Sometimes, when market requirements are forgotten, executives may go for machine loadings that give maximum efficiency of operation of each machine. One result could be over-production with many more products made than can be reasonably sold into the market. The unsold stock will raise the level of inventories and their cost. The executives do not realise that by acting in this way they may have sub-optimised not only the whole manufacturing operation but also marketing's and the company's.

On the other hand, marketing will be interested in having levels of output which are attuned to market demand and competition and are at acceptable prices. The prices should allow them to sell the output at specified profit margins to gain the targeted market shares. They aim to keep inventories down to levels consistent with demand and demand patterns, target market shares and the anticipated pattern of trade or purchase. They are usually not interested in increasing inventories of finished goods to levels that cannot be sold, regardless of what the theoretical improvement in unit production costs may be through better machine loadings. Nor are they interested in pushing quality higher than the standards required by customers, as this will increase unit costs and sales prices, often beyond the ability of customers to pay. Both sets of objectives are right and proper for the departments concerned but it will be realised that there are inherent conflicts in the different aims and purposes of these two departments.

Further, the financial department has to see that the assets of the company, especially money, are properly utilised and that too many are not kept idle or under-used for too long. They are also interested in maintaining cash flows at whatever levels are necessary for the company's business and future needs and to keep liquidity at acceptable levels. They see healthy cash flow and asset utilisation positions as positive indicators of good management. They believe these factors will persuade the company's backers to provide new capital at advantageous terms when it is needed. They see also as indicators of good management, good and effective credit control, consistent with marketing and other needs, and effective and sound budgetary control. Additional invest-ment for marketing or manufacturing has to be justified and shown to be worth the inherent risks. So here again, there are many areas of potential conflict with other departments or divisions. If the financial department pursues its objec-tives regardless of the countervailing needs of sister divisions, finance execu-tives may end up by frustrating the intentions of the company and its corporate strategy.

Thus, with all these possibilities of conflict even with legitimate departmen-tal objectives, it is clear that optimising corporate performance will only be possible with a fully integrated management. While each department must concentrate on carrying out efficiently and effectively its own tasks and respon-sibilities, this cannot be done without reference from time to time, to the needs of the other divisions or departments. Thus the quadrille concept approach is vital. Without it optimal corporate results are less likely. No matter how successful a company may be without integrated management, it would be considerably more successful if it adopted the concept.

K. G. Lockyer, in *Production Control in Practice* (Pitman, 1975), points out that before a production schedule can be prepared the following must be known:

1. existing commitments;
2. the resources available (which can be increased by (a) overtime, (b) shift-working, (c) sub-contracts);
3. efficiency of working of the various work centres;
4. the expected levels of sickness and absenteeism;
5. holiday periods;
6. maintenance commitments (and schedules);
7. other local factors affecting working — e.g. confined space may prevent multiple working at a work centre;
8. the work-content of the various products;
9. the proposed methods, route and sequence of manufacture;
10. the ancillary times implicit in the proposed methods;
11. allowances for scrap.

The above will involve considerable forecasting of the probabilities of these events happening as desired. The value of the schedule decreases as the accuracy of the forecast of activity diminishes. It is usual to prepare schedules at least twice, once when agreeing delivery dates and again later, when programming manufacture. The first 'pre-ordering for tendering' schedule is likely to be carried out in broader terms than the final manufacturing schedule. However it is important to establish a delivery date. Not to have such prior scheduling (however crudely it is done) is to invite disaster.

6.2.1 · Size, location and structure of plants

Manufacturing plants should not, necessarily, be designed to give the largest output (capacity) possible. To pursue the belief in the economies of scale to its ultimate conclusion may just result in disaster. Output must be related to the forecasted demand for the products in the market for which they are intended. Thus marketing colleagues must be involved in the work of planning factories so that the correct, relevant market statistics can be fed into the planning. The key factors here will be total size of current demand, changes taking place in demand patterns and forecasted future developments and trends. The locations of the plants also requires a multi-discipline approach in the planning and decision stages. When the transportation, road and rail congestions or bottlenecks, minimising the distance travelled between deliveries and minimising all distribution costs are taken into account, the best sites generally will not be in the 'obvious' locations identified from just looking at maps. Again, here is another potential area of conflict.

For manufacturing executives, the closer the factory is to its source of raw materials, energy or other major bought-in supplies, the lower should be the unit cost of production and the easier the delivery position. However, marketing requires the factory to be as close to the major markets it will serve, consistent with the transportation infrastructure. This will simplify distribution problems, reduce distribution costs (a substantial element of total marketing costs) and eliminate delivery delays which arise when long distances have to be traversed. Traffic hold-up due to bottlenecks is also minimised.

Seldom are souces of supplies and potential markets close together so, again, a compromise solution is necessary. The decision will have to be agreed by all interested executives. Their aim should be to select the best location for all considerations, one where unit costs of manufacturing and distribution are at a minimum, so optimising sales volume and profits. However it is not an easy task, as the merits of each conflicting need may not be easily identifiable. For example, in aluminium processing, because of heavy energy consumption, one good site would be wherever there was plentiful cheap electricity, e.g. a hydro-electric system. However the site may be right out in the wilds and transporting the raw materials there and bringing the finished aluminium back to its markets may prove difficult and very expensive. So the necessary compromise will not only involve the points mentioned earlier. It must also involve decisions on which product groups have the best short- and long-term profit and sales prospects and the order of priority that should be assigned to them. Also their growth prospects and the competition they will meet should be contemplated. Thus, product managers will also be involved at some time on decisions about factory locations! So will corporate planners, if only for their view of the future.

Wherever possible, location and size decisions must also try to meet long-term aims and not be decided solely on immediate needs. Then the life of the plant will be longer and so make the whole project viable and acceptable. This then means that future technological developments (for the finished products, their usage and manufacture) must also be considered. Otherwise plant layout may not be correct for future needs and major upheavals will occur when this has to be changed in order to accommodate changing requirements. Technical executives and the corporate planner will have a contribution to make on forecasts of future manufacturing and technical developments to ensure that the structure and layout of the plant would be right for immediate needs and reasonable future requirements. That is within the limitations of the site, its size, shape, location and the capital available, the fabric and general structural nature of the plant should be such as to make future adaptations and changes possible at economic costs and with minimum disturbance.

For example, if present needs are for large batch production but in a few years time, flowline or mass production requirements will arise, the general floor plan and layout of present machinery should take this into account as far as is practical and prudent. It is no good arranging boilers, chimneys and other ducting, for example, that would get in the way of mass production lines in a few years. Major structural reorganisation will be needed. The aim throughout should be for flexibility of approach. So again technical executives will be involved in discussions on the design and layout of plant. Research and development personnel may also have to submit their forecasts of when they would expect new technology, manufacturing processes, materials, products and so on to come to fruition. That is, they will set the time scale for long-term considerations in factory design.

6.2.2 The community and the factory

While economic and technological considerations predominate in decisions on the size, location and structure of plant, other intangibles must also be considered. One of these concerns the cultural life of the community in which the plant will be located and the cultural needs and satisfactions of employees. Will the proposed decisions enhance or retard the cultural life of the community and the employees? Is the provision of extra job availability in the area the main criterion? What are the pollution possibilities and problems? Will the community accept the factory or will there be aesthetic, economic, ecological or other strong objections against it? Will the opposition be total (i.e. no factory at all) or partial (i.e. requiring some alterations to the project)? Is the location in an acceptable climatic area? If not, what extra protection must be taken for the processes and the finished products?

These questions all have important bearings on the manner in which the local community will accept and welcome the factory and its workers; and this will affect the contentment and productivity of the employees. Also, while location in a remote area might have political and economic benefits (e.g. reducing unemployment in an area renowned for its high rate of unemployment), will the key employees be prepared to move to the area? Will they lead a happy and contented life when they are relocated? So, personnel executives must be present with technical colleagues and those from the marketing department when these decisions have to be taken. Financial executives will of course, always be present checking on the financial aspects of the proposals, especially the calculations on estimated costs and anticipated returns, cash flows, degree of risk etc.

Finally, plant location, size and structure are not things that can be decided once and for all. A regular review is necessary so that changes in market conditions, competition, transportation, technology and the depletion of raw material supplies, or the discovery of new, more economical sources can be considered. Modifications to the plant can then be made as soon as these are seen to be necessary. Further, new subsidiary or major plants can be designed for other locations and the original plant might then be used to produce some other products best suited for that location. It could continue to produce its original products but in the situation envisaged, this would lead to higher costs, smaller profit margins and various production problems because of the age or obsolescence of the equipment. Maintaining a flexible approach based on integrated management should ensure that quality standards will be maintained and can be altered to meet changes in the market in all situations except where outmoded equipment is being pushed beyond its useful, economic life.

6.3 Processes and technology

Even when national economies are suffering a period of depression, as in the west in the late 1970s, manufacturing processes and technology continue to change or improve. Indeed, pressures on profit margins in such circumstances may accelerate attempts to improve processes or bring about changes that will permit cost savings. This is, of course, assuming that the capital needs for this work are not excessive. Corporate survival may hinge on this work being done well and expeditiously. Also new technologies will be sought or tried for the same reason. Provided these moves do not change the product, its quality or performance beyond limits which the market will accept, there is nothing wrong in encouraging such changes.

If they are pursued without regard to marketing and financial requirements, however, the results obtained will harm the company (sales volume and profits may drop) and threaten its survival. If the costs, especially capital costs, involved in making the changes are greater than the company can afford, or prudence recommends, then there will be conflict of interest between manufacturing and financial executives. Then the proposed changes may lead to alteration in labour usage which may be unavoidable. The skills required may also be different. Making unwanted labour redundant, especially because their skills are no longer required can reflect badly on the name and standing of the company in the business world and the community in which it operates. This may impede future recruitment attempts. If the unwanted employees are not made redundant, labour utilisation figures will fall and create another problem for personnel executives. The latter will then find themselves in conflict with manufacturing executives because of the changes proposed or made in manufacturing processes and technology. So again, cooperation, balance and flexibility of approach are needed in all considerations of processes and technology.

In these discussions, note must be taken of the degree of specialised skills required and the disparity existing between the knowledge and capabilities of the experts and the non-specialists who have to work with them. Thus, when operational research was a new, scarce, unique and expensive skill it was held at some central point and provided assistance as required. Now that it is more plentiful and almost commonplace, operational research specialists can be located where they are needed. So, while in the first instance the training and development of non-specialists in the appreciation of operational research (its capabilities and limitations) was not possible, with the expertise more widely spread, it is possible to close this gap of knowledge existing between specialists and non-specialists. The situation arises with every important management technique and the extent of them will also influence decisions on the processes and technologies that will be used. If the majority of the people who have to work on an idea do not understand it they are unlikely to be able to operate at optimal efficiency.

6.3.1 Research and development

A company can never afford to relax in confidence. Market and technological conditions are changing and with them the nature and structure of competition. There is no longer any such thing as a product with an assured, profitable future for its manufacturer. Success has to be worked for continuously and involves hard effort. So in the context of products and processes, all companies will need research and development, whether they do it themselves or contract out to appropriate specialised research organisations or laboratories.

Research and development is a specialised activity requiring unique skills, abilities and knowledge. It cannot be left to eager amateurs who should in any case be giving their full-time attention to their main responsibilities. Research and development breaks down into three groups.

1. *Fundamental research* which seeks to push the frontiers of technical knowledge of the company even further outwards, seeking the fundamental laws of cause and effect for their own sake, without thought for what the results may be or if they will eventually lead to the development of profitable, commercial products.

2. *Applied research* whose purpose is to find solutions to some problem or

other that may have arisen in manufacturing or any other activity of the company.

3. *Development*, i.e. work designed to result in the development of some process or end-product that will assist marketing and the company in its development and growth or help it to counter competitive activity more effectively.

Type 1 work is necessary for all corporations particularly if they wish to remain with the other leaders of their industry. If a company wishes to maintain its position in market standing or market leadership and if it wants to attract the best talent to its workforce, the continuance of this type of research and development is vital. While some of it could be 'free ranging', i.e. left to develop as the work progresses and as the results dictate, objectives and guidelines should be laid down for all this work. Then the funds will be used wisely and not be wasted. Some guides to even the 'free ranging' studies would also be helpful as they would prevent unnecessary 'drift' in the work and thus waste of effort. Unstructured research provides scope for the development of initiative and knowledge, but its cost requires the application of self-discipline to avoid waste while maintaining a watch for opportunities for commercial development.

Type 2 work (applied research) will arise as a result of requests for solutions to problems by different departments. While manufacturing may be the main customer, marketing may also have requests stemming from the need for product improvements, new product development, cost and price reductions and so on, generally resulting from developments in the market. Purchasing may also ask for work to discover if cheaper alternative materials can be used, or to confirm that there are alternative materials to those in increasing scarcity. Financial executives could also initiate work where questions or doubts about costs and prices have arisen. For example, they (with marketing) may be seeking ways of making products more price competitive.

Type 3 work (development) will stem from the objectives and aims of the corporate plan, especially the parts dealing with future development needs. The plan may wish to open up new markets and enter new technologies at some future date. Research and development will have to show how, and when, this can be done. Its work would range over the development of new products, altering the methods and processes used in manufacturing and considering how the skills of the company can be altered over a specified period of time.

Thus at all levels of research and development, liaison and close contact with other departments will be essential from time to time, if not continuously. The reports on fundamental research (Type 1) should be studied by all departments or divisions to see if in fact any relevance exists or could be derived from the work and its results. The thoughts in executives' minds should be: is there anything here that will enhance or improve our present activities? Are there any results/conclusions which could, with some re-direction or addition to the work, lead to some product improvement, better manufacturing process, reduction in costs or the use of better/cheaper alternative raw materials? And so on.

In the case of applied research (Type 2) the line executives who requested the work and other interested colleagues should jointly have agreed with the research and development department, the terms of reference and objectives of the study. They should monitor progress of the work and its results continuously or at reasonable intervals of time. If the original objectives do not seem to be realisable: what change in plans is advisable to seek different possibilities? Or should the work be terminated? From the results are there any other avenues that should be researched? What unexpected benefits or products could accrue from the results being obtained, subject perhaps to more detailed studies in other areas? In this way the effort and money expended will not be wasted by just allowing the projects to continue to their bitter ends, regardless of their possible value or benefits.

Development work (Type 3) will evolve from the longer-term objectives and concepts of the long-range corporate plan. It will need close monitoring by representatives of all departments, especially the four main line divisions. There are so many unknowns and uncertainties in this area of planning that firm guidance is needed to save excessive waste of money and effort which could easily arise. The board, too, should have a direct interest in this work and results. Does the work show that original hopes and intentions can be translated into reality? Or should changes be made in the plans for long-term development and growth? What unexpected spin-offs may result and how will these affect the existing plans? How will the results alter the component parts of the long-term growth expectations?

6.3.2 Product development

Product development is usually seen as improving existing products, adapting them for new markets or applications, developing new products, improving quality and standardisation and exploring opportunities for diversification and expansion. However, there are other related aspects of corporate activity which have important bearing on the work of product development. These may be summarised as follows.

1. Improving existing production processes and developing new or more efficient ones.

2. Reducing production costs and exploring the possibility of use of alternative materials whether these are better, cheaper or are potential replacements for scarce resources.

3. Developing new uses for existing processes and materials especially waste or by-products.

4. Improving customer and public relations, and so meeting competitive pressures more effectively.

5. Enhancing the prestige of the company and increasing its acceptance and that for its products by all types of customers.

Thus product development and management is not the sole prerogative of the marketing department. According to what is involved, executives from all other departments can be members of the team, even if it is consultative rather than executive in nature. Manufacturing and marketing executives will be the major partners for this work, with finance colleagues making a positive contribution if only as honest brokers; but many others must be brought into the team, either permanently or from time to time as their expertise is needed.

Improving customer relations can stem from product development and research and development work if the end-results help customers in some way. It may provide them with products that fit their needs more exactly than before. The new ideas may accommodate changes which the customers have had to make in their own products or manufacturing processes. They may help customers to resolve problems that had not been capable of solution for some time. The new products may reduce customers' own manufacturing costs or the need for, or frequency of, maintenance. And so on. This benefit arises most in technical fields and, obviously, the greater the technical content of the business, the more room there is for this sort of customer assistance leading to improved customer relations.

6.3.3 Technology and the workforce

Too frequently, while corporations make adjustments and improvements to their manufacturing plant to accommodate changes in technology, similar improvements and adaptations are not made in the workforce. Manufacturing divisions do not take sufficient steps to retrain their workforce and teach them the new skills that a changed technology requires. Personnel executives must take some of the blame. They have not pressed home the importance of this requirement on the minds of executives from manufacturing. As a result their plans make no allowance for this. Yet, if the workforce is not properly trained to handle the ever increasing complexities of manufacturing (made so by technological advances), it is unrealistic to expect optimal production or output at acceptable unit costs.

Thus the manufacturing division needs to consult regularly with personnel colleagues about what training is required and how effective current programmes are proving. They should take detailed note of the technological changes affecting the company's manufacturing processes but should also appreciate the implications of similar changes occurring in customers' technologies. Where the manufacturing department is responsible for backup, technical or after-sales service to customers, liaison should be extended, on this point, to marketing colleagues. The performance of the manufacturing division can be effectively improved as a result of these consultations and advice.

The type of manufacturing processes which will be used are determined by the nature and type of products to be made, the quantities required and the unit costs that can be accepted. The timing of demand will also be an important consideration. Manufacturing, marketing and financial executives will be the main arbiters in this decision area. With the cost of plant and equipment rising, aggravated by the need for more sophisticated machinery and inflation, industry is becoming more and more capital intensive. Financial executives must, therefore, check that what is proposed is financially acceptable to the company. Marketing executives will state if the end-results of these decisions will provide products that they will be able to sell at a profit, to identified markets. Finally, the benefits of standardisation and simplification should not be overlooked. The former can ease manufacturing problems, especially costs. The latter can assist customers in the form of (perhaps) cheaper products, less frequent maintenance and lower cost of servicing and repairs. Again, financial executives would verify the money side of this work and marketing will advise if the intentions on these points would be acceptable.

6.4 Production planning, control and administration

In this part of the work by the manufacturing division, financial and personnel executives can help production colleagues considerably in the latter's efforts to improve performance and productivity. Also the interaction between manufacturing and marketing is probably most directly felt in the production control department. The latter depends on marketing executives for predictions of future requirements so that correct decisions can be taken rapidly on output, quality and other production matters. Without these forecasts, production planning and control would have to be based on internal considerations, with guesses about possible sales volumes, all of which might have very little relevance to actual market conditions.

Production planning defines the various manufacturing programmes that will be required at specified periods, to give the planned output that marketing will require for offers to potential customers. Unit costs will be kept down to agreed levels so that unit selling prices match those existing in the markets, i.e. ruling market prices or other criteria. Financial colleagues will watch to make sure that unit cost prices are a correct reflection of actual manufacturing costs. If the unit cost to marketing is less than the actual costs, the financial department must make sure this is in accordance with plans and necessary for future growth, or other valid reason. Thus marketing and financial executives can make positive contributions to the work of production planning.

This planning must also give consideration to the availability of machines, manpower of the right kind and materials. What machines are there, and are they accurate enough for the purpose? Can all the products that have to be made be handled efficiently by current equipment? What additional machinery is required? What is its cost? What is the manpower position? Are the right skills available? What are the costs? What materials must be used? What is their availability and cost? Are there alternative sources of supply, or substitute materials?

In answering these questions and others, production planners will obtain useful help from technical, personnel and purchasing executives while marketing would continue to oversee that the resultant products would be acceptable to them. Financial colleagues would check all facts about costs also.

Then when indications are clearer about output and the incidence of sales volume expected by marketing, physical distribution executives should also be consulted to make sure the system can handle the volume of business as it arises, with efficiency. Quality controllers should also be consulted in the planning stage. They will verify that what is intended regarding the use of machines, skilled labour and materials will produce products that meet the quality standards they have set in conjunction with marketing executives. When the plan is implemented it must, of course, be properly controlled and the progress made should be monitored regularly.

Poor production planning and control can lead to one or more of the following problems arising. First, there could be excessive build-up of inventories of raw materials and bought-in components if output falls below intended levels. There would be a shortage of them if output exceeded expectations. Second, similar situations may arise for finished goods and work-in-progress inventories. If marketing has overestimated demand, or given the wrong figures to production planners (it does happen!), sales will be less than anticipated and inventories rise. If the quality of the products or reputation of the company has been under-estimated, sales may exceed targets and out-of-stock positions would arise. The former incurs higher inventory costs and the latter loses potential profit and customer goodwill. If distribution has not been properly advised of production and marketing requirements and intentions, delivery delays and other associated problems will occur, further bedevilling customer relations.

Next, production planning may have got most of its figures wrong, in which case machinery might be under-utilised or overloaded as the case may be. In the first case, assets are being wasted. In the second, they are being over-stretched. If this also means working excessive overtime with no proper time for maintenance and repairs, leading to a high breakdown rate, the result for the company is rising unit costs or erosion of profit margins. Bottlenecks in production flow would arise and would be manifested by ever-increasing work-in-progress stores. With all these probabilities two certainties exist. First, there will be loss of business, possibly on an increasing scale. Second, the morale of the workforce — shopfloor and executive — would decline. They could be the trigger for other labour problems, worsening the labour relations problems of the company. These problems may have nothing to do with production bottlenecks but such manufacturing difficulties often act as the catalyst for increased industrial unrest, which can destroy the very foundations of the business. Thus careful planning and control is needed, right from marketing forecasts of demand through to final production plans. Close and regular contact between executives from all departments who have an interest in output matters is also essential.

6.4.1 Forecasts

It is generally assumed that marketing's forecasts are within acceptable limits of accuracy. This need not be so. If forecasts are consistently off target, production planning will try to compensate for this in its plans. If forecasts have continually under-estimated demand, as shown by past performances, manufacturing may tend to produce more than the forecasts so as not to be caught in an out-of-stock position. If there has been persistent over-estimation of demand, manufacturing will scale down its production plans so as not to be caught in an overstocked position, for any unsold stock of finished goods represents substantial increases in costs for the company. Whichever situation arises poses many problems for the management of the company. If solutions are not found quickly, the consequences for the corporation could be very serious.

To the manufacturing division, sales forecasts represent a statement of desired results. The figures of the forecasts are translated into specific production requirements at specified times of the planning period. These, in turn, are sub-divided into production targets for individual products. Where several products have to be made — as with most manufacturing organisations — the detailed work can be complex. Working out machine loadings and timings for the different products and dovetailing the whole production process is not as simple as it sounds. Inaccuracies in forecasting can thus cause considerable dislocation to the work of the manufacturing division. Marketing executives should strive continuously to improve their analyses of market demand and the accuracy of forecasting to give their production colleagues a chance of doing a good job of work for them.

6.4.2 Planning capacity and output

Deciding what capacity a plant should be designed for is a problem for manufacturing executives. Even when output and other matters have been agreed with marketing, financial, personnel and other colleagues, these executives have still to make certain difficult choices. For example, should they plan to meet peak demands or some lesser figure representing average demand over a normal trading year? If the plant is designed for peaks, there may be considerable periods in any year when substantial portions of the factory will be under-utilised. It will then be up to marketing executives to find other products which they can sell that can be made on this idle plant. The peak demand periods for these products must be such that peak loadings on the plant would be when equipment would have been standing idle if production were limited to the original product range.

If the plant capacity is designed for normal, average annual demand there is first the question of what 'normal, average' demand means in figures. Since the war, it could be argued that western countries have not had a 'normal' business year. Either there were years of boom, with sales rocketing, or periods of depression and gloom when sales fell equally quickly. No two years were very much alike; so how can executives decide which set of figures represent the norm which they should use to plan capacity? Even when some other figure is taken, and no attempt made to work to any mythical or real norm, the question is still posed: which figure should be used? If market demand is growing, the one used will approach the peak demand forecasted. When demand is declining, much lower, conservative figures may be used. In either case the company can be caught out. If demand stops growing suddenly, there will be overcapacity; if the decline is halted and demand increases quickly again, the smaller plant will not be able to supply all the products needed. If demand collapses, even the smaller capacity plant will be in trouble and any larger one would face almost certain disaster.

Thus manufacturing, marketing and financial executives must work closely together on this problem. Consideration must be given to more recent patterns of business or demand, how market and competitive conditions are changing, what political, economic and technological factors may arise and how all of these could affect future demand. Again the need is for very accurate analyses and forecasting, at least as accurate as can be afforded. It is also useful to look back at past attempts by the company to forecast events and perhaps make allowances for any defaults found in previous endeavours. However, it must be remembered that if some personnel have changed in the meantime the past performance may not be indicative of current abilities. While capacity represents the potential of the company to match customers' needs as characterised by market forecasts, there is also the question of the *ability* of the plant to produce the output required.

Immediate capacity (i.e. that which can be made available in the current planning or operational period) is limited by the size of the plant, availability of labour, finance and equipment and the general financial policies that affect the manufacturing decisions that have to be taken. *Effective capacity* (i.e. the amount used during the current operational period) is influenced by the technical abilities and knowledge available, organisational skills in the various manufacturing departments, the skills and versatility in purchasing and maintenance and the efficiency and versatility of the labour employed. *Potential capacity* (i.e. that which could be made available within some future, specified period) is dependent on the funds which will be made available, marketing's forecasts of future demand patterns, the objectives and aims of the corporate plans for that period and the ability, willingness and determination of the executives, especially senior ones, to achieve future objectives. Without the support of senior executives, growth in potential capacity will not be achieved.

For immediate capacity planning, manufacturing, marketing, financial and personnel executives would form the team dealing with this work. The same team might perhaps usefully analyse the effective capacity used also since this is a measure of the success of the company's management in past years and will have a bearing on decisions on immediate capacity planning. Appropriate members of the board should also take a direct interest in these studies and their findings. Future capacity planning will, from time to time, require the attention of the senior executives of all the company's main operating departments and the corporate planner or the team doing that work. In fact, the corporate planning team normally forms the main core of the group responsible for future capacity planning.

The time required to effect a change in capacity is directly proportional to the size of the change, its importance to the company, the equipment involved, its complexity, scarcity and size and the number of suppliers available. Thus, even before serious planning begins, the company has to have a good idea of how long the work might take, allowing for everything that could delay matters to occur. Then the team is formed, sufficiently in advance of the date when decisions are needed, to allow them reasonable time to do the work. The more important the decision, the longer the time that will be required; so, also, the earlier should the team be assembled and launched on its task. In other words, a critical path analysis of the task should be made before the team gets to work, or be its first job, so that the potential bottlenecks can be known from the start.

These consultations should continue when work scheduling, the preparation of detailed timetables of activity, is being done. (Scheduling is sometimes called, not quite correctly, 'sequencing'.) The scheduling will cover the machines to be used, the labour required and the raw materials and components needed in each operation. Effective scheduling should minimise production costs, inventory investment, storage space and cash outflows. It should maximise labour and plant utilisation, customer satisfactions, cash inflows and the balance between the different quantities required for each product.

6.4.3 Product design and quality control

The preliminary design of products is usually based on their marketing specifications. These are issued by the marketing department and are intended to interpret consumer needs in terms of product qualities, including dimensions if relevant. In the next stage the manufacturing department (i.e. the engineering and technical staff) translate and modify the original specification to suit the capabilities of the plant and to favour the most economical methods.

It is possible that some of the things requested by marketing are not physically possible, or technology may not have developed far enough to make the idea work on the factory floor. (E.g. it took many years before nylon and some other plastics could be used in the manufacture of some precision-engineered components. Even now they cannot match the high precision possible with most metals.) So marketing and manufacturing divisions will have to discuss the alternatives suggested by the latter. The former will then pick whichever alternative it believes comes closest to consumer requirements and which the potential customer could be persuaded to buy without incurring the company in heavy sales and promotional expenditures. The engineers and technical experts, with production and quality control colleagues can then design the product and produce a manufacturing specification, the document on which output will be based for the agreed product.

In practice, it pays to ensure that the product development team from marketing is strongly represented on the product design team (they could be one and the same, but with the latter including engineers and other production specialists as necessary) to ensure that the intentions of product development policies are not overlooked in the design of individual products. Not enough thought and effort are given to product design in Britain and this is probably why British designs, with honourable exceptions, have been so poor and why foreign manufacturers can often outsell British products with ease (e.g. motor-cycles and mopeds). Many executives are hesitant about getting involved with product design. It is something left to the 'arty' types. The sooner this attitude can be dispelled, the more effective product design might be.

With industrial products, product design is concerned mainly with the functional aspects of the thing. What will it do? How well will it do it? What will be its cost? What maintenance and repair requirement may there be? And so on. However, the product's size, shape, dimensions should also be considered in discussion with physical distribution management to see if less awkward, more compact shapes can be produced without ruining the product's operation. Too often, physical distribution is thought of only when the product is about to be made in bulk. By then it is too late. The cost of shipping awkward shapes, which means that even the best package will be wasteful because some of it will just contain air, as opposed to more compact designs, is quite considerable. For cost-conscious executives, this is one area where detailed study could lead to substantial savings in delivery charges, especially if big items going overseas are concerned. Then, of course, the requirements of customers should not be forgotten. (What do customers really want?) Neither should the strengths and weaknesses of the corporation.

For consumer goods and consumer durables, the potential customers' needs are usually well to the forefront of the discussions on product design. The problems arise in trying to interpret the intangible qualities that customers say they expect of a product. For example, how 'creamy' is a face cream? What do people mean when they say a product must 'taste nice'? If the associated technology is not being pushed too close to its current boundaries of knowledge, no great difficulty should present itself. However, appearance design is probably where the consumer goods team will face many hurdles. This is probably the most intangible point on consumer goods. What people say about appearance of non-existent products is difficult to interpret, if only because people use the same words but ascribe different meanings to them.

Also, with new products, potential users find it difficult to visualise them and so to express their opinions. Some help could be given by referring to current, substitute products but care is needed to ensure they are true substitutes. For example, this problem arose in the early 1960s when the electric toothbrush was being designed. Researchers in the markets tried to use the old handheld, 'waggled' model as a guide. This did not help and the findings were subsequently found to be off target, probably because the electric toothbrush and the hand one are worlds apart. The same can be said about 'waterpicks' that clean teeth by water jets under some pressure. About the only thing they could be compared to correctly are the similar devices used by dental surgeons.

Whatever the product being designed, it is clear that close liaison is needed between manufacturing and marketing executives and the former must also play a part in designing any marketing research where the findings could be of importance to manufacturing, especially product design. Yet it is sadly amusing to read books, even today, often written by production people, with phrases like: ' ... *even* seek information from the marketing staff'! (*Italics* and exclamation mark are the author's. The passage was discussing product design and specifications!) When money is short or marketing research is not possible, information should be gleaned (even?) from the field sales force.

Another point to remember is that the new product need not be better than the market requires unless there are good grounds to believe that potential customers are beginning to think along similar lines. If they are not, the new product may very well not be accepted by an unprepared public. An example in the 1950s was the massive 'Brabazon' airliner designed in Britain. Leaving aside the fact that technology had not advanced sufficiently to deal effectively with the problems posed by the idea, the public had not yet developed the need for, or accepted the idea of, mass inter-continental flights. Even if the plane had entered commercial operations it is doubtful if sufficient numbers of people would have wanted to use it. (It may, on the contrary, have triggered off such demand.) Years later when demand for such travel had developed, the big aircraft of the 1960s and 1970s found ready demand. In the early 1970s a similar problem was posed for supersonic flight and the 'Concorde'. In this case the passengers who have used it love the aircraft. It is the operators who worry because of the substantial losses incurred in the early part of its operations. All new product ideas are faced with such 'chicken-and-egg' problems regarding demand and consumer response. Does demand exist? If it does not, will the new product stimulate demand? These are just two of the questions that product developers and designers should always ask when contemplating new ideas.

Now even if product design is good, if maintenance and cleaning are difficult, the new product might fail after a brief introductory period. Difficulty in usage also turns away business. So there are many subsidiary points to be thought through carefully before designs are finalised and new products are made. Some examples include factory machinery and cars that have proved inconvenient for customers to handle, use, service or maintain; cartons and packaging that are difficult to open; consumer durables that need constant or regular and costly maintenance; and furniture that proves uncomfortable in use and too heavy for easy handling and movement. Thus the convenience and comfort of users must be kept in mind. However, they are too often overlooked by marketing and manufacturing executives who get carried away by the gimmick of the idea.

Maintaining high levels of quality seems to be a problem for many companies. Many lame excuses are made for lapses here. Sometimes the problem arises because sampling techniques have been incorrectly used and the resultant guidance on quality does not relate to the relevant facts. Or the mistakes may occur because of human error arising from boredom, fatigue, indifference to the job or simply lack of vigilance. Planning for good quality and quality control involves amongst many things, the preparation of specifications which take into account not only the obvious technical details but also the purpose of the product, the ability of the company to meet these requirements and the possible unit cost of production.

It should also be remembered that quality should cover reliability. When the specifications are written, they should be circulated to manufacturing, marketing, financial and personnel executives responsible for product design and quality control for comments and suggestions. When any changes have been made to the specification it can become the basis for the actual manufacture of the product. However, meanness with expenditure on quality control can result in excessive costs measured in terms of lost business and goodwill and the expense of replacing faulty goods. These 'costs' can be many more times the saving achieved by so-called economies on quality control and surveillance. Also, reworking, re-inspection and scrap costs will rise.

6.4.4 Controlling and reducing costs

The production control team has one continuous and important role to play amongst all its other responsibilities. That is to ensure that unit costs are kept down to agreed limits or possibly lower, if that does not mean there is divergence from the quality and other performance figures that have been set for the products. With weak control, costs will rise and so will prices leading to narrowing of profit margins. The last will be aggravated as customers turn away from the products because equally good and cheaper substitutes are available.

Where labour costs are concerned, production and personnel executives will find it necessary to work together to ensure that labour utilisation and turnover, and hence costs, are in line with plans and objectives. Part of the work involves making sure that the right skills are being properly used. The general training programme would also have a bearing here because the manufacturing division's part of a corporate training plan would include programmes that seek to improve the skills, extend the knowledge and boost capabilities and actions of the workforce to much higher levels of efficiency and effectiveness.

If a company wishes to improve quality control without increasing labour costs it could train its machine operatives to check the quality of their own work before passing it to the next stage. They would need training on how to use micrometers, calipers and the other usual tools of inspectors and how to draw the necessary samples for checking. Then the training programme should include sections designed to improve labour's operating skills and to motivate them, so that resultant high operating standards on their machines will ensure that the right quality products are produced.

A regular check is also needed on the effective performance of each operative and department. The various cost elements should be itemised and reported on in ways that will allow remedial action to be taken speedily. Finally, to summarise on labour cost control, the following list indicates the main areas of work that need constant or regular analysis or investigation.

1.   Use of different grades of labour. If the wrong grade is being used, the reason must be established and appropriate corrective action taken. It may be that there is an insufficient supply of the 'right grade' and the company has had to make do. Executives might compare all the costs associated with the use of the wrong labour with the cost arising from lost production if this labour was not used.

2.   Utilisation of capacity, especially idle capacity. Why is it idle? Can anything be done via re-planning of production, additional products or sale of the idle equipment to improve the corporate financial position?

3.   Effectiveness of labour and reasons for low effectiveness. Check on labour utilisation and turnover generally.

4.   Effect of premium payments such as overtime on costs. Is excessive overtime being worked? The time lost to training courses. What should be the net gain from the training programme?

5.   Extent and effect of waiting time. Are the jobs being planned and programmed properly? Are the machines being correctly loaded? Are the throughputs of the equipment being correctly estimated? Etc.

Material cost control requires study of a number of points. First, excessive material costs may arise if scrap or waste rise beyond planned or acceptable limits. This can be due to poor machine operation, ineffective working by operatives, bad planning or design or the use of wrong materials. Again, the right materials may not be available in sufficient quantity, or may be too expensive. Then the next best substitute will have to be used; and the increase in cost of waste will have to be checked against the increase in raw materials cost if the right ones were purchased, regardless of their high prices. This is a problem for purchasing and production executives to work out together but marketing must be informed as decisions here will affect the quality of the finished product. Also the substitute material may not be acceptable to customers.

Next, material costs can rise if the wrong production methods are used. Production, design and quality control executives will have to work out if the best design for production and material purposes has been chosen. What are the conflicting criteria and what trade-offs are advisable? Is the product design capable of improvement so that it will save on material usage and other production costs? Are the quality control standards too high, or too low?

The disposal of scrap needs to be properly controlled also and attempts made to find new by-products from proper utilisation of 'waste' material. A celebrated case was that of the company making paper sanitary products for women. Because of the high hygiene and other standards demanded in the production process, waste of materials was considerable. An observant operative noticed that women employees used this waste to clean their faces before leaving for home. From this sprang the idea of making paper tissues (handkerchiefs etc.) from this waste and so was spawned what is now a world-wide, multi-million dollar business, one that has greater sales value than the original products.

Material cost control can also be affected by purchasing policies. Good ones will help to keep material costs down, bad ones will put them up as replacement materials have to be purchased to make up for faulty supplies, or the apparent cheaper price turns out to be not so because of the doubtful quality and reliability of the purchases leading to higher reject rates in the company's manufacturing process. There are many more causes and effects. The points that must be kept in mind are as follows. Are materials being bought from the right sources and in the right amounts, at the right time, for production needs? Can better or greater use be made of cheaper substitute materials which do not lower or endanger product quality or performance? Would it be better from a cost point of view for the company to secure sources of supply by purchasing and owning them? Should a slightly higher price be paid for assured quality and supplies? When would it be safe and advantageous to go for slightly inferior supplies that offer substantial cost savings? Would these costs be real by the time any associated problems have been resolved? Etc. Thus purchasing executives and quality and cost control staff have to work together on these points and should keep marketing fully informed of their decisions and perhaps deliberations. Marketing could contribute useful comments to the latter.

With all these problems the greater use of value engineering or value analysis would be found to be helpful. Obviously the teams will vary in composition according to the problem being studied. However, there should be at least one person of appropriate stature and skill from each major division and the affected departments (ones with the problem or who will have to resolve it) plus others who have not the slightest connection with the process and problems, or even the product. Their unbiased and fresh minds can often shed startlingly new light onto old, intractable problems. These teams could also study the possible impact of technological changes on the company's business and methods and also the needs of customers.

6.5 Purchasing and inventory control

The mention of inventory control in this Section is merely for structural convenience of the book and because purchasing and inventories form another 'twin-set' of management similar to that of products and markets. However, while purchasing as a function belongs to the manufacturing division, if it is not an autonomous division, inventories are part of the physical distribution department which may or may not be part of the marketing division. So the logical discussion of related activities should not be allowed to confuse readers on their actual locations within a management structure.

6.5.1 Purchasing

The purchasing function, especially in Britain but in some other countries also, has too often been relegated to a 'Cinderella' role in management. Seen as just a part of manufacturing, it is frequently assigned the status of a clerical job with the purchasing officer or buyer reporting to the production manager (not even to a board member). Yet, as some of the preceding sections have shown, purchasing is a critical, specialist activity calling for considerable acumen and a wide-ranging knowledge of materials and industries. Where the company is in a technical field, purchasing executives must also have detailed knowledge of, and competence in, their own technology and those of their customers. In such cases, more widespread now than a few years ago, purchasing executives are required to have an appropriate engineering or technical degree and be qualified in economics as well.

Purchasing is often the largest single item of cost in a company's trading account. It can account for at least 45 per cent of the sales value of a company; but surveys in the second half of the 1970s indicated that the average for developed nations now exceeds 50 per cent. In the U.S.A. the equivalent figure was 56 per cent. In service industries, and for products requiring heavy expenditure on marketing, purchasing costs are equivalent to about 40 per cent of gross sales value. In highly technical, mechanised and process industries the comparable figure can exceed 70 per cent. Thus purchasing executives are responsible for the commitment of substantial sums of money. By their skills they ensure the money is spent effectively to give the best value possible. Also, they are always looking for ways of reducing purchasing costs for their employers. They do all this while ensuring that an adequately continuous supply of materials and bought-in parts flows into the company so that production schedules and plans are not disrupted. When supply difficulties arise they must find solutions speedily; ones that will not involve the company in excessive extra costs.

The purchasing department, like all the others, should agree policies for its operations with all who have a direct interest in the results of the work. These are, in particular, the marketing and manufacturing divisions. Financial colleagues will of course oversee the money aspects of the work. These policies will then provide essential guidelines to purchasing executives. The policies should also cover decisions whether items should be bought in or made by the company. In current conditions, many components and sub-assemblies can be made more economically and to high standards by sub-contractors. Their use would save on the capital investment that would be needed to have one's own manufacturing facility for the components without jeopardising the quality position. On this side of the work, purchasing executives liaise closely with production and financial colleagues about the proposed purchases, the amounts and timing of the purchases and the resultant quality and service that has been provided.

The question of 'best value for money' is not synonymous with obtaining the lowest possible purchase price. There are several permutations. These range from obtaining better quality articles at the same price as before to paying less for a lower quality product that is, nevertheless, regarded by engineering and technical colleagues as being adequate for the job in hand. The first allows the company to benefit from the better quality without having to accept increased costs. The second could allow the company to improve its profit margins (if it does not lower prices since customers see price as synonymous with quality) or offer slightly lower prices without narrowing its profit margins. Another possibility is obtaining the same quality at a lower price; but care has to be taken to ensure that the quality does not decline with future deliveries.

Alternatively, a much higher price could be paid for a much higher quality purchase. This could be justified if it proved to be of better value in the design of the product, if it greatly enhanced the life and performance of the product in which it was used, or if it greatly reduced the incidence of breakdown and the need for maintenance and repairs. Then it could be said that the added-value aspect of the purchase far exceeded the actual increased cost of the higher quality. There are, of course, limits to the degree of quality that can be accepted for any production job. In addition to this, there are the many possibilities posed by substitute supplies. Points to be checked include quality claims, performance in practice, whether quality is too low or too high, relative costs when wastage and scrap have been taken into account and so on.

Another point to be considered is whether purchases should be on short- or long-term contracts with specific call-off commitments or on an unspecified basis, or that buying should be against or according to market conditions, or on a bargain basis. It depends on the purchase, the company's need for it, the role it plays in the manufacturing cycle and the prevailing economic conditions.

Throughout all this the purchasing executives must maintain high standards of commercial morality, integrity and honourable practice in the conduct of this side of the company's business.

6.5.2 Inventories and inventory control

Inventories are now assigned to the physical distribution department but purchasing and financial colleagues have interests in them and their efficient control. Physical distribution involves not just the movement of finished products from the factory through the distribution channels to the customer. It covers also the movement into the plants of raw materials and other bought-in supplies, their storage and movement through the factory and their associated work-in-progress stores. However, physical distribution does not get involved with purchasing; but it is clear that there must be close liaison between purchasing and the physical distribution departments if there are to be no hitches in this operation. Also, many elements of cost are involved, all needing tight control and financial colleagues will be eager to maintain contact with the physical distribution and purchasing executives on these points.

Then there is the question of inventory levels: maximum, minimum and re-ordering. These should be fixed by consultation with manufacturing, marketing, purchasing and financial executives. Invariably a balance has to be struck between the ideal, high levels to ensure that production never runs out of supplies, the availability of supplies, the reliability of sources, the most advantageous order quantities for bulk or quantity discounts (consistent with what the company can afford) and the amount of money the company can afford (or wishes) to tie up in inventories of both bought-in supplies and finished products.

Physical distribution executives will also help purchasing colleagues to decide whether bulk quantities should be obtained with or without instalment deliveries, the timing of purchases to take advantage of inflation/deflation, with interpretation of the price situation and whether there is likely to be a glut or a shortage. It is difficult enough coming to decisions on these matters for standard or routine production of established products. They become more difficult when new products are involved. Indeed, in new product development more attention should be given to the inventory situation of the company, as well as the usual critical marketing points. A better timing for new product development might result if the inventory position was considered with other criteria. It could avoid bottlenecks in production or delivery and lead to a much smoother and more effective launch of the new product. It should be remembered also that decisions on purchasing matters will always have some effect on the inventory position. Decisions on inventories will also affect the purchasing position. Yet few companies think about these activities in this way. Thus like product-market aspects, decisions on purchasing should not be made without consideration of the effect on inventories and vice versa.

The financial executive's interest in inventories usually hinges around determination of inventory turnover, or the number of days supply of inventory there is on hand. These give approximate impressions of the effectiveness of control systems in the past. They are not sufficient as guides for reliable future order-size decisions. Most of the other points mentioned in this Section should also be considered and their effects on the company's supplies should be estimated. Inventory control is an area of management where decision-making under uncertainty is always experienced. This is so with decisions on the size of the order that should be placed and the timing of that order and delivery. Their uncertainties stem from uncertainty about demand and how sales will turn out. This reverts back, again, to the degree of accuracy of forecasting and the uncertainties associated with that. It is important, therefore, that decisions on inventories and inventory control should be reached by mutual agreement between marketing, manufacturing, financial and purchasing departments. These agreements would cover strategy and policies and the physical distribution department, which would have played a major role in those discussions, would be responsible for implementing the policies and taking all actions necessary for this purpose.

It is obvious then that in purchasing and inventories there are several conflicting interests involved. First, manufacturing want to get their machine loadings as high as possible to reduce the unit cost of production. (This will push up finished products' inventories.) They will wish to maintain output at a steady level without peaks and troughs, if possible, to improve machine loadings and utilisation. Marketing will wish purchasing and inventories to reflect patterns of demand and will want to avoid out-of-stock positions. They want inventories to be right for the forecasted pattern of sales. Purchasing wish to obtain a regular flow of purchasing orders placed at the most advantageous levels consistent with supply and demand, prices, inflation and other economic factors. The financial executives will be keen to keep inventories as low as possible. The board will be interested in obtaining the maximum return on capital; and part of this will be reflected by determined moves to keep all stock down to the lowest level throughout a trading year. Compromises are necessary but are not always easily achieved.

The effects of inflation and taxation must also be taken into account when considering inventory policies. When tax or inflation are at high rates, greater stringency in inventory control may be vital. (*See also* Section 7.5.2.)

6.6 Costs and prices

The subject of cost control is discussed in Chapter 7 and the relationship between prices and profit planning has been dealt with in Chapter 5. Here the cost/price relationship will be considered from manufacturing's point of view, although of course, pricing work is normally the responsibility of the marketing department.

6.6.1 Costs

In a manufacturing company, executives are interested not only in the items purchased and sold, as in a pure merchandising operation, but also in the cost of bought-in materials and components, the cost of work-in-progress as represented by the various processing costs incurred, overheads and the final cost of the finished products. The cost items or accounts that require regular study to check actuals against budgets are as follow.

1. Labour: direct and indirect.
2. Materials: direct and indirect.
3. Other supplies and consumables needed in manufacture and the maintenance and servicing of the plant, including also the power consumed in heating, lighting and manufacturing processes.
4. Depreciation costs.
5. Manufacturing overheads including, where appropriate, insurance, rates and other taxes and administration.
6. Other technical and engineering costs.
7. Research and development costs.

How these are actually allocated to products is primarily the responsibility of the manufacturing and financial executives, but marketing will have a say also. For too heavy a loading on one product would reduce its chances of sales volume if this means having to put up its price. A fair and equitable system should be devised. These items comprise the design and manufacturing costs of products to which, of course, must be added marketing, personnel, overhead and other costs to arrive at total product costs, the figure on which unit sales prices are normally based. Thus it is important that marketing executives be consulted regularly on cost matters and should have a permanent representative on any formal or informal group dealing with this subject. Marketing too are the ones who will decide what the terms of trading, discounts etc., should be and these can influence the decisions on the design and manufacturing costs that should be obtained.

The relationship between the main items of cost and prices is illustrated by Figure 6.2. In this diagram, *administrative costs* are taken to include *non-manufacturing overheads* while *manufacturing overheads — indirects and variances* would include *depreciation*. The cost of replacing goods due to errors in filling orders would be taken into *marketing costs* (or more precisely, physical distribution costs) while those arising from errors or faults in manufacture would

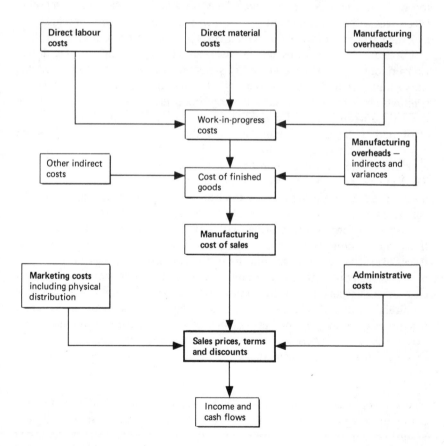

Fig 6.2

be included in *other indirect costs*. This last item would also take in *personnel costs*. In fact, each of these items would be recorded separately under its own heading and such reports would show actuals against planned results and the variances. The groupings mentioned above are made purely to keep the diagram as simple as possible; but they represent the correct group headings for these itemised costs.

The level of any one of these costs will affect the level of prices that would be required and the discounts possible. Too great a variance in either direction (positive or negative) of any major item of cost could interrupt the marketing process and policies and plans may have to be changed. Setting the standards for each item of cost is not an easy task. Executives have to arrive at decisions that are a fair representation of whatever is considered 'normal conditions'. But as the world has not had a normal year, economically, since 1945, it is difficult to know which set of figures should be used as the norms for these decisions. However, if standards are set too low, i.e. high cost figures as targets, and are easily attained, they will not provide good cost control. If set too high, i.e. very low cost targets that are almost impossible to achieve, executives will ridicule and ignore them, with disastrous results for marketing and the corporation as a whole when costs and prices rise out of control.

There are many ways by which costs can be allocated in manufacturing. Conventional approaches involve decisions on whether, and to what extent, the various cost items are connected with the manufacturing process, and even products, in some way. Variable costing procedures require total costs to be divided between fixed and variable items and only the variable elements are attributed to the cost of manufacturing the product. The fixed costs are regarded as period costs; costs that would always be incurred by the very existence of the company, regardless of the volume of output being achieved. They are charged directly as an expense on income. Variable costs in this instance are costs that change in total in some direct relationship with the volume of output or production. It is a simple concept, confused somewhat by the use of the term 'direct costing' to describe it. It eliminates income distortions when producing for inventories is necessary. It is useful because it also forces executives to think specifically in terms of fixed and variable costs and makes them appreciate all the implications of the latter while basing their cost/price decisions on this information. Arguments for and against variable (or direct) costing procedures will no doubt continue for some time. However, it requires close cooperation between manufacturing, financial and marketing executives and in enhancing the use of an integrated management approach, may have many hidden benefits to commend it.

6.6.2 Prices

The subject of cost cannot, however, be isolated from consideration of the prices to be charged and the profits to be earned and how these will alter according to the volume of output offered to the market and market demand at the time. Thus, analyses of the cost/volume/price/profit situation are necessary and, once again, involves a team drawn from marketing, manufacturing and financial departments. Decisions on the levels of production and inventory to be maintained are more easily derived if this relationship is studied. The executives have not only to identify the break-even points for the production of each product but also the variation in the level of profit that would be earned at different sales volumes, prices and costs. This requires further consideration of the pricing policies and objectives of the company and its profit plan and objectives.

Pricing policies can range from following the market to attempting to price comparable products below those of major competitors. Or, if a prestige market is involved and the company enjoys a high status for quality and reliability, the pricing policy may be to set prices higher than competitive products. Then pricing policies could be followed that set prices low enough to discourage the entry of new competitors into a market, or prevent a severe price war (price cutting). (In Britain in the 1970s price controls and the Prices and Incomes Board made it very difficult to raise prices again once they had been set or lowered. However in 1979 price control was abolished.) In the last instance, and in prestige markets, marketing and promotional activities would stress other factors considered important by people who make the buying decisions. The emphasis on price is reduced as far as possible. Or the pricing policy could be aimed at optimising the profits of the company, or at providing a good return on its investment, rather than at maximising the profits of each product. Or, when it is necessary or thought advisable to have large volume business, the policy may be to cut prices to the lowest possible level, with very narrow profit margins. If volume is really essential for manufacturing or marketing reasons, this is unavoidable. However, it contains a proportionately higher degree of risk than any other policy. It needs only a marginal drop in prices to put the company on its cost level or, worse, below costs. With a large volume this means substantial losses would be incurred. By the same token, if the large volume targeted is achieved, only a small unit profit will give good total profit figures. Whether these will be enough to cover other costs, dividends and so on is another question the executive team will have to resolve.

Pricing objectives are decided by other considerations than just optimising profit, though this remains the chief objective as a rule. Each objective has specific significance for the manufacturing and marketing executives in the decisions they have to make. For example, in current conditions, most companies would like to avoid charges of monopolising a market or industry or of dictating the level of prices for their products. This may relegate the optimisation of profits to a secondary position. In Britain and some other countries, Monopolies Commissions, anti-trust laws and income controls (which in Britain included dividend controls in the late 1970s) make this almost unavoidable. There may be other political, sociological and ethical reasons why the maximisation of profit should be avoided. These range from spoiling the company's image, losing its humanitarian reputation and being seen as just like any other big, capitalist profit grabber ('capitalist' in this context is usually meant in its worst connotations!) or the corporate tax structure is such that punitive taxation would fall on the company if it exceeded certain profit limits. (In Britain in 1975-78, 'excess profits' earned by companies had to be returned to the consumer in some way. In manufacturing industry this was through price reductions for an agreed period. For public utilities (e.g. telephones) this was done by a straight rebate to subscribers while the electricity industry planned a small percentage reduction in charges.)

More positively, a company may wish to improve its market share or its rate of growth and, at times, may be prepared to sacrifice or trade-off some profit to promote these other objectives. In difficult economic times the company may be more interested in survival in the short term with the hope that over the long term the situation will improve. So price objectives will, at first, aim to help the company defend its existing business and market share and when things improve, other pricing policies can follow depending on whether or not the company wishes to start a fresh push for growth and development. Or the company may wish to improve its prestige and standing in the public eye and build on good relations with its labour force and society at large.

The executives involved in costing and pricing decisions must, therefore, take a much wider view of the subjects than many have done in the past. Narrow, departmental objectives will have to take second place, at times, to the broader, long-term corporate need. The right balance between these two aspects of pricing should normally be taken into account, automatically, in an integrated management system. Then pricing objectives will be in accord with marketing and corporate aims and targets and will provide consistency in an area of management which has not been renowned for having supportive, consistent and cooperative policies.

6.6.3 Internal and external considerations

Many of the points mentioned above are what might be termed 'internal considerations', points which have to be taken into account because they will affect the internal workings and communications of the company and thus the effectiveness of its operations. Included in these would be the personal goals and aspirations of the employees themselves. Then there are other factors (the attitudes of customers, government and society, competitive activity etc.) which are external to the company, are usually beyond its control, yet have an important bearing on all aspects of pricing. The internal considerations will concentrate on views on the objectives and organisation of pricing, the role of price in the marketing programme, costs and the characteristics of the products or services.

However, maximum effectiveness in pricing work is achieved by the correct delegation of the responsibility for the formulation of policies to a specified executive. The executive chosen should, of course, have the right training and experience for the job and, if held responsible for other duties as well, these should be in some way related to pricing work. Having too disparate activities will often detract from the high performance of either. Generally, marketing seems to be the right recipient of such delegation. Marketing executives are the most *au fait* with market conditions and should be the most updated on the subject. However, as mentioned, close liaison with other company executives is always necessary.

The corporate planner may also be involved in some detail to check the consistency of pricing intentions with corporate short- and long-term objectives and future development plans and opportunities. The level at which pricing decisions are taken and the degree of consultation required will depend on the importance, difficulties and complexities of the task. Where pricing can be done on a fairly routine basis, the use of agreed formulae or procedures would suffice for most purposes. When pricing decisions are required rapidly, or frequently, established routines governed by precise rules would permit decisions to be taken at relatively low levels, often not above middle management. However where decisions covering very important matters, or considerable sums of money, or critical long-term aspects of the business are to be made, higher levels of management should play active roles and more and wider sets of consultations should be sought.

Although many companies have neglected the task of establishing pricing policies and several others do not follow their declared policies, pricing is a key activity of management. On its successful execution depends the success and survival of the firm. The ability and willingness to establish such policies vary from company to company so that the industrial approach to pricing appears haphazard.

Further, while interest is greatest in setting policies for new products, the same does not exist for ongoing products. Also, once a policy has been agreed, no attempt is made to update it to meet changes in markets, competitive, financial or manufacturing conditions. Thus, a flexibility of approach and willingness to adapt to changing circumstances are two further ingredients for success in pricing.

Marketing changes which can demand reconsideration of pricing policies include changes that have been made in other parts of the marketing programme, or the changed role of price in marketing policy and the (altered) characteristics of the product or services to be offered. The last is most applicable when an entirely new family of products is added to a company's range and they place quite a different emphasis on prices. The number and importance of buyers and potential customers and their views of prices and price levels may force pricing policy changes. So too would any substantial fluctuations in sales volume and the introduction of price or credit control regulations.

External factors of prime importance are of course, demand and changes in demand patterns, the nature of the industries being served, their market structure and the nature and extent of competition. Changes in competitors, especially the entry of new ones or the transformation of formerly insignificant ones to serious competitors, may all require reconsideration of pricing policies or plans. Changes in the environmental factors affecting the business, whether the company occupies the position of price leader, the age of the industry and the ease with which others can enter the market are all points that should be considered at regular times so that policy can be reformulated as necessary.

6.7 Human resources

This side of management is dealt with more fully in Chapter 8. However, it is worth noting one or two points here.

Besides the stability of labour supplies, especially skilled workers, labour costs and changes therein, the method of remuneration, wage incentives and labour productivity are all items that manufacturing executives must consider before they finalise any strategy, policy or plan decisions. The importance of incentives and the maintenance of good labour relations are also vital consider-ations. Thought should also be given to the possibility of devising group incentives. They are most effective when several members of the workforce are engaged in tasks which have common group characteristics which influence the inter-dependence of different operations. Some of these characteristics are unity of interest, the importance of mutual cooperation if everyone in the group is to operate successfully, and where each operation is directly depen-dent on the preceding one and strongly influences or delays the one that follows it and where there is physical proximity. Technical proximity, i.e. where the members of the group require the same technical know-how to operate well, is also important.

The successful working of groups requires good leadership also, not just mutual cooperation. This will be provided by a group leader who will usually emerge from each group. In their formation it may be that a leader is appointed but, in practice, it will be the natural leader, one with the experience, personal-ity and abilities required for the group task, who will head the group and motivate it, even if the nominated leader continues to carry the title and work with the group. Where there is mutual understanding between all members of a group who the actual leader is, this situation will not matter. If the appointed leader is constantly clashing on policy decisions and in other ways with the natural leader, the former should be removed from the group and found another post. It may be advisable also not to put such transferred persons into any other group if they still think that they will be the leader.

The effective use of manpower depends on such well-known things as better job evaluation and analysis which reveal the true facts about the various tasks, right levels of remuneration and more effective organisational planning. Recruitment, selection, training and industrial relations must all be well done to a high order. In addition, there is need for a change of attitudes, many of which have become virtual axioms in industrial activity. The first change should be towards trusting people rather than to distrust them, at least until they show they cannot be trusted! Then status should not be used to maintain power and prestige, but be seen as probably the only way people's knowledge and abilities can be used effectively in a functionally relevant way. If status is used to try to bolster prestige, will this not in fact destroy what prestige had existed before? Next, people should not be too strictly confined to a narrow segment of the company's operations as specified in their job descriptions. Many are capable of effective operations in other (usually allied) areas and, if used more widely in this way, could add considerably to their contributions to the company's success. If people are viewed as whole persons, with a variety of experience and successes behind them, greater utilisation of all labour is possible. This, in turn, would lead to greater job satisfaction and productivity. This requires acceptance of the view that people are not often fixed rigidly into given interests, skills or knowledge but are capable of development and of gaining new knowledge and skills.

6.8 Notes on overseas factories

It was not so long ago that most developing countries looked on modern technology, especially the advanced sectors, as the answer to all their industrial and economic problems. However, experience has shown that this is not necessarily true in every case and may only be correct in a few special instances. So the pendulum has swung back and some 'experts' are querying whether fully automated plants, for example, are really beneficial in nations with limited skilled labour and very high unemployment amongst the unskilled. Where advanced technology has been introduced, it has been blamed (not always correctly) for the development of a terrible, intractable problem: permanent and massive unemployment. It is suggested that with careful thought the highly-automated equipment could be modified to create as it were an intermediate technology that is better suited to the real needs of developing countries, whilst also being more profitable to all.

There is validity to the arguments in favour of automated plant, even in countries with high unemployment and low wage costs. The less automated plant can generate more managerial problems but these difficulties, of the intermediate technology, are often exaggerated. It can in fact be more difficult to keep an automated factory working successfully in a developing country, especially if the necessary backup skills, for servicing, repair, etc., are not available at all or are difficult to find. Even if the labour-intensive factory creates work for managers the greater benefits from better relations with the government and higher profits make it well worth the effort.

Another excuse given for not using local labour in manufacturing is that product quality cannot be guaranteed or held at some specified level, consistently. In a labour-intensive operation this is perhaps more often true than not; but not where intermediate technology is properly devised and managed. To avoid trouble, perhaps the main or critical processes can be automated or depend on a small number of highly skilled men while everything else (i.e. loading the machines with raw material, handling stocks of all kinds, final packing etc.) could be done with manual labour. Such operations will certainly require executives to keep a much closer watch on all operations than might be needed in a fully industrialised nation.

A reason given for choosing an automated plant is that output can be altered quickly to meet demand changes. Hence there is flexibility in the manufacturing process. If demand rose, it is argued, throughput could be increased and a night shift added to critical machines. This is much easier and quicker than training a large number of new workers for a labour-intensive operation. If demand fell, the machines could be slowed down, whereas with labour-intensive units a considerable number of workers might have to be made redundant. This does not take account of the fact that many modern plants are designed to work at optimal efficiency at maximum output, so that any slowing down of the operations could be very costly to them. In many countries labour legislation makes it extremely difficult to lay off workers and when they are laid off, the company's image suffers and later attempts at recruitment may be jeopardised. Then, again, if labour is under-employed it is very difficult to restore productivity to former levels. One answer can be found to this problem of adjusting to demand changes. It is better, or good, planning, based on sound forecasting, so that production runs steadily at some identified level of average demand with inventories taking care of the fluctuations. When demand falls, finished goods go into store and when demand rises above production levels, goods are drawn out of inventory to supply that peak demand. Or, where the work to be done is fairly unskilled, contract labour could be called in for specific periods to provide the quick, short-term boost to production.

Many expatriate executives in overseas plants assume that controlling a large workforce creates more problems for them than running a fully-automated plant. This may be so, but the problems of automated plants are plentiful when vital spare parts are not available locally and replacements have to be shipped long distances from the parent company. Or locally made components may be subject to frequent failures and the government still does not allow imports when local manufacture is available. Proper operation and maintenance become very serious problems for those enterprises which depend on automated plant for their overseas ventures. In labour-intensive plants, experience shows that absenteeism has lesser effects on productivity than in automated factories. While the rate of absenteeism may be no higher in automated plants, the absence of one worker has a much greater effect on productivity and output than the absenteeism of several workers in a labour-intensive factory. Also by a re-arrangement of the workloads, the labour-intensive operation can often neutralise the effect of even quite substantial absenteeism.

Further, in the majority of cases, the intermediate technology, labour-intensive approach for countries with low wage rates is usually more profitable. Where wages are high, investment in capital equipment for automated production is often more advantageous. This assumes, however, that the government will approve the import of expensive automated plant when it knows that equally acceptable labour-intensive equipment is available and will help to reduce the unemployment problem. However, intermediate technology may not be appropriate in every case in developing countries. Some highly automated plant may be unavoidable or may outweigh all the disadvantages mentioned (e.g. automated steel rolling mills). Then the form of the intermediate technology will depend on the technical abilities of the country, its industrial experience and record, the availability of skilled labour, the unskilled labour and unemployment situations, government policies on industrial development and employment, foreign exchange available for imports of specialised equipment and the extent of the government's aspirations for long-term development which may make unrealistic demands on the available foreign exchange. Then the importation of automated plant would be financially impossible.

In planning overseas plant, control is necessary of the engineers who will plan it because their enthusiasm for the project, especially the technical aspects, will tend to push them towards automation and excessively technical methods. Even when it has been decreed that the plant will not be automated but labour-intensive, their engineering bias will drive them to go for machines that guarantee high quality, which may be totally unnecessary for the operation in question. Then studies of the state of the local technological art is advisable so that the company will know what is available and possible, and what is not. Long years of working in wage-intensive, high-technology countries has made most engineers forget the simpler alternative production methods that may be available. In this connection also consideration should be given to the second-hand equipment that may be available, either from the home, parent company, or from local sources. Or, where new equipment is required, it may be possible to obtain it at advantageous prices if a developing country is able to make it to the required standards. If obsolete designs are involved, it should be checked first if these will be more appropriate for the project, given local conditions, than more sophisticated plant from developed countries. Finally, all bias should be eradicated from reports, first those on or about the projected venture and then the operating reports once the factory is in action. It is unreasonable to expect everything about production in a developing country to equal that in sophisticated, high-technology developed nations. Carping about the so-called failings helps no-one.

6.9 Implications for marketing, financial and personnel departments

The implications of the adaptation of the 'quadrille concept' to manufacturing, as explained in this Chapter, for the other three main divisions or departments of a company are indicated by Figure 6.3. It shows that as with marketing (Chapter 5) no decision can be taken without some consultations with colleagues from other interested or affected disciplines. To ignore this is to court disaster. It is no longer a question of whether one executive is talking to another. Each must talk to every colleague as and when necessary. Also, all must listen to each other and understand what is being said, i.e. the true message being conveyed, devoid of all embellishments.

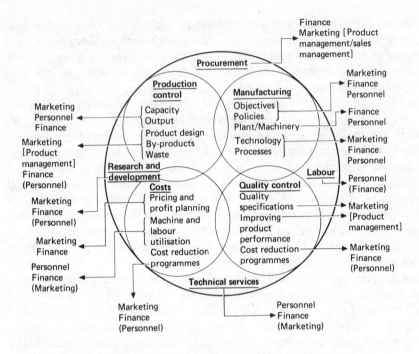

Where a major management discipline (e.g. marketing) is shown in ( ) this signifies possible/occasional involvement of this discipline or division.

Where sub-departments of division are shown in [ ] this signifies that that sub-department is primarily involved.

More extensive liaisons may be required at times.

Fig 6.3

6.10 Questions

1. What does the 'quadrille concept' mean for manufacturing departments? What are the implications and major liaisons which have to be established with other operational departments?

2. What changes of attitude should there be with the implementation of the 'quadrille concept'? What myths and fables have to be removed from managerial concepts?

3. What problems arise in the relationships between factories and the communities in which they are located? Why is this important when considering the size and location of plants?

4. Why is accurate forecasting important to capacity and output planning? What effects on production planning will good product design and quality control have under the 'quadrille'?

5. What relationships exist between purchasing and inventory control?

6. What are the important contacts or liaisons which must take place in decisions on the processes and technology, production planning and control systems, purchasing and costing methods that might be used by a company?

7. What is the cost-price relationship? How is it used to advantage by a corporation?

8. What major considerations arise with overseas plants?

7 Finance — marketing — manufacturing — personnel

Despite the many definitions and descriptions of 'management' there is no denying that managers are concerned with economic factors and questions as they affect the operation and survival of a business organisation. Their activities should be orientated towards the satisfaction of the economic needs of every party involved in the business, especially its customers. In following these precepts, good financial management has three main aims:

—to keep the business solvent with sufficient liquidity for its own needs and purpose;
—to provide the organisation with the finance needed to sustain operations and achieve growth;
—thus to provide the means whereby the organisation can satisfy at optimum levels, the economic and other needs of customers and all those who work for, or are associated with, the firm.

Money is the common denominator for all the activities carried on by a business organisation. Without money a business cannot function. It is like a lubricant. If there is too little the business will grind to a halt. If there is too much the company will be awash with numerous projects attempting to use the surplus funds. Some will be good risks and others bad. The total effect will be to clog the machinery of management by over-stressing executives and other manpower resources. It will smother the machinery, obscuring the vital and essential operations and will lead eventually to some malfunction of the management process.

Good management demands a proper appreciation of the role of money and its ability to measure the progress of a company. There must also be awareness that money, or appropriate money units, is the common denominator in management, for a given point in time and the purchasing power at that time. Thus *financial strategy formulation* is not something that happens after the 'real' managers (implied as manufacturing and marketing executives!) have made their decisions. Financial plans cannot be finalised until these executives have stated what they can, or plan, to do. The financial plan on paper may be one of the last links of the planning chain. However, financial strategy will have played an important part in shaping the other strategies of the company (corporate, marketing, manufacturing and personnel). Inability to appreciate the true role of money in a business could prove disastrous for the firm. Also, at the end of the planning process it may be advisable to conduct a final appraisal of financial strategy and to modify decisions made at the commencement of planning to bring them into line with reality.

The role of financial activities in the general scheme of things is illustrated by Figure 1.5 (The Basic Management Quadrille) while Figure 1.6 illustrated the relationships in more detail for an integrated management approach. The *financial quadrille* itself is shown in Figure 7.1. Here the major foursome, needing close cooperation at all times, is made up of *capital* (its raising, investment, utilisation) *and financial planning — management of funds* (all the funds at work in the company) — *cash flows* (inflows and outflows) — *budgetary control*. The second foursome, providing essential support, involves *credit control — resource allocation — acquisition and merger — project appraisal*. These eight form the essential heart of the financial operations of a company but cannot be carried out in isolation from the other divisions or departments of the company.

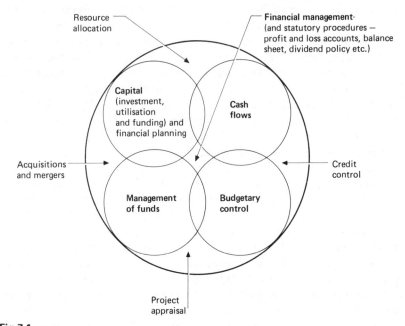

Fig 7.1

For example, cash flows and budgetary control involve all corporate activities and operations. Therefore their planning and control must involve appropriate executives from all departments. Then credit control is of particular interest to marketing executives. So the formulation of credit policies and their implementation must be achieved with the cooperation and assistance of marketing executives. Depending on the nature of the project, project appraisal will have to be undertaken in conjunction with manufacturing and marketing departments, and perhaps others as well. For example, personnel will have to be called in if new skills are involved in the project and there is need for an assessment on their availability and cost. The same is true about acquisitions and mergers; though in this case the board should be the prime movers, performing the leading role in investigations, analyses and decisions on this subject. If there is a corporate planner, that person will be included in all these discussions from time to time, especially when consideration is being given to the company's future role and activities.

7.1 Financial management

Financial management is responsible for the successful and efficient management of all the corporation's finance and financial activities, i.e. all the items, and more besides, shown in Figure 7.1 (which gives the main group headings only). It is not some superior form of accounting, or a financial information system. It is a related group of activities involved in decision-making and policy formulation for all financial and financially related aspects of a firm. These include capital, cash flow, credit, pricing and profit policies, performance planning and assessment and budgetary control policies and systems. The last, though considered primarily a province of financial management, also cannot be done effectively without the cooperation and agreement of every other division or department. Thus financial management represents the corporation's overall financial interests and is its watchdog for them. The work of financial management can be summarised as in Figure 7.2. Finally, the relationships between financial and other functions or activities in a firm are complementary and reciprocal in nature.

For example, senior management (or the board) is concerned with the allocation of capital and other funds for investment in the company's operations and is responsible for securing these from whichever source provides the most advantageous terms for both short- and long-term needs. They will also want to know if the resources are being used efficiently and effectively or if some resources may be better switched to other activities. Financial information is needed and the financial department is responsible for applying their expertise to making the most reliable, and unbiased, information available for these deliberations. The department is also responsible for overseeing that the financial decisions and intentions of the board, mutually agreed between all departments, are correctly carried out. They have also to recommend to the board when decisions or policies should be modified as changing circumstances dictate. This work must be well done for it is vital to the proper deployment and redeployment of funds. The financial reports must also give clear and correct pictures of the progress and status of the company and be precise in measuring the critical factors affecting the operation.

For the manufacturing and marketing divisions the financial department provides the essential support services without which there can be no certainty

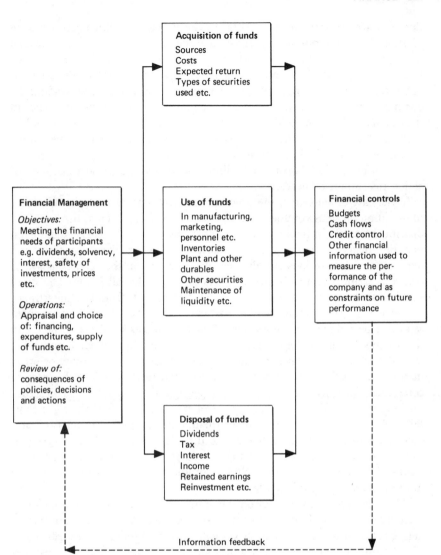

Acquisition of funds

Sources
Costs
Expected return
Types of securities
used etc.

Financial Management

Objectives:
Meeting the financial
needs of participants
e.g. dividends, solvency,
interest, safety of
investments, prices
etc.

Operations:
Appraisal and choice
of: financing,
expenditures, supply
of funds etc.

Review of:
consequences of
policies, decisions
and actions

Use of funds

In manufacturing,
marketing,
personnel etc.
Inventories
Plant and other
durables
Other securities
Maintenance of
liquidity etc.

Financial controls

Budgets
Cash flows
Credit control
Other financial
information used to
measure the per-
formance of the
company and as
constraints on future
performance

Disposal of funds

Dividends
Tax
Interest
Income
Retained earnings
Reinvestment etc.

Information feedback

Fig 7.2

that these two important activities are at optimal levels. For *manufacturing*, the
financial department's interests lie not only in matters concerned with the
investment in plant and inventories and fund utilisation. It is involved also in
keeping a check on the cost of production, ensuring that this meets standards
agreed collectively by manufacturing, marketing and financial executives. The
last will also maintain a watch on quality standards and quality control,
especially any variances in the cost in these respects. This, in turn, will involve
the financial executives in checking the correctness and cost of the purchasing
(procurement) activity, that correct materials, components, consumables and

durables are being bought at costs previously agreed with manufacturing division. Thus the purchasing department has a role to play in the financial management of a corporation, especially at the decision-making and policy formulation stages. Delays and faults in output are also of interest to financial executives especially if they cost more money than budgeted and so affect the company's profit plans and targets. If the remedy for output problems lies in the purchase of new or additional equipment, then financial executives will be very involved in those deliberations and decisions. In this case, personnel executives will also be in the team if new skills or additional labour is needed. They will have to advise on availability and costs and alternative courses of action that might be necessary.

In the case of *marketing*, the financial executives provide all the necessary information on sales volume, prices, profit and profit margins, turnover and distribution costs in total and sub-classified by products, markets and even possibly major customers and industries. Data on the cash flow and debtor/creditor positions are also usually furnished in the reports as are of course, variances from planned budgets or targets for all items. The more sophisticated reports may also contain brief comments from the department concerned on the reasons why a particular variance occurred in a given reporting period and most importantly what action has been taken to remedy the situation. Thus marketing executives can exercise more effective control of their department's activities. When changes in competitive activity or other market factor call for adjustments to prices and terms and possibly also to costs, financial executives work with marketing and manufacturing colleagues (including production and quality control executives) to find the right solutions. When changes in materials or quality are necessary, purchasing and quality control executives will join the three mentioned above to arrive at suitable, effective decisions. If changes in output (in total quantities or in the timing of production) need to be altered, production control colleagues will be in the team studying this matter.

While decisions and policies on the *distribution* system and methods to be used are the responsibility of physical distribution executives and other marketing colleagues, financial executives will work with them on cost, plant and labour utilisation aspects. Usually personnel colleagues have to be consulted also when labour questions arise. Manufacturing department must also be represented if discussions on distribution involve changes in output, production scheduling and even quality. The financial department is also interested in the financial outcomes or forecasts of decisions on the form of transportation to be used (own fleet — which would involve heavy capital expenditure, fixed and running — contract or casual hire), the number of depots to be used, their size and location and whether owned or leased, the average level of inventories, the flow of products through the system and the proposed administrative structure and systems to be used, hence their costs. They will be interested in estimates on the comparative costs and efficiency or effectiveness that would result. They will provide regular reports on the actual costs being incurred, will compare these with budgets and will show the variances (both positive and negative).

In *personnel* matters, financial executives help to provide the figures for, or estimates of, labour costs, labour utilisation, labour turnover, training and development costs, cost of industrial relations work, health and social services (including any subsidised canteen) and the actual administrative costs of the personnel department itself. Where labour turnover is the subject under study, appropriate manufacturing colleagues would join the team if the problem concerned factory labour; and marketing executives would join in if the problem concerned marketing staff. Should the labour turnover be high in another department, say research and development, then that department would be represented.

With regard to training and development matters, all departments would be represented if the corporate aspects were being discussed. If a specific section only is under scrutiny then only the affected department would join personnel and financial executives in their discussions. The accent is usually on actual expenditures compared with budgeted costs; for if the former is not kept more or less in line with the latter (assuming nothing untoward has occurred) the personnnel activity could become both costly and ineffective.

Thus financial executives are very much involved in all the expenditure and income centres of a company's activities. While the executives of the other divisions must play the lead roles in planning, policy formulation and decisions on the programmes or actions to be followed by their divisions, their financial colleagues provide vital support and advisory roles at almost every turn. Where the board has seen fit to delegate the control function to the financial department (e.g. in the planning, running and control of cost reduction programmes), these executives will play the leading role. However, even here the ready and willing cooperation, support and agreement of departmental executives are necessary for a successful operation.

The important role of financial management becomes clear when it is realised that the profitability and solvency of the company depend on their work. This is whether they are providing the information and data necessary, with associated advice, for effective decisions by line executives or taking direct control of some function. Survival depends on meeting both requirements and keeping a balance between them. (Increasing immediate profitability might lead to reduced solvency or liquidity, and vice versa.) Financial management has to see that this balance is maintained and that the right choices and trade-offs are made, through detailed consultation with line executive colleagues. As Professor R.J. Chambers has stated in his book *Financial Management*, the financial function is primarily a service function.

7.1.1 Financial director, treasurer and the 'upstairs maid'

The financial departments of companies may be organised in a variety of ways. Some have financial directors (or executive vice-president, finance) at their heads. Others do without, and share responsibilities between the chief executive or the chairman and the company secretary. Still others (usually not British companies) have treasurers. It was a British company secretary of long service and great ability who referred to himself and colleagues as the 'upstairs maids' of business, always having to do the detailed and dirty work for the masters upstairs. He also described the financial director as a waiter (they were either dancing attendance on the needs of the board and other departmental directors, or were just waiting for the right time to propose some new policy or other). The treasurer he saw as the porter, as he saw that role as being very similar to that of an hotel porter, always fetching and carrying in service to customers as well as his bosses. This company secretary always referred to these three titles or positions as 'The Waiter, the Porter and the Upstairs Maid', the title of a then current popular song that he hummed in moments of stress!

More soberly, the work of a financial director covers the management of all the work of that department. He has total responsibility for the effectiveness and efficiency of its work. The various activities could be conveniently listed as follows.

1. FUNCTIONAL
   (a) Accounting: statutory accounts and accounting procedures; credit control
   (b) Budgeting: cost and revenue budgets; budgetary control system
   (c) Treasurership: cash forecasting and control, raising capital, resource allocation, funds management

2. POLICY
   (a) Budget standards: recommends performance levels for costs and revenues
   (b) Credit: establishes credit policies for customers and suppliers
   (c) Investment: appraisal and recommendations on investment projects
   (d) Planning: plays leading role in discussions on all critical financial points in the planning process (see Chapter 4) and in setting agreed financial strategy and policies
   (e) Pricing: oversees discussions on pricing policies and standards between marketing and manufacturing etc.

Now it is clear that the financial director's responsibilities cover all the above. What is not quite so clear is the true responsibilities of treasurers and company secretaries. It all depends on how a company likes to organise this work, who likes doing what and the attitude of the chief executive and chairman towards subordinates, even at this exalted level. For example, they may just not like anyone else being involved in financial policy matters.

So, in theory, the company secretary without a financial director would normally be responsible to the chief executive for all the activities shown under item 1 (functional) above. If there is a financial director, the company secretary would be responsible to that person. However, there have been cases when, despite there being a financial director, the company secretary reported to the chief executive and sometimes the chairman. This arrangement is a potentially difficult one for a company secretary. In such arrangements, the financial directors concern themselves purely with the policy matters shown under item 2 (policy) above. Even then credit matters (item 2(b)) might still be the responsibility of the company secretary.

The position of the treasurer is even more mixed. In theory, the treasurer should look after item 1(c) (treasurership), often handles item 1(b) (budgeting) also and on occasions also deals with item 1(a) (accounting) when the treasurer has become the equivalent of a normal British company secretary. Some member of the board (either the chairman or president or some delegated colleague) would then be responsible for policy matters. However, some treasurers have also been in charge of budget standards, and/or credit and/or pricing matters. The only things that treasurers do not have direct responsibility for, but they will be brought into the discussions from time to time, are those concerning corporate strategy and policy formulation and planning (other than the areas indicated as their responsibility).

There are cases also of large corporations having a financial director (or vice-president), a treasurer and a company secretary. This is often dictated by the volume of work involved, or may be the result of a merger which was not correctly assimilated. In such a case, the financial director looks after policy and has overall responsibility for the financial department. The other two report to him and the treasurer looks after the budgeting and treasurership matters, and the company secretary deals with accounting matters. In the United Kingdom and some other countries, the company secretary also has certain legal responsibilities and liabilities mainly centering around the correct production and presentation of statutory documents, especially the balance sheet and profit and loss account and reports bearing on directorship matters (*see* Section 4.7). As the same company secretary mentioned earlier, remarked, if anything is wrong it is the company secretary who precedes the company chairman into prison! So when assigning responsibilities in the financial department, for those countries, the formal legal position must be considered carefully.

7.1.2 Financial planning

Financial executives have to interpret the nature, scale, scope and achievements of a business in financial terms to a company's executives and planners. In the planning stage the forecasts by marketing, manufacturing and the other departments will be presented in terms of expenditures, profit, return, cash flows and company worth. The managers can then see if the company is progressing as desired and what the anticipated return on capital would be for current plans. The board, in particular, would be interested in this information as it has the responsibility of keeping shareholders and financiers happy. Poor or indifferent results will handicap these efforts. If the results are inadequate, line executives will work together, and with their support operations, to see what can be done to remedy the position. If nothing can be done, they must consider other courses of action ranging from change of corporate strategy, product-market development, diversification or divestment and even the contraction of the business or voluntary liquidation. Throughout, their financial colleagues will be working with them, providing essential financial data and advice and sometimes, encouragement.

In financial planning and control, it is not enough to work by the profit and return figures only. The liquidity position must also be watched to ensure that the company can meet its liabilities. For example, growth of sales volume might have been achieved, but if this has been at the sacrifice of prompt payment or quick settlement of creditors' accounts, then the survival of the company may be endangered. The company may then be over-trading, i.e. operating at levels of business beyond the limits of its financial resources. Then, from the board's point of view, in dealing with shareholders and financiers and in preparing the ground for long-term development or growth, the net worth of the company and even the price/earnings ratio (p/e ratio) have to be planned and controlled. The board's aim is to improve these figures substantially, so that quick and inexpensive support in future from the company's backers will be assured; i.e. the company will pay advantageous rates for the new capital it will need. So financial planning and control encompasses much more than profit and return; yet many companies still believe that they have good financial operations when these two aspects only are being properly controlled. It is arguable also whether proper control is possible when all the other important aspects of financial management are left out of planning and control work?

Financial planning must express a corporation's forward plans in ways that identify clearly the needs, opportunities and problems that lie ahead in financial terms. This requires a clear expression of the financial strategy that should be followed in the acquisition, use and disposal of funds and in the performance standards that will be used to measure progress. The financial strategy will also act as a constraint on all other strategies, policies and programmes of the company. It should establish the points beyond which they should not go. At the same time it should also act as a spur to what should be done and could be achieved. It can stimulate capital investment, reducing liquid balances and ensuring more profitable use of funds. Thus, there is need for a close relationship and full cooperation between the financial and the other planning in a company.

Financial plans provide the main cash flow parameters by which decisions concerning profit targets, capital expenditure and inflows from depreciation and divestments are made. They should also include forecasts of movements in purchases and sales, and thus inventories and creditor and debtor levels. They estimate, in addition, the need for constant and variable capital. 'Constant capital' here is taken to be the fixed and working capital needed to sustain operations in the slackest period of a trading year. The 'variable capital' is the extra that is needed for operations above the constant or slackest level of activity. However, adequate financial control is possible only when a corporation works to regularly revised short-term cash flow forecasts, based on a budgetary control process.

In a large organisation with many operations, subsidiaries and international involvements which can include wholly-owned subsidiaries, partnerships, minority interests and other ventures, one big problem for financial planners is the consolidation of all the financial data from the individual projects and plans in hand. If the forecasted capital requirements are just totalled up, the resultant borrowing requirement is likely to be so huge as to be beyond achievement. Consolidation therefore requires executives to display discretion and discrimination in the selection of the plans and projects that will be implemented. Further, the localised and global effects of their choices, and of the omission of the projects not selected, have to be considered. Once again, this will involve executives from every facet of the enterprise at some time or other, in comprehensive and cooperative analyses and appraisals. Thus project appraisal, besides being necessary for every project as it arises or is proposed, takes on a much bigger role in this corporate process of project selection within the financial resources of the company.

Another difficulty facing financial management and planners in businesses with an international spread is that cash is not freely transferable from one country to another. A surplus of funds in one cannot compensate for a shortage in another. Yet the financial plans should treat capital as a corporate, not an individual subsidiary, resource. The strategy should allow for the funding of operations in one country from funds of another where this is legal, possible or desirable. But this should be in accord with local financial strategy which is itself approved by the parent organisation or at corporate level. These local strategies should also ensure that the mere existence of surplus funds does not lead to expenditure on inferior projects, ones that do not meet local or corporate strategy and objectives. The same strict rules as applied to all other project appraisals should apply in these cases also. So, the more complex the organisation, the greater is the need for integrated management between financial executives at different locations and levels of management and all associated executives from other interested divisions. Consultations are needed up and down the executive ladder and, also, laterally with colleagues of equal status in other departments.

Thus there will be many reasons why projects have to be rejected. Where sources of funds have to be reconsidered, or are inadequate for project needs, even desirable ventures have to be abandoned. Sometimes, when financial resources are limited and cannot be made up in any way, intended capital expenditure may have to be severely pruned and the whole corporate plan rethought. Further, while the cash flow position may not reveal any problems regarding the balancing of use of funds with sources and availability, some other financial weakness could force the postponement or rejection of projects. For example, liquidity or the ratio of debt to equity may be inadequate. Or, less frequently, if a company has a surplus of liquid assets, projects which will achieve good profit objectives may have to be postponed since they would only add to the liquid assets. This may increase the risk of a take-over especially by asset-strippers who are only interested in the free cash, not the future well-being of the company.

Financial planning is not only concerned with the investment of new funds into new projects. These opportunities arise in irregular batches. Other things requiring analyses or examination include plans to replace or expand present operations; divestments whether by closure, sale or merger; long-term contracts for goods or services; leasing and hire purchase involvements and cost reductions or savings. These should be analysed to indicate the optimal financial benefits to which they could contribute and their relevance to the corporate situation and objectives.

The performance of any company's management is usually judged in terms of earnings per share, profit, return on investment, growth in turnover and improvements in the profit/sales ratio. A few other ratios may also be used as guides; but rarely considered is the proper and effective management of the company's financial resources or funds. This only hits the headlines when the company has to announce, often abruptly, that it cannot meet its liabilities (i.e. pay its creditors) and is going into liquidation. (Some of the cases mentioned earlier in this book are examples.) This oversight occurs when executives leave everything to do with finance to the company's accountants or financial executives, while not giving the latter sufficient authority to do anything effective about them. Or when they believe that 'profit' means 'cash in the bank'. This last point is not true. The preceding sentence underlines the point made already in this chapter, that all executives must play an active part in financial planning and control. They need not be financial experts, but they must be aware of the implications of financial reports and the nature, scope and implications of the remedial action they may imply as vital for survival and growth.

7.1.3 Financial control

Plans are of little use if there is no effective control of them. Thus, with financial planning there is need for the creation of an appropriate financial control system. This can take many forms but the essential basic elements are:

—monthly cash forecasts, probably for 'next three months';
—short-term cash forecasts for the first two years of the planning period, probably on a monthly basis;
—long-term cash forecasts on a five or ten year basis, usually prepared annually.

The short-term forecasts should link with the operational plans and be on the same time basis. Thus if divisional operational plans are based on monthly forecasts and calculations, the short-term cash forecasts should be similarly timed. The aim is to see how the cash balances move, and to compare this with the operational results of the divisions. Yet many companies do not do this. They are then not making any real comparisons and should not be surprised when the operational results fail to meet the expectations of the short-term cash forecasts!

The long-term forecasts should also tie in with the long-term strategy planning and needs for the company. In this case, of course, the figures will be more generalised, less precise or accurate than should be the case with short-term forecasts. Finally, of course, all financial control systems should have as a very important element of them, a good budgetary control operation. This will help to keep the divisions within agreed expenditure and results targets.

7.1.4 Fund management and cash flows in corporate management

Since a business cannot operate without money, the effective and efficient management of the funds circulating in a company is important for sustained success. The funds cycle in a business is simply illustrated by Figure 7.3. This shows the links that exist between the various 'events' associated with cash flow, including the interest or involvement of colleague departments of financial executives. It will be appreciated that there are two aspects to every transaction: first, the supply or generation of funds; and, second, the utilisation of these. While considerable thought is given to the raising and injection of capital into an enterprise, far too many businesses still do not maintain the same depth of interest and involvement in the utilisation of the generated funds. Then on the operational side, considerable thought is rightly given to the subjects of profit and profit control; but less detailed attention is given to cash flows and cash control, i.e. the control of cash flow and the use of funds, until cash problems arise. It is then too late to try to correct a bad situation. The thing to do is plan and control matters so that cash problems do not arise.

These omissions are often the cause of corporate financial failure or difficulties. Much more attention must be given to the utilisation or use of funds and the control of cash flow. The several methods open to executives are well described in specialist books on financial management and are worth detailed study by all those responsible for financial matters in business. Then early warning will be given of any worsening situation in ample time for executives to carry out the necessary corrective actions. The reporting of cash flow situations should be made at least as frequently as reports on the profit position. Indeed some executives maintain that cash flow reports should be made more frequently. Thus if profit and other trading reports are made on a monthly basis, cash flow reports could be made fortnightly or even weekly, especially when considerable flows of funds is a natural part of the business.

As Figure 7.3 indicates, the other departments must be involved or consulted at the point of the cycle indicated in the illustration. Again, there is a strong body of opinion which maintains that senior executives of all departments must be continually involved in every aspect of funds, management and cash flow; or certainly in those parts that concern their own departments. Thus capital investment, if it is to do with new plant or machinery, would involve the

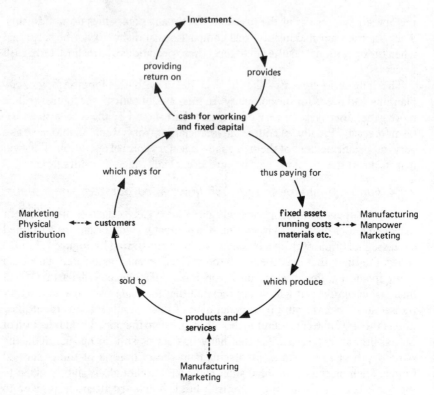

Broken arrows show the associated links or involvements in the cycle of the other departments of a business enterprise

Fig 7.3

executives of manufacturing division. If the investment is somehow due to the need for new skilled labour (e.g. extensive training programmes for existing staff), personnel executives will work with financial colleagues on this. If new or modified products will result from an investment, marketing executives must be in on all discussions and decisions. Throughout, of course, the principle of consistency must be applied. That is, the same concepts and principles must be used when preparing financial (and other) data for comparison. Otherwise executives will not be comparing like with like, and could stumble into faulty interpretations and wrong decisions.

Long-term cash forecasts and plans should also follow the same principles, and their consistency with the corporate and financial long-range objectives should be verified. Time and again decisions are taken on long-term cash aspects which at the time may prove convenient or may relieve overworked executives from having to find the time to consider the implications of their decisions. When in due course it is discovered that decisions taken a while back have diverted the company from its long-term objectives there should be no surprise. Also, when this deviation is discovered, much more time may have to be spent in trying to find the reason for this and thus the remedial action that must be taken. Executives must contemplate both the short- and the long-term implications of every major decision they propose to make before any irrevocable step is taken.

Given also that the mid-1970s not only heralded in an age of mediocrity but also an age of inflation, the old arguments for keeping inflation considerations out of the management of funds flow are no longer valid. It was contended that inflation need not be considered because sales prices could be inflated as costs rose and so profit margins could be maintained. When inflation reaches a high level, this is no longer true or possible since matching prices to cost inflation will eventually take products and services into price levels which customers and the nation will not be able to afford. Then it was contended that rates of inflation could not be forecasted. This may be true in absolute terms; but systems exist, and experience has been gained, to permit reasonably accurate forecasts to be made; and they should be. Then the short- and long-term implications for the business can be estimated and allowed for in the plans.

However, while some cost increases are beyond the control of a company (e.g. raw materials and import costs), prices should only rise as a result of decisions taken by management after full consideration of all the points and the implications concerned. Further, future cash requirements should be stated in future terms, not current ones; i.e. in tomorrow's values not today's. Finally, if inflation persists it must be taken into consideration in the planning exercise. The solution is to make more than one estimate of long-term strategy. It could first be considered in current money terms, and then with costs inflated at some anticipated future rate of growth of inflation to determine how much prices must increase to maintain margins or how much the business must grow to achieve the same gross profits. Then future cash needs and cash generation requirements can be more accurately determined. Also, it will indicate what change in strategy (including product-market strategy) and operations would be necessary to ensure the viability of the company within any official or governmental constraints in force. Further consideration of alternative strategies should then be undertaken.

While the terms 'cash' and 'funds' are often used synonymously, in balance sheet terms there is a strict difference. 'Cash' refers to the actual cash (sometimes referred to as liquid funds) in hand, or at the bank, or as represented by marketable securities; while 'funds' cover both sides of a balance sheet including the cash. However, in modern usage, cash flow has become identified with being identical with funds flow, covering cash and all the net sources and uses of all funds shown on the balance sheet. This flow appraises the impact and quality of management decisions over a given period of time. It indicates where abnormal or interesting flows have arisen which, therefore, should be investigated. The reasons for the beneficial changes can then be understood and used advantageously in future. The harmful ones can be noted and their recurrence avoided.

7.1.5 Use of capital

The concept presented by many books on capital investment and financial planning implies that, at a given date, the planners present to the board a list of opportunities, all graded in order of importance, potential and so on. In practice this situation only arises when some new field is to be tackled. For most existing businesses, executives have at random times to advise on the probabilities of additions to, or changes in, ongoing operations or plans. These opportunities arise in irregular patterns. Further, opportunities do not have to involve the expenditure of new capital in new projects to require serious analysis. All changed or new ideas need to be investigated, the degree depending on the time and cost permitted and the long- and short-term importance of the end-results of the ideas. Thus the investment of capital, new or recycled, to replace or increase current activities and for acquisitions and mergers should be properly investigated, planned, implemented and controlled. Saving of capital for reinvestment elsewhere, via cost reduction programmes, divestment or disinvestment, also needs the same careful attention.

In fact what is required in financial optimisation when every possibility is studied and analysed in some depth so that the optimum financial benefit can be identified and realised. This optimisation of usually mutually exclusive, viable alternatives can produce considerable financial benefit in the shape of higher profits earned and losses avoided. However, even the smallest problems can render worthwhile savings if properly tackled. These can range from consideration of expensive, long-life equipment v. cheaper short-life items to labour intensive v. automated production, air v. sea transport, and so on.

Thus optimisation studies must penetrate to the smallest part of a company's operations if worthwile savings and improvements in the use of capital are to result. However, the responsibility for this work and for indicating where it will be done rests with the chief executive, advised by a planning group drawn from executives of the financial and corporate planning departments with colleagues from the other divisions most likely to be affected by the outcome. Capital investment planning should, therefore precede the taking of all important financial decisions. While all executives are involved in this work at some time, it should be so organised that only minimal demands are made on the time of senior executives. They should be saved for concentration on factors that can only be assessed from experience and judgement (e.g. technical, personnel and political aspects). The decisions taken should be reviewed from time to time, to check on their continuing relevance in the light of changing conditions. This will ensure continuity of purpose and achievement to give a continuance of success in capital investment planning and action.

An equally thorough approach to the use and management of working capital is also necessary. Unfortunately this is often not the case. Yet it is very important to any business. The net working capital of a company represents the amount of current assets being financed from long-term sources and is of special interest to creditors. They regard these assets as the ultimate source of funds for the repayment of their loans to the company. It is also one of the responsibilities of financial managers, working with appropriate colleagues, to fund the company debt at the lowest cost consistent with the corporate objectives. The latter should also include statements on the acceptable levels of risk that could be incurred.

If finance is in short supply, joint decisions will be needed on whether to ration new capital according to the profitability and risk levels of projects, or on the strategic need of the company. Also, expenditure that can be postponed for a stated period can be identified and retimed accordingly. Or plans could concentrate on investments with the earliest payback. However, this last could put long-range objectives in jeopardy through the abandonment of projects which would take some time to repay investment but are still important for the future development of the company. Finally, the alternative ways a project could be implemented could be considered and the one needing least capital could be chosen. The alternatives could range from leasing or renting plant and equipment rather than owning them, hiring some assets rather than purchasing them, use of hire purchase generally and making maximum use of government and other grants which may be applicable to certain regions. Then there are the activities that could be sub-contracted, saving the company capital investment to set up and manufacture the components.

There are still companies with a flabby attitude to the management and controlled use of working capital. They are usually firms flush with money or assets that could be easily realised. It is only during times of economic recession that thought is given to better use of working capital. (Thinking about this after an asset-stripper has made a take-over bid is generally too late for effective action.) Reducing working capital through better efficiency improves the liquidity of the company and the return on investment while reducing the interest that has to be paid. Earnings are increased as a result of funds being placed to better use. On none of these aspects can financial executives be the sole arbiters. Colleagues from appropriate departments have to be consulted. For example, if spare cash is to be put behind an existing product-market venture by stepping up output with new equipment, marketing must first agree that this additional production can be sold without depressing prices or starting fierce competitive reactions. The manufacturing division will also have to confirm that they will be able to produce the extra items to the standards of quality and reliability required and at the times when extra output can be sold (i.e. times of peak demand not during slack periods). While fixed capital expenditure has to be considered at some time prior to its investment, with sound financial management executives should be encouraged to give daily thought to the effective use of working capital. Neither should they be satisfied that present usage cannot be bettered. It is possible that, by more careful consideration of the policies being implemented, executives could uncover some quite substantial additional flows which could be put to use on other activities. (*See also* Section 7.3.3.)

7.1.6 Dividend policy

Associated with these matters are decisions on dividend policy. Besides keeping investors happy, there is need to balance the payment of high dividends with the fact that lower ones will leave more after-tax profit available for reinvestment as new capital. While all the needs for new capital cannot be self-generated (found from internal sources), shortfalls in the raising of new capital from other sources can be made up in this way. Also, the more self-generated cash is used, the lower is the overall effective cost of this new capital. Or a deliberate policy to plough back a large proportion of the earned profits could reduce the immediate borrowing requirements, or overdraft, important during times of high interest rates. In Britain in the mid-1970s dividend controls were introduced as part of a national incomes policy which effectively removed the ability of executives to consider what dividend policy was necessary in view of corporate and economic facts. They removed executives' responsibilities in this matter. Companies had to follow dividend policies dictated to them. In 1979 these controls lapsed and executives could again follow dynamic dividend policies, according to the needs and aims of the company.

Whatever the decision, the reasons must be communicated to the shareholders in clear, unambiguous terms. It may also be advisable to give marketing time to consider the consequences of such decisions if it is thought that there might be some backlash on the demand for the company's products or services. Substantial shareholders (institutional) could also be substantial customers. If the dividend policy outrages them they may decide to break completely with the company and take their business elsewhere. This could be very damaging, with serious consequences for marketing if not the entire company. Further, some advantages may accrue from time to time if subsidiaries paid an attractive dividend even if this means that the parent company, or main partner, had to forego some of its share in the subsidiary's operating profit. It must also be remembered that a depressed dividend policy will lead to depressed share (stock) market prices. This could hold the company open to a relatively cheap take-over bid by an opportunist organisation.

7.1.7 Risks in investment decisions

The subjects of risk and risk management were discussed in general terms in Section 3.6. Here the points relevant to investment appraisal will be studied.

There is risk involved in every business venture. A risk-free business activity does not exist these days. However, risk can come in various disguises. First, there are the risks inherent in investment plans due to the various uncertainties there may be about them. Either it may not be possible to obtain or evaluate certain critical information, or assumptions made may be little better than hunches. Then it is seldom possible to be totally accurate with estimates on future costs and income. For one thing, the rate of inflation varies considerably between countries and can change drastically and dramatically almost overnight.

Further, the life of the project may be defined as a certain number of years, but it is never certain that this projected life will result. Sudden changes in technology, economic conditions, competition and international trading and political factors may extend the life of the project or, more likely, curtail it. Then projects may be judged on a single rate of return; but considering the imponderables always present, various rates of return may be possible. These are all contributory factors to increasing the risks inherent in all projects. It has already been stated that the degree of risk that would be acceptable must be decided by the board in discussions with senior line managers. However, while attention should be given to the risks and uncertainties involved in major capital expenditure decisions, equal attention is needed for all the risks inherent in the other activities or operations of a company. Risk evaluation spans a much wider field than is often realised.

7.2 Profit and cost centres

The concept of profit and cost centres is a simple one to expound, but it is not easy to implement. The main problems centre around the identification and selection of what should be a cost centre. Where the work of a factory is fairly straightforward, with the different processes in the chain of manufacturing occurring in clearly defined locations under the management of a specific department, each process and its location and department can become a cost centre. The centre is then responsible for achieving the cost targets set for it by the cost control system, after due consultation with the executives who will be in charge of the centre. Where a product has to pass through many processes which may be controlled by various departments, the definition of cost centres and the allocation of cost items and responsibilities, sets problems for management. The problems are greatest when overheads have to be considered.

For example, a company may be producing many products, most of which are standardised and are produced on some flowline, or in large batches, or by some other method. Most costs can be correctly assigned to the right departments and standard costing procedures could be followed. However, there may be other products produced to special order or on a one-off basis. Or the normal business of the company may require some small orders to be progressed from time to time. Cost allocations are then not so easy to achieve with precision.

The best solution is to have a sound physical organisation of the factory or plant so that important cost items can be isolated or specifically located. Then the executives in charge of that location can be given cost objectives to achieve for their areas of responsibility. For example, in Morganite Carbon a subsidiary of the British Morgan Crucible Group, small batch and one-off jobs were manufactured in a special production area where a simplified costing procedure was used. That department was designated a cost centre.

Responsibility for costs can only be assigned if complete control over costs and expenses can be clearly given to a specific executive, or group of executives. Yet the need to control costs is of such paramount importance that ways should be found to overcome the obstacles that may be presented. This can only happen if full and regular consultations take place between all executives and the board. A philosophy of accountability must be generated to ensure that executives will take positive action to achieve cost targets, reduce wastage, improve the efficiency of work and reduce the defective work which may otherwise result. The generation of a cost conscious atmosphere throughout a corporation is one of the aims of integrated management. This will only happen if it is generated and projected by the board and the control systems of the company reflect this emphasis. For example, all variances from target, including positive ones (i.e. where the company has performed better than target) should be reported and investigated as a matter of course.

The setting-up of cost groups, or clinics, to study cost items and results that beg investigation, is one way of putting the right emphasis on cost control. These groups can be formed from time to time as needed, but should not be confined solely to the executives responsible for the affected cost centre. Colleagues from other departments, as appropriate, and some who have no obvious connection with the area under study should be included. The meetings may take the form of brain-storming meetings as used by marketing for new product development and other creative work. Where manufacturing costs are to be studied, value engineering techniques are useful. The more general ideas of value analysis can be deployed against other cost-reduction targets. The composition of the cost groups should reflect the management quadrille, and their terms of reference should reflect the philosophy of zero-base budgeting. No traditional cost is carried forward uncritically.

The creation of profit centres does not pose such complex problems as does the setting up of a cost centre but the same rule must apply; the executives in charge must have complete control over its operations. (The problems associated with profit centres have been discussed in Section 5.4.5.) Profit and return targets are set for each centre through consultation between the executives in charge and the board. The targets must not be set too high or too low, or they will be self-defeating. If set too high, the executives will ignore them as they would be plainly unattainable. If set too low, the executives might not try hard enough. As with everything else throughout the company, the consultations take place throughout the year and not just during the annual planning period.

Further, the control system should also be designed to permit the effective operation of profit centres. Again, positive and negative variances should be investigated. If cost clinics are used as needed to investigate deviations from cost targets, it makes sense also to have profit clinics to do the same on profit matters, especially when results are deviating badly from plans. Again, the team should be widely drawn and not restricted to executives of the centres. The clinics could also be used as sounding boards for any contemplated changes in marketing operations that might affect profits, e.g. pricing policies, product-market strategy, credit and credit control matters. Finally, and obviously, if no benefits accrue from having profit and cost centres — most unlikely — then they should not be used.

7.2.1 The overhead trap

Overheads are whatever companies wish to make them. Controlling overheads is a subject that is mentioned vaguely in most companies, is talked about by most executives at some time or other but seldom is anything determined done about it. From time to time, chief executives thump their desks and demand that something be done because overheads are too high. Financial executives grumble about the difficulty in distinguishing and distributing overhead costs to the departments responsible for their occurrence. Other executives fight hard to prevent any overhead that is not directly attributable to them, from being charged against their departments.

This is the *overhead trap* involving much wailing but little effective action. This is due to lack of commitment to the work and cooperation between executives on this problem. This lack of interest may stem from the fear that any attempt to reduce overheads will mean that the size of a department (i.e. the number of people in it) will be reduced or its sphere of responsibility and authority diminished in any subsequent re-organisation. These managers do not appreciate that successful management is not judged by some headcount or other, nor by the size of the department, nor the spread of its authority but by its effectiveness plus its ability to achieve minimum costs and so optimise the company's profitability.

Overheads are simply expenditures which cannot be attributed directly to the cost of a product or service provided by the company. Most overheads exist simply because the company exists.

Overheads and indirect costs are usually the subjects of books on accountancy and finance rather than management. Yet the control of these expenditures is a management responsibility, not an accountancy one. However, the control of overheads is most effectively achieved through the design of a suitable budgetary control system. Of course, the system and methods must be defined by agreement between the controllers and the controlled since imposed budgets are useless as control mechanisms. Departmental executives must decide what has to be done and estimate the costs that would arise. Then they can agree with the financial department and the board, what the total expenditures should be and how they will be spread, i.e. their incidence, over each trading year. If these expenditures cannot be met by the company, then the entire strategy and all operations of the company will need to be reviewed.

The preliminary work requires all executives to seek the answers to a number of critical questions.

1. What capacities will be required to produce, market and administer the business at estimated volumes and timings?
2. What would be the cost of providing these capacities, in total and per unit, or per sales period?

3.   Which of these expenditures are fixed, and which would vary with volume?

4.   How should indirect expenses be adjusted if actual volumes vary from planned volumes?

5.   How should the operations and costs of non-productive departments (e.g. production control, quality control, marketing research, sales administration and personnel) and specialist departments with a high cost element (e.g. research and development, inspection, purchasing) be reviewed and controlled? How should their costs be allocated between all departments?

6.   Who are responsible for these expenditures? Are they aware of what is being spent currently? How may these expenses be controlled without impairing efficiency?

7.   What standards and budgets have been set? On what bases have they been formulated, and are they sound ones?

8.   Are all indirect expenditures incurred positively and deliberately in determined pursuit of corporate objectives? How many are due to simple carelessness or lack of proper control?

9.   How should overhead expenses be adjusted to meet changes in the company's business or needs? How can these be assessed?

It is important that managers have the right attitude to overhead costs and their control. Holding the view that they, are just an inevitable, expensive necessity, an unavoidable part of being in business, will itself lead to poor and ineffective control. Firm control and enhanced profitability are gained only when executives see overheads and their effective control as a vital part of their jobs and the whole profit-producing mechanism of business. Central overheads, e.g. the cost of head office and expensive specialist services such as operations research etc., pose the greatest problems when decisions on their allocation to operating units are required. To avoid arbitrary allocations, which may seem unfair to line executives, many of these items might be absorbed by head office during the process of the consolidation of the company's cost- and profit-centre accounting procedures.

However, whatever allocations are made, they should be on as equitable a basis as possible, and be seen to be so. Profit centres, for example, should not be seen as convenient venues for allocations of all central overheads. A fair system may be to estimate what the equivalent costs would be for the provision of such services from outside sources (e.g. consultants) and to charge proportional amounts according to the usage made by each unit of these services. Of course, individual departments should be discouraged from not using these services in order to 'save' having to contribute to them! If the units need such services, then they should use them and be charged the right equivalents for their proportionate use of them. If it is found that head office is making a 'profit' on this, i.e. allocations total more than the actual costs incurred, then suitable adjustments should be made to the proportional allocations.

A way in which overheads may be better controlled is to adopt the *return on investment* concept for them. This is particularly effective when decisions about increases in overheads, due to the appointment of extra staff or additional or new equipment have to be made. The return on investment, as usually used for major investment projects, forecasts the estimated or probable results by consideration of the factors that would have effect on the project. In this way the net earnings required can be estimated. Even when new plant is envisaged, executives have to satisfy themselves that extra speed of operation, or more modern methods of production, automation, improved quality and so on, will lead to lower running or labour costs or increased output, thus improving profitability.

The same approach can be brought to overhead considerations. For example, engaging additional staff is an investment and at today's cost, a substantial one. Thus, it is reasonable to estimate what benefits in equivalent money terms will flow as a result of having extra staff. Will office bottlenecks be overcome, permitting a more efficient throughput of the essential paperwork? Would it permit the administrative arms of the business to handle a greater volume of paper, and thus help increase production and sales by manufacturing and marketing colleagues? Will administrative delays be overcome, thus allowing the placing of orders on plant to be speeded up, resulting in increasing output or efficiency? Will the installation of a computer (or other equipment) save on labour costs and lead to more efficient working throughout the system? What will all these benefits mean in terms of saving in time presently being lost, saving on equivalent lost production, reduction of delays, increased throughput and volume of sales? What would be their effect on improved customer goodwill and what additional business is this likely to bring? These benefits represent the return that accrues to the company as a result of the investment in increased overheads. If there are no benefits, should the investment be approved because of the qualitative improvements they would bring? In most instances even these qualitative benefits can be costed and so their value in monetary terms can be gauged.

There are many reasons why companies have been reluctant to bring the return on investment concept to overhead costs investigations and decisions. First, they may believe that the department under consideration has no 'output' in statistical or monetary terms. In fact all departmental work can be sufficiently quantified in terms of its tasks and workloads for its efficiency to be gauged. This can be done for situations with and without the proposed additional investment. Second, very persuasive arguments have been mounted claiming that without the proposed investment disaster will strike, whatever the quantitative analysis might show. This is not true. In fact disaster is more certain if there is over-investment in any department. Third, the real impact of the new investment may be partly hidden by other factors and insufficient time and effort are given to making valid estimates of the benefits that would accrue. Finally, there may simply be a lack of understanding of the concept and application of return on investment approaches especially to 'non-productive' overheads. Yet the use of this concept focuses attention on the ultimate purpose of business: profitability. It reduces all studies of overhead budgets and projects to a common language which allows more effective comparisons to be made of different projects. Also, assumptions are explored and examined more fully and their implications for associated activities can be better understood. Thus more effective integrated management is possible. Once again, here is another area where close cooperation between all activities, at least at departmental head level, will repay dividends. Vertical and lateral liaison has also to be maintained if substantial benefits are to flow. Integrated management approaches are needed right down to the oft-neglected area of overheads cost control.

7.3 Capital investment

Section 1.5.11 discussed the more common mistakes that are made with decisions on capital investment that lead to corporate collapse. More detailed consideration is given to the subject here.

Capital investment decisions are amongst the most difficult to make in any business. Yet the capital employed in industry has grown to such unprecedented levels, that with its rising cost, aggravated by high inflation rates, it is imperative for the planning of capital investment to be based on very thorough studies. Further, once made, investments are difficult to alter. They can often be irreversible. For these reasons, capital investment propositions require detailed attention, the best management skills and complete cooperation between all relevant or affected departments, both in the planning and implementation stages. Yet this is not the case in many instances. Many companies are still not systematic or careful in their selection of investment projects. They rely too heavily on hunch or are too frequently swayed by the powerful arguments expounded by the strongest personality on the board or in the planning team. Yet these people may only be pushing the project for purely selfish reasons (to enhance their status or image, safeguard their position etc.). They may not have considered the short- and long-term implications for the company of what they propose. Also, decisions may be taken on projections of only one or two years ahead from the decision point. Yet if the studies were extended it may become obvious that in later years, problems and difficulties if not disaster, must occur. Realisation that this over-emphasis on 'present profits' may also restrict or prevent longer-term growth and development is often lacking.

How investment in private industry can be stimulated or restrained is still insufficiently understood. The uncertain approach to capital spending by private industry as a whole, excluding the few large corporations who try to be systematic about it, especially in countries with a 'mixed economy', leads to the government 'hunting' between various systems of investment incentives and restrictions. The latter only aggravate the atmosphere of uncertainty and doubt that pervades the whole question of capital investment. In many cases they produce results that are the exact opposite of what is needed by the company, industry and nation as a whole.

Yet the basic rules are simple, as far as executives are concerned. The appraisal of investment possibilities must be objective. They cannot be so, however, if any division or department affected or influenced by the decisions is excluded from the deliberations. The projections should also be on a moving three-, or preferably five-, year schedule if a true picture of the possibilities of the proposals is to be obtained. A specific figure should also be given as a target rate of return for all projects. This target, with estimated profitability and forecasts of the probabilities of this being achieved, should form the basis of comparison between competing investment possibilities.

Thus there is need for the provision of comprehensive data on every project. For example, marketing must provide forecasts of the business opportunities which the project will provide, with estimates on sales volume and profit, and with manufacturing estimating the costs that are likely. Manufacturing must estimate its ability to produce the new products in the quantities, quality and at the times when they would be required. They may also have to estimate the unit cost of production for batches of different quantities. Financial executives would, of course, provide estimates of the fixed and working capital that would be needed, the cost of that capital and the expected returns that could be achieved at different activity levels. Personnel would report on the availability of the labour required, the probability of its attainment and the costs. Thus, again, without an integrated management approach, capital investment decisions cannot be based on sound, comprehensive considerations and cannot be sure of standing much chance of achieving their targets.

In recent years in Britain and other countries, government involvement in business has increased. On the positive side, development grants, tax holidays, repatriation privileges and other incentives to capital investment have been welcomed (though not by all business executives or politicians). On the negative side are all the controls and restrictions which have also been placed by governments on business activity and planning. However, perhaps the most important development has been the growing realisation by governments that their taxation policies can have considerable effect (for good or ill) on business decisions and plans. (*See also* Section 7.4.3.)

7.3.1 Deploying resources

How resources are deployed between projects and between fixed and working capital depends on ruling economic and technical factors. The liquidity position, especially for new companies, is another critical consideration. Until a firm is well established, the funds employed are subject to greater risk than for an old-established company. However, with high rates of inflation it can be said that this type of risk has increased greatly for all enterprises. Unforeseen events may necessitate the re-appraisal of expectations and may call for major adjustments to the project if the solvency of the venture is to be safeguarded.

Again, studies in this connection must involve executives from all affected departments.

The estimated gain from investment in both types of assets must also be considered by all departments. If the business is thought to have a long life, liquidity may be discounted to a reasonable degree in order to increase investment in durable assets. This may provide a hedge against losses arising from discontinuity in the supply of services that would have to be purchased if the company did not have the investments to provide them for itself. Or, by being independent of suppliers, the company may avoid the worst aspects of the rising costs of these services.

However, decisions on the deployment of assets have to be made in the light of current demand conditions for the company's products, modified by expectations on the course of that demand, i.e. future demand conditions (including costs). The difficulties associated with forecasting future demand force executives to be as accurate as they can on their analysis of present demand conditions. It may include having to classify products as luxury or essential items. The implication is that demand for the former could decline rapidly if economic conditions worsen while that for the latter will hold up better, even if there is some drop in total demand. Even with some essential capital equipment, demand could tail off if users decide to keep their existing plant in operation for a few years more, i.e. delay replacement for a number of years beyond previously normal periods. With capital equipment usually used for seven or more years, postponement of replacement orders for two or more years, if it leads to users keeping their plants for ten years rather than the previous seven, could change the demand and demand pattern quite considerably. Then the company's income level and present and future wealth (especially liquid resources) should also be taken into consideration. For those in consumer goods, the income and wealth of consumers is another important factor to consider. If industrial and consumer wealth decline considerably the effect on spending patterns and total demand would be spectacular.

Present and possible future supply positions must also be taken into account. The size of the industry and its possible future growth or contraction have to be considered also, as they will affect the prospects of any project. In some industries (cement, iron and steel manufacturing, petroleum refining etc.) heavy initial capital expenditure is needed and the return may be long in coming. If the supply position is likely to become more competitive the prospects of the new ventures may be placed in doubt. In Western Europe in 1978, several expansion programmes in these and similar industries were cancelled or postponed indefinitely. If existing suppliers are leaving the industry should this be taken as a sign that things are getting so bad that a new venture would have little chance, or would it mean that a cleverly devised one, designed to exploit changing circumstances, would have a better chance of success? Then the existing costs of current products or services have relevance. If the new venture proves more expensive, the chances of success are reduced. If costs to customers can be reduced, the chances are enhanced.

Changes in the age composition of consumers and industries and racial composition of consumers can affect the demand/supply situation. Ageing industries can offer opportunities for new entrants with new processes, materials, methods and ideas. An ageing population will change the nature and pattern of demand as will any major alteration to the racial composition of a market. New entrants into established industries that are thought to be ageing or undergoing considerable change and those launching ventures into new industries, may consider it advisable to minimise investment in durables (land, plant, buildings and capital equipment). This will allow them to maintain a flexible stance and so be able to meet changes that occur in the industry and its markets. This will minimise the risk involved at times of rapid growth or substantial change.

Price levels also influence decisions on investment. When prices are rising the tendency is to increase investment in durable goods and plant with stockpiling of consumables as a hedge against rising costs. When prices are falling, new investment on plant and inventories will be reduced to avoid the risk of holding expensive items which may be purchased later at more reasonable cost. Further, cost of labour and other services will influence investment decisions and the deployment of resources. Cost of labour will vary from time to time and so will the availability of the type of worker and services required by the company. This may be due to more companies using such labour and the suppliers of the services not having adjusted quickly enough to any change in demand. The mobility of labour will also be another consideration. Whether it is low (i.e. workers refuse to move from their home regions) or high (i.e. because workers are prepared to move to find better employment) will indicate the chances of success for any project and will aid in decisions on resource deployment. Industrial unrest may also aggravate the labour supply position. None of these is easy to predict and this adds to the uncertainties and risk involved in investment decisions and those to do with resource deployment. Figure 7.4 summarises the main areas that have to be appraised before these decisions can be agreed and the departmental involvement in the work.

7.3.2 Managing working capital

The subject of the use of working capital was discussed in Section 7.1.5. Working capital will be studied further here from the point of view of its management in the context of capital investment considerations.

Working capital may be described as that proportion of a company's total capital that is used in financing short-term operations. Its management must take into consideration two distinct but inter-related sets of activities, the short- and long-term financial operations. The former involves managing the current asset balances of the gross working capital. The latter is concerned with providing the volume of net working capital required for the company's future and current operations. It must be remembered that the timing and pattern of the expenditures and receipts will determine the company's liquidity and solvency.

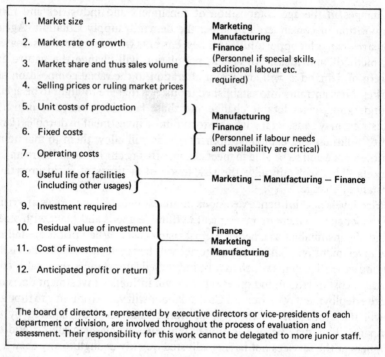

1. Market size
2. Market rate of growth
3. Market share and thus sales volume
4. Selling prices or ruling market prices

} Marketing
Manufacturing
Finance
(Personnel if special skills,
additional labour etc.
required)

5. Unit costs of production
6. Fixed costs
7. Operating costs

} Manufacturing
Finance
(Personnel if labour needs
and availability are critical)

8. Useful life of facilities
(including other usages) } — Marketing – Manufacturing – Finance

9. Investment required
10. Residual value of investment
11. Cost of investment
12. Anticipated profit or return

} Finance
Marketing
Manufacturing

The board of directors, represented by executive directors or vice-presidents of each department or division, are involved throughout the process of evaluation and assessment. Their responsibility for this work cannot be delegated to more junior staff.

Fig 7.4

The purchase of materials and components generates creditors or accounts receivable. Management of this is straightforward and should involve simply, control over the average age of the outstanding trade credit. The decision on when the accounts will be paid will be partly determined by the discounts received for prompt or early payment. However, payment should never be later than the due date for maintaining the credit standard of the company. Getting a reputation for being a slow payer could jeopardise future attempts to raise new capital or loans. However, settling accounts well in advance of the dates when maximum discounts are applicable will just put an additional strain on company finances by increasing cash outflows too far in advance of the anticipated inflows from the sales that are generated. How a company settles its debts can have either beneficial or adverse effects on deliveries of future supplies.

Finished products which have been sold generate trade accounts receivable (debtors). If goods are sold on credit terms the credit policy of the company must also be carefully considered. If the credit policy is too generous, cash shortages can be severe. If tax demands fall during a period of shortage of cash, the solvency of the company may be called into question. When a company needs cash urgently the risk of insolvency is at its peak and lenders are hard to find. Solvency can always be maintained by holding large amounts of cash, but this raises the level of working capital to higher limits than normal and holds the company open as an attractive target for asset-strippers. If the credit policy is too strict, it may inhibit sales, especially to small accounts that may become big customers. Then, in the long term, too strict credit policies can threaten future cash flows and raise solvency problems at some future date.

Thus the efficient management of the flow of funds or cash is an essential element of the management of working capital. The management of accounts receivable, in particular, requires careful attention to be given to the net cash values involved and the average collection periods permitted. It is a sad fact that the longer an invoice remains unpaid the less likely it is that payment will be made. If control of debtors is lax, customers will see this as a weakness not a kindness and will extend credit to very long periods. Thus bad debts will increase alarmingly. However, a decision to withdraw credit facilities and insist on cash payments on delivery has implications for the marketing and, ultimately, manufacturing divisions and they must therefore be consulted before the decision is taken. Factoring accounts receivable to a commercial factor may be another and better solution to the debtor problem. It has no immediate or direct effect on marketing opportunities and, for a small discount, the company gets its urgently-needed cash.

Managing inventories (finished goods, work-in-progress, bought in goods) is another critical area. If too much is held, then the cash absorbed here will rise and there will also be depot and storage problems which will probably also put up operating costs. If too low levels are held, there may be frequent out-of-stock positions which will affect sales and thus cash inflows. Ultimately, if goodwill is lost, sales might drop and both the marketing and manufacturing divisions will be affected. So this area of the management of working capital also needs close cooperation between finance, physical distribution, marketing and manufacturing executives. Thus the management of working capital is not the sole province of the financial department. Agreement on the policies, periods and amounts of capital that will be made available must be established by agreement with other departments. Sometimes the discussions can span a lengthy period, but unless agreement is achieved there is no point in pressing on further. Imposed budgets just cause more trouble and dislocation of the entire business.

7.3.3 Acquisitions and mergers

Section 4.4.2 considered these from the viewpoint of concepts relevant to corporate planning. Here acquisitions and mergers will be studied further as they relate to capital investment decisions.

Companies will be interested in selling all or part of their operations if there is a sudden crisis for which there is no other solution; or when their management has failed to earn adequate profits; or to provide for management succession; or for growth opportunities, if the company being sold will not be submerged by the acquiring organisation. Companies will buy others if a sudden bargain is presented to them or if the acquired company has surplus cash which the buyer needs. They may also respond if the purchase is seen as offering a chance to improve, or arrest, a falling return on investment position, or because the acquisition would provide growth opportunities. Whatever the reason, executives must ensure that the capital investment involved will prove advantageous to the acquiring company measured in terms of increased return and growth and, if possible, greater stability of the total operation.

Acquisitions and mergers are areas where managers find it difficult to be objective. Ambitions, livelihoods and reputations are involved and it is natural for good executives to seek growth for their companies. While acquisitions and mergers can provide rapid growth there is the danger that this can become so alluring that insufficient thought is given to the long-term financial and other considerations. The basic problems of the acquiring company may not be solved by an acquisition. They may be made far worse.

The question of whether to acquire or merge with another company requires executives from all departments to consider the following points about it.

1.   The investment resources available should be adequate for the proposed acquisition, as must the method and cost of raising any additional funds that may be needed.

2.   The return on investment expected of the acquisition should meet targets or requirements.

3.   The strengths and weaknesses of both parties should be known and preferably be compatible.

4.   There should be a statement on the operational aims of the acquisition, both for the short- and long-term and whether the acquisition fits into the long-range corporate plans of the buyer. This statement should be quantified, especially in money terms, wherever possible.

5.   The product-market range of the company to be acquired and the potential buyer should be considered and estimates made of how these will combine into the resultant joint operations. Are they complementary, and what will be the effect of the acquisition on the buyer's long-term product-market strategy and plans?

6.   Then the possible effect on the overall competitive situation should be studied, as should any improvement in customer satisfaction (or dissatisfaction with the takeover). Does it comply with any anti-trust or anti-monopoly laws and regulations?

7.4 Budgetary control

The nature of control in business is frequently misunderstood. It is often associated with restraints or restrictions rather than having a more positive meaning. Yet control systems are meant to guide the activities of a business so that correct executive judgement, decisions and actions will result and agreed objectives be attained. It should also indicate when remedial action is required when operations are veering badly off course, away from plans, policies and targets. The benefits which should flow from correctly perceived and implemented budgetary control are listed below.

1. It helps to define the objectives of the corporation in financial terms.

2. It provides the standards by which to measure the efficiency of the operations of various parts of the organisation and the company as a whole.

3. It measures the extent by which results have varied from declared objectives and provides guides to the remedial action required.

4. It provides centralised, coordinated control with correct delegation of responsibility.

However, a formalised procedure can induce complacency on the part of executives when the paperwork becomes routine and little notice or action is taken on the reports received (cf. the Rolls-Royce case history). If the system is too massive, beyond the needs of the organisation, the additional personnel required together with the paperwork and costs may negate any benefits that flow from having a budgetary control system. In addition, the reaction times of large systems may be long and so responses might be too late in coming for the situations reported. In addition, all systems will eventually outlive their effectiveness because of changes in the business or business environment. Then the budgetary control system must be brought into line with the organisation's new requirements.

In situations of economic recession, falling demand, rapidly rising costs and high inflation it is imperative that budgetary systems recognise the need to anticipate future sales, costs and cash flows in a dynamic and hostile business environment as well as aggressive political, legal and international conditions. In these circumstances, comparing actual results with budgets and targets made six or more months previously is of little value. The deviations from budget may be due to so many new factors that executives are not in a position to identify, quickly, the correct remedial actions that are necessary. In such circumstances a shorter-term rolling budget, rather than an annual one, may be advisable. In conditions of such uncertainty, forecasts and predictions are best updated on a monthly basis.

Thus the budget figures can be compared with these future forecasts. Where executives feel that there is no value in trying to get the operations back on course with the original budget, a revised future forecast taking into account all the latest changes, should be made. In adverse conditions, comparisons between the latest forecasts and the previous one will indicate why it has been necessary to change the forecasts. They will also allow estimates to be made on the effects this will have on the cash flow situation. The remedial action necessary should then be clearer, or easier to perceive. If in subsequent months the executives compare actual performance with past forecasts, they will be able to find out why the performance could not be maintained as originally intended. This leads to more positive budgetary control and positive responses and actions.

This approach will also prevent the establishment of any aura of sanctity over budgets. Once accepted the budget too often becomes enshrined as some rigid target that must be achieved at all costs. This attitude misses the point of planning. It is not an exercise in seeing how clever executives are in forecasting, but rather one that allows them to make better decisions than would be possible without effective planning and control systems. The short-term rolling budget approach, imposed on initial annual and five-year planning processes, makes it difficult for such an aura to survive.

In the budgeting exercise the economic, financial and political factors at play in the organisation, or on it, will influence decisions. It is unrealistic to ignore the fact that even in the best-managed organisations, powerful political pressures will be at work endeavouring to influence decisions on budgets. These may be countered by ensuring that all departments are equally represented at the budget discussions and that realism and impartiality should be applied with some rigour. To this end the role of the chief executive is an important one. That executive must act as adjudicator between competing departments and must prevent his or her own prejudices and preferences from biasing the attitudes, advice and final decisions adopted.

7.4.1 Credit control

The subject of credit control has been discussed in earlier sections in different contexts. Here a few comments will be made about the financial department's responsibilities in this area of work.

Credit management is a vital part of financial management. It is not something that can be left to some relatively inexperienced executive who has the time for it and may report to the chief accountant. A suitably senior experienced financial executive, capable of amicable negotiations with colleagues from other departments, with an appreciation of the duties, aims and problems of marketing, manufacturing and personnel matters, should be appointed to this task and should report to the financial director (vice-president). The work involves close liaison with the major divisions of the company and also with the chief executive. It cannot be done by an 'office boy' or equivalent junior.

Besides establishing the credit limits, the risks involved with each customer or group of customers must also be established. In setting credit limits, the importance of each customer should be known; for this will influence the level at which the credit will be set for each. Attention has to be given also to small customers. Can the company help them to grow and develop into major customers at some future date? If this is possible, credit limits might be set more liberally. However, care should be taken to ensure that the debt portfolio for any single customer does not become unreasonable nor that much of the debt is concentrated in too few customers or one sector of industry. This would put up the inherent risk to too high a level. Finally, credit limits should be reviewed regularly and kept abreast of changes in the business environment, the growth of individual customers' businesses and their reputation for being prompt payers.

7.4.2 Information flows

Budgetary control systems cannot operate efficiently or effectively unless there is an adequate flow of financial and other relevant information from all departments. This flow should be so designed that it allows executives to take a view and decisions on the corporate activity as a whole and not just on isolated sections of it. It must also provide a means of communicating the objectives to be attained, provide all the details required for planning and control purposes and keep all key executives fully informed of what is happening in other parts of the organisation and its operations. Otherwise the degree of cooperation needed will not be maintained. Thus the information system must pass vital data to and from all the operational groups of the company, ensuring effective communications vertically and laterally throughout the organisation. It should pick out the significant variables in operational reports so that the necessary corrective methods can be introduced quickly. The information system itself should be able to identify what this action should be.

However, all companies have integrated and overlapping sub-systems of information which individual departments, or sub-groups, require if they are to work satisfactorily. Some examples include marketing-production control, sales-physical distribution, pricing-costing, production planning-personnel, research and development-quality control, and so on. Thus it is necessary for a total systems concept to be adopted for the information flows in an organisation so that all these sub-groups can be properly integrated into a corporate system. This also recognises that a business entity is made up of a number of inter-dependent sub-systems, all needing their own special information flows, i.e. the 'quadrille' concept again.

The form and nature of the system used will depend on the size of the organisation, the permitted costs and the degree of accuracy, reliability, timeliness and security that must be achieved. However, it must segregate non-controllable factors from ones that can be controlled by the company so that assessments of the latter will not be confused or misled by the inadvertent inclusion of any of the former. In addition, attention should be given to the volume of information that will have to be handled and the pattern of flow that would be experienced, i.e. to the capacity of the system. Again, executives will find themselves facing a familiar quandary: should the system be designed to handle peak flows at the speed specified for the system, or should it be planned for a lesser, or more normal, flow? In the first instance, the system will be under-utilised at non-peak times. In the latter, the system will be strained and information flows will slow, with some departments not getting the data they need when they need it. The executives will have to ponder the pros and cons of both possibilities and select one which appears to safeguard the company's interests and information needs at acceptable levels of cost and speed of operation. Finally, the system used should be such that executives accept the presented information as worthy of their consideration and not just more, unnecessary paper that is consigned to the waste paper basket without serious study.

7.4.3 Taxation

With the economic conditions that prevailed in the mid-1970s, many companies' financial decisions have been influenced mainly by considerations of their tax liabilities. Also, making investment decisions without thinking about the project's anticipated after-tax results has become a dangerous pastime. However, the tax position and laws of a country can change frequently. Britain, for example, has had many supplementary or 'mini-budgets' in a fiscal year in recent times; the frequency depending on how the authorities read the economic situation. So, making due allowance for the tax position of a project is yet another exercise in guessed 'forecasts'. This is another reason why the short-term rolling forecasting plan, mentioned in Section 7.4, is preferable. It will allow for adjustments to be made in the tax forecast element of a plan, as changing circumstances make this necessary. In modern times it is difficult for any executive to fortell with accuracy, what next year's tax position will be. As politicians are always stating, one week in politics is a long time.

However, it is important for executives to time the payment of taxes carefully, as far as the system will allow, with the receipts of any grants or allowances due. Where the tax due is large and the receipts (allowances etc.) are vital to the financing of a project, mistiming these two activities can threaten the company's liquidity and solvency. Ideally, large slabs of taxation should not be paid before due allowances have been received; assuming that the delay in payment of taxes is permitted within the current laws and regulations. Otherwise there will be a heavy drain on cash without the corresponding inflow of grants and allowances to ease the liquidity position. Further, if grants are delayed for a year although the related expenditures have been made, perhaps due to the new plant being late in coming into operation, their value to the company is reduced by whatever percentage is used for discounting purposes. For capital-intensive projects the timing of these transactions can have a marked effect on the return on investment. Thus, effective tax management is important, but in the latter case, so too is efficient new project management.

How can effective tax management be achieved? First, there must be sound tax planning. This involves arranging the affairs of the company to minimise, legally, the incidence and impact of taxation. Steps must be taken to ensure that the amounts payable are not unnecessarily increased through poor timing of all operations and any failure to bring projects on stream at the right time. Second, there must be a correct computation of the tax liabilities and their timing or incidence. Then, while still complying with the laws and regulations in force, tax payments can be spread over the period of a company's operating year and so minimise the strain on its liquidity.

The subject of taxation is an important responsibility of the board and the person responsible for the planning and execution of the company's taxation policies must have regular, direct access to the board, preferably the chief executive. Normally the responsible person is the financial director (vice-president) so there is no difficulty in the establishment of this communication link. However, where a lesser executive has been delegated this responsibility then direct access to the board (not only to the financial director) is essential.

Only in this way can tax advice and plans be kept clear of internal company politics and the risk that advice may be distorted in transmission be avoided. The advice should also be given in conclusive, unequivocal terms, without recitation of the legal arguments for both sides of the argument on every tax question. Otherwise, the executives and the board will be confused by the legal jargon.

It will be of interest to note here some findings of a study made by Professor Gerald Lawson of Manchester Business School, England, of United Kingdom public companies especially during 1954–75, (published by the *Sunday Times* of July 30th, 1978). Although this study was more in connection with discussions on what system of inflation accounting (current cost accounting) should replace historic cost accounting, its findings on taxation and dividends *v.* earnings are startling. First, and as everyone predicted, the profitability of United Kingdom companies after the Second World War had been seriously overstated, especially during the period 1954–75. This overstatement had dramatic effects on the corporate tax burden on them. Interest paid and dividends to shareholders exceeded earnings after tax. The study showed—

1.   the effective rate of tax on United Kingdom companies averaged 71 per cent over 1954–75 and actually exceeded 100 per cent in three years;

2.   the effective rate of tax on United Kingdom equity earnings averaged 83 per cent and exceeded 100 per cent in six years;

3.   distributions to shareholders exceeded equity earnings in each of sixteen years, causing deficits financed by the banking system with overdrafts and short-term loans.

[Since 1975 in the United Kingdom, capital, stock and other allowances have meant that many companies in effect pay no corporation tax (advance corporation tax excluded). The report nevertheless is an object lesson on the debilitating effects of company taxation.]

Historic cost accounting systems generally cause profits to be overstated and Professor Lawson considered that corporation tax in Britain, is a totally debilitating burden and a severe deterrent to industrial investment. If nothing else these facts underline the essential need for a sound accounting system, associated policies and controls by all businesses, particularly for tax management, dividend and budgetary controls. (*See also* Section 1.2.7.)

7.5 Role of accounting in business

Accountancy is the language of all business enterprises and accounting provides many of the tools by which executives can make decisions. It is one of the means of collecting and providing useful information for managerial purposes but too frequently it is allowed to produce irrelevant, or so much, information, as to confuse its recipients and lead them to make wrong decisions. It also collects and provides information of a financial nature about an enterprise for all those who have an interest in the company (shareholders, creditors, debtors, customers, financiers, executives and other employees). Again, discretion is required as to the extent and format of the information provided. The aim should be to provide a correct and comprehensive picture of the financial aspects of a company while avoiding a form of presentation more likely to confuse rather than inform, the different recipients. Financial reports must also, obviously, comply with the laws and practice of the different countries in which an enterprise operates. Thus, while meeting the statutory requirements of the home country is the main concern of managers, the special requirements of nations in which subsidiaries or partners are operating must not be overlooked.

The financial statements resulting from the accounting process used to report only past events. They were financial reports on the company's achievements for some specified past years. Now, with the acceptance of planning as an essential preliminary role of management, financial statements also provide projections of what the immediate future (up to five years ahead) offers the company in possible opportunities. Attempts to project further forward usually lead to even financial reports appearing like little more than hopeful gazes into a dark crystal ball. These reports are also the only reliable sources of financial information that recipients within the company have on which to base their decisions and recipients outside the company have to judge if the decisions taken have been sound.

Accounting's role is, therefore, a dual one. First, it must provide information for decisions on the future. Second, it provides information whereby past decisions can be judged. A distinction between these two roles must be made if accounting activities are to be performed satisfactorily. In the first role, the significant criteria are those of relevance to the decision to be made and usefulness to that process. In reporting progress, the criteria are adherence to accounting principles and concepts (and the laws of the land) and provision of data which permit accurate assessments of past decisions. In the latter role, accounting is seen by many as being independent of the management process itself.

Unfortunately, the distinction between these two roles is frequently forgotten. The result is that no single recipient is served satisfactorily by the data provided. Thus, the standards to be followed should be based on the relevance, fairness and usefulness of the data provided to all interested parties. The reports themselves should be so drafted, if necessary in more than one form, as to serve the needs of the different types of recipients and be presented in a manner easily understood by them. Thus for effective management, a coherent system of financial reports is needed to keep all departments and recipients correctly informed about the company's progress and future intentions.

The compilation of these financial reports was formerly considered the sole responsibility of financial executives and accountants. Now they are more effectively produced in cooperation with executives from line departments or divisions who become involved in the detailed work for those parts of the reports relevant to their responsibilities. Full effectiveness is only obtained if these executives cooperate between themselves on all aspects of financial reporting and forecasting. It should be recalled also that the accounting process and its reports form very important elements in the total corporate communications system. The processes by which the information is derived and the means by which it is communicated should be so devised that recipients will respond to the reports they receive in the same dynamic fashion they adopt for facts they observe or experience directly.

7.5.1 The wider role of accountants and financial executives

Accounting is an abstractive activity and, as mentioned already, is seen by many as something apart from the management process itself. Further, some others hold the view that the accounting function has nothing to say about the technical properties of the products of a company, nor about the psychological and social consequences of a company's actions. In the light of modern experience, these are narrow or restrictive views of financial management's responsibilities and a denial of the social responsibilities of one section of management, if not all of it. While it is true that financial executives know little about the technological aspects of a company's business, they have the responsibility and right to question all expenditure proposals and events in that area, to ensure in a positive sense that the company's assets are being put to the best use.

Part of this depends also on the impact of the company's actions and products on the public as a whole. If public opinion moves against it, demand for the company's products will decline rapidly, the acceptable rate of return will not be achieved and the company will not be employing its assets for the maximum benefit of investors, employees, distributors, customers and even the nation as a whole. Financial executives have very real interests in such unfortunate developments. They are also concerned about activities or products which may prove harmful to customers or the ecology of the regions in which they operate and which pollute the atmosphere. Indeed, they should play a positive role in preventing these occurrences from happening, if only because when they become known to the public there could be widespread rejection of the company and its products. If other executives are allowed to follow policies and activities that assist in the destruction of the world, can the accountant stand back and take a detached view that this is not a direct, associated responsibility of financial management and thus nothing to do with financial executives? Would this ultimate destruction of the company's markets not have something to do with financial executives' responsibilities for ensuring the continuance, well-being and growth of the company's business? For similar reasons, financial executives cannot stand by and watch colleagues pollute the environment (by industrial processes or products) to extinction. They themselves are involved, as indeed are all business executives.

They discharge their roles as watchdogs over the activities of their companies and the financial consequences that flow from them. They must also be concerned and involved with what may look like unrelated events but which, in the end, will undermine the business survival and prosperity of the company. They discharge this responsibility by questioning whether proposed activities will be beneficial or harmful to society at large and the environment in which it must live. In serious cases they could block events by refusing them funds! Thus accountants and financial executives have much wider roles to play than just keeping their noses down to the financial aspects of the business. The roles of the financial executive and accountant have been simply illustrated in Figure 7.5. The non-financial points discussed above have been shown simply as 'sociological aspects' as an input into the management information system.

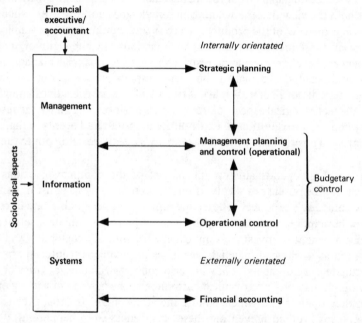

Fig 7.5

7.5.2 Inflation or current cost accounting

In Britain in the mid-1970s, discussions have raged long on the subject of traditional, historical cost accounting methods *v.* current cost (or inflation) accounting as the way in which company accounts should be rendered. During periods of inflation, especially if they span a long time and the rates are very high, historical cost accounting methods are less and less able to convey a true and fair view of a company's real current financial position. Graphic examples of this were given in 1978 by Professor Lawson's researches, reported in Section 7.4.3. The historic cost approach significantly overstates companies' 'true' earnings (therefore their taxable capacity) and profitability. This promotes claims or expectations for dividends, wages, taxes and interest, which exceed a company's true earning capacity. There is erosion of capital and even bankruptcy as a result, or less dramatically, the need to sell up. Thus the usefulness to its recipients of a report based on the historical cost method has been called into question more and more. Hence the pressure to move to current cost, or inflation, accounting methods.

At the time of writing (1979), firm decisions had not been taken on the form or detail of any revised method that might be used. The discussions continue and no doubt whatever is written here could be out of date by the time the book appears in print. The comments should be taken therefore, as only reporting the present state of play. The nature of the necessary change has been debated by the accountancy profession for many years and a number of solutions have been suggested. Each has had its adherents and detractors. However, it can be agreed that historical cost accounting suffers from its inability to show the impact of changing price levels and costs, especially for capital expenditure, on the earning capacity of companies. The inflation rates of recent years have made it imperative that this defect be remedied.

Management needs updated information on true costs and values if it is to run business effectively and efficiently. More realistic information is required and it would not be sufficient, merely to provide a once-a-year adjustment in annual accounts still based on historical costs methods. The general body of opinion seems to be swinging towards agreement on the following points.

1.   Depreciation should be calculated on the value to the business of its assets, not on their historical costs. This could be replacement value at balance sheet dates.

2.   The cost of sales could be calculated on the cost of replacing the goods sold and not on their original, or historical costs.

3.   There should be an appropriation account which brings together current cost profit; revaluation surpluses, the amount which the board considers necessary to maintain the value of the business; and dividends. (Current cost profit = profit after deducting all costs calculated at current values.)

4.   Balance sheets should show current values for most assets, not their historical costs. (Some suggest that both current values and historical costs should be shown side by side for comparative purposes.)

5.   There should be a statement on the change in the amount attributable to ordinary shareholders (stockholders) — the equity interest — after allowance for changes in the value of money have been made. (In Britain this would be determined by changes in the index of retail prices.)

The last point is the only concession to the concept of current purchasing power and recognises the shareholder's interest in the current purchasing power of investments.

Companies which have tried this approach at a time of high inflation have seen how the true current profits of their activities were considerably reduced from the figure thrown up by historical cost accounting methods. The problems posed included the lack of a consensus of opinion on what is the substance of any business. Is it the physical assets, or all the assets, or the owners' capital, or the long-term capital? Should this 'substance' be maintained and expressed in real terms, or in money terms? In Britain, also, the attitude of the Inland Revenue is important.

On past record the Revenue may be unwilling to permit a treatment of profit which could open the doors to full indexation of allowances. This would remove its authority to tax companies without the specific authority of Parliament through what the Commissioners of Inland Revenue call 'buoyancy of revenue' and others more commonly refer to as 'fiscal drag'. It is still to be seen if the government of the day and/or public opinion will exert enough pressure on the Revenue and other agencies not to stand in the way of progress.

7.5.3 Financial analysis

The interests of the recipients of financial reports are not so much in the statements themselves but in the inferences which can be drawn from them. The investing public is not generally interested in the fine details of the financial affairs of a company. Perhaps if they had been, many of the problems of industry and especially of the spectacular failures, might have been avoided. It is the failure of investors, especially the large institutional ones, to probe into the fine details and demand action when situations dangerous to a company's performance and survival arise, who must rightly take the blame for the lethargy of too many companies and their continued poor performance, especially in Britain. The individual investor is interested mainly in profitability in the shape of the resultant dividends, and solvency. The major investors should increase their interest in the strengths and weaknesses of a company, its policies and activities and seek to have something done about the weak points.

The objective of financial analysis is to draw out the implications of what is in the statements. However, if the information provided is defective, the deductions made will be equally defective. The investors will then be misled as to the true condition or state of the company. Investors and executives alike, in addition to profitability, dividend yields, solvency, policies and programmes should give attention to the company's gearing or leverage (debt to equity relationship). This indicates the relative safety of the investment. However, while the method of analysis involves simple mathematical processes, no one indicator, or small group of them, will necessarily prove a financial point. No single feature can be deemed, necessarily, to be the cause of failure or success. Financial analysis must, therefore, encompass not only the financial aspects of the business but also take into account relevant parts of marketing, manufacturing and personnel activities. So proper financial analysis also depends on the application of an integrated management approach.

Nor should the analysis concentrate only on the company's performance but should compare it with that of like companies, competitors and others of similar size etc. (In the United Kingdom companies have recourse to the findings of Interfirm Comparisons, Ltd. when they wish to compare their performance with the norms for their industries.) These external comparisons should, however, recognise that companies use different accounting methods and timings and may be following different corporate and financial policies, and should make appropriate allowances. Nonetheless they will be useful in fathoming whether the company's performance is really as good as it seems, when compared with other enterprises.

It should also be remembered, and due allowances made, for the fact that companies are at different comparative 'ages' of their life cycle and may be operating in different national and business environments. Thus, their performances may vary for these reasons. In the latter case, the management philosophy may also be different as may their capabilities, experience and interests. Thus even two companies which seem identical may in fact be quite different entities as far as their operations and effectiveness are concerned. For these reasons it is advisable to use ratio analyses only to provide a reasonable if selective basis for interpretation and comparison. Many of these ratios will indicate the relationships between assets and claims in a company. Figure 7.6 is a simple *schema* of the main items and their relationships.

7.5.4 Controlling improvements in company performance

In this work, financial executives and colleagues work together to achieve improvement in performance in all departments. First, financial, marketing and manufacturing executives will work together to allocate manufacturing orders to the various units in ways which will minimise total manufacturing and distribution costs for each major product group. At the same time they plan to optimise the availability and output of products and so assist the marketing department to increase sales profitably. Marketing executives and their physical distribution colleagues will be working to reduce clerical errors in filing orders and mistakes in the despatch of finished goods, thus further reducing cost items. Manufacturing will be striving for better control of production to reduce the incidence of defective or faulty products being despatched to customers, yet another area where substantial additional costs can arise, especially with the replacement of these products.

All executives will be working together to optimise the profitable use of funds. Manufacturing executives will be seeking better scheduling of maintenance and plant repair or replacement so there is minimum disruption of manufacturing activities. This will reduce shut-down time and time lost due to breakdown. Finally, manufacturing would want to improve its forecasting of workload inputs for processing etc. This will depend on marketing improving its forecasts of demand and the company's market shares. In all these cases, financial executives will be interested in the anticipated and actual outcomes. In addition to this, personnel executives will wish to improve labour utilisation, reduce labour turnover and have more effective training programmes geared to the company's future needs. In this they will rely on other colleagues for accurate forecasts of their present and future personnel requirements.

Other areas where improvements would be beneficial include customer services of all kinds (marketing and manufacturing executives' responsibilities) and inventory management (physical distribution, marketing, manu-

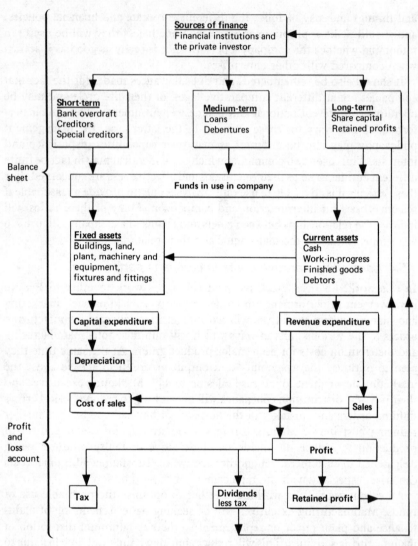

Fig 7.6

facturing and financial executives' responsibility). Then there is the question of cash management (financial and other executives, as necessary) and operations in the public sector (all executives, as necessary). The financial department will be the motivator of some of these initiatives and will be the adjudicator of their cost and efficacy. All such endeavours could contribute considerably to improvement in profitability and efficiency but, if not properly controlled, they could also contribute extra costs which might erode existing profits, without any benefits accruing to the company.

Financial executives should also be involved in attempting to improve the decision-making processes of the board. This is a vital area, yet very often little effort is made in this direction. It is as if executives believe the sanctum is too hallowed and the occupants so perfect that they are beyond the need for help from mere mortals. Perhaps if the directors (vice-presidents) were a little more forthcoming and invited constructive criticism, or set up means whereby their activities could be discussed to arrive at good suggestions of how things might be improved, more useful activity would result. First, there must be clear definition of objectives for the work of the board and identification of those activities that can only be done by it. Next, there must be determination of the detailed steps required to carry out these activities with the formulation of a method whereby the results can be evaluated. This would help to identify the shortcomings of the board and, thus, the opportunities for improvement that might exist. Finally, alternative courses of action to correct the shortcomings can be identified. The improvement programme for the board can then be planned and launched.

The inter-relationships existing in any business enterprise, as it will now be appreciated, are numerous. The coordination and cooperation have to be of a very high order if sound management and successful operations are to result. Ad hoc management approaches, especially on the financial side of a business, are no longer good enough. By comparison the inter-relationships between the main budgets of an enterprise are relatively straightforward. This is illustrated by Figure 7.7.

7.6 Financial management and the general management quadrille

The important role that financial management plays in the general management 'quadrille' has been stressed in the preceding sections. Besides helping to control marketing, distribution and manufacturing costs and producing a more effective budgeting system for them, the department plays an important role in other activities, especially those which represent problem areas for many firms.

7.6.1 Controlling research and development work

The first of these problem areas is the research and development function. More companies are prepared to allocate a growing proportion of their resources to this department because of increasing competition. Yet, if the financing of these activities is not based on reasonably accurate forecasts of costs and likely returns, this department could become one of the greatest non-productive users of funds in a company.

The difficulty in formulating a research budget is obvious. Even when the objectives of the work are clearly defined, the ultimate results of any project are rarely predictable. Nor can the completion date of a project be forecast with accuracy, since the work must deal with many unknown factors that are hard to predict (otherwise there may be little reason for doing the research and development work). The formulation of needs and associated budgets often

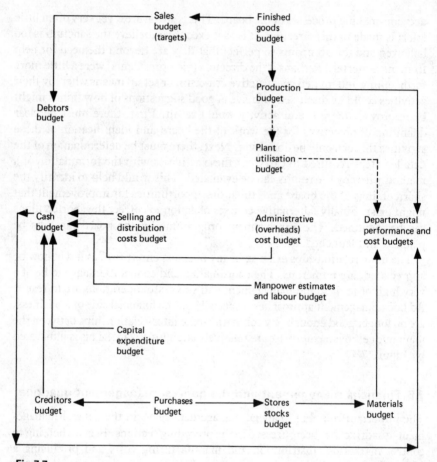

Fig 7.7

begins in the laboratories but should, in appropriate cases, stem also from marketing and manufacturing divisions (including production and quality control executives). While some degree of budgetary control is needed over this expenditure, the nature of the work dictates that control should not be applied too rigidly, or follow the elaborate formal system too precisely. A flexible approach is needed to permit the playing of hunches when some result of the process suggests that this is advisable and may be profitable. Preferably, an 'elastic' budget, nonetheless with upper limits for time and money clearly specified, should be used. (*See also* Section 6.3.1.)

7.6.2 Controlling the cost of the personnel department

The next potential problem area is the personnel department where proliferation (i.e. uncontrolled growth in size without justification) can lead to costs rising to very high and unnecessary levels. The application of budgeting and costing techniques, and associated control systems, can improve the efficiency of operation of this department as a whole. One of the more neglected areas is the costing of the replacement of people, whether blue or white collar worker. Also, the more senior the person being replaced, the higher is the total cost of that replacement. This cost includes the relative cost of the time when the executive is not in post and the cost of training and preparing the new worker to take over the job. This is not an argument for not replacing unsuitable or incompetent people, but a better understanding of the cost aspects of this by senior management would perhaps persuade them not to continue with cavalier approaches to the hiring and firing of employees. Perhaps they would take the whole subject of recruitment and training far more seriously.

Many personnel managers argue that the costing of their activities is not possible. The usual reasons given in support of that claim include the belief that there is no general principle which decides how much should be spent on personnel activities and it is not possible, a year in advance, to decide how any given sum can be apportioned to different personnel activities. Further, it is stated, there is little point in attempting more specific approaches to costing in the department as there is no way of assessing the 'direct' return from such expenditures. These arguments in fact stress the need for better control of expenditure.

The first point illustrates the lack of control that exists and blind reliance on the belief that it cannot be done. The second implies that the personnel department does not know what it will be doing next year or what demands will be placed on it. (The next chapter will show how untrue all this is.) The third point if true, could argue the same point for all other departments (e.g. sales administration) where there are no means of assessing the returns. Since the budgeting and cost control systems have been shown to work well in these other departments, the argument is really that these systems would be equally beneficial for the personnel department.

The budget for the personnel department should also cover the training and development work that has to be done for blue and white collar workers. The work needed will be indicated by the future growth objectives in the corporate plan and assessments by departmental heads of the training needed by their individual staff to help them improve their capabilities, performance and knowledge for future purposes. The size of this part of the budget will have to be decided by discussions with line managers and financial executives. They will indicate the amount and timing of the personnel and training work which will be needed. Then knowing the departmental costs (salaries and administration) and the ruling market prices for the services that will have to be bought in (personnel selection, or head-hunting, or training, or manpower planning, or job evaluations, etc.) a budget, with contingency allowances, can be devised.

Then the department should always be exploring ways of doing things just as well but at lower costs. If the work produces what line managers have asked for and costs are kept down to pre-set target figures, without loss of quality, then it can be considered that the personnel department is working as effectively as possible. The budgetary control system may also be judged as to be working reasonably effectively.

7.7 Questions

1. How does the 'quadrille' concept alter the role of financial control in the management process? How does it also widen the role of accountants and financial executives?

2. Why is financial planning so important to managers today?

3. What are the important reasons for having good and effective management of funds employed and cash flows? How can this help to improve the overall profitability of a corporation?

4. What work is entailed in financial management? Why is cooperation with other line departments essential for success?

5. Discuss the different roles and responsibilities of a financial director (or vice-president), treasurer and company secretary.

6. What responsibilities and work are involved in what is normally described as financial planning and control?

7. What important points have to be considered when planning the use of capital? What are the more common errors or omissions?

8. What is meant by 'profit centres' and 'cost centres'? What are their advantages and disadvantages? How should executives set them up? How are they controlled?

9. What is the 'overhead trap'? Discuss fully.

10. What are the important points to remember when having to deploy resources (e.g. money)?

11. Why is budgetary (and cost) control important? Can they be applied to the personnel department? How can research and development work be controlled?

12. What effect does taxation have on management initiative, efficiency and corporate performance?

8 Personnel — marketing — manufacturing — finance

As it will have been seen from Figure 1.5, the personnel function is a major partner in the general management of a business. Figure 1.6 also shows its relationship with the other disciplines of management in the 'quadrille' concept of integrated management. Without the right amounts of labour and executives with the requisite skills and capabilities, a company cannot hope to perform satisfactorily over the long term. It may be able to fudge along for short periods but sustained, high levels of success are not possible. Yet for too long, especially in Britain, personnel executives have been accorded a status far below their rightful level and worth, or importance, to a company. Happily, management concepts are improving and the personnel function is being seen more and more as an equal partner with the other management disciplines. Even so, the personnel director (or executive vice-president) is still something of a rarity in Britain and some other countries, being confined mainly to the larger corporations. In other firms the chief of personnel is often barely accorded departmental manager status and does not report to the chief executive. At best, he or she reports to the financial director or even just to the company secretary.

Thus the status and responsibilities of the personnel function varies from company to company, industry to industry and country to country. In most cases it is the character and opinion of the chief executive that influence the development, structure, responsibilities and methods of operation of the department. If it is allowed to develop properly, the department's objective is to create the right environment within a company to help recruit, develop, motivate and retain the employees needed to fulfil its business objectives. It should be involved in the planning and policy-making activities associated with personnel matters (including the terms and conditions of employment, remuneration and so on). It must also provide essential personnel services such as recruitment, training, development, personnel information and guidance to line executives on all these matters and on the important subjects of industrial relations, the motivation of white- and blue-collar workers and human resource planning and development.

As the stature of the head of personnel, however titled, has grown so, coincidentally, have the available techniques increased. Also, the arguments marshalled by personnel specialists are based more and more on fact or collective experience and wisdom rather than subjective judgements or hunch. Salary, benefit and attitude surveys, with other research studies, have helped personnel executives to quantify collective opinions and experience and identify trends in applications and principles. However, these have all to be interpreted in terms that are easily understood by executives in other departments. Thus the personnel executive must be like a good salesperson; able to sell the intangible as well as the tangible.

The personnel function is in fact involved with the task of selling ideas and concepts, while with industrial relations it fulfils an advisory role though at times it may have to exercise (delegated) line authority in this matter. Personnel's purpose is to maximise the use of human resources at all times by ensuring that the correct terms and conditions of employment, remuneration, opportunities for development and other benefits are provided. Thus the entire payroll can be motivated and, with enhanced promotional prospects for all, a high level or standard of work can be sustained.

However, personnel management is not the sole preserve of the specialists comprising the personnel department. It is one of the responsibilities of all executives who manage or are in charge of departments or work groups. They all have to manage people. Therefore managers must have a clear idea of their responsibilities for the personnel matters of their departments and not be preoccupied only with the central activities or main functions of their departments. Personnel matters are not side issues to be considered as and when the departmental head has the spare time. They are central to the department's needs and are perhaps the sector of operation wherein the quadrille concept of integrated management has its greatest or most important role.

One of the major responsibilities of management is to maximise the use of scarce and expensive human resources at its disposal. Personnel management is thus an essential and basic function at every level of management from chief executive to shopfloor supervisor. While the work covers a wide spread of activities, the main components of the *personnel quadrille* are illustrated by Figure 8.1. The main quadrille is made up of *personnel management — human resource utilisation and costs — training and development — manpower planning*. The essential support quadrille is comprised of *remuneration and incentives — industrial relations — organisational development — participation*. Again the axle around which these all revolve is the management core of the department.

The personnel function in most countries is susceptible to change and in Britain's case, several changes have occurred in the 1970s. Increases in labour legislation have made heavy claims on the personnel management resources of most companies. Executives from that department are having to give close consideration to many new legal aspects and spend more time in consultation with the company's lawyers. This is a significant re-orientation and the function has become more bureaucratic and reactive. The department's ability to be creative has been maintained only through significant increases in staff, noticeably specialists in new aspects resulting from recent legislation. The

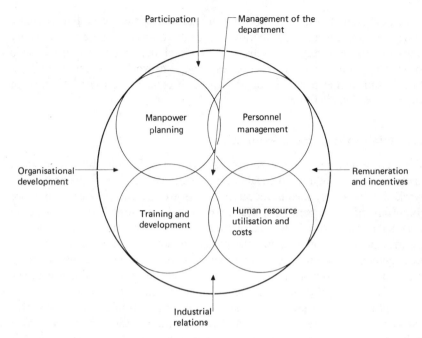

Fig 8.1

growing importance of better human resource utilisation and the holding down of associated costs, with the growing importance of industrial relations work, have brought about the need for new professional skills and experience. Thus the personnel executive has become an essential member of an integrated management team in Europe and other countries as much as in America.

The personnel function is responding to the greater bureaucratic nature of the work by spawning more structures, systems and committees as legislation on labour matters proliferates. A personnel executive now has to act as a mediator in a number of new areas for line executives, as well as being the latter's expert on such matters. Social issues are also growing in importance. Thus the personnel function could be in danger of losing its professionalism and executives must guard against being swamped by these new developments. They must keep one eye firmly fixed on the importance of their professional role to colleagues in other departments and must be allowed to play a full part in the concept of integrated management.

In Britain, nearly 75 per cent of all heads of personnel departments are now qualified at least to graduate level. They are undoubtedly well experienced. Apart from the specialist training they have received as practitioners in personnel matters, their educational specialisations also appear very appropriate, e.g. degrees in economics; study of sociology etc. Most are in the forty to sixty year age group, which dispels the belief that the personnel function is a haven for ageing incompetents. However, only about one third of all senior personnel executives have seats on their company's main board and far too many still do not report direct to the chief executive or chairman of the board. Far too many still report to the technical or manufacturing directors, as if these were the only departments requiring the skills and advice of personnel executives. This situation requires early correction especially as worker representation on boards and worker participation are sure to become mandatory in Europe in the not too distant future.

8.1 Role of the personnel function

Frequently, the personnel executive is involved in finding the solution to a crisis in the form of an industrial relations negotiation. This is the part of the work that receives maximum publicity. However, the greater, and more important part of a personnel executive's role is concerned with influencing personal relations (not industrial relations) by the formulation of dynamic and positive personnel policies and the pursuit of sound principles of personnel management. Therefore, the executive must be sensitive to changes taking place in the company's environment so as to be able to advise line executives correctly on the principles and policies that should be followed.

In practice, the personnel executive's responsibilities fall into two categories. First, the executive implements and administers the personnel policies of the company. Second, the executive operates as the company's specialist in the behavioural sciences, interpreting the behaviour of individuals and groups within the organisation and advising colleagues on the implications of such behaviour for the achievement of departmental and corporate goals. The executive has also to keep pace with the development of new techniques especially in areas like personnel selection, training, remuneration and 'manpower' planning. ('Manpower' in this chapter is used as a convenient generic title to cover both men and women.) However, given the plethora of 'new' concepts of recent years, the executive has to be very discerning in the selection of new ideas to be used by the company and those that should be rejected as gimmicks, or as not relevant to the company's needs. Then the need to improve the company's profitability and productivity also requires personnel executives to ensure that working conditions and environment (both physical and emotional) are such as to optimise the performance of the individual employee, as well as groups. Thus again, close and regular consultation with other executives, to decide which techniques are relevant or best for the company, are essential to the satisfactory execution of the role of the personnel function and more effective management.

8.1.1 Personnel strategy

The attraction of personnel work, it is claimed, lies in its involvement in tactical or immediate situations and the immediate need for solutions. So long as this absorption in tactical aspects falls within a framework of overall strategy on personnel matters, no harm may arise. Where the framework of thought and action is confined to narrow tactical aspects, the tendency is for neither side to show any initiative until some external event achieves importance. (In Britain, the external matters that eventually drove sense into union and management heads included the need to bring the rise in the cost of living, or inflation, under control; political needs; etc.) The strategic long-term aspects of personnel policy can also be forgotten when a narrow view is taken of personnel activities. Defence mechanisms come into play and the problems are fought in the old-fashioned way when there is no long-term strategy to guide the tactical moves.

Because there had been no strategy to guide both sides, until the advent of an incomes policy, under one name or another, the annual wages battles in the United Kingdom led to the wage/price spiral taking an ever faster upward movement leading to massive price increases, especially in 1975–76. Early attempts by governments to impose wage restraints, albeit on an ad hoc, basically short-term (tactical again) basis, seemed only to aggravate the position. It was not until the much-vaunted, but derided, 'social contract' was formulated in Britain and the government of the day refused to consider this only on a one-year basis but extended it for three years, that some sense returned to wage and allied bargaining. Then some stability was imparted to the economic environment and high rates of inflation (20 per cent plus) were reduced to single figures (approximately 8 per cent). (However towards the end of 1978, the then Labour Government in Britain was meeting stiff resistance from the trade unions to its proposed Stage 4 of its wage control policy. Measured in terms of actual increases in earnings obtained in Stage 3, some observers held the view that this was not all that successful either. These arguments and the subsequent disagreements between the Labour Government and unions were seen by some to be a major reason why the Labour Party lost the 1979 general election.) Painful though the incomes policy had been, it forced both sides of industry to realise that while they were fighting a tactical battle, there would be no winners until a strategic framework, involving the wider context of the national economy and public interest, was evolved to set the tactical discussions on a sound base. Individual companies can learn important lessons from past national events. Personnel executives have to make sure that these lessons are driven home to executives and union leaders. (The 1978 mid-western coalminers' strike in the U.S.A. is another illustration.)

There are several factors which can help to identify the strategic framework in which personnel activities should be conducted. They represent, also, strong constraints against continuation of old freebooting approaches. First, as stated, the incomes policy forced all parties to take into account in personnel strategy formulation, government criteria and public opinion. Second, the development of corporate planning has encouraged all executives to think from a strategic base to tactical operations. Then, there is a vital inter-relationship between corporate planning and personnel and manpower planning. While it is possible to develop personnel strategy and policy based solely on personnel matters, the results obtained would be inferior to those that accrue when personnel strategy is thoroughly integrated with the company's business objectives and corporate strategy. Then, personnel executives must be fully appraised of the business plans and objectives which have been identified for the company so that recruitment, training, remuneration and all activities of the personnel function can be totally supportive to their attainment.

Personnel strategy will also be influenced by the strengths and weaknesses of the company on the personnel side. What level of managerial and shopfloor skills exist and what should be obtained for the future according to the corporate plan? What capacity exists for the effective handling of the more likely personnel questions and problems that will be met in normal operations and in any attempts to expand the business? What personal and collective attitudes exist, including the degree of resistance to changes? How will these problems be handled, and how good is the department in handling them effectively and efficiently? What type of unions are involved? How do they react to proposals especially concerning major changes in operations, employment, manning and work rates, remuneration etc.? How good is the department at handling these questions? What is its past record? What inter-union relationships exist? Are there any demarcation problems? What changes are taking place in union structure, policies and attitudes and relationships between unions? How good is the personnel communications network? Does the department have the capability for the efficient handling of all these points? The impact of each of these points will vary from company to company. However, the answers will indicate what the strengths and weaknesses of the department are at any given time.

Other unique factors could influence the position. For example, Standard Oil of New Jersey realised that its Esso Petroleum subsidiary would be more competitive and managerial quality could be improved, if a productivity bargaining system could be introduced. This required, automatically, long-term or strategic planning. Without the resultant forecasts it would have been impossible to evolve a realistic and workable, long-term productivity bargaining plan. Then on a more general plane, there is the increasing professionalism of personnel executives and their growing involvement in general management and corporate planning. This, again, requires more constant and consistent contact and cooperation between personnel and other executives.

8.1.2 Organisation behaviour

In the past, many business organisations 'just growed', like Topsy. Yet the primary reason for the existence of organisations is the need for people to cooperate and work together in an efficient and effective way to achieve common objectives. Just allowing the organisation to be thrown together without thought or purpose negates this aim. How successful an organisation is can only be judged in terms of the contribution it makes to the attainment of declared objectives. When the objectives or scope of the operations change, the organisation may need to be changed, not on an ad hoc basis but in a carefully planned way relevant to the changes which have occurred. Nowhere is this more important than in a business enterprise where untidy and unplanned development of the organisation invariably leads to major problems, even forced mergers and liquidations. (*See also* Section 1.5.10.)

Personnel executives have very important parts to play in organisational development. While this is one of the areas of managerial activity where executives from all departments must work together collectively if success is to result, the personnel executives, as experts in their own field, play critical consultative and advisory roles. It is not a case of the board, or the personnel department, or some-one else dictating what the organisation should be. It is here that personnel executives' powers of persuasion and reputation for knowing their specialism must have greatest play. Yet, too frequently, personnel executives are hardly consulted on organisational changes. They are left to look after the mechanics of the organisation, while executives in the upper branches of the management tree pontificate and decide on what changes should be made. While departmental heads must lead in these discussions and indicate what they want most for their departments, for valid reasons, they are not so knowledgeable on personnel and manpower matters as to be able to exclude personnel executives from their deliberations.

The classic writers on organisational theory think of organisations as formal structures. However, their approach has serious limitations. Organisations are also groups of people; social units formed deliberately to fulfil specific purposes and to achieve stated objectives. Each organisation is a system of social relations as well as work activities. The system is an attempt to break down the total task into sub-groups of manageable workloads performed by the people assigned to them. So managers tend to think in terms of the people who make up the organisation and how they relate to each other. Therefore, how well people work together will affect the performance of the organisation. In other words, the individual personalities of the people forming the organisation and the resultant corporate personality (something more than the sum of the individual personalities and behavioural patterns) determine the potential effectiveness of an organisation. The form is of least importance. What is important is how well people work with each other.

Human beings do not confine their behaviour at work to the performance of that work. They interact as job-holders and as people. Their relationships with each other, attitudes to management, work and the organisation as a whole and their fears and hopes for the future, have considerable impact on their individual and collective performance. The social system, which executives should study and understand, comprises a set of shared beliefs and values with, superimposed, a network of informal social and business roles and relationships. That is in the internal work environment. The external environment in which people live and have their social intercourse, the family, neighbourhood, clubs and associations of all kinds, also affect situations, attitudes and values associated with their work.

Thus the model of organisational behaviour stemming from the classical theory has been challenged and criticised by behavioural scientists. They do so on the grounds that the theory failed to reflect the reality of people's situations and that it does not do justice to the complexities of organisational life. Also, since the overriding purpose of the classical approach was to maintain close control of activities, initiative and enterprise were stifled. In very formalised companies this certainly seems to be the case. The same argument is levelled at the systems approach to organisational development since this tends to ignore the individual and individuality. Hence initiative, enterprise and job satisfaction can be subsumed to the needs of the system. Social scientists continue to point out from their studies of industry that workers at all levels are frustrated and alienated from their work. The degree of frustration and antagonism increase as responsibility and status decrease, i.e. the lower down the executive ladder a person is, the more frustrated, antagonistic and resistant to change will that person be.

These represent some of the key factors often overlooked in personnel work on organisational development. Thus executives must give consideration to:

1.   the organisation as a whole, both the system of work activities involved and the social system at play—plus the inter-actions between them;

2.   the place and attitudes of individuals and the avoidance of their subsumption to the benefit of the system to be used;

3.   the dynamics of organisational life and the need for growth (in its fullest meaning), adjustment to change and organisational development and job satisfaction;

4.   the relationships of the organisation to its environment, especially that it is just a part of a much wider socio-economic system.

Personnel executives today need command of a much wider span of knowledge, experience and appreciation than would have sufficed some years ago.

In deciding whether organisational change is necessary, the theory is that executives should analyse in depth what the actual state of the organisation is, its performance and its ability to meet existing and projected future needs. Then, by study of these future needs, the organisation required for the next stage of the company's life can be deduced. However, in trying to decide the strategy and details of the change needed, executives will find that they never have enough information on which to base decisions. For example, what constitutes 'better performance' when the question of job performance has to be considered? It may be that the starting point for the analysis of the organisation is the identification of the degree and nature of the training executives are going to need for future effectiveness. Or should it be an analysis of the skills available, and the matching of these to future needs?

Further, should the new organisation be designed from the point of view of what the company needs regardless of the availability of the skills in the present organisation? If this is what is wanted, will the company have to recruit new executives to fill the gaps, while sacking those whose skills are inadequate or no longer relevant to future requirements? Would this be socially acceptable? The alternative is then to tailor the organisation to fit the talents available. An intensive training programme may be necessary to add the skills that are missing to the organisation in time. At first the compromise will operate below desired levels of efficiency but, as training continues, the standards should rise. There is always the prospect that at the end of the training another company will entice staff away; the former being too lazy or mean to mount its own training programmes. Or some members of the staff will not be able to learn or may be unable to change and adapt to meet the new requirements. Then the compromise organisation may never work well. The first possibility, with its inherent ruthlessness and subsequent redundancies, however, would never be accepted socially during times of high unemployment.

Planning the strategy for organisational development can start at any point in the system. It could begin with an analysis of present operations, or of future requirements, or with the selection of executives who would form the planning team and their training in the analytical skills they would use on the job. Whatever the case, personnel executives will have to be the specialist leaders in the work, advising their colleagues on all the personnel matters involved. Their own knowledge and experience must, therefore, be more extensive than was the case thirty years ago in old-fashioned personnel departments involved almost exclusively in selection and recruitment on the instructions of departmental managers. (*See also* Section 1.5.10.)

8.1.3 Recruitment and selection

The detailed work involved in recruitment and selection will always form a major part of the personnel executive's work but this will be done in a specialist capacity. That is, the personnel executive is dependent on line executives to specify clearly what staff they want and what cost range is permitted. The personnel executive will then go through the process, hopefully, to produce a short-list of acceptable candidates. The final selection must be left to the line managers for whom the candidate is intended. Only they can interpret correctly which candidate is the best for them in terms of personality, ability to fit in with the team, performance, initiative, etc. To expect personnel executives to undertake the final selection for line managers is totally unrealistic. Even in companies with fully integrated managements, the personnel executive cannot be expected to know, in detail, all the critical points on which the success of the new recruit will depend. In every important case personnel and line management must agree a job description (these should exist anyway for important posts) and from that agree a candidate specification. Otherwise personnel's work will not be closely directed and therefore, will stand less chance of success.

In addition, the company should have an agreed policy on recruitment and selection and its associated activity, promotion. Then consistency in these areas will be achieved. When the policy includes a commitment to promotion from within whenever possible, employee morale should remain high. In heavily unionised companies the application of this policy to blue-collar workers, and some clerical jobs, should also be agreed or approved by the appropriate unions. The method of recruitment and selection for promotion and the relative importance of merit, ability and seniority should be specified. Then the selection procedures are simplified, the personnel executives know what has to be done, how it should be done and, possibly, when it should be carried out. The number of new recruits and their level of entry should be harmonised with internal promotions to give the right balance to the development of skills and the acquisition of new ones. With this approach, human resource utilisation will be improved and labour turnover reduced to acceptable or 'normal' levels.

Such a policy will also require a more intensively planned training programme for employees at all levels. Decisions will have to be made on how this should be arranged (in-service or through external organisations whether colleges, universities, training consultants, trade and professional associations and institutes etc.) and the costs (i.e. training budget) that can be afforded. Care is needed however, to guard against too much in-breeding through too many internal promotions, especially if there are any doubts that the candidates will be able to achieve the degree of improvement and learning that would be necessary. (Note the Great A. & P. case in Section 1.11.3.) Caution is also required about recruiting new people capable of obtaining rapid promotion which will not be immediately realisable for several reasons. Frustration will result and some recent recruits of high calibre would leave and the company may get itself a bad image that will inhibit future recruitment. Many companies in the 1960s recruited newly qualified MBAs and then found they did not have the scope or calibre of work that these people could do. There was much wailing and gnashing of teeth! Happily things have now settled down to more balanced and common-sense approaches to the recruitment and use of MBAs and others. So again, personnel executives must constantly liaise closely with line departments to ensure that policies and practices are correctly balanced to meet short- and long-term needs while overcoming the problems and difficulties that will be encountered along the way. There should be better and more open communication between the recruiting company and candidates.

Setting correct time and cost horizons to the work is also essential. Then there should be agreement on the methods of recruitment and selection to be used (personal selection or executive head-hunting), on the personal appraisal methods (for external and internal recruits), job and performance evaluations and how future prospects should be correctly outlined to all applicants. Again, this shows that an integrated approach to management throughout a company cannot be avoided if a high level of success is to result.

8.1.4 Training

It has been stated already that a properly planned training and development programme is an essential part of personnel work. It is essential when the company's policy is to enhance the prospects of internal promotions in the right mix with recruitment from external sources. Even if promotion did not enter into the considerations, the evolution and development of new or improved management concepts and techniques, improvement in support services like statistics and computers, not to mention the growing use of techniques like operational research, mean that even if a person is doing the same job in five years' time, that job will have grown in content, specialism and professionalism. Training will be essential if present incumbents are to be given a chance to improve their capabilities and knowledge in line with such developments. Where they are to be given the chance of promotion, their training needs will increase still more.

The training and education given by universities and some colleges is aimed at improving the knowledge and abilities of individuals along basic, theoretical lines. In-company programmes, however, should be orientated more to practical requirements so that the company's organisation will be helped in its main aim: achieving stated corporate objectives, including long-term development and growth. This does not mean that it should ignore completely the study of basic theory. Theoretical knowledge is vital if sound practical knowledge and applications are to result. However, the in-company training programme should be based on the company's corporate needs in terms of skills, ability and applied knowledge. The following objectives apply to most training programmes, should be made clear to line managers and the resultant plans should meet them.

1. Provide the skills, knowledge and attitudes needed for jobs at all levels, for immediate and forecasted future requirements and developments, in order to improve performance.

2. Assist in the development of individuals so that they can reach levels of untapped talents and enhance their promotional prospects.

3. Improve individuals' decision-making abilities, encourage the greater use of their imagination and experience leading to a better understanding of the roles they are playing and the subsequent short- and long-term consequences of their decisions.

4. Improve individuals' understanding of the inter-relationships of their jobs with other related activities in the company, i.e. a better understanding of the implications and results that can stem from an integrated management approach.

To achieve these objectives, personnel executives with line managers will first have to review the organisation (present and possibly future structures), products and processes of present activities and projected future ones, the structure and composition of the workforce (its characteristics: e.g. age, turnover, sources of supply etc.), its performance and problem areas. In other words, there should be a thorough corporate appraisal exercise beforehand.

This appraisal will identify training needs and so permit a more effective training plan to be devised. Personnel executives will be responsible to line managers for the implementation of agreed training programmes and must evolve ways of monitoring and evaluating the effectiveness of them. They should issue reports from time to time, to the different departmental heads assessing the progress that the latters' staff have achieved. Evaluation includes assessing the extent to which the training plans have attained their objectives at all levels of management and shopfloor activity. The immediate gains include changes in job-related knowledge, attitudes and skills. In the intermediate term, evaluation checks on the changes in on-the-job behaviour. The ultimate goal is to achieve an improvement in the results obtained by managers, supervisors and all levels of employees.

8.1.5 Management appraisal and development

This aspect of personnel work seems to cause many companies some difficulty. They seem unable to decide what the concept of appraisal actually means. They are confused about the distinction between appraisal systems, appraisal skills and behaviour. Neither are they certain about the nature of the discussion process that should be used to ensure an acceptable and workable system of management appraisal. Perhaps their problems can be overcome if personnel executives stress that before an appraisal system can be devised and used, there must first be a clear understanding of who makes the decisions, what skills are needed for the appraisal and whether there is in fact need for any appraisal and, if so, what form the system should take, There should also be agreement on what levels of decision are involved, which line executive has to make the final appraisal decisions for each person being appraised and who will be the final arbitrator in the event of any major disagreements.

Again the personnel executives fulfil the role of specialist advisers and should not be responsible for making the final appraisals. These can only be done by the appropriate senior or departmental managers. Most appraisal systems employ forms on which ratings are given for intelligence, personality, initiative, performance, potential, attitudes, punctuality and so on. The ratings can be based on semantics (excellent, good, average, poor, etc.) or on some numerical scale where the top figure represents the highest rating and one or zero represent the worst. However, the appraisal should also take into account the past, present and potential value of the executive in the current job and some forecast of value and capabilities in future jobs of a higher status or responsibility. The evaluations should also be done in conjunction with the executives concerned who should be invited to comment (approve or disapprove) on any point raised. If these comments are also recorded on the form and both manager and executive sign it at the end, the report forms a basis for consistent assessments.

On its own, however, the above requires definitions of the different properties 'measured' (e.g. what is 'intelligence'? how is it measured?). Even fully trained psychologists have difficulty in quantifying many of these. In the example cited, intelligence can only be measured relatively to behaviour and behaviour patterns. So, to avoid the appraisal system becoming mechanistic and to inject justice and fairness into it, it should be remembered that assessments can only be made through the observation of actual behaviour. The latter involves actual performance and has little to do with future expectations or intentions. The performance cannot be considered independently of the circumstances in which the work is performed and an individual's performance is unique to each person. Further, individuals can learn from past experience (though they do not always do so) just as an organisation can; and both can change their behaviour in the future if they are prepared to learn from these experiences.

Individuals, however, need help and guidance to change their work behaviour patterns. Current poor performance may be due to many work or social circumstances beyond the control of the employee. Managers and subordinates should work together to try to overcome such problems. There should also be recognition that an excellent improvement in performance may be a major breakthrough for some, while for others it is just the next logical step in their development. Personnel executives, therefore, need to respect what executives do and the ideas they have on these matters, while assisting them in seeing their work role in a different and more helpful perspective. For the personnel executives this is a demanding role to play, requiring great intellectuality and emotional stability. Cooperation with departmental managers is again essential. Further, the more senior the executives are, the more blind they are to the impact on others of decisions taken and actions carried out by them. Many executives lack the ability and training to assess individuals effectively. The personnel executive can provide the vital role of observer and interpreter in these instances.

There are three conceptual approaches to management development planning. First, there is the manpower planning view that attempts to fit the current situation to future requirements will indentify the relationship of the present to future situation through the use of specific plans. These deal with training, recruitment, redeployment, redundancy and so on. They identify the personnel and management gaps which would have to be filled in the future. These comparisons are done in terms of numbers and skills presently used and likely to be needed in the future. Where corporate planning exists, the resultant model is an operational one simple to use, especially when computer facilities are available for the various simulations that should be made. It is essentially a numerical model which encourages the organisation to explore operational possibilities.

Another concept, based on the pioneering work of people like Fayol and Urwick, involves the structure of the organisation. In this the approach starts with consideration of the overall purpose of the organisation. With a careful definition of objectives, the various tasks to be done can also be defined if these objectives are to be achieved. This involves specifying the jobs that have to be done and then finding the people to do them. This method is also based on concern for specific issues such as authority and responsibility, delegation of the former, the relationships between line executives and specialists, the span of control and so on. Its strength lies in the fact that it lays down clearly the rules of operation of the organisation and these are expressed in the language of management and should thus be readily understood. Its weakness is in its mechanistic approach and that sufficient attention is not given to the informal structure or discussions that take place and which play important roles in the management process. It does not recognise the inevitability of the formation of informal groups in a business organisation and the fact that all organisations represent a plural society. Nor does it allow for the lateral pulls that these groups will exert, especially in times of change or threat.

Finally, there is the behavioural view based on the work of Rensis Likert and others. This sees the organisation, its management theory and philosophy and the people who make up the organisation as the three main variables in a business structure. Together, these are considered to evolve human policies, i.e. policies on organisation, job design, communications, control, training and development. This requires an understanding of the interactions between the three main variables and how the policies will combine to affect the fourth variable, performance. This concept is not an operational model since comprehensive information reflecting fully this behavioural view does not yet exist. This approach has an important bearing on the personnel policies that can be followed. Performance is dependent on the relationship of policies as they apply to the people in the organisation. In working with people, all executives make assumptions about human behaviour and the collective impact of these assumptions, especially by managers, have a significant effect on the performance of the organisation.

If management development plans are to be successful and effective, all three views should be considered. In theory, these have areas of conflict, but, in practice, they can give a composite foundation for management development. Their strength lies in the fact that they focus on different aspects of the problem. The behavioural view is intent on the use and development of the human potential in the organisation. Understanding of the structural approach is relevant to the sequencing and organisation of management activity and the nature and interactions of formal and informal systems. The manpower planning approach provides a solid quantitative base for overall planning and direction of the organisation and the selection of an appropriate rate of growth. However, a fourth ingredient is necessary. That is line management, especially senior executives, must maintain and engender a positive, responsive and responsible attitude to management development, both for the individual and the organisation as a whole.

8.1.6 Relationships with other departments

It will be clear that personnel management involves all departments and the personnel function must pervade the entire company. Personnel executives must inculcate the spirit and the purpose of their specialism to all parts of an organisation. They cannot carry out any of the work effectively without cooperation from, and involvement with, colleagues from the other departments. Only then can they ensure that personnel activities will help the organisation to achieve its goals.

A high degree of integration is necessary if effective control of personnel activities is to be achieved. However, personnel executives must avoid the development of a purely bureaucratic set of systems which, in becoming fully mechanistic in their use, destroy the basic purpose of integrated management: more effective and efficient management. The formal systems should not be allowed to swamp entirely, the essential informal systems which provide the lubrication whereby organisations operate efficiently and are capable of early response to changing business circumstances.

8.2 Manpower planning

Manpower planning (which in this book refers also to the ladies) is all about labour supply and demand, labour here covering both white and blue collar workers of both sexes. It is concerned with forecasting future requirements of all types and levels of employees to match the plans and objectives of the company. It specifies the strategy to be followed for the acquisition, utilisation and performance of human resources and their preservation and improvement.

In recent years in Britain, more emphasis has also been placed on manpower utilisation for there is little doubt that, compared with other nations, Britain uses manpower wastefully. This has helped to aggravate the economic problems of the 1970s. The aim of full employment, the political *credo* of all British governments since the end of the Second World War, has been allowed to disguise the serious under-employment of labour in many industries. This misuse of labour can be traced to restrictive practices by unionised labour and lack of managerial ability and determination to achieve high levels of effectiveness in the management of human resources. It is understandable, therefore, for personnel and other executives to give more time to the question of utilisation, even if the effort is somewhat belated.

Manpower planning is a far from easy task especially for business enterprises subjected to political and economic changes beyond their control. Further, as corporate objectives change, manpower requirements will also alter. Manpower planning and activities will have to be modified from time to time to match these changing requirements. Thus it is useless, if tempting, for personnel and other executives to think of manpower planning in the short-term, tactical, context only. While this is important, like training and other personnel policies, if manpower policies are not keyed into longer-term considerations, as expressed by the corporate plan, especially the long-term strategic element of it, they are not likely to achieve maximum effectiveness. There must also be commitment of adequate resources to do the work properly combined with a numerate approach, if possible with the aid of a computer. After all, the consequence of success in this work, is the long-term survival and growth of the business.

Projections of manpower requirements on their own are of little value. The studies must be related to the measurement of current utilisation; the purpose of the latter being to curb under-employment. The work involves forecasting present and future supply and availability of all types of labour required, on a local and national basis. This will include estimates of population, population drift or movements, educational and technical training standards and transport, with measure of labour's willingness to travel to work. For example, one group in Britain encountered difficulties when it moved from its old factory in a suburb of Birmingham, where all its employees lived, to a new country site some ten miles west of Birmingham, with limited transportation facilities. Apart from the labour not being prepared to travel to the new location (a five minute walk sufficed for the old), the lack of transport made the journey difficult and arduous. Laying on special transport was not a complete answer as the workers had still to get up much earlier than hitherto and there were limited shopping facilities near to the new site. Women employees in particular could not make their usual lunch-time forays on family (food) shopping expeditions.

8.2.1 Wider implications of manpower planning

Manpower planning for the major line departments of a business must also take into consideration the implications and associations with other company activities, especially those normally called 'management services'. These include operational research, data processing, corporate planning, finance and accountancy and payroll work and other personnel activities and services. Figure 8.2 is a simple schematic illustration of the overlapping relationships that exist. As manpower planning aims to improve the ability of a business to achieve its objectives through strategies designed to optimise manpower utilisation and contributions, it requires extensive flows of information drawn from these other activities.

For example, it needs data from the personnel department on recruitment, training, selection, career development and promotion needs or prospects of the organisation. It requires also details of current and projected payroll costs and financing, as well as data on corporate long-term intentions and objectives. Operational research and associated activities will have to provide information on methods currently being used and the bottlenecks that are encountered, hence indicators of current resource utilisation. Other services such as data processing will help manpower planning executives to analyse all this information through a computer. Speedy simulations can be made of possible decisions. This will allow manpower planning executives to present the most likely solutions to management for consultations and decisions.

Thus the work requires periodic reports on the manpower situation and the development of procedures which permit estimates to be made of requirements for different types of labour over various periods of time as indicated by corporate objectives. It will also allow the identification of untenable corporate objectives, especially those that would make unrealistic demands on manpower and thus may need modification to suit practical realities. Then ways must be found to increase utilisation while the factors that limit the contribu-

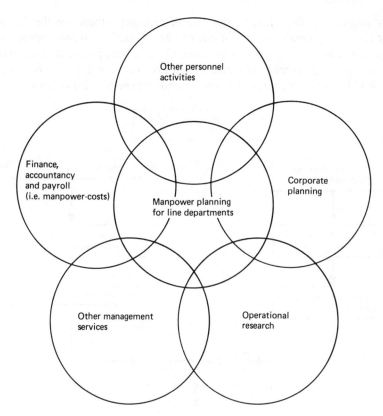

Fig 8.2

tions of individuals and work groups can be identified and corrective action taken to eliminate or avoid them.

Personnel executives must keep in mind also that manpower and capital form an inter-dependent productive system and that manpower is an increasingly costly resource. Manpower is thus the primary asset of a company, its main income generator. At the same time, it is becoming a scarce resource, particularly where skilled labour is needed and high quality is increasingly being demanded. This is especially true for managers who take long-term and important decisions committing other resources to the company's activities. Another aspect that must be kept in mind is the relative immobility of labour despite the encouragement given by trading blocks such as the E.E.C. to increase mobility between member States. Resources, therefore, should be committed to research into manpower aspects, to identify the long-term effects of manpower decisions as they affect the income generation abilities of a company. Control of manpower is not simply a question of cost control. It must also acknowledge manpower's relative inflexibility (since retraining and the learning of new skills takes time) and plan accordingly. In most instances also, retraining is beset by psychological and economic problems which further delay progress in this area. In the case of managers, there are the further complications generated by questions on the promotion, remuneration and retirement aspects of manpower planning. Thus again, personnel executives have to work closely with colleagues when involved in manpower planning. Figure 8.3 illustrates simply the process and information flows involved.

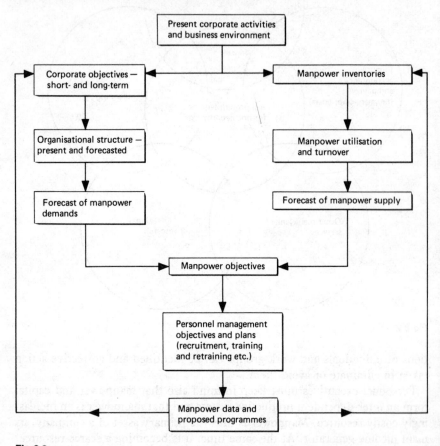

Fig 8.3

8.2.2 Human resource development

Often considered just a fancy name for 'training', human resource development is a much more comprehensive approach to the training and development of personnel, the acquisition of skills needed in the future and the maximisation of the utilisation of these resources. It starts with consideration of the main areas of interest where labour utilisation of a high order is essential. To achieve this the company must, first, create an organisational climate that is conducive to the development of people; second, it must ensure that jobs are clearly defined; and, third, it must make sure that only suitably qualified persons are recruited to fill these jobs, while identifying employee potential for future development relevant to the growth intentions of the company. Finally, these development opportunities are provided while the remuneration (tangible and intangible elements) is seen to be fair and equitable.

The definition of jobs is made in the context of both present and future needs as identified by the corporate plan. The work covers job analysis and design, and attempts are made to chart the career patterns and prospects, at least for key employees. The last is not easy to do and the degree of accuracy achieved will depend on the skills of personnel and line executives, working together, in this type of forecasting. However, even the most generally outlined career path is better than vague promises. When defining future job needs note must obviously be taken of the work that is being done for the company on manpower planning.

The need to select suitably qualified people is obvious and has been discussed earlier. However, it should not be forgotten that candidates should not come exclusively from external sources. Many employees of the company are worthy of promotion or transfer to other jobs with or without further training and encouragement. It is vital for corporate morale that suitably qualified internal candidates have equal chances of being selected as external applicants.

Too often with existing employees, senior management holds prejudiced views of them because of previous mistakes or failure to perform. These prejudices arise also because senior executives usually know their own staff and colleagues too well. These seniors usually forget that people usually learn by their mistakes and those who appear not to have made any are lucky (in that their mistakes have remained hidden). Those who claim they do not make mistakes are liars, or imbeciles. Senior executives when considering promotions must put aside personal prejudice and replace it with unbiased and objective assessments of the people and the new jobs for which they are being considered. The selection of employees must also be made by reference to principles, plans or intentions regarding career planning and the development of the jobs themselves as the result of the implementation of corporate plans. The criteria of the selection process must be clearly defined and understood by those making the selection.

One aspect of the work which receives scant attention is that of identifying and encouraging the development of employees' potential. This is a serious omission not only from a narrow sociological aspect, but also because it means the company is not realising the full potential of skills and abilities it possesses in its employees. Thus, regular and consistent appraisal of performance is needed. The areas to be studied are not just the basic or normal duties of the employee but also any special assignments which have been carried out. The last often indicates where an employee may be used more effectively and will hint at hidden talents. Assessment of potential requires careful analysis of appraisal results, may require further tests or interviews and must take into consideration career planning aspects.

Only then will it be possible to perceive what human resource development opportunities exist or can be provided. The comprehensive training needs will also become clearer to define. These should cover basic training (to improve performance in the basic skills required for the job), technical development (to add new skills), leadership development (to prepare the ground for future promotion) and any other development that is seen to be useful for the future. Figure 8.4 illustrates the main segments of work involved in human resource development.

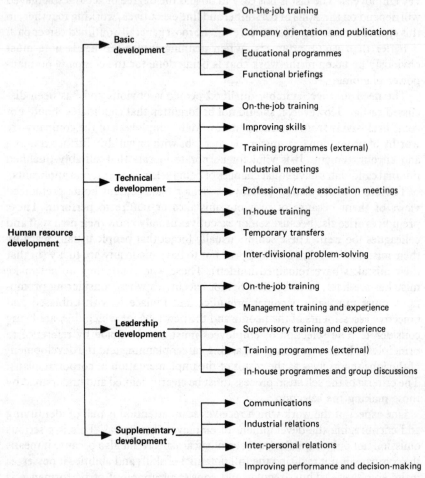

Fig 8.4

8.3 People and systems

When devising management systems of any kind, it should not be forgotten that they will be operated by people and that all organisations are social systems involving people and their personal inter-relationships. Personnel executives should act as watchdogs to ensure that systems are not devised in a mechanistic way, ignoring the people involved. This is particularly critical now that computers are in widespread use. If people are ignored this will lead to frustration, dissatisfaction, friction and increased resistance to systems as well as any essential changes of method that may be necessary. Thus, if good industrial relations are to exist, the points made here should be kept in mind.

Further, the nature of computers requires resultant programmes to be specified in precise terms. If a mechanistic perception of a system is maintained then the work of the system is certain to fail, or be rejected or be ill-used by the persons who should depend on it for the essential data they need for their work. Nor should it be forgotten that the influence of systems operatives will depend on their personal credibility to other executives and the climate or relationship that exists between executives and systems specialists.

8.3.1 People at work

People at work respond to the colleagues with whom they have contact in some way of other, both in the personal context and in what these people mean or represent in the work situation. The reactions depend less on the personalities involved than on what the contacts represent to the executive. Also the executive's expectations of the colleagues and past treatment by and experience of them, influence reactions. The personnel executive has to keep in mind the researches and findings of the many thinkers on management (*see* Chapter 1, especially Sections 1.1, 1.2 and 1.9) ranging from Taylor's 'scientific management' approach to Maslow's 'hierarchy of needs' and modern thought on organisational behaviour.

Taylor's assumptions were that people by nature are lazy, passive and usually not at all ambitious. (In modern times this has been translated to mean that most people want only a quiet, peaceful, self-indulgent life for themselves.) Close supervision is required if latent talents are to be properly exploited. The human relations school bases its emphasis on personal job satisfaction. The Hawthorne experiments still provide part of the basis for the human relations approach. Maslow's theory is based on the thesis that there are levels of needs to which people aspire. The hierachy of needs spans psychological and safety aspects, love, esteem and self-actualisation. A complementary feature is that some people never rise above a certain level because of deprivation of some sort or another in their early lives. Maslow's theory supports the human relations approach to management. In addition there are Herzberg's motivation/hygiene theory and McGregor's Theory X and Theory Y approach. In practice, all of these have some relevance, to differing degrees, to the subject of people at work and puts additional requirement of knowledge and application, on personnel executives. High levels of success in planning systems and methods cannot be achieved if these theories are ignored.

8.3.2 Handling a team

Planning, creating and handling any team in a business organisation is not, therefore, as simple as it may first appear. Apart from the points mentioned earlier, ignoring how members of a team and the team behaves, can limit the quality and consistency of the performance of that team. If human resource utilisation is to be improved one thing that is needed, in addition to those already discussed, is economy of effort to avoid wasting time and duplicating work. Attempts are also necessary to define and create a social environment that will stimulate people to strive for agreed objectives. If this is possible the members of the team will achieve job satisfaction of a high order and so attain the objectives that have been set. High productivity and low absenteeism should result. Cooperation is stimulated, minimising strife and dissatisfaction. The alternatives are frustration, aggression, resignation and regression of individuals.

Inter-group behaviour must also be considered. Generally when an inferior or lower status group makes direct demands on higher status ones, conflict results and efficiency is lowered. Experiments by Sherif and others (Sherif M., 'Superordinate goals in the reduction of inter-group conflict', *American Journal of Sociology* 1958) suggested that when superordinate goals (i.e. goals desired by two or more groups in conflict but which cannot be achieved except by their combined effort) are introduced, conflict is reduced. Other steps to reduce conflict include the creation of intermediary groups to act in a liaison capacity (e.g. production planners who act as intermediaries between marketing and manufacturing executives), using a lower status member of a higher status team to deal with the lower status group and indicating that the lower status person is acting on behalf of a higher status executive. For example, a young specialist demanding information from a department may be resented unless it is made clear that the youngster is acting on behalf of higher management. Even then, care and circumspection are needed in handling the department.

Then there is the question of leadership. This has been discussed in Sections 1.9.2 and 2.6 and in general terms the natural leader will emerge according to the prevailing circumstances. For example, the pilot or captain of an aircraft in flight will be the leader, being sufficiently trained and experienced for the task. However, if the plane crashed into a jungle, the leader would be one who is trained in jungle survival or who has the personality, inclination and drive to survive. This may not be the plane's captain. In normal work-group situations, the leader will probably be the person whose activities and attitudes coincide with the norms of the group's behaviour, i.e. the person seen most likely to achieve group goals or needs. This concept has important ramifications. The leader cannot deviate too quickly or too greatly from expected patterns of (group) behaviour or he or she will be rejected as leader by the group. Thus, winning over the leader to a point of view need not necessarily win over the group. Pressing the view too strongly on the group may lead to repudiation of the leader and replacement by a more intractable personality.

8.3.3 Relationships

The superior-to-subordinate relationship is often considered the main (or even, only) relationship formally existing in an organisation. However, lateral relationships between people of the same status, but in different work situations, also exist and are important. If they are not managed properly the effectiveness of management and the success of the company will be endangered. For example, if the product manager and the quality controller are not on speaking terms, unless an intermediary (production planner) intercedes, product quality and thus sales may suffer. Neither of these relationships exists in a vacuum.

In the case of the superior-subordinate one, cultural and organisational aspects have effect. In the lateral relationship, job satisfaction, the individual's needs, attitudes and expectations, probably stemming from educational and other social backgrounds, have play. In superior-subordinate situations the culture of the country sets the stage. Note for example the (often false) camaraderie of American business and the more deferential attitude of Japanese executives to their seniors. In some countries (Germany, perhaps?) the manager is expected to be autocratic. In Britain, informal attitudes are the exception rather than the rule. In other countries, a more democratic and participative approach is taken as normal. In China, managers are expected to spend two or three days a week in manual work. These cultural differences can offer hazards to expatriate executives who do not understand them. It is something that should be considered carefully in international or multinational companies when executives are posted to other countries. Then there are the organisational aspects. In formal organisations where the manager has many subordinates, only close supervision of a few is possible and a more democratic relationship builds up, naturally or unavoidably. Where the formal organisation supports the manager's authority, a more autocratic relationship will evolve.

These are just some of the points which personnel and other executives must consider when planning organisational structures. Will the structure provide the form of management and associated relationships seen as normal for the company in its national or business environment? If it does not, then conflict may arise and the management team will fail to achieve its desired level of effectiveness. Rank and status established by formal organisation creates a 'social distance' between superior and subordinate. This may increase the superior's formal authority but it is equally likely to impede the free flow of information between the two. Early research suggested that employee-centred leadership gave the best performance but later studies indicated that there is no one best method. What proves best depends on the needs of the people supervised and the nature of the work that has to be done. The more superior the work, the greater will be the natural cooperation existing in the work group involved in that activity. Above all, it is important for the superior to have one recognised style so that the subordinates know where they stand!

8.3.4 Communications

It has already been stated that all companies require a good communications system. Having one minimises the problems that arise with people and in other operational areas. When investigated it will be seen that most management 'problems' stem from some mis-communication or other. People respond according to the meaning they perceive in the situations in which they find themselves. Often these are not deliberate judgements but automatic reactions or assumptions, the bases of which have not been examined. This is particularly true where moral judgements are concerned. (*See also* Section 1.3.)

The assumptions made are not observable but are inferred from observed behaviour. The more commonly recurring assumptions that impede communications include beliefs that economic motives are the main motivators of on-the-job behaviour; poor performance due to lack of initiative and interest can be isolated to a single department or section of the company; persons newly promoted can immediately implement their new responsibility and authority without training or assistance; personnel problems once solved should remain solved; attitudes of employees are not important, or are no concern to senior executives; junior executives have little to contribute outside their daily tasks; and too informal an attitude destroys authority. Not one of these assumptions is correct, though one or two may sometimes appear to be valid. Thus, the work of improving the communications system must include efforts to eradicate these false assumptions and to make executives and others aware of the automatic and incorrect assumptions they have and how these impede the formation of a good communications system. Thus a sound system, i.e. one that is effective, is not just a question of dealing with the communications techniques and methods to be used, but requires attention to the psychological and sociological questions that always arise in any human system.

8.3.5 Participation

Employee participation in the decision-making process of corporations can be at two levels: first, through representation on the board of directors; and, second and more usually, by the involvement of employees in decisions made at all levels of the operation. The question, especially the first form of it, has been engaging the attention of management experts and industrial sociologists for some time for two reasons. First, society is accepting that it is right and proper for members of any organisation to have a say in decisions which are likely to affect their prosperity and job security. Second, greater effectiveness is achieved in implementing decisions and plans, or in optimising the utilisation of facilities, if employees are involved in the discussions and planning that led to them. Another central point, often forgotten however, is that if participation is to prove successful, it must command the full commitment of all employees to the idea of the company being profitable, even if it is state-owned. If the social objectives of participation are to be achieved, this commitment can only come about if there is a trading surplus sufficient for these objectives. This approach will help to bridge the gap between management and blue collar workers and keep intact the primary objective of any business: making profits to ensure future growth and prosperity.

Participation faces all employees with three key issues. First, there is the question of industrial democracy in the use of power and the sharing of that power with employees at different levels of the decision-making process in a business. Then there is the question of job restructuring so that each job becomes significant in its own right, providing an element of challenge to its incumbent and identifying the decision-making role it plays in the corporate structure. This will ensure better utilisation of each employee's mental, physical and other skills. Finally, there is the question of disclosure of information. Making effective decisions is not possible unless the employees involved have the relevant information made available to them. Unless careful thought is given beforehand to the information that should be disclosed, when and how it should be, and to whom, it can be misunderstood or misused (as in wage bargaining) to create greater conflict and friction than before. This will worsen, rather than improve, a company's industrial relations.

Thus, before the personal involvement required for effective participation is possible, the communications network must be good enough to permit a satisfactory dialogue to take place over every decision situation. This must cover not only the information flow needed for the discussion-decision process but also show that the decisions made have been implemented and what results are being, or have been, achieved. The information flow should also allow the decision groups to consider both the short- and the long-term implications of possible decisions for the company; and how these will enhance or hinder the achievement of corporate objectives, particularly growth and survival. This is important since what emerges as a result of decisions taken is often different from what was initially intended because, for example, assumptions on external matters beyond the company's control (e.g. price controls, taxation, competition etc.) have been overtaken by events during the implementation of the agreed decisions. As this is a general and frequent experience, other questions that should be considered include: what future discussion or participation is needed? When and how should this be done after decisions have been taken? In other words, what role should participation play in monitoring the results being obtained?

These problems vary according to the level at which decisions are taken. For task-orientated managers concerned with technical matters and the meeting of deadlines, it is the end-result that is more important than the method by which the results are obtained. Quality, costs and quantity of output are often merely secondary considerations. Managers concerned with the overall operations, i.e. coordination of the supply and utilisation of men, machines, materials, have as their prime concern the scheduling of these and the complex human relations problems which could arise. Executives responsible for the strategic aspects of the business are concerned with the long-term aspects and in effect, negotiations with external partners (e.g. shareholders, financiers, governments, trade unions) and in interpreting the effects of changes in external factors (economic, technical, legal and social developments). All face and respond to different groups of people with different interests and goals. There is thus an inherent conflict of interests in any management team, however organised.

In such a situation there is need for trust. Information disclosures by one group should not provide the ammunition for another's insular interests. If there is no trust, the release of information must be carefully planned and perhaps some training given in the interpretation of that information. Often this is an essential first step if future conflicts are to be avoided. The roles and relationships of the different groups should also be carefully structured. Initially, there could be formal committees in which motions are passed or rejected. Only when employees have realised the true implications and value of participation and that the aim is to advance the common good (not promote sectional interests) can a move be made to a less formal approach seeking 'consensus' views on whatever requires collective decisions.

There are four ways in which participation can occur. First, there is participation in the ownership of the company. Second, there is participation in the control of company operations. Third is participation in the day-to-day management of the business and finally there is participation in determining terms of employment, remuneration and so on.

Participation in ownership involves various schemes for employee shareholdings, co-partnerships and profit-sharing. Many consider these as not providing effective participation since the rewards are remote from immediate effort and from employees; that they are unpredictable and provide too meagre rewards. Shareholders in practice exert little control over the management of a company and over decisions which have significant effects on the interests of employees. British trade unions have criticised such schemes because they take little account of the pluralistic nature of the different interest groups. They see them as ways of weaning members away from the unions. The interest of British employees in such schemes has been low, as witnessed by the numbers who sell the shares they receive in share-owning schemes almost as soon as they receive them. Thus union criticisms seem justified in practice.

Participation in control is exemplified by the notion of worker-directors sitting on main boards whether such representation is 'direct' or 'indirect'. In direct representation, the worker-directors are elected by the employees from candidates drawn from their own number. (This has yet to happen in Britain or most of Europe.) Indirect representation is where management appoints, for example, former trade union leaders, to their boards for the expertise they can bring to the board. (Recent examples in Britain include the Post Office and the British Steel Corporation.) They are not drawn from the employees of the organisation nor do the employees have any say in the appointments. Attempts in Britain began with such (latter) appointments to the boards of nationalised industries and to the National Enterprise Board, the holding organisation for companies taken over by the State for one reason or another (e.g. B.L., formerly British Leyland).

The presence of worker-directors has led to some reduction of friction and strike potential but has not significantly improved industrial relations or discipline within companies. Nor has it reduced the inter-union rivalries that exist in Britain. On the other hand, the conflict of interests that was feared has not emerged. However, while senior executives, especially board members, liked the appointment of worker-directors, albeit on an indirect basis, many middle and junior managers were resentful of office and shop-floor workers having access to information and power denied to them. British interest in worker-directors has been stimulated by Britain's entry into the E.E.C. and by the Community's plans to harmonise company law. The E.E.C. Commission's view is that such directors can be appointed in two ways. First, the employees could appoint up to one-third of the members of the board or all members could be appointed jointly at shareholders' meetings and through employee appointments, with all parties being able to oppose the appointment of any proposed candidate.

Participation in day-to-day management could be through the appointment of semi-autonomous work groups, a task-based organisation. Then all members of a group would participate in making decisions for their group and controlling the resultant operations. Through job enrichment also, employees could participate in decision-making at immediately superior levels of work. For example, a machine operator could be a member of a team making decisions on inspection and work supervision. There is thus the possibility for each employee to achieve psychological growth. By improving motivation, job satisfaction and performance through this approach, favourable results have been obtained.

Participation in decisions on terms of employment etc. is achieved through extending collective bargaining to more levels, types of employees and issues. These include areas formerly regarded as being within the management's prerogative. The weakness of this approach is clear when it is realised that the interests of weaker groups of employees can be submerged by the interests and demands of stronger groups. The history of British trade union activities during the 1950s and 1960s throws up many examples of this.

European attempts and experience of participation are varied. In Holland, employees can influence the composition of boards, but are not directly represented on them. French law permits employee representatives to take seats on their boards. This is, however, in a purely consultative capacity and these worker-directors have no voting rights. Belgium, Ireland, Italy, the United Kingdom, Switzerland and Finland (at the time of writing) have made no provision for employee representation on boards of directors as a mandatory requirement. The countries which have made some provision for employees to influence the composition of boards (Holland, Norway, Sweden, Austria, Luxembourg and Denmark), have only done so relatively recently (1973–74).

These provisions followed decades of effort to expand employee participation, and no country contemplated this without long experience of operating a works council structure. These councils were designed to increase industrial democracy at the place of work. Further, they were legally backed and covered all employees whether union members or not, even if the councils were in fact dominated by trade union members. Where employee representation at board level exists it applies generally to the supervisory board of a two-tier system (e.g. Austria, Germany, Denmark, Luxembourg, Norway and Holland). In France, the option is either a unitary or two-tier board structure, though the latter is rare. In Sweden, employee representatives sit on a unitary board which is primarily a supervisory body, day-to-day activities being delegated to a management team. In all seven countries, the shareholders' representatives on the board retain ultimate control though in some German companies their voting majority is less than totally dominant.

The perils posed by participation are many. First, worker participation does not ensure automatic removal of all problems. Some of these problems are simply built into, or are the result of, the industrial situation that has developed over many years. For some there are no known remedies except a long-term and slow change of attitude of worker representatives, and especially trade union leaders. It could involve a total reappraisal of the role of trade unions in industry. Other problems do have remedies but not one has any easy solution. The remedies may be of infinite variety but the problems are fairly universal.

One is the surprising incidence of executives and others developing a Messianic faith in participation. They tend to move faster than the rest of the organisation or country on this, beyond the first, carefully planned steps of the process. They develop an emotional commitment to the idea and when frustrations and delays are encountered, they will leave their companies. Other enthusiasts may overstep some boundary or other and be forced to resign.

Another problem is encountered when an executive starts to operate in a participative manner with subordinates. The executive becomes less docile and may even be excessively aggressive with superiors, questioning, challenging and criticising everything the superiors say, propose or do. The experience can be uncomfortable for colleagues and lead to further, unnecessary, friction. Executives who change their style in this way are often looked upon as heretics by senior management and may be ignored, or pushed into dead-end jobs. This is a pity; what personnel and senior executives should try to do is to find some way of channelling this new aggression so that it will prove beneficial and productive to the company.

Yet another problem arises when top management is not fully committed to the decision to accept participative management. In this case discontinuities can arise in the management processes and the autocratic management team, masquerading as a participative one, only aggravates the problems and increases friction and discontent. The trouble is worse for large companies which because of their size, are not easy to control. The head office team may then be reduced to holding on tightly to the crucial set of financial ratios by which the performance of subsidiary companies is measured.

Participation in management requires managers to evolve new priorities in the use of their time. Executives are forced to listen to what subordinates, equals and superiors are saying. They must follow up ideas and ensure correct feedback to the others involved with the progress of ideas and decisions. Executives, instead of making decisions on their own, must seek collective decisions and be able to judge themselves by their ability to communicate with subordinates, equals and superiors, and the encouragement they give to subordinates to participate in the decision-making process and in carrying through these decisions. Personnel executives therefore have a complex and full programme ahead of them when called upon to assist line colleagues and the board, in bringing participation to their company's management style.

8.4 Industrial relations

Much money is lost in companies through the incompetent handling of personnel matters, often due to ignorance of new legislation and other trends in employment matters. Nowhere is this more true than in attempts to improve the industrial relations of a company. In any group of people, differences of opinion and interests arise and in industry, negotiations are necessary to resolve these differences. In Britain, the approach to industrial relations negotiations tends to be pragmatic rather than systematic, with little reliance on legal backing or constraints. While in the past this has seemed to suit the British character, in the 1970s increasing legislation found its way onto the statute book in attempts to formalise labour relations. It has been difficult for personnel executives to keep pace with this legislation and they are faced with an ever-increasing volume of negotiations to handle in situations of uncertainty and changing environments.

The basic changes which have occurred range from moves in emphasis from industry-based negotiations to negotiation at the workplace, and the widening of the matters subjected to negotiation from the original packet of wages and working hours to many other work practices and conditions. At the same time, some unions now attempt to block decisions by management to which their members object, if the union has not been party to negotiations on the matter. Next, while collective bargaining remains the preferred way of negotiating wages and working conditions, despite having been subjected to increasing criticism, there have been attempts to strengthen it and extend and formalise the approach, including the codification of grievance procedures. The groups covered by collective bargaining are also increasing and now include technical and administrative workers including supervisors and (some) managers. Finally, areas which were dealt with by management unilaterally, or by negotiation, in Britain are becoming more and more subject to decisions by outsiders such as industrial tribunals or to recommendations, often arguable, by bodies such as ACAS (Advisory Conciliation and Arbitration Service). These changes are likely to continue with an increasing involvement by existing and possibly new public agencies. The personnel executive thus has much to learn and contemplate in the field of industrial relations. However, the basic relationship will involve managers and workforce at the place of work.

While legal requirements must be met, it is still essential for managers and all workers to create sound, constructive relationships which will improve the efficiency of the company and give greater job satisfaction to all employees.

Developments in recent years, therefore, have increased the industrial relations problems and the difficulties faced by most companies. In some cases companies have been reluctant to hire new or additional labour. First, many job categories have generated insupportable wage differentials and thus union rivalries. Second, previously successful policies have failed as a result of increasing economic and social pressures and the irrelevance of many national and industrial pay agreements to the increasing problems of productivity (or rather the lack of it). Third, remuneration systems have increasingly become irrelevant or incoherent. Fourth, the motivational content in industrial relations planning has declined with insufficient attention being given to job content and job satisfaction. There is too great a tendency to reduce the individual worker to little more than a mindless cog in the 'machinery' of the company.

The development of successful industrial relations policies requires a comprehensive approach that considers every aspect of the subject. Not only must personnel executives work with all colleagues in devising these policies, but they must also take into account all the other objectives, policies and plans of the company. Too often, in many companies, functions are acutely compartmentalised to the extent that any one group encounters extreme difficulty in discovering and understanding what other groups are doing. Thus disputes and difficulties arise because executives are ignorant of what is happening outside their own departments. For example, marketing may know that a product's life is ending and will have planned for new products to replace it. However, the consequential changes in the composition or location of the labour force required may be known to manufacturing but may not be disclosed to those responsible for industrial relations matters in the company. Or, the latter may not be ignorant of the changes, but they may not have been made aware of the depth and significance of the planned changes in the labour force. Where redundancies are involved, they may not have been consulted. They may also be kept in ignorance of the changes in the economic, technological and social framework in which the company will be operating in the immediate future, never mind the longer-term period.

Thus in policy formulation, consistency with the conditions under which the work will have to be done is an essential ingredient for success. Also the policy should be based on clearly-defined objectives, but should be flexible, avoiding restrictions on management action. Industrial relations policies should be part of a coordinated, corporate personnel policy and the corporate plan.

The objectives of industrial relations policies include the development of an atmosphere of trust and cooperation at the workplaces so that problems and disputes are prevented from arising or, when they do, are kept within reasonable bounds. The solutions to problems which arise should be through agreed procedures and involve minimal expenditure of time, disruption of work and subsequent expense or losses. The policy should also encourage employee motivation, high productivity and the development of appropriate skills. Finally, it should help to improve control of activities and reduce or stabilise labour costs.

The standards to which the policy should conform include the existence of a written policy statement which, couched in broad terms, permits various or varying local conditions to be met. This is essential for international or multi-national corporations. It will give a framework within which procedures and actions may be developed which are consistent with the basic policy. The policy should be justified by its long-term impact on profitability and whatever other measure of effectiveness is used or deemed to be necessary. It should be capable of universal application within a company, applicable to all plants and all countries (within their legal constraints and requirements) and be regarded as inviolate, as far as this is within the power of management and the unions.

8.4.1 Motivation

Few people consider their jobs merely as means of providing the necessary money with which to pay their bills. Most seek other satisfactions besides the simple one of money. Thus the personnel executive, working with line managers, must ensure that they are aware of the various goals which motivate all employees. As stated already, these range from job satisfaction to status and having a favourable work environment. In the latter case, productivity and cooperation will be higher than for a team working under unsatisfactory conditions. Having identified the various motivations that are important to employees, personnel executives and line managers must try to match these goals to the work situation.

Research shows that amongst the goals connected with job satisfaction are psychological aspects such as job security, status and prestige, approval by seniors and a sense of achievement. These give clues to the work incentives that should be created. Another basic need of humans is that of being accepted as a valuable integral part of a closely-knit group. For lower grades of workers, prestige and status are important but these are related more to the individual's position within the work group rather than in the company's hierarchy. The leadership style and social relationships created by managers can contribute positively to employees' interpretations of their prestige and status. Finally, within a cohesive work group, even if the work is repetitive, undemanding and monotonous, individuals will still gain a sense of achievement. When executives understand the power, value and importance employees place on their primary working groups, they will better understand the reasons for irrational behaviour when instructions are issued that, to the employee, appear to destroy or undermine the cohesion of the group. This is an important consideration when it is necessary to change systems, procedures or methods of working. (*See also* Section 2.2.3.)

8.4.2 *The realities of change*

Senior managers too frequently embark on changes of systems, methods, procedures, techniques and structures without due regard to the effects these will have on the people concerned. Considerable research may be carried out on what changes are necessary and how they should be implemented, but little is done to take account of the human factor and how workers will accept the proposed changes. Even less frequently do executives take the time to explain the necessity of the proposed changes and the anticipated results to their subordinates. Yet they are surpised when they encounter antagonism and resistance to these changes. Managers are annoyed when subordinates become defiant, aggressive or simply uncooperative. This is especially confusing to executives if the changes appear obvious to them, but they do not stop to think of the effect on people to whom the changes come as a surprise. If they are ignorant of the reasons for the changes and why they are necessary and if they have not participated in the planning of them, it is natural for employees to oppose the proposals especially if their status and prospects appear to be threatened by the changes.

Unexpected changes cause resentment and suspicion. All changes, unless explained, are seen as threats by the people affected by them. They fear that their jobs might disappear and their work group be broken up. They may also believe that they will not be able to adapt to new needs nor learn new methods and skills. All people are afraid of the unknown and thus personnel executives and line managers must never forget the need for full consultations and explanations when changes are necessary. Otherwise it may prove impossible to push through the changes so that the desired effect of improving company performance may not be realised. (*See also* Sections 1.3.1, 1.3.2 and 3.5.1.)

8.5 Remuneration

The subject of remuneration is a lengthy one and, again, this Section will deal only with the more common problem areas and the points which are often overlooked.

To start with, remuneration strategy and policy should be clearly defined to act as guides for action programmes. Yet seldom are they so. They must, of course, be consistent with corporate strategy and policy and assist, through the attainment of the correct manpower and skills, in the achievement of short- and long-term objectives. However, they seldom achieve this as many remuneration plans seem to be only remotely related to the corporate plan. Nor should economic wage and salary costs mean paying the lowest rates going, as this will just mean that poor quality labour (blue and white collar) will be obtained.

The basic objectives of a remuneration policy should include acknowledgement of the need to attract and retain a workforce of the right quality and skills needed to provide successful company operations. It should provide other forms of encouragement and incentives to tempt employees to give of their best. Finally, it should achieve all this at minimum long-term costs consistent with the quality and performance standards required. Once the policy and objectives have been established, the methods of remuneration to be used can be decided. These can be based on job evaluations by grading, ranking, points and other established systems, or by merit ratings. The question of incentives and pensions must also be considered and it should not be forgotten that for the average employee, a pension is a very important element of the remuneration package. The question of equal pay for men and women must also be considered. The pressure for this is growing and, in Britain, it has become mandatory by law.

Again, the personnel executives cannot work in isolation. Close cooperation with line managers and especially financial executives and board members will be essential. Otherwise the strategy, policy and objectives will not be properly defined and resultant action programmes may prove unproductive, i.e. fail to achieve their goals.

8.5.1 Incentives

A properly planned incentive scheme should result in the improved stimulation (or motivation) of employees. They are thus more likely to put greater effort than normal into their work in return for rewards that make that effort worthwhile. The scheme should be designed to make the aims of the company and the employees' coincide. The main objective of incentive schemes is to improve the profitability of the firm through increased profits. Thus, another aim would be to ensure that the employees' desires are directed to increasing the profit of the company and to sustain these gains over the long term, thereby earning themselves attractive rewards which satisfy their desires or expectations.

It is important that any scheme launched is within the ability of the company to keep its side of the bargain. This includes ensuring that opportunities are presented to employees to earn the bonuses offered by the incentive scheme. Thus schemes for salespersons should not set such high qualifying levels that intelligent staff will realise there is little chance of earning a worthwhile bonus. In this connection, the potential of each sales area should be considered so that the targets can be correctly related to potential. For example, while London-based salespeople may have no difficulty in earning good bonuses, those covering northern Scotland may have difficulty in qualifying if the same qualifying level is set for both areas. Finally, it should be remembered that even good incentive schemes are no substitute for bad, or poor, management. Indeed, poor management may often mean that even good incentive schemes fail to realise their full potential due to the incompetence of the managers. If the latter create friction and antagonism among their subordinates, the best incentive scheme in the world will not balance these negative factors and motivate employees to achieve maximum performance.

To summarise, incentive schemes should match the aims of employees participating in the scheme with the objectives of the corporation. They should be flexible to allow for adjustments should the basis of the scheme need to be changed because of changes in the company's business environment. The firm should ensure that reasonable opportunities are presented to employees to earn their bonuses. The incentives must be acceptable to participants and be seen by them to be worth the extra effort. The incentives should be bonuses paid for extra effort and should not be in lieu of proper basic wages. They should be in addition to good basic wages.

8.5.2 Pensions

As mentioned earlier, pension schemes are considered by most employees as an integral part of the remuneration and terms of employment for the jobs they do. While many, especially the dynamic employee with initiative, will not rely entirely on the pension for provision for their old age, it forms a good base for whatever else the employee might be able to provide through careful investment of savings from salary etc. In addition to the basic pension, prospective employees may be tempted to join a company if the scheme includes benefits for widows and the children of employees, disablement pensions, death benefits and advantageous share purchase schemes. They all form part of the package that may prove a strong incentive in the personnel executive's task of recruiting and retaining employees, thus reducing the labour turnover figure.

The purpose of a pension is to make some provision for the old age of employees and the greatest advantages are naturally accorded to faithful long-term employees of the company. However, pensions are usually payable at some distant time and, in periods of high inflation, their value is rapidly eroded. Attempts to overcome this problem, e.g. by index-linking them to the rate of inflation or to the rise in the retail prices index, are still being discussed intensively. The move in Britain that resulted in public service pensions being index-linked has caused considerable jealousy on the part of managers and employees in private industry. The problem with index-linking is the cost though private industry could manage something with skilful investment of pension funds. For public services the extra cost tends to fall as an increased burden on taxpayers.

8.5.3 Redundancy

The economic problems of the mid-1970s put paid to most western industrialised countries' aim to maintain full employment. In 1977 for example, over 6 million people were unemployed in Western Europe and projections in 1978 envisaged this rising to 10 million or more in the 1980s. Similarly substantial figures prevailed for the U.S.A. The question of high unemployment poses a whole new set of problems for politicians, managers and especially personnel executives; problems which so far no-one seems capable of solving. The situation is depressingly similar to those pertaining in the second half of the 1930s.

All that executives seem able to do is attempt to maintain their level of activity at rates which will minimise redundancy for their employees. This includes development of new and unique products which will have profitable levels of demand and allow a firm to retain its market shares and profitability. It is up to the governments of all nations, working together, to try to follow economic policies which will boost international trade. Unfortunately, at the time of writing, no real effort in this direction has been made. There has been much talk, and little action. Indeed there has been fear that there will be a movement towards greater protectionism, with tariff barriers raised to inhibit imports of goods which could otherwise be produced in the home country. Unfortunately this trend, if it continues, could lead to even higher unemployment. Then the role of personnel and other executives will be restricted to trying to lessen the impact of redundancy on the unfortunate people. Even this will be of such a limited nature as to be of little value to those facing many years of unemployment.

Policies which industry could follow to mitigate redundancy include incentives to increase the mobility of labour to areas with jobs where labour demand still exists. In the public domain new public attitudes and policies are required. The greatest risks lie in dogmatic faith in old policies and texts which have long lost their relevance. New ideas on how to resolve the unemployment problem will no doubt have flaws, but they will have the merit of recognising the true nature of today's conditions. They would represent a determined effort to set society at large towards a correct solution of this apparently intractable problem.

One possible salvation may lie in the fact that some industries are still experiencing shortage of skilled labour. Promoting the retraining of redundant workers may, therefore, limit the impact of unemployment and may help to reduce the unemployment rate to less horrific proportions. Unfortunately, many workers are still averse to retraining and finding new jobs. This is particularly so if a move of home to new and unknown areas is also required. Thus personnel executives have a major re-education job on their hands if these particular resistances to change are to be overcome. The ostriches must be made to withdraw their heads from the sand and realise that the good old days will not return. This is particularly true for old or ageing industries whose products are no longer needed. Salvation may only lie in the development of new industries with good long-term product demand. Change of jobs, skills and home locations are then unavoidable and provide the only positive alternative to long-term, if not permanent, redundancy.

8.6 Personnel management and the management quadrille

It will be seen from this chapter that the personnel function is one management activity that is least able to function effectively on its own. Since the management of personnel pervades all departments and personnel executives act as specialists and advisers to colleagues on all personnel matters, close if not continuous cooperation and liaison with other departments is vital. Without this, personnel activities will not prove as effective and productive as they could otherwise be. Nor should line executives underestimate the important contribution the personnel department can make to their success. Personnel activities can no longer be accorded the low status that they have hitherto had to suffer.

8.7 Questions

1. What is the role of the personnel function?
2. Why is it important for a company to have a clearly-defined personnel strategy?
3. Why is it important for a company to have good industrial relations? Have recent developments helped or hindered the creation of sound industrial relations?
4. What are the main functions comprising the personnel quadrilles? How does personnel work integrate with that of other departments in a company?
5. Why is the role of personnel executives becoming more complicated? In which areas must their knowledge and experience be extended to allow them to handle modern personnel requirements?
6. What major points must personnel executives keep in mind when working on organisational development?
7. What points must be kept in mind when formulating selection and recruitment strategy/policy and when carrying out the detailed work?
8. Why are training and development so important? What guidelines have to be met here?
9. What is meant by 'human resource development'? How may this work be segmented?
10. What aspects of personnel work is covered by manpower planning? What are the major problems it seeks to overcome and what implications are there in this work for company executives?
11. What are the key points to be remembered in dealing with people at work and handling work groups or teams?
12. Discuss the importance of the various forms of 'participation'. How have more recent thought and concepts helped or hindered participation in business organisations?
13. Why should a good remuneration policy be used in a company? What supporting role do incentives play?
14. Discuss the superior–subordinate relationship that should exist in any company. What problems bedevil this aspect of management?

Bibliography

(Mainly relevant to Chapters 1 to 4)

Ansoff, H.Igor. *Corporate Strategy*, Penguin (1968)

Ansoff, H.I., Decleck, R.P. and Hayes, R.L. Eds. *From Strategic Planning to Strategic Management*, Wiley (1976)

Argenti, John. *Corporate Planning: a Practical Guide*, Allen & Unwin (1974)

Argenti, John. *Corporate Collapse — the Causes and Symptoms*, McGraw-Hill (1976)

Brooke, M.Z. & Remmers, H.L. *The Strategy of Multinational Enterprises*, Longman (1970)

Donnelly, J. et al. *Fundamentals of Management, Functions, Behaviour, Models*, Business Publications (1975)

Drucker, P. *The Practice of Management*, Heinemann (1965)

Drucker, P. *People and Performance*, Heinemann (1977)

Foster, D.W. *Planning for Products and Markets*, Longman (1972)

Franko, L.G. *The European Multinationals*, Harper & Row (1976)

Golightly, H.O. *Managing with Style and Making it Work for You*, Prentice-Hall (1977)

Grant, J.V. & Smith, G. *Personnel Administration and Industrial Relations*, Longman (1969)

Haimann, T. & Scott, W.G. *Management in the Modern Organisation* (3rd edn), Houghton Mifflin Co. (1974)

Hussey, D. *Corporate Planning; Theory and Practice*, Pergamon (1974)

Jones, Harry. *Preparing Company Plans*, Gower Press (1974)

Lorsch, J.W. et al. *Understanding Management*, Harper & Row (1978)

Louden, J.K. *Managing at the Top; Roles and Responsibilities of the Chief Executive Officer*, Prentice-Hall (1977)

Macfarland, D.E. *Action Strategies for Managerial Achievement*, Prentice-Hall (1977)

Malloby, M. *The Gamesman*, Secker & Warburg (1977)

Margerison, C. & Ashton, D. *Planning for Human Resources*, Longman (1974)

Pollard, H.R. *Development in Management Thought*, Heinemann (1974)

Reddin, W.J. *Managerial Effectiveness*, McGraw Hill (1970)

Stewart, R. *The Realities of Organisations. A Guide for Managers*, Macmillan (1970)

Stewart, R. *Contrasts in Management*, McGraw Hill (1975)

Stopford, J.M. & Wells, L.T. *Managing the Multinational Enterprise*, Longman (1972)

Taylor, B. & MacMillan, K. Eds. *Top Management*, Longman (1973)

Woodward, J. *Industrial Organisation: Theory and Practice*, Oxford University Press (1968)

Woodward, J. Ed. *Industrial Organisation: Behaviour and Control*, Oxford University Press (1970)

(Mainly relevant to Chapters 5 to 8)

Attwood, P.R. *Planning a Distribution System*, Gower Press (1977)

Boyce, R.O. *Integrated Managerial Control*, Longman (1967)

Chambers, R.J. *Financial Management*, (3rd edn) Law Book Co. Ltd., Australia (1967)

Cuthbert, N.H. & Hawkins, K.H. *Company Industrial Relations*, Longman (1973)

Drucker, P. *People and Performance*, Heinemann (1977)

Fitzroy, P.T. *Analytical Methods for Marketing Management*, McGraw Hill (1976)

Foster, D.W. *Planning for Products and Markets*, Longman (1972)

Grant, J.V. & Smith, G. *Personnel Administration and Industrial Relations*, Longman (1969)

Glautier, M.W.E. & Underdown, B. *Accounting Theory and Practice*, Pitman (1976)

Hacon, R. Ed. *Personal and Organisational Effectiveness*, McGraw Hill (1972)

Jantsch, E. *Technological Planning and Social Futures*, Cassell/Assoc. Business Progs. (1972)

Kotler, P. *Marketing Decision Making; a Model Building Approach*, Holt, Rinehart, Winston (1971)

Lockyer, K.G. *Production Control in Practice*, Pitman (1975)

Margerison, C. & Ashton, D. *Planning for Human Resources*, Longman (1974)

Merrett, A.J. & Sykes, A. *The Finance and Analysis of Capital Projects*, Longman (1969)

Mitchell, J. *Price Determination and Prices Policy*, Allen & Unwin (1978)

Morris, W.J. *Principles and Practice of Job Evaluation*, Heinemann (1973)

Revons, R.W. *Developing Effective Managers*, Longman (1971)

Schwartz, D.J. *Marketing Today; a Basic Approach*, Harcourt, Brace, Jovanovich (1973)

Westing, J.H. & Albaum, G. Eds. *Modern Marketing Thought* (3rd edn), Macmillan, N.Y. (1975)

Wilson, M.T. *Managing a Sales Force*, Gower Press (1970)

Wilson, R.M.S. *Management Controls in Marketing*, Heinemann (1973)

Woods, E.G. *Costing Matters for Managers,* Business Books (1974)
Woods, F. *Business Accounting,* Vols. I & II, Longman (1968)

Index

The letter-by-letter system has been adopted, and, except for Case Studies, names of firms and of individuals have mostly been excluded.